Authoritarianism in All its Guises

Authoritarianism in All its Guises provides an interdisciplinary assessment of contemporary experiences of authoritarianism.

Drawing on psychoanalysis and critical theory, contributors from a range of academic backgrounds consider authoritarianism as it manifests in a range of movements and contexts. The chapters investigate, interrogate, and, in some cases, clash creatively and revealingly over the meanings of contemporary experiences of authoritarianism across the political spectrum. The issues raised here not only compel us to come to grips with and clarify what constitutes modern authoritarianism but also what defines the "Left" in this stubbornly neoliberal age.

Authoritarianism in All its Guises will be essential reading for academics and students of psychoanalysis, political and social psychology, sociology, history, and media and cultural studies.

Daniel Burston is a Professor Emeritus and former chair of the Psychology Department at Duquesne University, Pittsburgh. A historian of the mental health disciplines, he has authored several books and numerous journal articles on the history and politics of psychology, psychiatry, and psychoanalysis.

Kurt Jacobsen is a Lecturer in Social Sciences and Faculty Associate in the Department of Political Science at the University of Chicago. He is author or editor of a dozen books and is co-editor of the UK journal *Free Associations*.

Authoritarianism in All its Guises

Perspectives on Right, Left, and Center

Edited by Daniel Burston and Kurt Jacobsen

Routledge
Taylor & Francis Group
LONDON AND NEW YORK

Designed cover image: Cover image © Kunstpalast / ARTOTHEK
Peter Ludwigs, Der Krieg, 1937

First published 2025
by Routledge
4 Park Square, Milton Park, Abingdon, Oxon OX14 4RN

and by Routledge
605 Third Avenue, New York, NY 10158

Routledge is an imprint of the Taylor & Francis Group, an informa business

British Library Cataloguing-in-Publication Data
A catalogue record for this book is available from the British Library

ISBN: 9781032486130 (hbk)
ISBN: 9781032485997 (pbk)
ISBN: 9781003389927 (ebk)

DOI: 10.4324/9781003389927

Typeset in Times New Roman
by Newgen Publishing UK

Contents

Contributors

Daniel Burston is a historian of psychology, psychiatry, and psychoanalysis, and the author of numerous books and articles on the intersections between the mental health disciplines and politics, religion, and philosophy. His latest books include *Antisemitism and Analytical Psychology: Jung, Politics and Culture* (Routledge, 2021) and *Critical Theory and Psychoanalysis: From the Frankfurt School to Contemporary Critique*, co-edited with Jon Mills (Routledge, 2022).

Donald Carveth is emeritus professor of sociology and social and political thought at York University in Toronto. He is a training and supervising analyst in the Canadian Institute of Psychoanalysis; a past Director of the Toronto Institute, and past editor-in-chief of the *Canadian Journal of Psychoanalysis*. He is the author of *The Still Small Voice: Psychoanalytic Reflections on Guilt and Conscience* (Karnac, 2013); *Psychoanalytic Thinking: A Dialectical Critique of Contemporary Theory and Practice* (Routledge, 2018); and *Guilt: A Contemporary Introduction* (Routledge, 2023). Many of his publications are available on his York website (yorku.ca/dcarveth) and his current website (doncarveth.com); his video lectures are available on his YouTube channel (YouTube.com/doncarveth). He is in private psychoanalytic practice in Toronto.

Samir Gandesha is Professor of Global Humanities and the Director of the Institute for the Humanities at Simon Fraser University in Vancouver, Canada. He is a co-editor of the *Journal of Adorno Studies* and has written extensively on fascism, authoritarianism, and populism.

Cheryl Goldstein, Ph.D., Psy.D. is a research psychoanalyst in Los Angeles with doctorates in Comparative Literature/Jewish Studies and Psychoanalysis. She writes on the intersection of Jewish thought and psychoanalytic theory and practice, specifically on the importance of difference and otherness in psychoanalytic thought. She has a clinical practice in Los Angeles, CA.

Kurt Jacobsen is Lecturer in Social Sciences and Faculty Associate in the Department of Political Science at The University of Chicago. He is coeditor of the UK-based journal *Free Associations*, and the author or editor of a dozen books.

Russell Jacoby is Professor emeritus in History at UCLA. His latest book is *Intellectuals in Politics and Academia: Culture in the Age of Hype.*

Lauren Langman is a professor emeritus of sociology at Loyola University of Chicago. He received his Ph.D. from the University of Chicago and analytic training at the Chicago Institute for Psychoanalysis. He is the past chair of Marxist Sociology of the American Sociological Association where he recently received the Lifetime Achievement Award. He is a founding member and board member of the Global Studies Association, the International Herbert Marcuse Society, and the North American Erich Fromm Society. Recent publications include *Trauma Promise and Millennium: The Evolution of Alienation*, with Devorah Kalekin, *Alienation and Carnivalization* with Jerome Braun and a special issue of *Current Sociology* on Arab Spring, the Indignados, and Occupy. His recent books include *God, Guns, Gold and Glory* (with George Lundskow) and *Inequality in the 21st C: Marx, Piketty and beyond* (Brill). He is on several editorial boards, including *Critical Sociology*, *Current Perspectives in Social Theory*, and *Populism.*

Neil Mclaughlin, Ph.D. is a Professor of Sociology at McMaster University in Hamilton, Ontario, and has a courtesy appointment at the Institute for the History and Philosophy of Science and Technology at the University of Toronto. His most recent publications include *Erich Fromm and Global Public Sociology* (2021, and 2023 paperback: Bristol University Press). He studies public intellectuals, the politics of higher education, and Soros conspiracy theorists.

Ilene Philipson, Ph.D. holds doctorates in sociology, clinical psychology, and psychoanalysis. She is a Training and Supervising Analyst at the Institute of Contemporary Psychoanalysis in Los Angeles, and a Supervising Analyst at the San Francisco Center for Psychoanalysis. She is the author of many books and articles in the field of psychoanalytic sociology.

Javier Sethness Castro is a primary-care provider, a libertarian socialist, and the author or editor of five volumes, including *Queer Tolstoy: A Psychobiography* (Routledge Mental Health, 2023).

Michael J. Thompson is Professor of Political Theory, Dept. Political Science, William Paterson University and is a candidate in the Division I Program in psychoanalysis at the William Alanson White Institute in New York City. His books include, *The Politics of Inequality* (Columbia, 2007), *The Domestication of Critical Theory* (Rowman and Littlefield, 2016), *The Specter of Babel: A Reconstruction of Political Judgment* (SUNY, 2020), *Twilight of the Self: The Decline of the Individual in Late Capitalism* (Stanford, 2022), and the forthcoming *Descent of the Dialectic: Phronetic Criticism in an Age of Nihilism* (Routledge).

Charles Thorpe is Professor of Sociology at the University of California, San Diego. He is author of *Oppenheimer: The Tragic Intellect*, *Necroculture*, and *Sociology in Post-Normal Times* as well as a contributor to numerous professional journals.

Neil Wegenschimmel, MA Sociology, MA Psychology is a Ph.D. candidate in social psychology at the University of Waterloo where he researches cultural change, nihilism, extremism, and authoritarianism, particularly how perceptions of societal extremism might influence social norms. He is broadly interested in meaning and belief in different contexts (religion, extremism, polarization, and nihilism), media and information consumption, and the effect of digital social life on what we see as being real or true.

Introduction

Daniel Burston and Kurt Jacobsen

In December of 2022 one of us called up an old friend, a colleague of ten years who now teaches in a different university. She was a lawyer before she became an academic, and because of her knowledge and experience in legal matters, was chosen by her colleagues to represent them to the administration as their Faculty Chair. After the customary exchange of greetings and personal news, she related an unsettling conversation that she had recently with her university's Vice President of Diversity, Equity and Inclusion (DEI). This newly-hired administrator told her that her office's first priority was to set up a Bias Response Team. Being a lawyer by training, our friend tactfully suggested that perhaps this new administrative unit should be called the Allegations of Bias Response Team to preserve the presumption of innocence. However, the new VP replied that no, that would not be appropriate; if a faculty member's actions or utterances were experienced as biased, they *were* biased. That's all there is to it. Nor do the faculty member's intentions or contextual factors in the situation have any bearing at all on the case. The impact of the faculty member's utterances on the complainant is all that matters.

The Faculty Chair was stunned by the Vice President's declaration, since the presumption of innocence is a fundamental principle of Anglo-American jurisprudence, and the presumption of bias can easily become an insidious kind of bias all on its own when left unchecked. Furthermore, the absence of due process here puts faculty at a dramatic disadvantage to their accusers, who may harbor ulterior motives for lodging complaints. Indeed, this stacked arrangement can empower students or colleagues to ruin the careers and livelihoods of dedicated teachers and scholars solely on the basis of aggrieved feelings that are entirely subjective and/or unjustified. And if faculty are denied the opportunity to face their accusers and offer their own side of the story—which is usually the case in situations like this–they, like accused miscreants in Mao's China, must apologize for their alleged misdeeds, and undergo, if not expulsion, a ritualized process of "re-education."[1]

This is an all too familiar story. Similar things are happening—or indeed have already happened—in universities across the country, rendering university teaching an even more precarious profession than it hitherto was. No wonder university instructors tend to be apprehensive around their students nowadays and placate them with inflated grades and other indulgences.[2] After all, if they make a minor misstep, or get on someone's bad side, students, administrators, and many faculty caught up in the hue and cry may gang up on them and have them dismissed on flimsy pretexts. The hot button issues, interestingly, are almost always ones of identity or culture, never class which, as Michaels trenchantly remarks, is "harder to get rid of."[3] And for decades now, university administrators in the US and UK have pounced on the extreme sensitivity of student groups and accommodated even bizarre demands in their overarching quest to diminish or erase any degree of faculty autonomy.[4]

In the ensuing days we gave this grim situation more thought and several dark parallels readily came to mind. The first was the odious Stalinist show trials of the 1930s, where the presumption of guilt was a foregone conclusion, and the accused's efforts at explaining or justifying their actions or utterances were routinely taken as clinching evidence of their guilt.[5] In that judicial travesty, there was absolutely no way to establish one's innocence. The Nazi regime embraced strikingly similar policies and practices.[6] Even in a democracy, the disgraceful antics of the House Un-American Activities Committee displayed how uninhibited and unhinged authorities can be when they have temptingly powerless prey in their crosshairs.[7]

Another fitting, if melodramatic, parallel was the practice of "trial by water" for unfortunate women accused—often due to unslaked lust of their accusers for them or their property, or both—of practicing witchcraft. In such cases, the accused was forcibly submerged under water for lengthy intervals. If she drowned, she was grudgingly judged to be innocent, because the Devil had not rescued her. And though she died, sadly, at the hands of supposedly wise and upright judges, she would assuredly ascend to heaven, thank the Lord. If she survived, however, her resilience was deemed to be proof that she was in league with Satan, and she would be promptly burned at the stake or hung. In all these scenarios, the accused never stood a chance. You lost either way; by protesting your innocence or by surviving the ordeal.

In a Stalinist courtroom or Salem witch trial you often forfeited your life. By contrast, when academics are unjustly accused of bias in a classroom setting today, whether because of a misunderstanding or malice, they only stand to lose their voice, reputation, livelihood, and employment prospects, rather like the blacklists of the McCarthy era (which faded but never really expired).[8] The fact that a faculty member rubbished in this fashion spent many years, and often accrued considerable debt, in the process of preparing to teach (and to "publish or perish") in a university is not deemed relevant. And if this ordeal cost their marriage too? Well, sorry, but that's not the authorities' problem. Did it render the scholar incapable of feeding, clothing, and schooling their children properly? Well, they should have thought of that *before* they stepped out of line and offended the exquisite sensibilities of the complainant.

Over the past few years, Burston has been contacted by many people who thanked him for calling attention to these issues, but who were too intimidated to speak out themselves. Why? Because they are afraid of losing all that they worked so hard to achieve, usually in a field they love—or loved, at any rate. Several are highly accomplished teachers, clinicians, and researchers working at Ivy League level institutions who have made significant scholarly contributions; people who, in normal circumstances, would feel secure, appreciated, and even acclaimed in their professional roles. But now, after decades, they feel obliged to keep secrets from their colleagues, and to hold their tongues in public, to avert awkward confrontations and perhaps even a personal catastrophe. And who can blame them? It would be bad enough if insidious situations like this were confined to universities alone. But unfortunately, this is not the case. Whether in politics, business, journalism, sports, or the entertainment field, people are too often "cancelled" for questionable or patently absurd reasons and have no way of exonerating themselves or recouping their losses.

Observers suggest various diagnoses for the malignant collective behavior we're addressing. A Jungian would speculate that we are witnessing an instance of *enantiodromia*, or the psyche's tendency to overcompensate for a one-sided (and ultimately untenable) attitude by abruptly adopting its opposite. From a purely descriptive standpoint, this is an apt description of the postmodern portion of the global Left's recent shift away from a kind of squishy relativism to a harsh, hasty, and judgmental mindset that confers a false sense of moral clarity for "true believers," who believe they are in possession of immutable truths. An especially striking and marvelously apt term for this sub-group is "Brahmin Left" (if not "Charlatan Left"), connoting a caste-like section of purported radicals who have downgraded or ditched class politics and instead elevated their own precious sensitivities to the supreme social standard.[9] The crusaders who champion the new moralism—variously called Critical Social Justice Theory, "equitism," and other things—at first ran no risks in this fervid campus climate (though the Right especially in Texas, Florida, and Arkansas and North Carolina quickly rejoiced over these juicy targets). But while the concept of *enantiodromia* works well at a purely descriptive level, it doesn't really address the how or why of such a stunning and worrisome collective reversal. Perhaps these testy exemplars of extreme "wokeism" were bubbling up among us all along.

To many aghast onlookers, this astonishing about-face seems to herald a newly emergent strain of progressive or "Left-wing" authoritarianism. And as several contributors to this volume point out, our current malaise—or whatever you call it—has roots in postmodernism and other intellectual movements that germinated in the 70s, 80s, and 90s; movements which, even then, were widely criticized by many lifelong leftists as diversions from and dilutions of the Left's historic commitment to class struggle and emancipation.[10] These movements were inspired by the abstruse work of post-modern philosophers and theorists who at first exerted scant impact outside the universities. But that is, as contributor Russell Jacoby attests, no longer the case. So, before we go any further, let's briefly consider what defines the Left, and what constitutes Left-wing authoritarianism, and why it is not parsed out and discussed more clearly nowadays.[11]

The concept of Left-wing authoritarianism was introduced in the 1930s by two Marxist psychoanalysts urgently conducting separate studies of the psychology of fascism (Burston, 2022). When discussing the Left-wing variant, Wilhelm Reich and Erich Fromm referred to Stalinism, which they both repudiated as a grotesque distortion of Marx's message and methods. However, after the defeat of the Axis powers, Right-wing authoritarianism continued to be studied intensively while the concept of Left-wing authoritarianism lapsed into obscurity. This was chiefly because *The Authoritarian Personality*, a classic in 20th-century social psychology, which focused on antisemitism, racism, and the potential for a revival of Right-wing demagogy in a HUAC-ridden US, ignored this issue altogether (Burston, 2022). Indeed, social psychologist Bob Altemeyer, a leading authority in the field, even remarked that Left-wing authoritarianism, according to the Adorno team's criteria and his own RWA measures, is "the Loch Ness monster of social psychology – shadows, yes, but no monster" (Altemeyer, 1996).

Many people on the Left, including at least one co-editor, still believe this statement to be true and claim that the persecutory excesses we are witnessing on many college campuses have nothing to do with the Left's historic priorities and perspectives, even if they do brandish a self-proclaimed "progressive" label. Indeed, a frequent accusation is that self-styled progressives, while acutely aware of Right-wing authoritarianism, are oblivious to the authoritarianism in their own ranks and are therefore prone to dismiss anyone who calls attention to it as an agent of the Right (which, as contributor Lauren Langman points out, is sometimes very much the case).[12] And here is where the customary media equation of "progressive" with "Leftist"—and either of these terms with "Liberal"—produces humongous confusion. Many Leftists in the USA dub themselves progressives because it is the most acceptable public term under which to present themselves in mainstream discourse. Nevertheless, many purported progressives exhibit little or no interest in the bedrock Leftist goals of redistributing wealth and power, or else imagine that they can do so by installing administrative mechanisms or processes that would presumably insure "equity," rather than equality.

Granted, grabbing your piece of the action is an archetypal goal associated with many progressive causes, but it need not (and generally does not) entail the systemic change for which Leftists have advocated historically. For Adorno and his associates, being Left of center entailed "opposition to the status quo, a tendency to think in sociological rather than moral-hereditarian terms; a tendency to identify with labor and the 'common man' and to oppose the power of business, support for the extension of the political and economic functions of government."[13] So it is important to remember that however "woke" they may be, or pretend to be, most college administrators, like others in the professional managerial class and aspirants to it, come to a screeching halt well short of endorsing many of the foregoing criteria for fear that donors might form lynching parties, or at the very least abandon them.[14] University administration buildings should never be mistaken by sober parties for Leftist strongholds any more than windmills should be mistaken for hulking giants.

Recently, several teams of researchers contested Altemeyer's assessment of Left-wing authoritarianism, devising new instruments to measure it—although here too, the terms 'liberal" and "Left-wing" are used interchangeably and indiscriminately by researchers; muddying the waters by conflating these often antagonistic stances (e.g. Conway et al. 2021). But without prompting from psychologists, many seasoned Left-wing theorists and commentators confront this incipient problem forcefully, arguing that the detected presence of authoritarian attitudes and practices in progressive movements impairs their effectiveness and credibility to a considerable and even crippling degree. These Left-wing critics stress that earlier generations of Left activists advocated the liberation of specific racial groups, ethnic and/or sexual or gender minorities, etc., but only as a prelude or accompaniment to the emergence of a more egalitarian and humane society for all. Moreover, they hasten to point out that the 1962 Port Huron Statement, founding document of Students for a Democratic Society, extolled participatory democracy and staunchly opposed restrictions on hard-won rights of free speech and other civil liberties, which are absolutely necessary to achieve universalist goals.[15]

By contrast, many contemporary progressive activists claim to be anti-capitalist but are so deeply enmeshed in identity politics, an outgrowth of postmodernism, that they seldom suspect or care whether the working class, however defined, harbors revolutionary potential (Lange & Pickett-Depaolis, 2022, introduction). Unlike their Stalinist and anti-Stalinist socialist predecessors, who courted the working class, the new authoritarian progressives tend to ignore working-class people—who are not all white, by the way—or else view them as an *impediment* to social change.[16] In fairness, perhaps, the fact that a significant portion of working-class people vote against their own interests is not exactly news.[17] This tendency was evident to Reich and Fromm and in fact motivated them to study Right-wing authoritarianism in the first place. Still, the upper and middle classes are not without their "class traitors" too (Marx counted on it), and perhaps of the same proportion, though they are not nearly as numerous as those who must live paycheck to paycheck.

The fact that this trend persists, and indeed seems to have been aggravated, suggests that progressives, liberals, and the Left have yet to fully grasp the underlying causes (including their own contributory role) for this phenomenon, much less to find appropriate remedies for it. In the US and UK since the 1990s the Democratic Party and the Labour Party, as their platforms attest, clearly chose to shrug off working-class voters for middle-class professionals and minorities instead in a continuous regressive cycle, interrupted only by Jeremy Corbyn's and Bernie Sanders' thwarted campaigns.[18] What is happening is not so much that working-class people are voting for knuckleheaded demagogues but that, increasingly discouraged, they aren't voting at all or going independent. Voter turnout follows family income very closely.[19] But while it may be far-fetched to expect a stereotyped working class to pave the way for general human emancipation, as Marx expected, it is equally (if not more) foolish to imagine that a lasting social transformation can be accomplished *without* engaging working-class people and enlisting their active participation in the transition to a sane society. And at the end of the day, the rallying cries of many progressives seldom speak to the experiences or concerns of working-class people in all their diversity. If anything, they often repel them.

So, why, in many circles, are authoritarian progressives regarded to be exclusively Leftist, rather than, say, as opportunistic centrists and liberals? Adorno and his associates clearly discerned that in the American context, the "Liberal approach is not as broadminded as it may appear" because "it often hides the conviction that there is no objective truth in politics, that every country as every individual, may behave as it likes and that the only thing that counts is success. It is precisely the pragmatization of politics which ultimately defines fascist philosophy."[20] This "pragmatization of politics"—the hoary creed that the end justifies the means—is what we plainly witness as the creed of the growing techno-managerial class and in the excesses lamented above. We therefore argue that authoritarianism as a mode of action—rigid, dogmatic, monomaniacal, and exclusionary—can be manifested by anyone on the political spectrum: Right, Left, and Center.

As our contributors demonstrate in the pages that follow, progressive and Left-wing authoritarianism not only alienates working-class folk but also many Left-wing activists whose sensibilities and political priorities were formed in the tumultuous struggles of the 1960s onwards. Consider Slovenian philosopher Slavoj Žižek. He calls attention to the shocking decline in ethical standards among Right-wing politicians in the United States, Russia, and Israel—and rightly so, of course. But then, significantly, he turns his attention to incipient Left-wing authoritarianism, saying that the Left, as he understands it,

> . . . has become increasingly authoritarian and intolerant as it advocates permissiveness for all forms of sexual and ethnic identity – except one. . . . All sexual orientations and gender identities are now acceptable unless you are a white man whose gender identity corresponds with your biological sex at birth. Members of this cisgender cohort are enjoined to feel guilty just for what they are – for being "comfortable in their skin" . . .

After furnishing examples of the trend, Žižek concludes that

> . . . under a woke regime, we never know if or when some of us will be canceled for something we have said or done (the criteria are murky), or for simply being born into the forbidden category.
>
> Far from opposing the new forms of barbarism . . . the woke left fully participates in it, promoting and practicing an oppressive discourse without irony.

> Though it advocates pluralism and promotes difference, its subjective position of enunciation – the place from which it speaks – is ruthlessly authoritarian . . . That said, we should bear in mind that this mess is largely confined to the narrow world of academia (and various intellectual professions like journalism), whereas the rest of society is moving more in the opposite direction.

While many observers agree that the Woke or "Brahmin Left" has become more authoritarian and intolerant, they seldom reckon that these trends are mostly confined to the university. For example, Russell Jacoby notes that since the 1950s Left intellectuals, who could no longer find employment as freelance intellectuals, writers, and organizers, often gravitated towards academia for comfort and camaraderie, hoping to find (or create) a convivial and economically sustainable milieu for themselves. And for decades, many thrived there because enrollments were rising steadily and their services were in demand. However, by the late 1990s, employment opportunities in academia grew scarcer. Worse yet, the universities could not place all the eager postmodernist students, but that wherever they went, they brought along the sensibilities and jargon they learned on campus. "The leftists who would have vanished as assistant professors in conferences on narratology and gender fluidity or disappeared as law professors with unreadable essays on misogynist hegemony and intersectionality pushed out into the larger culture."[21]

Jacoby's assessment of Leftish newspeak is withering, but calling this kind of talk "blather," while hardly flattering, may risk minimizing the harm it can do. In a recent article Julia Suissa and Alice Sullivan point out that

> the kinds of statements that routinely lead to people (overwhelmingly women) being denounced as transphobes include: that humans, like all mammals, have two sexes, male and female; that females are the sex that produce large immobile gametes called ova; that males are the sex that produce small mobile gametes called sperm; that women are adult human females; that women do not have penises; that homosexuality is same-sex attraction; that only women have cervixes; that a transwoman who transitions as an adult has not always been female; that non-gender conforming young children should not be encouraged to believe that they may have been 'born in the wrong body' and that they can change their sex.[22]

They go on to lament

> the hounding of Labour MP Rosie Duffield, who 'liked' a tweet commenting 'do you mean women?' in reply to a campaign recommending cervical cancer screening to 'individuals with a cervix'. To imply that cervix-bearing people might prefer to be described as women, or that only women have a cervix, was sufficient for her to face calls for the removal of the Labour whip.[23]

Suissa and Sullivan go on observe that in the present climate[24]

> the traditional Left basis for no-platforming fascists is often misunderstood. This rests on the view that fascists will shut down democratic debate and organizing through the use of violence against opponents (Trotsky, 1944). The argument was not that fascist speakers have dangerous ideas which might influence their audience, but that there is no sense in trying to reason with violent thugs . . . But it seems that no-platforming has now been turned on its head, as those who oppose the democratic civil liberties of freedom of speech and association use no-platforming to silence dissent (Ditum, 2014). None of the feminists who have been no-platformed for gender-critical views have committed or incited violent acts. Accusations of fascism and 'literal violence' levelled against these women may appear comical, but have real consequences in dehumanising and monstering them, thereby justifying harassment and even violence against them.

Despite their different emphases, certain common concerns are being articulated here. One is that the progressives' current emphasis on diversity often masks other, less laudable (and perhaps unconscious) attitudes and agendas. Another is that the policy of no-platforming and silencing dissenters is incompatible with the beliefs and practices of earlier generations of activists and is undemocratic in nature. There is no scenario in which silencing opponents advances democratic leftist goals, and indeed historically censorship ploys are always turned against an ever vulnerable Left. Finally, there is the perception that the "progressive" Left's refusal to allow debate on certain subjects attests to the prevalence of a trait that is highly correlated with Right-wing authoritarianism, namely, dogmatism. Dogmatism consists in the fervent embrace of claims, statements, or beliefs that are either demonstrably false or are open to reasonable doubt, but which are nonetheless embraced by large numbers of people who are inclined to impose them on others. Among those who share a set of dogmatic beliefs, those who do *not* celebrate them are usually viewed as ethically or intellectually deficient. And among extremely dogmatic authoritarians, people who *challenge* their beliefs publicly are deemed to be depraved or dangerous to society and targeted for reprisals of one sort or another. Dogmatism of this sort is nothing new, of course. On the contrary, it has dominated and disfigured many political and religious movements and organizations through the ages.

According to Altemeyer, an eminent expert on Right-wing authoritarianism, dogmatism is often associated with cognitive distortions such as dichotomous, either/or, all or nothing thinking and with "doublethink," or a lack of cognitive dissonance when the subject *should* be aware that they are affirming two contradictory ideas or positions simultaneously.[25] Cognitive anomalies and blind spots like these serve much the same purpose as Freudian defense mechanisms, keeping inconvenient truths out of conscious awareness. But leaving these cognitive distortions aside for the moment, on the motivational side of things, dogmatism often conceals a desperate desire for certainty and a search for unanimity and belonging.

Correlatively, it may mask a "will to power." Unfortunately, both the desire to belong and the will to power tend to warp our judgment and to stifle rational doubt. So, for example, in bygone ages, doubting the existence of the afterlife, or the heritability of sin, the inerrancy of scripture, the Divine Right of Kings, the existence of witches, Ptolemy's astronomy, the infallibility of Popes, or the fixity of species (and so on) afforded doubters an opportunity to discover and develop a more realistic understanding of the world and their place within it. But it also placed them at odds with the majority of their peers, rendering them vulnerable to shaming, shunning, exile, torture, or death. That being so, it took a good deal of courage for heretics like these to challenge and resist these widely shared beliefs in their search for a humane truth.

While religious belief and organized religion are decidedly in decline, many of beliefs shared by postmodern Leftists are embraced with a seemingly religious fervor, prompting their adherents to wage vicious campaigns to hound heretics out of academe. Meanwhile, we're apt to forget that religious authority *still* holds considerable sway is much of the Muslim world (though Indonesia and, intermittently, Pakistan are democratic states) where many of the same features found among authoritarian Leftists flourish among ruling Islamists. Consider Salman Rushdie, a British citizen of Muslim heritage who lost an eye and the use of one hand in a near fatal attack from a Muslim assailant at the Chautauqua Institution in New York State on August 12, 2022. Rushdie's long ordeal began in 1989, roughly one year after the publication of a Swiftian and iconoclastic novel, *The Satanic Verses*. As Rushdie relates in his memoir, *Joseph Anton*, his novel was a satirical outgrowth of a proud Muslim intellectual tradition that dates back many centuries; one that accepted, indeed encouraged rational doubt and open debate, both of which are inimical to the Islamist mindset.[26] Rushdie's literary audacity provoked Ayatollah Khomeini, the religious and political leader of Iran, to declare him an apostate, and to issue a *fatwa* (or religious decree) calling for his death, offering substantial financial rewards—up to $3 million—to his would-be killer.

With generous help from friends, the British secret service, Susan Sontag, and the writers' organization PEN, Rushdie eluded his would-be assassins—until recently. But when his novel was first published, his publishers and their offices were menaced with bomb threats, and two of his translators were murdered by religious zealots for bringing his work to non-English speaking audiences. In response to these encroaching threats, Rushdie went into hiding for an entire decade, only gradually returning to public life. Samir Gandesha, another contributor to this volume, observed that[27]

> The Rushdie fatwa and its aftermath set the tone for a series of encounters that expose some of the contradictions between, one the one hand, the freedom of expression and the press, and on the other, religious freedom. It would be followed in 2005 by the Danish Cartoon affair and then the massacre in the offices of the irreverent and provocative magazine Charlie Hebdo in 2015, which left

> twelve people dead and eleven injured. The violence was justified, in part, by the idea that transgressive representations of Islam were harmful, which is to say that "retaliatory violence" could be justified if not enjoined by the faith. The rationalism and anti-clericalism that had heretofore been the pillars of the Left back to the Italian Renaissance, if not before, now come to be seen as potentially serving Eurocentrism, Orientalism, and a now discredited modernity and its literally *incredible* meta-narratives.

While a dismaying number of contemporary progressives are indulgent to plainly authoritarian Islamist groups, not all Left-wing sympathizers are so blinkered. For example, in *Living in The End Times*, the Lacanian Marxist Slavoj Žižek deplores the[28]

> . . . all too easy and uncritical acceptance of anti-American and anti-Western Muslim groups as representing "progressive" forms of struggle, as automatic allies; groups like Hamas and Hezbollah suddenly appear as revolutionary agents, even though their ideology is explicitly anti-modern, rejecting the entire egalitarian legacy of the French Revolution. (Things have gone so far here that some on the contemporary Left even consider an emphasis on atheism as a Western colonial plot.) Against this temptation, we should insist on the unconditional right to conduct a public critical analysis of all religions, Islam included – and the saddest thing is that one should even have to mention this. While many a Leftist would concede this point, he or she would be quick to add that any such critique must be carried out in a respectful way, in order to avoid a patronizing cultural imperialism – which *de facto* means that every real critique is to be abandoned, since a genuine critique of religion will by definition be "disrespectful" of the latter's sacred character and truth claims.

Žižek's complaint overlaps with familiar charges elsewhere that an imputed surge in antisemitism and an ambivalent attitude toward Islamic fundamentalism is symptomatic of the Left's basic impotence, and the absence of any meaningful class struggle in Europe and the United States. But for purposes of this discussion, the important point is that endorsing or excusing Islamism (whose rise owes a great deal to cynical realpolitik ploys)[29] by some Leftists and progressives does seem indicative of authoritarian leanings, and a willingness to silence those who question their respective world-views; a sorry state of affairs that Lars Rensmann argues against in his book *The Politics of Unreason: Critical Theory and the Origins of Modern Antisemitism.*

Though they overlap and converge to varying degrees, the essays gathered in this volume are somewhat disparate in tone and emphasis, and, in some particulars, they conflict. This was a deliberate choice on our part, and we've made no effort to minimize or obscure these differences. After all, these essays are not intended to be comprehensive in scope, nor are we aiming for uniformity of perspective. As we argue at the outset, authoritarianism takes many different forms today, including centrist and Left-wing ones, and neither of us is invested in trying to have the last word on this subject. On the contrary, our hope here is to kindle deeper reflection and more robust and searching debate among Left-leaning thinkers and activists about these "other" authoritarianisms—although Right-wing authoritarianism remains by far the most potent American threat, especially after January 6, 2021.[30] Of course, we also recognize that many readers may have already pledged their allegiance to movements and ideas that we and our contributors critique, and as a result, may be tempted to dismiss some or perhaps *all* of our efforts. We hope that they give us a fair hearing, but if not, so be it. Heretics have always had to take risks to express dissenting points of view. And if they hadn't done so, historically, where would we be today?

Despite many striking differences in tone and emphasis, the contributors to this volume do share some common convictions. We believe that transitioning to a sustainable eco-system to ensure the future of humanity and indeed, of all life on this planet, requires more than merely ending our reliance on fossil fuels and spurring public and private investment in new and better energy technologies, no matter how breathtaking in scope they may be. A truly sustainable future requires economic justice, and a massive downward redistribution of wealth in the not-too-distant-future. Meanwhile, on a pragmatic level, we support raising the minimum wage, universal healthcare, educational reforms, and the return of robust unions to insure a more equitable distribution of wealth and opportunity. We support a foreign policy style that will at least ask questions first and foremost, and search for means of cooperation and compromise, before it entertains the prospect of shooting anyone. Will this lead to a democratic and socialist future? We certainly hope so. However, in the interim, as readers will gather shortly, many of us regard identity politics as a massive distraction that siphons energy and attention away from the more pressing issues at hand. Perhaps if we address the issues that directly threaten our near-term survival we can turn our attention to the vexing issues of race and gender that preoccupy many on the postmodern and identitarian Left, in the hope and expectation that the tensions and ideologies that drive the Left's internal divisions will abate considerably once the neo-liberal order has been replaced with a more just and sustainable world.

Contested Legacies: Marx, Freud, and Nietzsche

The first paper in our anthology is entitled "Three Way Fights: From the First International and the Russian Revolution to Today," by Javier Sethness Castro. It addresses the issue of Left-wing authoritarianism through a Left-wing libertarian or anarchist lens, arguing that the tragedy of the Russian Revolution and the authoritarian features of many Marxist and Left-wing groups today were foreshadowed in Marx's decades-long efforts to discredit and eventually expel Bakunin, Guillaume, Proudhoun, Herzen and other anarchists from the International Working Men's Association in 1872 (The First International) and subsequently.

Anarchist perspectives are seldom incorporated into contemporary debates on authoritarianism, but even those who dispute Sethness Castro's characterizations and conclusions regarding Marx and his followers will acknowledge that Sethness Castro is extremely well informed and approaches his subject matter with clarity and rigor. Moreover, to his credit, Sethness Castro recognizes the contradictions and defects of anarchism, and freely acknowledges "the misogyny, antisemitism, violence, and proto-fascism of certain anarchist and syndicalist thinkers," which he documents convincingly. At the very least, this essay merits a careful read and a thoughtful response.

Our next essay is entitled "The Superego: Our Inner Authoritarian," by Donald Carveth. Like Sethness Castro, Carveth is quite critical of the authoritarian trends in Leninist Marxism. But whereas Sethness Castro celebrates the *Narodniki*, or the anarcho-populist faction in the lead up to the Russian revolution, Carveth sides with the *Mensheviks* (or Social Democrats), whom Lenin and Stalin both abhorred. (In Weimar, Stalin's followers labelled them fascists!) However, as a psychoanalyst, Carveth is not nearly as focused on interrogating the historical record as he is on illuminating the psychodynamics of authoritarianism, which he explicates in neo-Kleinian terms. As he has done for many years, Carveth stresses a crucial illuminating distinction here between the superego and conscience proper, arguing that the former is at the root of authoritarianism (on the Right and the Left) while conscience, properly understood, is the psychological antithesis and/or the antidote to authoritarianism. To conflate the two, as many psychoanalysts do routinely, is to invite a subtly corrosive kind of confusion about our underlying motives for action. Although he brings an original perspective to bear on these issues, Carveth recognizes the priority of Erich Fromm in making the crucial distinction between conscience and superego, which Fromm termed humanistic and authoritarian conscience, respectively. Again, like Fromm, Carveth stresses the presence of authoritarian trends in the history of psychoanalytic organizations, including—but not limited to—the International Psychoanalytic Association.

Carveth's piece is followed by "The New Moralism: From Agonism to Antagonism," an essay by Samir Gandesha. Unlike Sethness Castro, who stressed the historical importance of the First International and the Russian Revolution, and Carveth, who stresses the importance of Freud and Klein, Gandesha trains our attention on the problems that flowed from the Second International's philosophy of history and the contemporary Left's rejection of it, which is predicated on a near total (and ultimately disastrous) rejection of the Enlightenment's legacy, accompanied by a descent into melancholia and a kind of sweeping irrationalism that reflects the Left's decline and thwarts its ambitions to transform society in meaningful and effective ways. Gandesha does borrow somewhat from psychoanalytic theory, but lays much greater emphasis on the need for a "shift from Hegel to Nietzsche," and with it, a reconsideration and novel application of Friedrich Nietzsche's concept of *ressentiment*; a very useful heuristic for understanding the "new moralism" and the complexities, problems, and blind-spots of contemporary anti-racist and anti-colonial theory and practice, and the way they facilitate an unhealthy "desublimation," i.e. a resurgence, of violence.

Politics and the University

Apart from the postmodern Left's repudiation of reason and the abandonment of universalism, another trend that Gandesha laments is the growing popularity of the Afro-pessimist movement inspired by Frank B. Wilderson III. Similarly, in the following essay entitled "Questioning the Universities Anti-Blackness," Charles Thorpe addresses some of the problems entailed in the (more or less open) embrace of Afro-pessimism by contemporary anti-racist activists, providing us with a detailed and searching analysis of how the sudden surge of anti-racist activism and identitarian Leftism on the UC San Diego campus thoroughly eclipsed and derailed years of class-based politics and struggle there. Thorpe's essay is a detailed micro-historical analysis of events on a single university campus over a period of a few years but is clearly illustrative of more pervasive trends in academe.

Next up is an essay entitled "Silencing Dissenters: Academic Authoritarianism in Response to Two Hoaxes" by McLaughlin and Wegenschimmel, which gives us a brief history of the Sokal hoax and a clear-eyed, more detailed account of the Grievance Studies affair and its impact on the fortunes and political views of its protagonists Peter Boghossian, James Lindsay, and Helen Pluckrose. It raises serious concerns about the level of scholarship and the integrity of the peer review process in a number of different fields and academic journals. Like Gandesha, albeit from a different standpoint, McLaughlin and Wegenschimmel believe that the postmodern Left's unwillingness or inability to entertain or address competing points of view is a dangerous trend; one that alienates many thoughtful and well-intentioned people, pushing them in this case to the Right, politically.

McLaughlin and Wegenschimmel's essay is followed by another meditation of the vicissitudes of university life by Russell Jacoby. Called "Back to School: Academic Dogma Invades Public Life," it is a scathing and hilarious—but in the end, quite serious—analysis of how ideas that incubated in the halls of academe hatched and entered society at large, creating a new and unprecedented collective malaise that is difficult to address.

Fluid Identities: Who (or what) is "Woke," a Woman, a Jew?

By contrast with the essays that precede it, which address authoritarian trends in contemporary social movements and university life "The Transformation of *Woke*: Weighing the Mischievous Role of the Right," by Lauren Langman, takes a much more optimistic view of the contemporary Left, arguing that the term "woke" does not denote or describe anything that is intrinsically problematic. Instead, he argues, the term "woke" is a merely sliding signifier that originally referred to laudable progressive ideals but which quickly became a rhetorical cudgel that the

Right deploys to bludgeon and dismiss progressive movements of all shades and stripes, tracing the shifting significations of the term over time in some detail. Langman's reflections on the shifting meanings of "woke" and "wokeness" is followed by "Gender Trouble, Authoritarianism, and the Flight from Womanhood," Ilene Philipson's critique of Judith Butler, Queer Theory, and its impact on the growing influence on contemporary feminism. Philipson laments the trans movement's efforts to silence, discredit, and marginalize women who embrace and espouse gender critical views, and affirm the material—as opposed to merely cultural or symbolic—basis of sexual difference. She explains the growing popularity of Queer Theory since its inception in 1990 to a widespread desire to be "in the know," or a member of an epistemic elite and a "community of the righteous."

Philipson's essay is followed by "The Challenge of Jewish Difference: Antisemitism and the Progressive Left" by Cheryl Goldstein. Drawing on psychoanalysis and Adorno's ideas, she calls attention to the feeling of helplessness and rage that animate much contemporary political discourse, prompting the progressive Left's over-reliance on simplistic binaries, its inability to understand or acknowledge Jewish difference, its insistence on categorizing Jews as "White," as oppressors, etc., and its growing antisemitism, which are all inextricably linked to its deepening symbiosis with Islamist movements.

Left-Wing Authoritarianism: Truth or Fiction?

Echoing many of Goldstein's concerns, in "Psychoanalysis, Authoritarianism, Antisemitism, and the Left: A Critical Theory Perspective" Daniel Burston briefly chronicles the psychoanalytic roots of the concept of authoritarianism, and the ways it entered and impinged upon the lives of psychoanalysts and critical theorists immediately before and after World War II. He argues that despite its recent neglect, Left-wing authoritarianism is a genuine phenomenon which shares several traits with Right-wing authoritarianism, notably a pronounced tendency to dogmatism and rigidity in the form of binary thinking, a derisive attitude toward liberal democratic norms and practices, and, in its more extreme forms, a penchant for violence. Nevertheless, today's Left-wing authoritarianism looks quite different from its Stalinist precursor, having undergone significant metamorphoses since the late 1960s, when it soured the life of Theodor Adorno in the German university setting. Unlike Right-wing authoritarianism, which is rooted in identification with the aggressor and therefor prone to fostering conventional normativity, contemporary Left-wing authoritarianism is shaped by identification with the victim, and is marked by an anti-conventional ethos and an uncritical embrace of both postmodernism and Islamism. Indeed, the co-mingling of Left-wing and Islamist movements—which are authoritarian to the core—is possibly its most salient and worrisome feature.

In an essay entitled "From Solidarity to Identity: Group Narcissism and the Demise of Left Politics" Michael Thompson takes a different (though no less pessimistic) view. Like Burston, he acknowledges that dogmatism and a propensity to lean on simplistic binaries are increasingly prevalent on the Left today, but argues that the source of these trends is not authoritarianism per se but a regression to group narcissism brought about by the ravages of neo-liberalism and an increasingly cybernetic society. Echoing earlier ideas of Adorno's, and citing a diverse range of social theorists—including Herbert Marcuse, Anthony Giddens, Paul Verhaeghe, Peter Berger, and Erich Fromm, among others—Thompson cites "ego weakness" as the cause of the newly emergent "anaclitic self," its intolerance for ambiguity and complexity and its retreat from solidarity into group identity, which weakens the capacity for genuinely critical thinking and effective political action.

Finally, Kurt Jacobsen's essay, "Centrists Askew: The Muddle over the Authoritarian Middle" casts a cold eye on self-serving conceits and blind spots that make up too much of conventional political stances. What Arthur Schlesinger Jr. long ago dubbed the "vital center" is not devoid anymore, if it ever was, of its own authoritarian tendencies.[31] The political "middle" constitutes a moveable zone between the right and left poles in any given society, and as those poles shift over time so will the positioning of the middle (which in the US and UK since the 1970s has been ever rightward). As a key criterion of authoritarianism, the Adorno and Altemeyer studies each emphasize a strong conformist adherence to what is deemed approved thought within the relevant in-group, with a consequent repulsion and indeed aggression directed at troublesome outsiders. Jacobsen notes that Stanley Milgram's most compliant "killer" subjects in the famous obedience experiments typically ranged up to the mid-60s as a percentage, which implicates much, if not all, of the middle anywhere.[32] Jacobsen also briefly compares the centrist authoritarianism at play in the British Labour Party during the advent of Jeremy Corbyn and his initially invigorating grass roots movement, with the Democratic Party's centrist leaders determined effort to derail Senator Bernie Sanders' presidential candidate bids. While unscrupulous and deceitful activities are often the norm in politics, in these instances the wily perpetrators regarded themselves as shining saviors of their Parties and their nations from what they portrayed as the forces of darkness—an authoritarian trait worthy of scrutiny. Centrism, alas, is no easy refuge from simple binaries, dogmatism, prejudice, or any other malady accounted above. Reason requires humility, openness, and critical self-reflection—always in short supply—which we hope are modeled and encouraged by this volume, which includes quite a few papers that were first presented at a conference also entitled *Authoritarianism in All Its Guises: Right, Left and Center* in September 2023, co-organized by David Morgan and co-sponsored by *Free Associations* journal and London's Freud Museum.

While it should go without saying, we hasten to affirm that the authors in this volume are all acutely aware of how much members of sexual and racial minorities suffer under oppressive conditions of various kinds, and we distance ourselves from venal Right-wing jeremiads that occasionally and uncomfortably overlap with some concerns expressed here. (Allan Bloom and Herbert Marcuse both rued the alleged "closing of the American Mind," but for vastly different reasons.)[33]

Yet not all the remedies and ideologies spawned by liberation movements reflect reality, and indeed some may engender dogmas that render the causes they champion less plausible and effective politically, or oppressive in unexpected ways not evident to their most passionate adherents. All the more reason, then, not become a "true believer," but to strive for a reflexive self-awareness of one's own agendas and biases, to acknowledge the incompleteness of all knowledge, and to address contrary cases, data, and arguments that bring to light neglected or overlooked aspects of an issue honestly. If these qualities were more valued and more actively embraced nowadays this volume probably wouldn't have been necessary in the first place.

Notes

1 See Robert J. Lifton, *Thought Reform and the Psychology of Totalism in China* (New York: Norton, 1961). The resonances with McCarthyism and "lesser" phenomena in the West did not go unremarked upon.

2 See a student newspaper editorial defense of the practice at Harvard where 4 of 5 now get A range grades, "The Inflated Fixation on Grade Inflation" Harvard Crimson 20 October 2023. https://www.thecrimson.com/article/2023/10/20/editorial-grade-inflation-compression/https://www.thecrimson.com/article/2023/10/20/editorial-grade-inflation-compression/ A Harvard Report noted the direct correlation between high grades and high student evaluations of faculty.

3 Walter Benn Michaels, *The Trouble with Diversity: How we Learned to Love Identity and Ignore Inequality* (New York: Holt, 2006), p. 7. "We are getting to the point where there are more Black people than poor people in the universities . . . so treating classes as if they were cultures or races is a strategy for managing inequality rather than diminishing or eliminating it. (p.10)

4 See Benjamin Ginsberg, *The Fall of the Faculty: The Rise of the All-Administrative University and Why it Matters* (New York: Oxford University Press, 2013).

5 Yet another option, explored by Arthur Koestler in his novel *Darkness at Noon*, was that of innocent people collapsing before the volleys of adamant accusations and embracing the charges. A more recent counterpart case, arising in the Satanic abuse panic of the 1990s, is examined in Lawrence Wright, *Remembering Satan: A Tragic Case of Recovered Memory* (New York; Vintage, 1995).

6 Ingo Muller, *Hitler's Justice: The Courts of the Third Reich* (Cambridge: Harvard University Press, 1992).

7 See, for example, Paul Buhle and Patrick McGilligan, *Tender Comrades: A Backstory of the Hollywood Blacklist* (New York: St Martin Press, 1997) and Thomas Doherty, *Show Trial: Hollywood, HUAC and the Birth of the Blacklist* (New York: Columbia University Press, 2018).

8 See Ellen Schrecker, *Many are The Crimes: McCarthyism in America* (Princeton: Princeton University Press, 1998) and *No Ivory Tower: McCarthyism & The Universities* (New York; Oxford University Press, 1986).

9 One of us heard Catherine Liu use this deadly accurate evocative term at a conference on "Neo-Feudalism" at the University of Chicago in April 2024. See Liu's book *Virtue Hoarders: The Case Against the Managerial Class* (Minneapolis: University of Minnesota Press, 2021).

10 The 1970s debate between Noam Chomsky and Michel Foucault is a landmark illustration of mutual and irritable incomprehensibility between two major figures who both tend to be counted by outsiders as among the "Left."

11 For a recent worthy, if far from definitive, attempt see John T. Jost, *Left and Right: The Psychological Significance of a Political Distinction* (New York: Oxford University Press, 2021).
12 Also see the account of conservative antics choreographed with the "hope of purging liberal ideas, professors and programming wherever they could" in Nicholas Confessore, "Inside the Crusade against Woke: 'America is under Attack': How Conservative Activists Took Aim at 'Woke.'" *New York Times* 21 January 2024. p. 14.
13 Theodor Adorno et. al., *The Authoritarian Personality* (New York: Harper & Row 1950), p. 157.
14 "On the origins of the Professional Managerial Class" An Interview with Barbara Ehrenreich, Dissent 22 October 2019. Also see Erich Fromm, *The Pathology of Normalcy* (New York: American Mental Health Foundation, 1991).
15 See Saul Landau and Paul Jacobs, *The New Radicals: A Report with Documents* (New York: Random House 1966). Of course, SDS fatally splintered in 1969 into three factions, the two smaller of which, in their different ways, are ripe candidates for a left-authoritarian label: the Weathermen and the Progressive Labor Party. See Kirkpatrick Sale, *SDS: The Rise of Students for a Democratic Society* (New York: Random House, 1973), Maurice Isserman and Michael Kazin, *America Divided: The Civil War of the 1960s* (New York: Oxford University Press, 2015, 5th ed), Bryan Burrough, *Days of Rage* (New York: Penguin, 2016), and the rueful, if not quite repentant, reflections in Mark Rudd, *Underground: My Life with SDS and Weatherman* (New York: HarperCollins, 2009).
16 The "New Left" of the 1960s viewed its constituency as consisting of more than the traditional working class, but rarely downgraded the importance of the latter. On vexing aspects of assigning people in an objective manner to class "positions," see for example, Eric Olin Wright, *Classes* (London: Verso 1998).
17 Times have been tough. For a scorecard on the success of the conservative counter-revolution see Thomas Piketty, *A Brief History of Inequality* (Cambridge: Harvard University Press, 2022). Also see the summary of a RAND report on income maldistribution in Nick Hanauer, "The Top 1% of Americans have taken 50 Trillion from the Bottom 90% – and That has made the US Less Secure." *Time Magazine* 1 September 2020. https://time.com/5888024/50-trillion-income-inequality-america/
18 See Zach Grant and Geoffrey Evans, "A New Dilemma of Social Democracy? The British Labour Party, the White Working Class and Ethnic Minority Representation," *British Journal of Political Science* 54, 3 (July 2024) and Geoffrey Evans and James Tilley, *The New Politics of Class: The Political Exclusion of the British Working Class* (Oxford: Oxford University Press, 2023). Also see Nesrine Malik, "Emerging from the Landslide is a Sad truth about British Politics." *The Guardian* 15 July 2024.
19 Rob Urie, "Who Elected Donald Trump?" *Counterpunch* 16 October 2020.
20 Adorno, *Authoritarian Personality*, p. 726. "Being intelligent today means largely to look after one's self, to take care of one's advantages whereas, to use Veblen's words, 'idle curiosity is discouraged.'" (p. 662)
21 Russell Jacoby, 2022. "The Takeover: Self-Righteous Professors Have Spawned Self-Righteous Students and Unleashed Them on the Public Square." *Tablet Magazine*, Dec. 19.
22 Judith Suissa and Alice Sullivan, "How Can Universities Promote Academic Freedom?". *Impact: Philosophical Perspectives on Education Policy*. 27 (2022), p. 14
23 Debbie Hayton, "How Keir Starmer can make it up to Rosie Duffield," *The Spectator* 5 July 2024.
24 Suissa and Sullivan, "How Can Universities Promote Academic Freedom?" p. 20.
25 Bob Altemeyer, *The Authoritarian Specter* (Cambridge: Harvard University Press, 1996). Chapter 8.
26 Salman Rushdie, *Joseph Anton* (New York: Random House, 2012).

27 Samir Gandesha, "Max Weber on Authoritarianism" OpenDemocracy, 27 October 2021 p. 120.
28 Žižek, *Living in the End Times*, 2011, p. 137.
29 On the funnelling of US arms to fundamentalist groups see, for example, Ahmad Rashid, *The Taliban* (I.B. Tauris, 2022).
30 Jason Wilson, "Violence by Far Right is Among US Most Dangerous Threats, Study Finds." *The Guardian* 27 July 2020.
31 He emphasized that "unmolested inquiry is essential." Arthur Schlesinger Jr., *The Vital Center: The Politics of Freedom* (New York: Houghton Mifflin, 1949), p. 208.
32 Stanley Milgram, *Obedience to Authority* (New York: Harper & Row, 1974).
33 Compare Allan Bloom, *The Closing of the American Mind* (New York: Simon & Schuster 1987) with Herbert Marcuse's much earlier and more prescient *One Dimensional Man* (Boston: Beacon Press, 1964).

Chapter 1

Three-Way Fights

From the First International and the Russian Revolution to Today

Javier Sethness Castro

Formally speaking, Imperial Russia ended when the socio-political revolution of February 1917—inspired by the preceding, abortive uprising of 1905—succeeded in deposing Tsar Nicholas II. Although Great-Russian imperialism persisted in the Union of Soviet Socialist Republics (USSR) and in the post-Soviet State—especially as reflected in the genocidal assaults on Chechnya, Syria, and Ukraine ordered by Vladimir Putin—the overthrow of three centuries of despotic rule by the Romanov dynasty was tremendously progressive. This world-historical opening allowed peasants to launch a "Black Repartition" of the land until then owned by the feudal lords. In parallel, soldiers and urban workers self-organized in councils known as *soviets.*

Beyond the subsequent transitions toward a Provisional Government and Bolshevik dictatorship in the political realm, such vital social aspects of what the Russian-Jewish anarchist Vsevolod Eikhenbaum (Voline) calls the "Unknown Revolution" would not have been possible under Tsarist domination, which banned trade unions up until the 1905 Revolution, and systematically crushed agrarian revolt.[1] Indeed, Boris Mazurin, founder of the "Life and Labor" Commune (1921–1936), which followed the Christian anarchism of artist Lev Tolstoy, writes that "the powerful stimulus to the formation of independent agricultural communes [… was] the February Revolution."[2] Tragically, however, within a decade, these horticultural communes, based on mutual aid, had either been crushed by security forces or forcibly integrated into the State as *kolkhozy* (collective farms).

Still, even before Joseph Stalin notoriously defeated his rival Lev Trotsky and took the reins of the Communist Party of the Soviet Union after their leader Vladimir Lenin's death in 1924, the Bolsheviks in power had nullified the autonomy of the *soviets* (or workers' councils), repressed the urban anarchist movement, crushed the radical mutineers at the Kronstadt naval base, and destroyed the peasant-anarchists of the Revolutionary Insurgent Army of Ukraine, led by Nestor Makhno. This is not to mention the Red Army's counter-insurgent war against Muslims of Central Asia (so-called *Basmachi*), waged in alliance with Russian settler-colonists starting in 1918, much less its reoccupation of newly independent Georgia in 1921, or its subsequent disarticulation of the Georgian Democratic Republic, led by rival Mensheviks.[3]

DOI: 10.4324/9781003389927-1

In this sense, the fall of the Romanovs arguably set off a *three-way fight* involving anarchists, autonomists, and Populists (*Narodniki*) against Marxist-Leninist pseudo-revolutionaries and Tsarist-sympathizing reactionaries that persisted through the Russian Civil War (1918–1920) and the rest of the Soviet period (until 1991), though greatly dampened by Stalin's Terror (1936–1938).[4] In effect, the model of the three-way fight demonstrates that political struggle is three-dimensional: it is not only waged between either the left and the State *or* the left and the extra-parliamentary right, and the State can both help *and* hinder the cause of the right.

Accordingly, in this essay, I provide a historical spin on Matthew Lyons's concept of the three-way fight for Russia's immediate post-revolutionary period, whereby anarchists represent leftists; Leninists, and especially Stalinists, are the newfound "*Sov-bourg*" (Soviet bourgeoisie) denounced by the Spanish anarcho-syndicalist Vilkens; and the "Whites" symbolize the insurgent far-right.[5] My approach will focus mostly on the struggle between the left and the State, both in Tsarist and Soviet times, as on competition between anarchists and Marxists, both before and after the Russian Revolution, over who would spearhead the left (see Figure 1.1 below).

The tragedy of the Russian Revolution—to ossify into a state-capitalist nightmare—repeats the pattern established by Karl Marx's expulsion of leading anarchists from the International Workingmen's Association (IWMA), or First International, in 1872 (see Figure 1.2 below). It also hearkens back to the eclipse of Russian Populism (*Narodnichestvo*) by Marxism at the turn of the 20th century, due to the tireless efforts of Georgii Plekhanov and his protégé Lenin (until their own 1903 split). This Freudian repetition compulsion calls out for recognition that Marxism is "part of the very problem of domination," and that the cause of liberation "necessarily entails a movement against Marx," in the words of political scientist Isaac Balbus.[6] Rather than fetishize capitalism and the State "dialectically," as Marxist theory does, Russian Populists (*Narodniki*) in the 19th and 20th centuries proposed that the intelligentsia organize the peasantry *against* the ruling class and State, with the aim of creating a free-socialist society based on the principles of the peasant commune (*mir*, or *obshchina*).[7]

Therefore, in this chapter, I seek to outline the theoretical and historical differences between Marxism and anarcho-Populism (or anarchism), in the context of Imperial and post-revolutionary Russia. Through an in-depth historical

Actor	Late Imperial Period	Early Soviet Period
State	Tsarist	Communist (Marxist-Leninist)
Left	*Narodniki* (Populists)	Anarchists
Non-State Right	Marxists	Whites

Figure 1.1 Russian Three-Way Fights

account, I will contrast anarcho-Populism from Marxism and Marxism-Leninism in theory, and discuss the intimately related tragedies of the First International and of the Russian Revolution. My guiding hypothesis is that, due to their anti-statist stance, anarchism and anarcho-Populism provide more liberatory frameworks than Marxism and its authoritarian, state-capitalist derivatives—including Leninism, Trotskyism, and Stalinism. Before concluding in the spirit of a critical anarchism, I will consider some objections to my hypothesis, acknowledging that anarchists are in no way exempt from affirming right-wing politics, and connect the argument to a critique of left-wing authoritarianism today, especially over such pressing questions as the Syrian and Rojava Revolutions, the Russo-Ukrainian War, and Israel's war on Gaza.

Admittedly, some self-described Marxists may balk at my framing here, which accuses their tradition of authoritarianism and conservatism. By contrast, most Marxist-Leninists would not deny such charges. Rather, they openly seek to mobilize domination in the interest of socio-political and economic transformations directed by themselves. Accordingly, in Figures 1.1 and 1.2 in this chapter, the term "Non-State Right" should by no means be taken as suggesting that the corresponding groups advocate anti-statist or anti-authoritarian politics. Instead, this term merely means that the groups in question are relatively more conservative than their leftist counterparts, and not in State power.

Introducing Anarcho-Populism

Russian Populism (*Narodnichestvo*) was born from the ashes of Tsar Nicholas I's death in March 1855 and Imperial Russia's defeat by British, French, and Ottoman forces in the Crimean War (1853–1856). Spurred by these historic setbacks for established authority, dissident intellectuals known as *Narodniki* sought to mobilize and politicize the People (or *Narod)* toward an "anti-establishment and anti-corruption agenda" rooted in anti-authoritarian, anti-capitalist critique. Their primary influences were Charles Fourier, Pierre-Joseph Proudhon, and Alexander Herzen.[8] These *Narodniki*, including writers Nikolai Chernyshevsky and Tolstoy, felt a "deep hatred of oppressors and a deep personal love for the simple-hearted heroes of human emancipation," in the words of anarcho-communist Peter Kropotkin.[9]

To realize their mission, Russian Populists preached "a moral community, vaguely stateless in political form, localized in activity, mutual in human relations, and religious in spirit."[10] Many *Narodniki* framed their revolutionary aims as the millenarian seeking of a religious utopia akin to the mythical *Belovode*, a realm freed of war and exploitation. In reality, both the courage of the Populist youth who committed "revolutionary suicide," and the *Narodniki*'s goals of liberating the peasantry and overthrowing Tsarism, inspired the boldness of the Russian Revolutions of 1905 and 1917.[11] Seen from this perspective, the Revolution had been consciously prepared for at least two generations by countless activists, political prisoners, and martyrs for the cause. Indeed, radical students and *Narodniki* organized Imperial Russia's first public protests, "sights [that] had never [before] been seen": namely, a student demonstration held in St. Petersburg on a "wonderful September day" in 1861, and a public demonstration in the same city in 1876, which took place in front of Kazan Cathedral.[12]

Anarcho-Populism, then, is a messianic political philosophy first theorized by the Russian anarchists Herzen and Mikhail Bakunin, as based on their observation of and passion for the toiling People, defined by a "distrust of [all] liberal democracy; belief in a possible autonomous development of Socialism in Russia; faith in the future possibilities of the *obshchina*; [and] the need to create revolutionaries who could dedicate themselves to the people."[13] The Populist hero's "symbol of faith," hence, "is *the people's welfare*."[14] In Imperial Russia, the maximalist doctrine of anarcho-Populism referred and appealed to the peasantry, fused together with the revolutionary intelligentsia, as the emancipatory subject that would overthrow the despotism of Tsarism and landlordism, avert the bleak imposition of Western-style capitalism, and institute a counter-modernity characterized by agrarian-socialist federations of self-governing communes.[15]

In contrast to the Marxist and Lenino-Stalinist strategies of State capture and central planning, anarchists propose an approach known as interstitial metamorphosis, whereby communalist, self-managed, syndicalist, and reconstructive popular movements function to transform society without central authority.[16] Many, though not all, *Narodniki* adhered to anarchist political principles, which can be summarized as including anti-authoritarianism, anti-statism, anti-parliamentarism, federalism, libertarianism, and social revolution.[17] As the Ukrainian scholar Anatolii Dubovyk observes, "[m]ost socialists in the 1870's Russian Empire belonged to the followers of anarchist ideas, either of Bakunin or [Peter] Lavrov," with the latter figure being another radical Populist.[18] Russian researcher Sergei Ovsiannikov adds that, historically speaking, Russian anarchists tended to be more philosophically-oriented, whereas Ukrainian anarchists were more practical-minded.[19] In terms of the situation before the 1917 Revolutions, Russian anarchist Grigori Maximoff writes that

> Russian Socialism, notwithstanding its tactic of revolutionary terror applied toward the Tzar's government, was never bloodthirsty, terroristic and inhumane. It never viewed society as a disciplined battalion, never lost sight of the living personality with its needs and interests. The Socialism of Chernishevsky, Bakunin, Lavrov, Kropotkin, and Mikhaylovsky was based upon the ideas of individual freedom, of regional and communal federalism [...].[20]

Hence, it becomes clear that anarchism and anarcho-Populism defy the Marxist vision of a "dystopian, industrialised future," with "capitalist modes of production under new ownership"; the vulgar "barracks communism" imposed by so many Marxist-Leninist regimes in the 20th century; and the overall bleakness of Marx's theory, which "equates production with the human condition" and would "turn the whole world into a giant workhouse."[21] In an attempt to rescue Marx from such grim associations, in their new translation of the "Critique of the Gotha Program" (1891), Kevin B. Anderson and Karel Ludenhoff seek to present Marx's allusions to the *Staatwesen*, or "State apparatus," of the future dictatorship of the proletariat as meaning "body politic" instead.[22] Yet, this venture to recast Marx as less authoritarian than he was is linguistically unconvincing.

While the late autonomist Antonio Negri developed his *Marx Beyond Marx* (1979) from the master's *Grundrisse* (1861), and despite the convergence between anarchism and the humanism of Marx's early economic-philosophical manuscripts, history proves that Marxism epitomizes left-wing authoritarianism, as it "directs those below for the benefit of those above."[23] In parallel, the German anarcho-syndicalist Rudolf Rocker had a point when he accused Marxism of reducing workers to "a mass to be manoeuvred."[24]

Anarcho-Populism vs. Marxism in the Russian Revolution and First International

Historically speaking, the political and strategic tensions between Marxists and anarchists have played out numerous times, yet perhaps never more significantly than during the struggles that raged between them in the First International (1864–1872) and the Russian Revolution. In both cases, with reference to the framing of the three-way fight in the pre-revolutionary context, anarchists functioned as the left and Marxists as the right, as long as capitalism or Tsarism dominated (see Figures 1.1 and 1.2 above). Anarchists still served as the left after the October 1917 Revolution, when the Bolsheviks seized State power.

In his theoretical critique of the Marxist proposal for a "People's State" (*Volks-Staat*), made in the 1870's, Bakunin declares this idea to be nonsense: an "(imaginary) emancipation of the proletariat by means of the State." This is so, his argument goes, because all States are based on the domination of a small minority over everyone else. As bureaucracies and pyramidal organizations, they seek "self-perpetuation" and the indefinite future reproduction of the "slavery" of their subjects.[25] Likewise, in his final manuscript, "On Socialism" (1910), Tolstoy criticized Marxian statism and economic determinism, instead avowing Kantian-Christian moral law.[26] Thus, due to their anti-authoritarian prescience, these thinkers can be likened to Cassandras of the Russian anarchist movement. After all, Marx cynically dismissed Bakunin's misgivings about using the State to effect social change,

Actor	Mid- to Late Nineteenth Century
State	Capitalist
Left	Federalists, Libertarians, Anarchists
Non-State Right	Marxists

Figure 1.2 The Three-Way Fight in the First International

and even expelled him and his Swiss comrade James Guillaume from the First International over this disagreement. Marx called these two "rotten" and "feeble-minded elements" who needed to be excluded—even "excommunicated"—from the movement, while Engels defended their decision to keep the International "pure and unadulterated."[27]

Such contempt for other radicals, involving the mobilization of lies and a rejection of pluralism, prepared the ground for purges in the First International and after the Bolshevik takeover of the Russian Revolution.[28] Indeed, Lenin's Communists imprisoned and executed numerous Tolstoyan conscientious objectors during the Russian Civil War.[29] Given how closely the Bolshevik leaders mimicked their master's example, the anarchist critic Alan Carter charges Marx with responsibility for the catastrophic outcome of the Russian Revolution.[30] In a similar vein, the Christian anarchist Nikolai Berdyaev believes the USSR to have amounted to "the third [historical] appearance of Russian autocratic imperialism," thus mimicking Russia's Muscovite and Tsarist rulers, who themselves had succeeded the Roman, Byzantine, and Mongol Empires.[31] In this vein, Lenin wrote in April 1921 that the Communists should "learn from the Germans how to run state capitalism, [...] doing [so] at an even more rapid pace than the one followed by Peter the First in Westernizing barbarous Russia."[32]

Along these lines, the Bolsheviks' fetishization of political centralism, discursive privileging of the proletariat, and rejection of workers' control over production should be understood as severe *reactions* to the decentralism, humanism, and class inclusiveness of Russian Populism.[33] Lenin's dual rejection of utopian socialism and Populism—positions that proved instrumental in the ruthless replacement of the *Narodnik* emphasis on freedom and ethics with statist brutalism—was "remarkably consistent" throughout his career.[34] Tellingly, in this sense, Lenin slandered the authentically revolutionary Kronstadt mutineers, whose *Petropavlovsk* program (1921) was remarkably anarcho-Populist, as counter-revolutionary White agents.[35]

In reality, what mattered to Marx and Lenin was to defeat one's competitors by any means necessary, including slander and hatred. This would clear the way to taking power. As the fate of the Kronstadt Commune proved, Marxists converge with the Tsarist "administrative utopia" in proposing and celebrating societies that are "disciplined, united," and organized "vertically [...] by a central authority."[36] Stalin thus merely took Marx and Lenin's critiques of utopianism and anarchism to a higher level through his totalitarian assaults on equality, metaphysical speculation, and social experimentation. After all, the Soviet General Secretary dismissed egalitarian calls for social leveling as "leftish chatter" and "reactionary petty-bourgeois nonsense"—leading to a "fantasectomy" of the collective radical imagination, and the global Communist movement.[37] In this sense, the atrocities involved in Stalin's reign built on the Tsarist inheritance and the pre-existing cults to Lenin and Marx. After all, Bolsheviks principally differentiated themselves from Mensheviks through their pledging of allegiance to Lenin, not to mention their less-consistent commitment to democracy.[38] Although such sado-masochistic political dynamics would prove highly detrimental to the fate of the Russian Revolution, they served Lenin's authoritarian goal of Party domination over State and society.

In fact, just two months after the Bolshevik seizure of power in October 1917, the loyalist Council of People's Commissars raised a political police force known as the All-Russian Extraordinary Commission, or CheKa. The CheKa was first based in the headquarters of the Tsarist Okhrana, the successor of Nicholas I's Third Section, or secret police.[39] Rather than be designed for accountability to the peasant, worker, or soldier *soviets* that emerged in the Revolution, the CheKa and its successor organizations—namely, the (O)GPU, NKVD, and KGB—were wielded by Red authorities to consolidate power and eliminate adversaries.[40] Grimly, during the suppression of the Kronstadt Commune, Chekists worked closely with rearguard "Blocking Detachments" to ensure that Red Army soldiers carried out their fratricidal orders—and to swiftly execute anyone who might refuse.[41] Such dystopian scenes highlight the extreme risks involved in pursuing the Marxist goal of political domination, which is to be achieved by strengthening "[State] power above society."[42]

The First International

Before proceeding, let us step back to consider the unfortunate history of the First International, or International Workingmen's Association (IWMA). The IWMA was a prefigurative workers' association, which had been founded in London in 1864 by French and British proletarians, who proclaimed that "the economic emancipation of the working class is the great aim to which [...] all political movements should be subordinated."[43] If the French anarchist Élisée Reclus was right to perceive in the International's founding a potential turning point in the history of freedom, its collapse in 1872 may have amounted to "one of the major achievements in the history of domination."[44] Divided between its vociferous Marxist sections and General Council, run by Marx and Engels, and its federalist-libertarian majority, the First International was a promising, though vulnerable, initiative. Whereas the anti-authoritarians in the group envisioned a transformative strategy rooted in direct action, unionization, and collective self-management, the Marxists advocated statist-electoral approaches, in keeping with a social-democratic program.

At the IWMA's Geneva (1866), Lausanne (1867), Brussels (1868), and Basel (1869) Congresses, the distinctions between the federalist-libertarians and the Marxists became increasingly pronounced. It was around the time of the Basel congress, at which the IWMA's majority had endorsed revolutionary syndicalism, that Marx and Engels's attacks on Bakunin intensified.[45] They repeated libel they had first circulated in 1848 about Bakunin being a Tsarist agent, now adding that he sought to establish a dictatorship over the International.[46] At the private London

Congress (1871), participants aligned with Marx's aims of organizing through political parties and empowering the General Council, provoking protest from libertarian-federalist sections that had not been invited.[47] For Guillaume, these London proceedings sought "to transform the International from a free association of independent sections into an authoritarian and hierarchical organization in the hands of the General Council."[48]

Eventually, Marx used Bakunin's closeness to his *protégé* Sergei Nechaev—who notoriously murdered his own recruit, the agronomy student Ivan Ivanov, in Moscow in November 1869, after the youth objected to Nechaev's authoritarian leadership style—to expel Bakunin and Guillaume from the International at the September 1872 Hague Congress. This bureaucratic scheme, which included the sudden transfer of the General Council to New York, utterly wrecked the organization, for Marx's Blanquist allies and libertarian rivals quit in disgust.[49] The anti-authoritarians immediately regrouped by founding an Anarchist International in St. Imier, Switzerland, eight days later, declaring that "the destruction of all political power is the first duty of the proletariat." Plus, several of Marx and Engels' comrades joined the libertarians, feeling "revolted by the conspiratorial behavior" of their former leaders.[50] Later, in 1896, the Marxists comprising the Second International (1889–1914) expressly banned anarchists.[51]

Ultimately, the expulsion of Bakunin and Guillaume from the IWMA illuminates the fundamental disjuncture between Marxism and anarchism. It is apparent that the homophobic Marx used guilt by association to condemn Bakunin over his supposed infatuation with Nechaev, in line with his political compulsion to eliminate critics and centralize power.[52] While Bakunin erred in associating himself politically with a terrorist like Nechaev, this was mere pretext for Marx. Even the sympathetic biographer Franz Mehring chides Marx's opportunistic use of a threatening letter written by the young Jacobin as evidence against Bakunin.[53] Plus, on the charge of Bakunin's undermining the International through his leading the International Alliance of Socialist Democracy (the "Alliance")—a charge that Marx used as grounds for expulsion—the investigative committee could not even prove its existence.[54] In this sense, such Machiavellian aggressiveness may have been related to Marx's reductive understanding of power as being purely economic in nature. As Carter argues, such a narrow definition "opens the door for political and ideological tyranny."[55]

Ultimately, the German Communist appears to have felt anxious that the combination of Bakunin's charismatic personality; the strength of the Bakuninist program; and the federalist-libertarian sympathies of the International's French, Swiss, Spanish, Belgian, and Italian sections threatened both his position within the organization, and the authority he derived from proposing that it adopt an international electoral strategy.[56] In sum, at the Hague Congress, Marx and Engels chose schism and collapse rather than accept a minority position in a pluralist context, thus confirming their own narcissism and authoritarianism, while anticipating the nightmares of (neo)Stalinist reaction.[57]

The Populist Emphasis on Freedom vs. the Marxist Fetishization of Power

In the eyes of anarcho-Populists, the lives of peasants confirmed what outsiders like Herzen, Bakunin, and Tolstoy presumed to be the People's affinities for anti-authoritarianism and egalitarianism. Such emphases on spontaneity and rural life form important reference points for both anarchists and *Narodniki*. In contrast, Marxists tend to welcome the bourgeoisie's proletarianization of the peasantry as a supposedly historically "necessary" precondition for the development of communism, which is to be achieved through the concentration of the urbanized proletariat in large-scale industry.[58] In keeping with such dogma, during the Russian famine of 1891–1892, Lenin believed the peasants should be denied aid, according to the mantra, "the worse, the better."[59] In fact, the Fordist and Taylorist management styles implemented early in the Soviet period merely conveyed Marx's own enthrallment to capitalism and technocratic politics.[60]

Implicitly echoing Proudhon against Marx in their fierce debate about the former's *Philosophy of Poverty* (1846), writers associated with the *Narodnik* organization *Zemlya i Volya* ("Land and Liberty") lampooned the determinism of Hegelian-Marxian dialectics in 1878 by declaring that "[n]othing is more stupid than to say that Socialism is possible only in a highly developed society." In reality, it "spr[ings] up wherever inequality and exploitation [a]re to be found."[61] These views anticipate the thought of the 20th-century Greek-French philosopher Cornelius Castoriadis, who argues that

> socialism is not a necessary stage of history. It is the historical project of a new institution of society, whose content is direct self-government, the direction and collective management by human beings of all aspects of their social life, and the explicit[ly autonomous] self-institution of society.[62]

Grounding themselves like Castoriadis does in faith in human freedom, Populist humanists committed themselves to, and sacrificed themselves for, the struggle against Tsarist authority out of a belief that the fight for socialism was just, not out of any belief in the inevitability of its victory, or its putatively superior efficiency.[63] Rather than accept the repressive and self-serving arguments made by liberal and Marxist Westernizers alike about the supposedly "progressive" or "necessary" nature of capitalism, Russian Populists—from Bakunin and Nikolai Speshnev in the 1840's, to Chernyshevsky in the 1850's and 1860's, Lavrov in the 1870's and 1880's, and the Socialist Revolutionaries in the early 20th century—rejected deterministic ideas about historical stages. Instead, they proposed steering society directly to socialism, so bypassing further capitalist development.[64]

In contrast to Marx's privileging of the urban proletariat as the presumably revolutionary subject, and of capitalist industry as the principal site of class struggle, Herzen and Bakunin's notion of socialism was much closer to the rural anarcho-communism of Kropotkin. Herzen envisioned a non-industrial agrarian socialism, and an improved version of the peasant village; he stressed the social life of the *Narod* as a promising base for revolutionary social transformation. As he writes, it had not been gentry intellectuals who had introduced to the Russian peasants the systems of communal property and the periodic redistribution of the land and collective labor they themselves instituted. Bakunin felt a similar pride for the revolts of the Russian peasantry, and turned his gaze to the less industrially developed regions of southern Europe for anarchic inspiration. Unlike Marx, these thinkers found great revolutionary potential in decentralized rural communities.[65]

Rather than make "dialectical" excuses for authoritarianism and the perpetuation of class society, as Marxist theory does, anarchists and anarcho-Populists effectively employ "producerist populist ideology" to advocate direct control of the means of production by workers and peasants (see the *Rt* → *At* curve in Figure 1.4 below).[66] Indeed, anarchist internationalists look forward to abolishing the State and replacing it with an economic system based on contracts forged among communes and workers' collectives.[67] The profound radicalism of the *Narodnik* and anarchist strategies suggests that, had these been implemented in the former Tsarist Empire after the Russian Revolution, they may have provided a better chance of arriving at a post-capitalist future that would have led to workers' control (*At*) and communism (*Pt/Ct*), rather than state capitalism (*Ft*), according to the Marxist and Leninist doctrines (see Figures 1.3 and 1.4 below). After all, eyewitness visitors to the early Soviet Union like the Spanish anarchist Vilkens confirm that it was stratified by class and lorded over by the "*Sov-bourg*."[68]

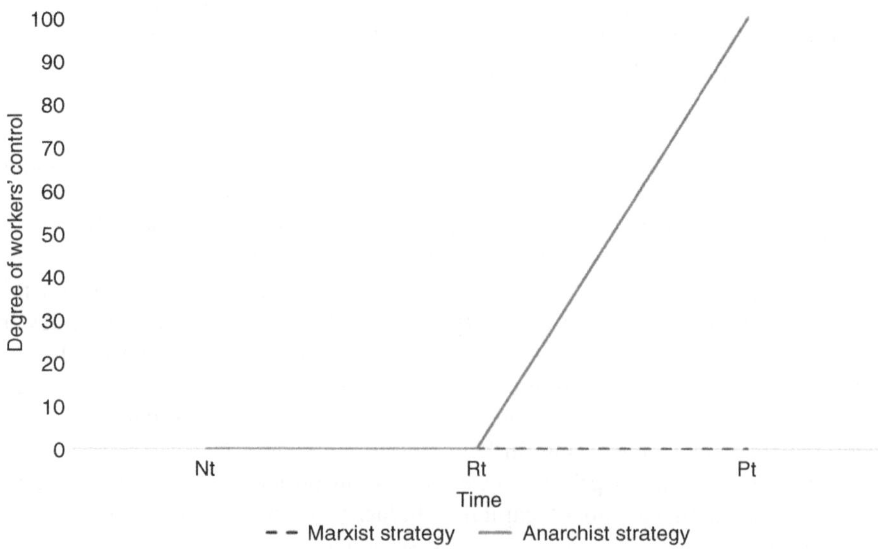

Figure 1.3 Communism, or State Capitalism?

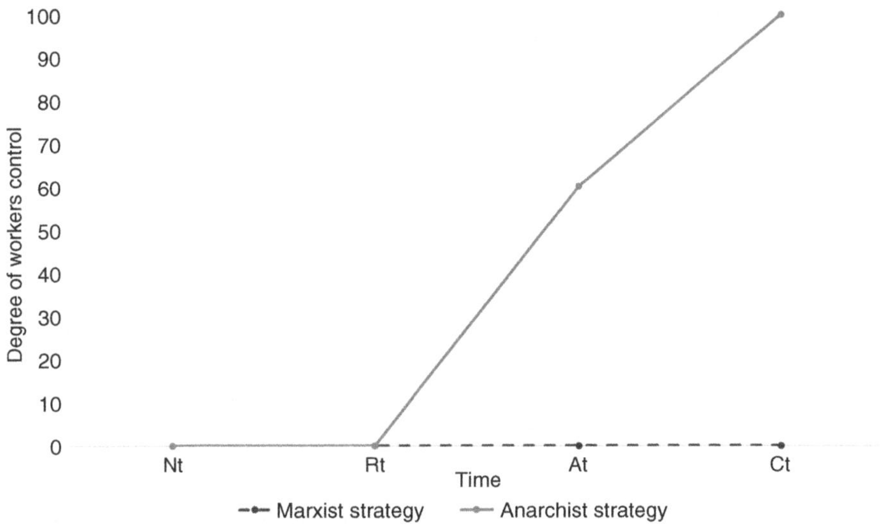

Figure 1.4 Revolution and Workers' Control

Figures 1.3 and 1.4 contrast Marxist (dotted line) and anarchist strategies (solid line); Figure 1.4 details anarcho-syndicalist/anarcho-communist strategy (adapted from Carter 241–3). The x-axis refers to time, and y to the degree of workers' control in a given society. In both stylized graphs, *Nt* corresponds to the present time, and *Rt* to the future time of revolution. In Figure 1.3, *Pt* refers to the ideal arrival of communism, while *Ft* indicates the stabilization of state capitalism: that is, an ostensibly post-capitalist society lacking any sort of workers' control. By contrast, in Figure 1.4, starting to institute workers' control at point *Rt* leads to *At*, direct control of the means of production. Thus, by using anarchist strategy, the associated producers can realistically achieve full communism at a later point (*Ct*).

As though tracing asystole, or cardiac death, on an electrocardiogram, the legacies of Marxism and Leninism can be visualized in the *Rt* → *Ft* curve of Figure 1.3. Without a doubt, the April 1986 nuclear disaster at the Vladimir Lenin Nuclear Power Plant in Chernobyl starkly illuminated the horrors of Soviet state capitalism, just as the genocidal wars waged by Putin on Chechnya, Syria, and Ukraine, and the nuclear blackmail to which he subjects all of humanity, replay the Red Army's brutal invasion and occupation of Afghanistan, as well as the madness of the Cold War. Prior to this, the Russian Communists had crushed the Kronstadt Commune, the Revolutionary Insurgent Army of Ukraine, and the *Basmachi*; recolonized Ukraine and Transcaucasia; suppressed the anarchist CNT-FAI in the Spanish Civil War; imposed forcible collectivization, famines, mass-deportations, and mass-imprisonment in the Gulag; desiccated the Aral Sea; signed the Nazi-Soviet Pact; partitioned Poland with Hitler; and perpetrated the Katyn Massacre, among other things.

While Marxism is not exclusively responsible for these crimes, considering how Great-Russian chauvinism, statist illogic, power politics, and the domination of nature have also contributed, it is apparent that the Marxist tradition features less critique of socio-political hierarchy, compared to the anarchist one—to its great credit. At the same time, libertarians must come to terms with the misogyny, antisemitism, violence, and proto-fascism of certain anarchist and syndicalist thinkers.[69] (See the next section on Anarchist Contradictions.)

Anarchist Contradictions

Considering the breadth and depth of setbacks and atrocities for which Soviet authorities were responsible between 1917 and 1991 (as referenced above), it would seem that Marxists and Marxist-Leninists have much more to atone for, compared to anarchists. In this sense, consistent with the analysis of the three-way fight, Voline aptly accused bureaucratic Communists of being red fascists.[70] After all, Marx welcomed the modernization of India by British imperialism, even if he decried the brutality of this process, and he appears to have subscribed to the racist pseudo-science of phrenology.[71] Meanwhile, Engels celebrated the outcome of the Mexican-American War (1846–1848), when the victorious Anglo-American settlers took California from the "lazy Mexicans, who could not do anything with it [*sic*]."[72]

Although, in light of such evidence and Figures 3–4 above, one may be prepared to conclude that anarchism is truly more progressive than Marxism, one must first confront some of the objections that might be raised in good faith against this claim. For instance, in his zeal to raise a regional revolt against Tsarism in 1863, Bakunin conveniently overlooked that the rebellious Polish gentry had been even less willing to accept Tsar Alexander II's abolition of serfdom than landlords in central Russia.[73] Likewise, in "Federalism, Socialism, and Anti-Theologism" (1867), Bakunin seems to sympathize with the Confederates in the then-recently concluded U.S. Civil War, when he comments baselessly on the "democra[cy] par excellence" practiced in the antebellum Southern states—thus forgetting their widespread enslavement of African workers.[74] By contrast, Marx consistently supported the Polish cause, the Union during the U.S. Civil War, *and* Reconstruction.[75]

With his friends Proudhon and the composer Richard Wagner, Bakunin moreover shared conspiratorial antisemitic views, and Wagner's operas—so beloved by Adolf Hitler—likely paid tribute to Bakunin's combination of revolutionary anti-capitalism and hatred for Jews.[76] Besides, Proudhon and Tolstoy were deeply misogynistic, although Herzen, Bakunin, and Chernyshevsky admittedly were feminists, and Tolstoy's *War and Peace* (1869) has now been banned from educational curricula in Ukraine, on the charge that this classic glorifies the Russian military.[77] While *War and Peace* certainly criticizes militarism, Tsarism, and Napoleon Bonaparte's imperialism, the novel admittedly does at times convey Russian-chauvinist and sexist sentiments. Likewise, despite his revolutionism, Chernyshevsky rejected self-determination for oppressed nations in the Tsarist

Empire.[78] Marx, for his part, was no feminist, and his theory often promotes Eurocentrism, pan-Germanism, and antisemitism.[79]

Crucially, Ze'ev Sternhell's insightful study, *The Birth of Fascist Ideology* (1994), traces the deformation of revolutionary syndicalism into Italian Fascism a century ago, due to the tireless efforts of the French revisionist Marxist, Georges Sorel. Although he was not an anarchist, Sorel found Proudhon's defense of private property and fetishization of violence inspiring. He proposed a socialist-nationalist synthesis that rejected Enlightenment principles of rationalism, humanism, and liberalism. Besides welcoming Italy's colonial invasions of Libya and Ethiopia, Sorel's futurist Italian acolytes viewed World War I as a bloody opportunity to destroy the bourgeois world, and Benito Mussolini ended up adopting the corporatist, class-collaborationist strategy preached by Sorelian anti-humanism for the working class.[80]

Along similar lines, in *Anarchism and Eugenics* (2019), Richard Cleminson uncovers the startling engagement with eugenics taken up by European and Argentine anarchists at the turn of the 20th century. According to Cleminson, anarchists, feminists, and neo-Malthusians intervened to advance "positive" eugenics by promoting contraception, preventive health, and social-hygiene campaigns, in line with classical anarchism's anti-clerical, anti-militarist, and perfectionist ideals. Despite Kropotkin's dismissal of sterilization regimes as reproducing class oppression, some anarchists came to advocate voluntary *and* compulsory sterilization for certain hereditary conditions, on the pretext of improving the future health of the working classes and thus, ostensibly, improving the chances for social revolution. Indeed, two articles published in the Spanish anarcha-feminist newspaper *Mujeres Libres* in 1937 call for the "euthanasia" of people with disabilities, presumably in keeping with syndicalist and ableist ideas about heroic "producers" and contemptible "parasites."[81] That being said, anarchists generally lost interest in the field, alongside British and Soviet Marxists, once the Nazis started implementing their dreadful eugenics programs in the 1930's.

Last, Sean Patterson's *Makhno and Memory* (2020) brings to light important evidence about atrocities perpetrated by Makhnovists against German Mennonites in Ukraine during the Russian Civil War. As members of a landowning ethno-religious minority that allied itself with the Central Powers in World War I, and then with the Whites during the Civil War, while organizing self-defense units (*Selbstschutz*), Mennonite communities became targets for peasant radicals once State power collapsed in 1917. Dehumanized as class enemies, Mennonites suffered pillage, mass-rape, and mass-murder at the hands of Makhnovists and Ukrainian peasants. These tensions culminated in the Eichenfeld and Sagradowka massacres of late 1919, which took the lives of hundreds of Mennonite civilians.[82]

While it appears that Makhno did not himself lead or participate in such atrocities, they may perhaps be attributed to the utilization of terror as a form of anarcho-communist vengeance, given that many poor Ukrainians had been exploited as workers on German and Mennonite estates.[83] Considering the pressing nature of the land question in post-revolutionary Ukraine, the ultra-violence wielded by Makhnovists against Mennonites appears to have aimed at "level[ing] society by eliminating the wealthy rural classes."[84] Yet, as Ukrainian anarchist V. Azarov soberly observes, this approach "allows any kind of abuse to flourish on the grounds of the just struggle with the exploiting classes."[85] Indeed, Voline was critical of the *Makhnovshchina*'s warlordist tendencies, especially its practice of rape.[86]

Marxism, Anarchism, and Left-Wing Authoritarianism, Past and Present

Both implicitly and explicitly, the argument made throughout this chapter has highlighted the intimate overlap between Marxism and left-wing authoritarianism. Fatefully, Marx and Engels preached an authoritarian-centralist strategy for confronting capitalism. As Bakunin and Tolstoy foresaw, and as Carter recognized, Marx's highly instrumental and amoral attitude toward workers and fellow radicals was readily mobilized by state capitalists and "Red hangmen" like Lenin, Trotsky, and Stalin.[87] Wolfgang Eckhardt adds that Marxian centralism became reality only in 1919 with the founding of the Soviet-sponsored Communist International, which would outcompete the anarcho-syndicalist International Workers' Association (IWA, founded in 1922) for two decades.[88] It follows that so many Marxist believers fervently defended the USSR while it existed, and that publications like *Monthly Review*, *Jacobin*, and *The International Marxist-Humanist* still champion the Bolsheviks to this day. By so identifying with the despotic authority of the Red State, the editors of these journals continue to illuminate the primary contradiction of Marxist theory, which is to sell out the working classes (see Figures 3–4 above).

In parallel, it has been neo-Stalinists who have spearheaded the legitimization of neo-fascist "anti-imperialist" States—including Syria, Russia, Iran, and China—in the wake of the catastrophic U.S.-led invasion and occupation of Iraq in 2003. In the U.S., Workers' World (WW), the Party for Socialism and Liberation (PSL), and their various front-groups and allies have poisoned the well of left-wing internationalism by establishing an orthodox "left" approach which sacrifices our common humanity in the name of "anti-imperialism." Simply put, WW and PSL function primarily to critique U.S. foreign policy and defend genocidal regimes abroad through dominating the anti-war protest movement and aggressively reproducing gross disinformation about, and inciting racist dehumanization against, those whom many leftists consider "unworthy victims."[89]

Socialist writer Rohini Hensman calls such "supporters of Assad and Putin" *pseudo-anti-imperialists*, for they present as trenchant critics of Western imperialism. Yet, in reality, they function to legitimize Russian expansionism and assert "the right [of 'anti-imperialists'] to practice mass murder in the name of the principle of sovereignty under international law."[90] This same propaganda model has been adopted not only by opportunistic pseudo-radical outlets like *The GrayZone* and *Multipolarista*, but also by Donald Trump and his neo-fascist, isolationist, COVID-denialist followers and congressional minions. What unites these seemingly disparate elements is a common disregard for the truth; strong aversions to egalitarianism, humanism, and internationalism; and a fetish for violence.

Hence, this phenomenon of the "red-brown alliance" represents yet another instance of left-wing authoritarianism, also known by Jürgen Habermas's formulation of "Left fascism."[91] Such a noxious alliance corresponds to Marx's conservatism and naïveté about the State, the related failure to come to terms with Soviet atrocities carried out in the name of Communism, and the denial of present-day genocide perpetrated in Syria and Ukraine by Russia. Yet, to echo the discussions from the introduction and the previous section, while anarchists are generally less susceptible to pseudo-anti-imperialist and left-wing authoritarian traps, they are not exempt from authoritarian tendencies, and have unfortunately not always provided adequate alternatives to the status quo.

For instance, although Sorel was no anarchist, a degree of Sorelian bloodlust against liberals is evident in parts of the anarchist movement, as "insurrection envy" over Trump's failed January 6, 2021, coup attempt has revealed.[92] Plus, in confronting COVID-19, anarchists have responded well with mutual aid, but have drawn less attention to the pandemic's eugenicist tendencies toward "social murder," and not prioritized resistance to the capitalist compulsion to return to "normal."[93] That being said, thanks in part to intersectional theory and burgeoning resistance to White supremacy, anarchists have improved on certain archaic forms of discrimination, including sexism, racism, and heteronormativity. Still, the movement's horizon is very far from the rationalist optimism expressed during the late 19th and early 20th centuries, as explained below.

Since 2012, Western anarchists have strongly supported the Rojava Revolution, led by the local affiliate of the formerly Stalinist Kurdistan Workers' Party (PKK) in northern Syria, but have sympathized considerably less with the Syrian Revolution against the Ba'athist regime of Bashar al-Assad (see Figure 5 below). This is likely due to a number of factors: for one, pseudo-anti-imperialist loyalties, in light of Assad's place within the pantheon of "resistance" to Western imperialism;[94] the prevalence of anti-humanist and anti-Muslim attitudes; and stark ignorance of the reality of Syrian anarchism, from the activist Omar Aziz, martyr of the Assad regime, to the Local Coordinating Committees (LCC's). Such a puzzling lapse—accentuated, in turn, by most Western anarchists' sympathies for Palestinians—is arguably anticipated in the Mennonite-Makhnovist conflict in Ukraine a century ago, when "a movement [...] massacred innocents in the name of liberty and justice."[95] This racist dehumanization and exclusion is also sadly consistent with the enthusiasm evinced by some historical anarchists for eugenics.

Moreover, many Euro-American and Eastern European anarchists boldly denied the threat posed by Putin's massing of troops on the Ukrainian border before the launching of Russia's "special military operation" in February 2022.[96]

Actor	Syrian Revolution	Rojava Revolution	Russo-Ukrainian War	Israel-Hamas War
State	Assad Regime	Turkey/Syria	Russia	Israel/U.S.
Left (supported by Western anarchists?)	Civil resistance, LCC's, early Free Syrian Army units (No)	Party of Democratic Union, TEV-DEM, Syrian Democratic Forces (Yes)	Solidarity Collectives, Resistance Committee, *Commons* (Yes/No)	Humanitarian organizations, Standing Together, Anarchists in the '48 Area (Yes/No)
Non-State Right	Hayat Tahrir al-Sham	Islamic State	Wagner Group, Azov Brigade	Kahanists, Islamic Jihad

Figure 1.5 Present-Day Three-Way Fights

Subsequently, a week after Russia's full-scale invasion commenced, the Serbian Anarcho-Syndicalist Initiative (an IWA affiliate) regurgitated Putinist disinformation about the Ukrainian government being an "undoubtedly nazified regime" that came to power through a "coup."[97] By contrast, Ukrainian Holocaust survivors have belied such distortions.[98] In fact, while Ukrainian anarchists like those in Solidarity Collectives organize humanitarian relief and support for anti-authoritarian and internationalist fighters on the ground, too many Western anarchists overlook Ukrainians' rights to independence, self-defense, and self-determination.[99] This is apparently so, because Western governments are supporting Ukraine, and whatever these governments are doing, leftists and anarchists must reflexively oppose.

That being said, Israel's genocidal assault on Gaza (October 2023–present), which has been entirely facilitated by Western States—the Biden administration, second to none—lends a great deal of credence to such instincts. After all, many leftists, including anarchists, have sought to save face for their lukewarm or even non-existent support for Ukrainians confronting Russia's genocidal attack by not only centering the similarly genocidal suffering and mass-death of Gazan Palestinians at the hands of Israel (and the U.S.), but also calling for an immediate ceasefire. In parallel, Russia has aimed at rehabilitating its reputation on the international stage by opportunistically championing the Palestinian cause, even as it intensifies its war on Ukraine.[100]

Conclusion

In this chapter, I have discussed the major theoretical and historical differences between Marxism and anarcho-Populism in detail, while considering Lyons's framework of a three-way fight among leftists, the State, and the right during the First International and Russia's late Imperial and post-revolutionary periods. I have shown that anarchist and anarcho-Populist programs are generally more profound and progressive than Marxism's bureaucratic, authoritarian, and state-capitalist prescriptions. They are, in other words, more consistent with human emancipation.[101]

Although anarchism is a uniquely promising approach for resisting the worldwide onslaught of reaction, authoritarianism, and counter-revolution, we cannot overlook the serious contradictions posed by the prejudices and violence perpetrated and re-entrenched by some of the tradition's most-revered figures and movements, historical or contemporary. To reiterate, by contrast, the equivalent contradictions are much deeper, and likely irreconcilable, for Marxism and Marxism-Leninism. Yet the case of Makhnovists attacking Mennonites, together with the apparent pseudo-anti-imperialist tendencies of many anarchists, underscores the ongoing need for a serious "struggle against authoritarian political relations within a[ll] genuinely revolutionary transformation[s]" and movements.[102]

In turn, one of the most important lessons of the First International and of the Russian, Syrian, and Rojava Revolutions is to recognize the imperative need for autonomy and dissent to be respected, even and especially in organizations fighting for collective liberation.[103] Another major lesson in this vein, acutely reinforced by the Russo-Ukrainian and Israel-Gaza Wars, is to acknowledge the importance of international solidarity in defending the cause of humanity. Following the anarcha-feminist writer Ursula Le Guin, this ever-vigilant commitment to rooting out domination and promoting participatory decentralization across the globe would be a *critical* anarchism, or "an ambiguous [anarchist] utopian[ism]."[104]

Notes

1 Voline 1975; Tolstoy.
2 Mazurin 70.
3 Rywkin; Lee.
4 Lyons.
5 Vilkens 36.
6 Balbus 4.
7 Marx 1976; Berlin 210; Mamonova.
8 Berlin.
9 Kropotkin 297.
10 Stites 26.
11 Newton.
12 Venturi 227; Figes and Kolonitskii 37, 151.
13 Venturi 35; Berdyaev 58; Smolski et al.
14 Frank 136 (emphasis added).
15 Bulgakov; Berlin 211–19.
16 Ferguson.
17 Graham 2015: 3–4.
18 Dubovyk (translation by Dmitriy Ivanov).
19 Ovsiannikov.
20 Maximoff 19; Rublëv.
21 Kinna; Balbus 17; Jay 57.
22 Marx 2023: 33, 68, 77 n39.
23 De George 97.
24 Bernardini 3.

25 Bakunin 1953: 286–8.
26 Gustafson 393.
27 Zurbrugg 399 (emphasis in original); Eckhardt 408; Berthier 9.
28 Eckhardt 418–20.
29 Bartlett 431–7.
30 Carter 204–18.
31 Berdyaev 120.
32 Lenin (translation modified).
33 Voline 1975; Figes and Koloniskii 114–6; Wetzel.
34 Frank 154.
35 Avrich 1970: 96, 171.
36 Sorel 135; Stites; Honneth 80; Shlapentokh.
37 Stites 45, 232–6.
38 Figes and Kolonitskii 100–1.
39 McKay.
40 Maximoff 57–8; Morgachëv.
41 Croll.
42 Balbus 326; Carter 187.
43 Angaut 11; Berthier 3–5.
44 Clark 45.
45 Graham 2015: 109–37; Berthier 8–9.
46 Graham 2015: 173–81.
47 Angaut 4; Berthier 69.
48 Mehring.
49 Avrich 1974; Graham 2015, 2022; Goodwin.
50 Zurbrugg 402.
51 Graham 2015: 198–9; Graham 2022.
52 Kennedy.
53 Mehring.
54 Berthier 76.
55 Carter.
56 Graham 2015; Eckhardt; McKay.
57 Eckhardt 409; Berthier 66.
58 Marx 1976: 873–6.
59 Figes 1996: 144.
60 Schonfeld and Chang 9; Marx 1976: 873–95; Balbus 109–21.
61 Graham 2015: 33; Venturi 622.
62 Castoriadis 229.
63 Berlin 224–30.
64 Berlin 214; Berdyaev.
65 Malia; Carter 253.
66 Abromeit; Bakunin 1973.
67 Graham 2022.
68 Vilkens.
69 Abromeit; Castro and Sethness Castro.
70 Voline 1934.
71 Ahmad 236–8; Marx and Engels 181, 218; Marx 1862.
72 Engels.
73 Berdyaev 66; Evtuhov et al. 424.
74 Bakunin 1867.
75 Anderson 56–67, 79–114.
76 Castro and Sethness Castro.
77 Фокус.

78 Bulgakov 43.
79 Balbus; Bakunin 2005.
80 Sternhell.
81 Cleminson 13–188, 205; Abromeit.
82 Patterson 9–10, 141–3.
83 Patterson 42–7, 62–6, 84–6, 130.
84 Patterson 52.
85 Patterson 125.
86 Patterson 31–2, 67–70.
87 Skirda 2004: 389.
88 Eckhardt 419; Garner.
89 Chomsky and Herman.
90 Hensman 10–19; Horkheimer and Adorno 414.
91 Gandesha.
92 Helmore.
93 Small.
94 Hensman.
95 Pearson 3.
96 Sethness.
97 Anarcho-Syndicalist Initiative.
98 AFP.
99 Price.
100 Wintour.
101 Balbus 84–125.
102 Balbus 326.
103 Angaut 15, 18.
104 Angaut 3; Le Guin.

Bibliography

Abromeit, John 2015. "Transformations of Producerist Populism in Western Europe." *Transformations of Populism in Europe, the United States and Latin America: History, Theories and Recent Tendencies*. Ed. John Abromeit. 367–413.

AFP 2022. "Ukraine is 'not Nazi', Holocaust survivors tell Putin." *France 24*, 25 September. Available online: https://www.france24.com/en/live-news/20220925-ukraine-is-not-nazi-holocaust-survivors-tell-putin. Accessed 28 September 2022.

Ahmad, Aijaz 1992. *In Theory: Nations, Classes, Literatures.* London: Verso.

Anarcho-Syndicalist Initiative 2022. "Let's turn capitalist wars into a workers' revolution!" *IWA-AIT*, 5 March. Available online: https://iwa-ait.org/content/lets-turn-capitalist-wars-workers-revolution. Accessed 28 September 2022.

Anderson, Kevin B. 2010. *Marx at the Margins.* Chicago: University of Chicago Press.

Angaut, Jean-Christophe 2007. "Le conflit Marx-Bakounine dans l'internationale: une confrontation des pratiques politiques." *Actuel Marx*, vol. 41, no. 1. 112–29.

Avrich, Paul 1970. *Kronstadt 1921.* Princeton: Princeton University Press.

Avrich, Paul 1974. *Bakunin and Nechaev.* Freedom Press: London.

Bakunin, Mikhail 1867. "Federalism, Socialism, Anti-Theologism." *Marxists Internet Archive*. Available online: https://www.marxists.org/reference/archive/bakunin/works/various/reasons-of-state.htm. Accessed 6 July 2022.

Bakunin, Mikhail 1953. *The Political Philosophy of Bakunin: Scientific Anarchism.* Ed. G. P. Maximoff. London: The Free Press of Glencoe.

Bakunin, Mikhail 1973. *Selected Writings.* London: Jonathan Cape Ltd.
Bakunin, Mikhail 2005. *Statism and Anarchy.* Trans. and ed. Marshall Shatz. Cambridge: Cambridge University Press.
Balbus, Isaac 1982. *Marxism and Domination.* Princeton: Princeton University Press.
Bartlett, Rosamund 2011. *Tolstoy: A Russian Life*. New York: Houghton Mifflin.
Berdyaev, Nicolas 1966. *The Origin of Russian Communism.* Ann Arbor: University of Michigan Press.
Berlin, Isaiah 1978. *Russian Thinkers.* London: Penguin.
Bernardini, David 2021. "A Different Antifascism. An Analysis of the Rise of Nazism as seen by Anarchists During the Weimar Period." *History of European Ideas.* DOI: 10.1080/01916599.2021.1963629.
Bookchin, Murray 2005. *The Ecology of Freedom.* Oakland: AK Press.
Bulgakov, Sergei 1994. "Heroism and Asceticism: Reflections on the Religious Nature of the Russian Intelligentsia." *Vekhi: Landmarks*. Trans. Marshall E. Shatz and Judith E. Zimmerman. New York: Routledge. 17–49.
Carter, Alan 1988. *Marx: A Radical Critique.* Boulder, CO: Westview Press.
Castoriadis, Cornelius 1997. *The Castoriadis Reader.* Ed. David Ames Curtis. Oxford: Blackwell Publishers.
Castro, María and Javier Sethness Castro 2019. " 'Dangerous Minds': Wagner and Bakunin's Social Imaginaries – Nationalist or Anarchist?" *Institute for Anarchist Studies*, 19 October. Available online: https://anarchiststudies.org/dangerous-mindswagner-and-bakunins-social-imaginaries-nationalist-or-anarchist. Accessed 15 December 2020.
Chomsky, Noam and Edward S. Herman 1995. *Manufacturing Consent*. London: Vintage.
Clark, John P. 2019. *Between Earth and Empire: From the Necrocene to the Beloved Community.* Oakland: PM Press.
Cleminson, Richard 2019. *Anarchism and Eugenics: An Unlikely Convergence, 1890-1940.* Manchester: University of Manchester Press.
Croll, Neil 2004. "The Role of M.N. Tukhachevskii in the Suppression of the Kronstadt Rebellion." *Revolutionary Russia*, vol. 17, no. 2. 1–48.
De George, Richard 1978. "Anarchism and Authority." *Nomos*, vol. 19. 91–110.
Dubovyk, Anatolii 2022. "Anarchists in the Workers' and Trade-Union Movement of Ukraine in the Late 19th and Early 20th Centuries." Presentation at Seventh Anarchist Studies Conference, 24 August.
Eckhardt, Wolfgang 2016. *The First Socialist Schism: Bakunin vs. Marx in the International Working Men's Association.* Trans. Robert M. Homsi et al. Oakland: PM Press.
Engels, Frederick 1994. "Democratic Pan-Slavism." *Marx-Engels Institute.* Available online: https://marxists.architexturez.net/archive/marx/works/1849/02/15.htm. Accessed 6 July 2022.
Evtuhov, Catherine et al. 2004. *A History of Russia: Peoples, Legends, Events, Forces.* Boston: Houghton Mifflin.
Ferguson, Ann 2018. "Socialist-Feminist Transitions and Visions." *Radical Philosophy Review* vol. 21, no. 1. 177–200.
Figes, Orlando 1996. *A People's Tragedy: The Russian Revolution, 1891–1924.* New York: Penguin.
Figes, Orlando 2002. *Natasha's Dance: A Cultural History of Russia.* New York: Metropolitan Books.
Figes, Orlando and Boris Kolonitskii 1999. *Interpreting the Russian Revolution: The Language and Symbols of 1917.* New Haven: Yale University Press.

Фокус 2022. "Роман Л. Толстого *Война и Мир* исключат из школьной программы в Украине (видео)." *Фокус*, 7 June. Available online: https://focus.ua/ukraine/518171-roman-l-tolstogo-voyna-i-mir-isklyuchat-iz-shkolnoy-programmy-v-ukraine-video. Accessed 6 July 2022.

Frank, Simon 1994. "The Ethic of Nihilism: A Characterization of the Russian Intelligentsia's Moral Outlook." *Vekhi: Landmarks*. Trans. Marshall E. Shatz and Judith E. Zimmerman. New York: Routledge. 131–55.

Gandesha, Samir 2019. "The 'Authoritarian Personality' Reconsidered: The Phantom of 'Left Fascism.'" *American Journal of Psychoanalysis*, vol. 79, no. 4. DOI: 10.1057/s11231-019-09227-w.

Garner, Jason 2016. *Goals and Means: Anarchism, Syndicalism, and Internationalism in the Origins of the Federación Anarquista Ibérica.* Chico, California: AK Press.

Goodwin, James 2010. *Confronting Dostoevsky's Demons: Anarchism and the Specter of Bakunin in Twentieth-Century Russia.* New York: Peter Lang.

Graham, Robert 2015. *We Do Not Fear Anarchy; We Invoke It.* Oakland: AK Press.

Graham, Robert 2022. "The Birth of Revolutionary Anarchism." *Black Flag* vol. 2, no. 2. 3–9.

Gustafson, Richard F. 1986. *Leo Tolstoy: Resident and Stranger.* Princeton: Princeton University Press.

Helmore, Edward 2022. "'I'm Deadly Serious': Why Film-maker Michael Moore is Confident of a Democratic Midterm Win." *Guardian*, 23 Oct. Available online: https://www.theguardian.com/us-news/2022/oct/23/michael-moore-democratic-party-win-midterm-interview. Accessed 24 October 2022.

Honneth, Axel 2017. *The Idea of Socialism.* Trans. Joseph Ganahl. Cambridge, UK: Polity.

Horkheimer, Max and Theodor W. Adorno 2002. *Dialectic of Enlightenment.* Trans. Edmund Jephcott. Redwood City: Stanford University Press.

Jay, Martin 1973. *The Dialectical Imagination: A History of the Frankfurt School and Institute for Social Research, 1923-1950.* Berkeley: University of California Press.

Kennedy, Hubert 1995. "Johann Baptist von Schweitzer: The Queer Marx Loved to Hate." *Journal of Homosexuality*, vol. 29, nos. 2–3. 69–96.

Kinna, Ruth 2020. "Interview: Ruth Kinna." *Freedom News*, 21 April. Available online: https://freedomnews.org.uk/2020/04/21/interview-ruth-kinna. Accessed 2 July 2022.

Kropotkin, Peter 1991. *Russian Literature: Ideals and Realities.* Montreal: Black Rose Books.

Kropotkin, Peter 1992. *Words of a Rebel.* Trans. George Woodcock. Montreal: Black Rose Books.

Lee, Eric 2017. *The Experiment: Georgia's Forgotten Revolution, 1918–1921.* London, Zed Books.

Le Guin, Ursula 1999. *The Dispossessed: An Ambiguous Utopia.* New York: Harper Collins.

Lenin, V. I. 1921. "The Tax in Kind." Trans. Yuri Sdobnikov. Available online: https://www.marxists.org/archive/lenin/works/1921/apr/21.htm. Accessed 24 November 2020.

Lyons, Matthew N. 2018. *Insurgent Supremacists: The U.S. Far Right's Challenge to State and Empire.* Oakland: PM Press.

McKay, Iain 2017. "The State and Revolution: Theory and Practice." *Bloodstained: One Hundred Years of Leninist Counterrevolution.* Eds. Friends of Aron Baron. Chico, Calif.: AK Press. 62–117.

Malia, Martin 1961. *Alexander Herzen and the Birth of Russian Socialism*. New York: Universal Library.

Mamonova, Natalia 2018. "Vladimir Putin and the Rural Roots of Authoritarian Populism in Russia." *Open Democracy*, 3 April. Available online: https://www.opendemocracy.net/en/vladimir-putin-and-rural-roots-of-authoritarian-populism-in-russia. Accessed 31 May 2018.

Marx, Karl 1862. "Marx To Engels in Manchester." *Marx Engels Archive*. Available online: https://marxists.architexturez.net/archive/marx/works/1862/letters/62_07_30a.htm. Accessed 6 July 2022.

Marx, Karl 1976. *Capital, Volume I: A Critique of Political Economy*. Trans. Ben Fowkes. London: Penguin Books.

Marx, Karl 2023. *Critique of the Gotha Program*.Trans. Kevin B. Anderson and Karel Ludenhoff. Oakland: PM Press.

Marx, Karl and Friedrich Engels 1974–2004. *Collected Works*, vol. 12. New York: International Publishers.

Maximoff, G. P. 1940. *The Guillotine at Work: The Leninist Counter-Revolution*. Globus Printing: Chicago.

Mazurin, Boris 1993. "The Life and Labor Commune: A History and Some Reflections." *Memoirs of Peasant Tolstoyans in Soviet Russia*. Trans. William Edgerton. Bloomington, IN: Indiana University Press. 27–108.

Mehring, Franz 1935. *Karl Marx: The Story of His Life*. Trans. Edward Fitzgerald. New York: Covici-Friede. Available online: https://www.marxists.org/archive/mehring/1918/marx. Accessed 9 October 2022.

Mett, Ida 2017. "The Kronstadt Commune." *Bloodstained: A Hundred Years of Leninist Counter-Revolution*. Eds. Friends of Aron Baron. Oakland: AK Press.

Newton, Huey P. 2009. *Revolutionary Suicide*. New York: Penguin.

Ovsiannikov, Sergei 2022. "Anarchist Underground in Kharkiv (late 1918–early 1920s)." Presentation at Seventh Anarchist Studies Conference, 24 August.

Patterson, Sean 2020. *Makhno and Memory*. Winnipeg: University of Manitoba Press.

Price, Wayne 2023. "Anarchists Support Self-Determination for Ukraine." *Anarkismo*, 28 May. https://www.anarkismo.net/article/32774. Accessed 17 August 2023.

Rublëv, Dmitriy 2021. "P.A. Kropotkin: His Individualist Communism." Life, Freedom, & Ethics: Kropotkin Now! International Conference, 5 February. Available online: https://www.youtube.com/watch?v=WaMEi12gH9M. Accessed 13 February 2021.

Rywkin, Michael 1990. *Moscow's Muslim Challenge: Soviet Central Asia*. Armonk, NY: M.E. Sharpe.

Schonfeld, Irvin Sam and Chu-Hsiang Chang 2017. *Occupational Health Psychology: Work, Stress, and Health*. New York: Springer.

Sethness, Javier 2022. "Assembly, a Ukrainian Anarchist Magazine, on Politics and a Possible Russo-Ukrainian War." *The Commoner*, 27 Jan. Available online: https://www.thecommoner.org.uk/assembly-a-ukrainian-anarchist-magazine-on-politics-and-a-possible-russo-ukrainian-war. Accessed 7 April 2024.

Shlapentokh, Dmitry 2019. "Marx, the 'Asiatic Mode of Production,' and 'Oriental Despotism' as 'True' Socialism." *Comparative Sociology* vol. 18. 489–521.

Skirda, Alexandre 2002. *Facing the Enemy: A History of Anarchist Organization From Proudhon To May 1968*. Oakland: AK Press.

Skirda, Alexandre 2004. *Nestor Makhno: Anarchy's Cossack*. Oakland: AK Press.

Small, Raia 2022. "Why Has the Left Deprioritized COVID?" *Midnight Sun*, 14 September. Available online: https://www.midnightsunmag.ca/why-has-the-left-deprioritized-covid. Accessed 28 September 2022.

Smolski, Andrew et al. 2022. "Case Studies in the Sociology of Absence and Emergence: Anarcho-Populism in Russia and Mexico." *Theory in Action*, vol. 15, no. 1. 1–24.

Sorel, Georges 2004. *Reflections on Violence*. Trans. T. E. Hulme and J. Roth. Mineola, NY: Dover.

Sternhell, Zeev 1994. *The Birth of Fascist Ideology: From Cultural Rebellion to Political Revolution*. Trans. David Maisel. Princeton: Princeton University Press.

Stites, Richard 1989. *Revolutionary Dreams: Utopian Vision and Experimental Life in the Russian Revolution*. Oxford: Oxford University Press.

Struve, Petr 1994. "The Intelligentsia and Revolution." *Vekhi: Landmarks*. Trans. Marshall E. Shatz and Judith E. Zimmerman. New York: Routledge. 115–29.

Tolstoy, Leo 1960. *The Kingdom of God Is Within You and Peace Essays*, trans. Aylmer Maude. London: Oxford University Press.

Venturi, Franco 1960. *Roots of Revolution: A History of the Populist and Socialist Movements in Nineteenth Century Russia*. Trans. Francis Haskell. New York: The Universal Library.

Vilkens 2017. "On Women." *Anarchist Encounters: Russia in Revolution*. Ed. AW Zurbrugg. London: Merlin Press. 35–9.

Voline 1934. "Red Fascism." *The Anarchist Library*. Trans. Paul Sharkey. Available online: https://theanarchistlibrary.org/library/voline-red-fascism. Accessed 7 July 2022.

Voline 1975. *The Unknown Revolution*. Montreal: Black Rose Books.

Wetzel, Tom 2022. *Overcoming Capitalism: Strategy for the Working Class in the 21st Century*. Chico, California: AK Press.

Wintour, Patrick 2024. "The New World Disorder: How the Gaza war Disrupted International Relations." *Guardian*, 6 April. Available online: https://www.theguardian.com/world/2024/apr/06/world-disorder-israel-gaza-war-international-relations. Accessed 6 April 2024.

Wittfogel, Karl 1957. *Oriental Despotism: A Comparative Study of Total Power*. New Haven: Yale University Press.

Zurbrugg, A. W. 2016. "Revisiting Marxism and Anarchism." *Science & Society*, vol. 80, no. 3. 395–403.

Chapter 2

The Superego: Our Inner Authoritarian

Donald Carveth

In attempting to clarify our stance toward the many pressing moral, social and political issues of the day, we can become so focused on the ends we promote and the evils we oppose that we lose sight of the question of the legitimacy or illegitimacy of the means we intend to employ. Those who assume that the ends justify the means don't have to think about this, so convinced are they of the righteousness of their cause that other values, such as free-speech and democratic principles, are expendable.

As a politically naive young man I was so focused on the evils I opposed that I initially failed to notice that I differed from many like-minded comrades with respect to the methods or strategies to be employed in pursuit of our common aims. The scales began to fall from my eyes when I was invited to join secret committees devoted to caucusing, plotting and manipulating the wider movement. When an enthusiastic comrade attempted to allay my fears and belie my scruples by introducing me to the arcane doctrine of "democratic centralism" my thoughts went to Orwell and "double-speak" and I began to recognize my Menshevism, my social-democratic commitment to both a Marxian critique of capitalism and anti-authoritarian principles, procedures, and attitudes.

While excellent work on right-wing authoritarianism has been done by political psychologists, a blind eye has often been turned toward left-wing authoritarianism. For example, Robert Altemeyer's (2006) description of his authoritarianism scale as measuring right-wing authoritarianism is problematic (Carveth, 2008). Authoritarian followers tend to support whichever authorities are in control. In the former Soviet Union, for example, these were politically left-wing. It would seem odd to refer to such people as right-wing left-wingers, but Altemeyer does exactly this, explaining that he is using the term "right-wing" in a psychological not a political sense. He acknowledges that left-wing authoritarians can be found here and there, but not in sufficient numbers to threaten democracy in North America. But Altemeyer was writing a quarter century ago. In the current era of "cancel culture" and what might even be called the McCarthyism of the left, this is clearly no longer the case. Historically contingent situations do not justify building a political concept into the very definition of authoritarianism and to include it in the name of the scale designed to measure it. Political bias should not be allowed to creep into the

DOI: 10.4324/9781003389927-2

way we formulate scientific constructs: we need to be more conscientious in our analysis of conscience and its corruption.

Many of us who have backgrounds in social science have long been alert to class, gender, racial, generational and related patterns of social injustice. But today we see that many people who identify as "progressive" have taken to pursuing their goals in distinctly authoritarian ways. When Jorden Peterson was invited to speak at McMaster University he was shouted down by "leftist" students and faculty opposed to his critical stance toward attempts to legislate and enforce "correct" pronouns in referring to people who identify as transexual.

A young woman psychologist I supervised was hired by a prominent university to teach a summer course on psychodynamic theory. When she made it clear that she was going to try to teach, not just bash Freud, many of her students were outraged. She overheard some of them saying they planned to punish her. Feeling intimidated, unsupported and unsafe, she resigned and quickly left the campus. Even in psychoanalytic societies, teachers whose views are poorly understood and misrepresented by student activists can be disinvited to teach by committees of colleagues who would rather throw them under the bus than risk displeasing social justice warriors and possibly losing customers of their programs.

Although it is not easy to critique those with whom we share many values, it is nevertheless incumbent upon the "woke" who are not authoritarian to call out the "woke" who are. Why? Because absent this kind of internal critique, movements and organizations that are ostensibly devoted to good causes can have unintended consequences and produce either bad or very mixed results. This is true in psychoanalysis and the mental health professions, as well as the academy at large.

Regrettably, while it provides many useful tools for self-examination and reflection, psychoanalysis is not free of authoritarianism, either. For example, in 1914, in the wake of Jung's "defection," Freud organized his secret committee (see Grosskurth, 1991). He also organized the International Psychoanalytic Association along patriarchal, hierarchical lines, such that former Bolsheviks and card-carrying members of the CPUSA, such as Charles Brenner, Jacob Arlow, and Ralph Greenson (Richard's 2016), could feel quite at home there.

On entering New York harbor in 1909, Freud is reputed to have said "They don't realize we are bringing them the plague." I like to think that what he had in mind was his demonstration of our intrinsic contradictoriness: that there is no unitary ego; that we are permanently divided selves, all are both Dr. Jekyll and Mr. Hyde. Because we lack a unitary self we cannot entirely trust our judgment, for we have another self who may judge very differently. Even while proclaiming my Menshevik leanings and democratic principles my inner Bolshevik may be stirring beneath the surface.

Though she approached this issue from a somewhat different theoretical perspective than Freud did, Melanie Klein (1946) reaffirmed Freud's insight along these lines through her elucidation of the two distinct mental worlds or "positions" which we oscillate between throughout our lives. So, for example, when, possessed by a bad mood, I may bark at my wife and later apologize saying "Sorry honey,

I wasn't myself." But the truth is that I was merely myself in the *paranoid-schizoid position.*

The paranoid-schizoid world is characterized by narcissism, omnipotence, splitting, and envy. Authority in the paranoid-schizoid position is represented by the sadistic, authoritarian superego, which by Klein's reckoning begins in infancy, well before the Oedipal phase, as Freud had imagined. Like Freud, however, she acknowledged that vestiges of this earlier developmental phase linger on in the adult unconscious.

By contrast with the paranoid-schizoid position, the *depressive-reparative position*, which people evolve into to varying degrees, is characterized by greater realism (whole object relations), gratitude, and a capacity for empathy and concern for others. The emergence of democratic values depends upon our growth into the depressive-reparative position.

The paranoid-schizoid position gives rise to authoritarianism, with all of its cognitive distortions and emotional rigidity. In the depressive-reparative position, however, we acquire what Erich Fromm (1947) called a "humanistic conscience" characterized not by rigid and moralistic rules (superego), but by what Winnicott (1963) called a "capacity for concern" for the other.

By contrast with our humanistic conscience, the superego is formed out of both oedipal and pre-oedipal reactive (as distinct from primary) aggression turned back against the self, plus internalization of parental and social authority. In *Civilization and Its Discontents*, Freud (1930) described the superego as something like a good cop saving us from a descent into barbarism. But in his clinical work he described it increasingly as harsh, sadistic and tyrannical, and viewed it as at the root of most psychopathology. According to Freud the superego is formed through submission to the Oedipal rival due to castration anxiety and operates thereafter "like a garrison in a conquered city" (Freud, 1930, p. 123). Melanie Klein claimed it originates much earlier as the internalization of and identification with the all-bad persecutory part-object.

I hold that the roots of conscience (as distinct from superego) lie in our primate inheritance and our early internalization of and identification with the "good object" and, more generally, with the nurturers who gave us comfort and safety (Sagan, 1988; Carveth, 2013, 2023).

Only by developing and aligning ourselves with our biologically-grounded humanistic conscience, our "true self" (Winnicott, 1960), are we empowered to stand up to inner and outer tyranny. In masochism we submit to the superego; in sadism we identify with it and, marching under its banner, deploy its aggression against scapegoats, sometimes developing what Heinrich Racker (1957) called a "mania for reproaching" (p. 740).

In enacting superego aggression against self and others we are out of synch with conscience. As our "inner authoritarian" the superego can function like a fifth column. In our struggle against authoritarianism we ourselves can easily become authoritarian, for authoritarianism is a part, but not the whole, of our nature. Those of us who oppose authoritarianism in the name of democratic principles need to keep the superego under regular surveillance.

Franz Alexander 1925) saw the superego as a vestigial organ. Freud (1940) called for its "demolition" (p.180). Ferenczi (1928) argued no analysis can be complete without its "complete elimination" (p. 100). Although James Strachey (1934) acknowledged the superego's severity and its central role in psychopathology, unlike Freud, Alexander and Ferenczi who called for its "demolition," he adopted a more moderate position, calling for the modification rather than elimination of the superego. He was right to do so for two reasons.

First, Freud, Alexander and Ferenczi were naive to think the moral issues could be adjudicated by the rational ego. As David Hume famously observed in the 18th century, reason cannot "deduce an ought from an is." Science is descriptive not prescriptive. It can tell us *how* to build a bridge but not whether we *ought* to. Second, we need laws to proscribe and, when necessary, to punish antisocial behavior, even if the socially constructed norms are culturally relative. But while he was correct to call for modification rather than elimination of the superego, Strachey gave us no clue as to in what directions it ought to be modified. The very value judgement that the superego ought to be modified comes from somewhere. What is the source of that value judgment? It seems we need a judge to judge the judge. It is for this reason that I call for us to reverse Freud's decision to fold conscience and ego-ideal into the superego and instead posit conscience as a separate psychic structure and function capable of conflicting with, judging and calling the superego to account.

Such a conscience may be conceived either as a separate mental structure along with id, ego, superego, and ego-ideal, yielding a five-fold structure to the psyche, or as having its roots in the prosocial, as distinct from the antisocial part of the id.

The distinction between superego and conscience parallels Martin Luther's differentiation between law and gospel, Moses and Christ. For Luther, "[T]he only 'real theologian' was one who 'knows well how to distinguish the gospel from the law'" instead of confusing the two and teaching "the very opposite, namely, that Moses is Christ and Christ is Moses" (Pelikan, 1984, p. 168). I advance a parallel claim: the only real psychoanalyst is one who knows well how to distinguish the conscience from the superego instead of confusing the two and teaching the very opposite, that the superego is the conscience and the conscience the superego.

Luther's distinction is an elaboration of that proclaimed in the six antitheses of the Sermon on the Mount *(Matthew* 5:21–48 KJV)—"Ye have heard. But I say unto you"—in which Jesus distinguishes an ethic of rules and reproach (superego) from an ethic of the heart (conscience). As Pelikan points out,

> It was the special ministry of Moses to proclaim the wrath of god in the law, and the death that was the consequence of man's disobedience. Thus Luther portrayed Christ as saying to Moses: 'I will not preach as you, Moses, are obliged to preach. For you must proclaim the law. ... Therefore your preaching produces

> only wretched people; it shows them their sins, on account of which they cannot keep the law.'
>
> (p. 168)

But as Pelikan goes on to point out, it is a superficial reading of Luther's distinction that rejects "the authority of Moses and the Old Testament in favour of the sole authority of Christ and the New Testament" (p. 169). According to Pelikan,

> [F]ar from equating the Old Testament with law and the New Testament with gospel, he [Luther] found the message of the gospel throughout the Scriptures. ... Moses had predicted his own surrender of authority to Christ, as the prophet whom men were to heed. At the same time, Luther recognised that there were commands throughout the New Testament. This meant that there was gospel in the Old Testament and law in the New.
>
> (p. 169)

Is it then an error to suggest that law can be displaced by gospel, superego eliminated and replaced by conscience? I think the answer to this question, as for so many others, may be found in Jesus's own statement on the matter: "Think not that I am come to destroy the law, or the prophets: I am not come to destroy, but to fulfil" (*Matthew* 5:17 KJV).

In psychoanalytic discourse, the distinction between conscience and the superego was prefigured as early as 1947 in Erich Fromm's distinction between authoritarian and humanistic conscience, albeit without being tied to the paranoid-schizoid and depressive-reparative positions posited by Klein. According to Fromm (1947):

> Humanistic conscience is not the internalized voice of an authority whom we are eager to please and afraid of displeasing; it is our own voice, present in every human being and independent of external sanctions and rewards. [...] Conscience is thus a reaction of ourselves to ourselves. It is the voice of our true selves which summons us back to ourselves, to live productively, to develop fully and harmoniously—that is, to become what we potentially are. It is the guardian of our integrity.
>
> (p. 158f)

In a remarkable (1958) essay, Carl Gustav Jung clearly differentiates conscience from superego and argues that conscience has an archetypal basis, by which I understand him to mean a natural foundation. Just as Bowlby (1969-80) argues that we come into the world with an unlearned need for attachment so, like other primates we arrive with unlearned needs to respond altruistically to our fellows (see De Waal, 1997). Paul Bloom's (2010; 2013) research at Yale shows that infants as young as three months of age already have a rudimentary conscience, preferring characters who help others over those who obstruct or frustrate them.

I am often asked how we can distinguish the voice of conscience from that of the superego in the clinical situation. While some superegos are more authoritarian than others, the superego generally speaks in a language that is more or less harsh, dictatorial, dogmatic, and unforgiving. In contrast, although conscience has a bite, it generally speaks in the language of concern and mutual aid (Kropotkin, 1902). It does not wish to punish, berate or humiliate, but only to call the errant subject back to conscientiousness and, like the father of the prodigal son, to welcome him home.

In the conflicts currently dividing American psychoanalysis, the proponents of CSJT (critical social justice theory) are full of political passion and moral indignation. They are quick to accuse analysts who do not share their ideological orientation of unexamined racist biases (Burston & Nelson, 2023). Whether their call to their fellow psychoanalysts to become activists entails being an activist either outside or inside the clinical consulting room is not always clear from the context. But on reflection, the prospect of carrying our political, religious or other passions into the clinical setting is utterly incompatible with the time-honored ideals of abstinence and technical neutrality. Without the ongoing struggle to contain our countertransference psychoanalysis would be replaced in favour of education, indoctrination, or conversion. Instead of really analyzing a patient it would become more a matter of urging him or her to become a "Mini-me." There is no doubt a parallel danger on the other side: being so dispassionately ensconced in the depressive position that one becomes complacent in the face of the serious issues of the day. This is the pathology of the depressive position. On the other hand, the therapist's forbearance, self-control, even at times self-abnegation preserve the boundaries that are essential to a successful analysis.

So, in the final analysis, we have and need a superego, but we also need a conscience. We live at times in the paranoid-schizoid position and strive to advance into the depressive. Beyond oscillating between these polarities, we might, at times, manage to advance dialectically to a kind of"transitional area" (Winnicott, 1955) in which we can do justice to both. This is an ideal from which we usually fall short, but it is an ideal worth striving toward.

While we need to be alert and responsive to the many injustices of the world, and the ways in which they may shape or distort psychological development, we also need to acknowledge that the pursuit of our progressive ideals can sometimes yield (and yield to) anti-democratic and authoritarian modes of functioning. Progressive ends do not justify authoritarian means.

People on the right have long sought deregulation of the economy, with disastrous consequences for public health, environmental integrity and the ever-increasing population of poor and homeless citizens, and the restless migrants fleeing unbearable conditions in their countries of origin. Those of us on the left must acknowledge the importance of regulation in our psychological lives and disavow the flight from guilt by embracing a superego that is modified and disciplined by a robust and intact conscience.

References

Alexander, F. 1925. "A Metapsychological Description of the Process of Cure." *International Journal of Psychoanalysis*, vol. 6. 13–34.

Altemeyer, R, 2006. *The Authoritarians.* Winnipeg: University of Manitoba Press.

Bloom, P. 2010. "The Moral Life of Babies." *New York Times Magazine*, 3 May 2010.

Bloom, P. 2013. *Just Babies: The Origins of Good and Evil.* New York: The Crown Publishing Group.

Bowlby, J. 1969–80. *Attachment and Loss*. Vols. 1–3. London: Penguin.

Burston, D & Nelson, C. 2023. "Under Siege: Political Activism and Psychoanalysis." *Free Associations* 89. https://freeassociations.org.uk/FA_New/OJS/index.php/fa

Carveth, D. 2008. "Conscience Aside. An online review of John W. Dean's *Conservatives Without Conscience* and Robert Altemeyer's *The Authoritarians*." *Literary Review of Canada: A Journal of Ideas* (Jan–Feb. 2008).

Carveth, D. 2023. *Guilt: A Contemporary Introduction.* London: Routledge.

De Waal, F. 1997. *Good Natured: The Origins of Right and Wrong in Humans and Other Animals*. Cambridge, MA: Harvard University Press.

Ferenczi, S. 1928. "The Elasticity of Psycho-analytic Technique. In: M. Balint (Ed.), E. Mosbacher and others (Trans.), C. Thompson (Intro.), *Final Contributions to the Problems and Methods of Psychoanalysis* (pp. 87–101). New York: Basic, 1955.

Freud, S. 1930. *Civilization and Its Discontents. S.E.* vol. 21. 57–146.

Freud, S. 1940. *An Outline of Psycho-analysis. S.E.*, 23: 139–208. London: Hogarth.

Fromm, E. 1947. *Man for Himself.* New York: Rinehart & Co.

Fromm, E. 1950. *Psychoanalysis and Religion.* New Haven: Yale University Press.

Grosskurth, P. 1991. *The Secret Ring: Freud's Inner Circle and the Politics of Psychoanalysis.* Boston: Da Capo Press.

Jung, C. G. 1958. "A Psychological View of Conscience." In *Civilization in Transition*. 2nd ed. Vol. 10 of *The Collected Works of C. G. Jung*, Herbert Read, Michael Fordham, and Gerhard Adler (Eds), R. F. C. Hull (Trans). 437–55. Princeton, NJ: Princeton University Press, 1970.

Klein, M. 1946. "Notes on Some Schizoid Mechanisms." *International Journal of Psychoanalysis*, vol. 27. 99–110.

Kropotkin, P. 1902. *Mutual Aid: A Factor in Evolution.* New York: McClure, Phillips & Co.

Pelikan, J. 1984. *The Christian Tradition: A History of the Development of Doctrine*, Vol. 4: *Reformation of Church and Dogma, 1300–1700.* Chicago: University of Chicago Press.

Racker, H. 1957. "The Meanings and Uses of Countertransference." *Psychoanalytic Quarterly*, vol. 26. 725–777.

Richards, A. 2016. "The Left and Far Left in American Psychoanalysis: Psychoanalysis as a Subversive Discipline." *Contemporary Psychoanalysis*, vol. 52, no. 1. 111–29.

Sagan, E. 1988. *Freud, Women and Morality: The Psychology of Good and Evil.* New York: Basic Books.

Strachey, J. 1934. "The Nature of the Therapeutic Action of Psycho-analysis. *International Journal of Psychoanalysis*, vol. 15. 127–59.

Winnicott, D. W. 1955. "Transitional Objects and Transitional Phenomena—A Study of the First Not-me Possession." *International Journal of Psychoanalysis*, vol. 34. 89–97. [Reprinted in *Playing and Reality.* London: Tavistock, 1971.]
Winnicott, D. W. 1960. "Ego Distortion in Terms of True and False Self." In: *The Maturational Processes and the Facilitating Environment* (pp. 139–52). London: Hogarth, 1965.
Winnicott, D. W. 1963. "The Development of the Capacity for Concern." In *The Maturational Processes and the Facilitating Environment* (pp. 73–82). London: Hogarth, 1965.

Chapter 3

The New Moralism: From Agonism to Antagonism[1]

Samir Gandesha

> Where they burn books, they will, in the end, burn human beings too.
>
> —Heinrich Heine

In this chapter, I address what I call the "new moralism." Such new moralism has shown up in a wide range of spaces but, in my view, most clearly crystallizes in what has been called "third wave anti-racism."[2] While aspiring to protect Black, Indigenous, and other racialized peoples from *harm* such anti-racism can, paradoxically, be considered deeply *harmful* because of its own unconscious racism. In contrast with conservative commentators, who see third wave anti-racism as a function of the rise of the power of the left, particularly within the university, media, and government, I suggest that the exact opposite is true. The emergence of the new moralism in recent years is a result of the left's short-comings, failures, and defeats, both domestically as well as globally. This has led to a pessimistic and rather melancholic sensibility—the exact anti-thesis of Herbert Marcuse's hopeful and revolutionary call for a "new sensibility" during the height of the Students' and Anti-War movements in the 1960's. Such melancholia is most clearly expressed in that form of identity politics that goes by the name of "Afro-pessimism," particularly that of Frank Wilderson III. The logic of this new morality can be clarified, counter-intuitively and perhaps somewhat transgressively, with the help of Friedrich Nietzsche's concept of *réssentiment*; a process which has led not to a robust, militant revolutionary *esprit* in an age which desperately needs it, but the rather the opposite.

It can also be understood as the collective response to a series of traumatic failures both within the left opposition in North America as well as truncated decolonization processes in Africa and Asia, not to mention the decline of the secular-nationalist left in the Arab world and the concurrent rise of its authoritarian Islamist rivals. The former, moreover, must no doubt also be seen in the context of the Israeli's state's policy of "feeding the enemy" vis-à-vis Hamas up to the precipice of October 7, 2023.

Civilizational as opposed to individual traumas can be understood as occurring at two distinct though related levels. We might term the first one *first order* trauma, because it happens at the level of the event itself, for example a riot, an

DOI: 10.4324/9781003389927-3

uprising, or a revolution, war, occupation, genocide etc. *Second order* trauma, in contrast, happens at the level of the *hermeneutics* of the event; a crisis of interpretability of first order historical traumas, which pushes against the limits of existing conceptual knowledge, models, or paradigms. Second order trauma results from the impossibility of integrating the traumatic event into existing frameworks of intelligibility.

The dominant framework of intelligibility of European modernity was and perhaps remains in order global neo-liberal order historicism or the philosophy of historical progress in the idea of universal history articulated by Kant, Hegel and the orthodox Marxism of the Second International (of which Walter Benjamin was, of course, immensely critical).[3] The genius of this philosophy of progress was that it intuited the need to relate two orders of trauma through the notion of contradiction which, ultimately, was understood to lead, via what Hegel calls "the cunning of reason," to reconciliation or "the identity of identity and non-identity."[4] This is ultimately an apologia for historical violence and suffering not unlike the historical justification of colonial domination (the so-called "White Man's burden") in the form of a kind of secularized theodicy.

A sympathetic reading of the identity politics upon which the new moralism is based suggests that it registers a second order trauma produced by the bloody, terroristic, colonial histories of Western modernity, to which it is related both past and present. It therefore registers the profound damage to existing universalistic frameworks of intelligibility. However, identity politics seems to disavow enlightenment universalism in *toto* to the point where the question of its own "progressive" credentials must inevitably arise. It is precisely here that identity politics throws the *rational* baby out with the *colonial* bathwater and, consequently, takes a dangerous authoritarian turn.

The throwing out of the emancipatory baby of reason with the colonial and White supremacist bathwater (and the corresponding embrace of irrationalism in various guises) could be described by the shift from a Hegelian to a Nietzschean account of the relation between master and slave. The Hegelian version of the master-slave dialectic is to be found in Chapter IV "The Truth of Self-Certainty" of the *Phenomenology of Spirit*.[5] It posits an encounter between two solipsistic consciousnesses, their struggle to the death, and the eventual triumph of he who values his honor above all, and is therefore unafraid to risk his life over the other, who clings tenaciously to it. The former becomes the master, the latter, a slave. However, the original hierarchy is reversed when it becomes clear that the master's dominance hinges on the recognition of an inferior being, which is to say, the slave, the slave seeks but obtains no such recognition from the master. Fortunately, however, the slave eventually learns to recognize himself in the products of his own labor, which Hegel describes as a process of self-objectification and self-affirmation. From that point onwards, presumably, the slave does not require the master's recognition. Insofar as the slave alone works upon and transforms nature, while the master enjoys an imaginary self-sufficiency, the slave alone has before him the possibility of genuine emancipation.

Nietzsche's account of the master-slave relationship appears in the first essay of the *Genealogy of Morals* simply entitled " "Good and Evil,', 'Good and Bad.' "[6] In direct contrast with Hegel's version, which is characterized by a search for recognition, in a crucial sense, Nietzsche's depiction stresses precisely the disavowal of such recognition. The master's morality is grounded in the opposition between "good" and "bad" which has to do with whether an action increases or enhances the feeling of life, what Nietzsche calls the "Will to Power," or does the opposite. In contrast with Hegel's master, who is entirely dependent upon the slave for his social position, for Nietzsche the master is all but indifferent to the slave, which is what is Nietzsche means by the latter's "pathos of distance." The slave, on the other hand, the beneficiary of the most significant "transvaluation of values" history has seen, begins not with what is good or bad for his own life and its "active, interpreting powers," but with the premise that he who is spiritually stronger is a priori "evil" and from that infers that he, the slave, alone, is "good."

So, in short, the Hegelian account emphasizes the autonomy and active, world-transforming power of the slave, which vividly prefigures Marx's account of the proletariat, who attains an "authentic" self-consciousness in contrast to the false-consciousness of the master, who prefigures Marx's bourgeoisie. In contrast, for Nietzsche the slave embodies what he calls " 'the spirit of revenge" or *réssentiment.* The slave accomplishes in thought and language what he is patently unable to accomplish in world-transformative praxis. The failure of subaltern classes to take power in a dialectic of liberation has led to what Gillian Rose calls in an authoritarian "paradox of empowerment." Rose argues:

> 'Empowerment' legitimises the potential tyranny of the local or particular community in its relations with its members and at the boundary with competing interests. It is the abused who become the abusers; no one and no community is exempt from the paradoxes of 'empowerment'.[7]

By this, Rose means the idea that while, foregrounding the differences between marginalized and dominant groups, identity politics sacrifices difference within such groups and in the process is in danger of *enacting the very violence of erasure it seeks to undo*?[8]

This shift from Hegel to Nietzsche can help us understand the contours of the "new moralism" in at least three ways:

1. This new moralism construes racialized subjects as always already victims in need of special treatment and protections by the state and other institutions such as, for example, campus speech codes, safe spaces, trigger warnings and the like. This is in marked contrast with, for example, the Black Panther Party's emphasis on self-organization, community building, and armed self-defence.[9] Far from challenging and undermining "Whiteness," therefore, the new moralism continually re-confirms its insidious power. Today, the prospect of a Black leader such as Huey Newton debating an open racist like William F. Buckley Jr. on the latter's own talk show *Firing Line* would simply be unthinkable.[10]

2. Far from seeking to go *beyond* racial categories, the new moralism perpetuates the subsumption of racialized persons beneath rigid and reified group categories as a new version of what Freud, following McDougall, called the "Herd instinct," (though now *positively* rather than *negatively* evaluated). And in such a logic, it fails to challenge the deeper underlying and essentializing logic of racism itself, the central harm of which is the negation of the individuality of the person by force of racialized subsumption.

3. Finally, and perhaps most troublingly, in its embrace of the tactics of cancelation or de-platforming offensive or "problematic" speakers, the new moralism disavows a strategy of contesting competing perspectives via discourse (broadly understood) and therefore hastens the slide already afoot globally from agonism to antagonism, which is to say, *a dangerous and unpredictable de-sublimation of violence and de-legitimation of democratic institutions.*

"The New Moralism"

Today we witness the re-emergence of a powerful new moralism that was set in motion several decades ago but has since become strongly amplified in the wake of the killing of George Floyd in the Spring of 2020 (one of a brutal litany of such murders) and the discovery of the unmarked graves of scores of Indigenous children buried on the grounds of Canada's infamous Indian Residential Schools about one year later—confirmation of the Canadian state's ignominious, genocidal history. This new moralism is expressed in diverse ways, whose adverse effects have injured the lives and livelihoods of those targeted by its often random and unpredictable vicissitudes from a spate of firings of White individuals who demonstrated insufficient support for racialized people or for #BLM. Elsewhere I have written about this trend in the university and in the art world.[11]

For example, in 2020, *New York Times* food writer, Alison Roman was suspended for criticizing *en passant* in an interview two women of colour for commercialism: Chrissy Tiegen and Marie Kondo. Also in 2020, Leslie Neal-Boylan, Dean of Nursing at the University of Massachusetts Lowell, lost her job because, after having acknowledged "Recent events recall a tragic history of racism and bias that continue to thrive in this country," she states "BLACK LIVES MATTER, but also, EVERYONE'S LIFE Matters." She was promptly reported to the University of Massachusetts administration and terminated. In the same year, a data analyst, David Shor, was fired from his position for tweeting data that showed that in the 1960s violent, as opposed to non-violent Black protests, were more likely to lead local citizens to vote for the Republican party.

After several decades of challenges to the metaphysics of presence (in the spirit of Nietzsche via Derrida's understanding of the logic of the trace, which is to say, the spatio-temporal, differing-deferring "play of the text," and Barthes' notion of the "death of the author,") the metaphysics of presence grounded in authorial intentionality has returned with a vengeance and is now anchored in ethical judgments, which is to say, a *new morality*, grounded in the binary of good and evil, which appears to function now as a kind of secular religion. This new morality reverses Max Weber's observation (with reference also to Baudelaire) about the modern differentiation of spheres of value in "Science as a Vocation" where he says that "...something can be true although and because it is neither beautiful nor sacred, nor good."[12] Today, it would seem, particularly in discussions of gender identity, that nothing can be accepted as true unless it is also deemed to be both *sacred* and *good.* The new morality is, in other words, taken up with a zealousness that suggests nothing less than quasi-religious fervour.

Social justice politics on the Left and the resurgence of ethno-nationalism on the Right both exhibit a form of collective enthusiasm that has much in common with religious fundamentalism. In other words, politics now is less about the realization of specific material interests, i.e., about addressing growing socio-economic inequalities between groups and classes, than about symbolism, grievance, and the redefinition of accepted *meanings*.

If the ascetic ideals that Nietzsche unmasked in the *Genealogy* were grounded first in a specific form of what he calls the "slave revolt in morality" in which "the wretched are alone good,"[13] then it is possible to say that the new morality grounds a new structure of religious feeling. But how are we to understand such a new moralism and its power? One way is to understand its role in contemporary US anti-racism which, as one of the few exports from a de-industrializing economy in decline, now meets an apparently insatiable global demand.

Dismantling Racism?

One expression of the new moralism is to be found in an influential text by Kenneth Jones and Tema Okun entitled *Dismantling Racism: A Workbook for Social Change Groups*, which seeks to define the components of what it calls "White Supremacy Culture." *Dismantling Racism* has been adopted by, and has informed the diversity policies of, several municipal governments and institutions across the United States and Canada.[14] According to Jones and Okun, "White Supremacy Culture" is comprised of the following characteristics: perfectionism, sense of urgency, defensiveness, quantity over quality, worship of the written word, paternalism, either/or thinking, power hoarding, fear of open conflict, individualism, progress is bigger or more, objectivity, and the right to comfort. Each characteristic has its own distinctive "antidote" or characteristics to be embraced.[15] Let's look more at those characteristics that could be said to apply especially clearly to educational institutions:

"Worship of the Written word"

— If it's not written down it doesn't exist
— Those with strong documentation and writing skills are more highly valued, whether this is related to the mission or not
— There is one right way to do things

Antidote
- Acknowledge that there are many ways of reaching the same goal
- Accepting and implementing decisions made in different ways
- Understand that there are many skillful ways of being in the world
- And it is desirable for all to flourish

Individualism
- Emphasize (supposed) individual achievement/competition over cooperation
- Fosters isolation
- Leads to focus on individual vs collective/organizational goals

Antidote
- Support teamwork and related skills
- Emphasizes collective goals
- Actively give credit to everyone contributing to a process/activity/goal

Objectivity
- Belief there is such a thing as "objective"
- Devalues emotion (and people expressing emotion), hyper values logic (and people arguing "logically")

Antidote
- Accept that there are many ways to experience a given situation
- Assume that everyone has a valid point and it is your job to understand it fully

Now many (though not all) of these characteristics, *when fetishized or seen in isolation*, may accurately describe the way in which contemporary corporate and bureaucratic institutions operate within the context of a particularly rapacious neoliberal capitalism. This is the case not just in the United States and Western Europe but globally and is the function of the drive to capital accumulation, ensuing competition between contending firms and monopolization, such as it is. But if these are properties of capitalist social organization everywhere, what purpose is served by describing them as qualities of a nebulous phenomenon called "White Supremacy Culture"? And what are the unintended consequences of doing so? It is here perhaps that a well-intended anti-racism shows its Janus face.

For example, in the context of secondary and tertiary education, if effective writing skills, individualism, and objectivity are taken to belong to White Supremacy Culture, then what will be the impact on Black, Indigenous, and otherwise racialized students in fields that require such skills and perspectives? Does it not imply that acquiring effective writing skills, aspiring to objectivity in, say, lab experiments, or simply exercising independent judgment (as opposed to the "herd mentality") is to be complicit with a culture premised upon one's own domination, suffering, and erasure? And if so, what of teachers and professors who are professionally obligated to teach these things in their classes? Does it not pose a serious dilemma to them/us? Would they not be guilty of engaging in more than just "micro-aggressions" towards their racialized students? Would they—even racialized teachers and professors among them—not, in fact, be guilty of promoting "White Supremacy Culture"? It scarcely needs to be pointed out that White Supremacy does exist, but not in the form of a *culture* of good writing, individuality, and the aspiration to objectivity, etc. but, as has become obvious after the events of January 6, 2021, as an insurrectionary and existential threat to the democratic orders of the US, Canada, and Europe. However well-intentioned, Jones and Okun's account of "White Supremacy Culture" egregiously misunderstands and indeed trivializes this very real threat.

Meanwhile, leaving the teachers' dilemma aside, for the moment it is not difficult to see where the logic of this account of White Supremacy Culture leads students: by convincing racialized students that this is what White Supremacist Culture looks like, it will become a self-fulfilling prophecy: fewer and fewer of these students will excel in these critical areas of study. They will consequently be less empowered to challenge *actual* White Supremacy which, to repeat, is a clear and present danger. We may regard the effects of such well-intentioned anti-racism as in the fact running directly contrary to its stated aims, which is to say, to improve the future life chances of Black and Indigenous and other racialized people more generally. The theorization of White Supremacy Culture effectively deconstructs and undermines itself.

Such an argument about the self-defeating nature of contemporary anti-racism is made by African American Columbia University linguist and *New York Times* columnist, John McWhorter in his 2021 book *Woke Racism: How a New Religion Has Betrayed Black America*, from which the first three examples I discussed at the outset are drawn. While deeply flawed in certain ways, the book is valuable because it identifies something very disquieting and profoundly disempowering about contemporary third wave anti-racism. According to McWhorter, the first wave of anti-racism heroically took on slavery and the Jim Crow legislation that arose in its aftermath, while the second wave confronted what he (somewhat vaguely) calls "racist attitudes" in the 1970s and 1980s. *Third wave* anti-racism only becomes mainstream in the first decade of the 21st century. By contrast with its predecessors, McWhorter suggests that third wave anti-racism:

> teaches that because racism is baked into the structure of society, whites' "complicity" in living within it constitutes racism itself, while for black people, grappling with the racism surrounding them is the totality of experience and must condition exquisite sensitivity toward them, including a suspension of standards and conduct.[16]

We see this reflected in Jones and Okun's description of "White Supremacy Culture" I referred to above. As the subtitle of his book suggests, third wave anti-racism is less of a social and political and more of a religious movement which, at its heart, entails what McWhorter calls a "contradictory catechism." For example, he points out the following:

> Silence about racism is violence.
>
> [Elevate the voices of the oppressed over your own.]
>
> Show interest in multiculturalism.
>
> [Do not culturally appropriate. What is not your culture is not for you, and you may not try it or do it.]

Such a catechism hits on many of the norms of the contemporary North American university, with its vocabulary of cultural appropriation, micro-aggressions, safe spaces, challenges to freedom of expression and so on. The underlying premise of these norms tends to be an equation of dissensus, disagreement with offence and offence, in turn, with violence and therefore *harm*. Or as Sarah Schulman has argued, there is a tendency to equate *conflict* with *abuse* hence conflict itself is construed as harmful. But the sublimation of conflict from a violently physical encounter into law and politics has been crucial to the history of the civilizing process and such an accomplishment ought not be taken lightly. The equation of conflict and abuse is an effective as a way of shutting down discourse and avoiding contestation. Schulman argues that

> people experiencing the inevitable discomfort of human understanding and misunderstanding often overstate the harm that has been done to them—they describe themselves as victims rather than as participants in a shared situation. And overstating harm itself can cause harm, whether it leads to social shunning or physical violence.[17]

Like the implications of Jones and Okun's understanding of "White Supremacy Culture," McWhorter argues that third-wave anti-racism is, itself, *racist.* Why? Because while aiming to protect Black and other racialized people from harm, it *actually does the opposite.* In other words, in the act of putatively protecting them from harm third wave anti-racism harms the very people whose lives it aspires to support and improve. Such an equation relies on an often-unstated premise and one which I suggest (and here I agree with McWhorter) that African Americans, and by extension Indigenous and other racialized peoples, are powerless victims who ultimately possess little if any agency, which is accorded solely to something called "Whiteness." This is what comes to a head in the anxieties leading to the multiplying of prohibitions on access to, and interpretation of, challenging art works. If the "message" of these works is not received in the correct manner, this can cause offence or be seen as abuse and therefore can cause harm. The fall out for museums and galleries (not to mention their patrons and sponsors) can be devastating to their "brands."

What is at the root of concepts such as "White Supremacy Culture"? One way of understanding its rise is the predominance of Identity politics and central Identity politics is standpoint epistemology. From its inception in the Georg Lukács' essay on "Reification and the Consciousness of the Proletariat" in his *History and Class Consciousness* to the Afro-pessimism of Frank B. Wilderson III, standpoint epistemology has stressed the transition from an active, transformative subject to a passive subject that is an effect of "subjectification" through the institutions of the modern, which is to say, Western and Euro-centric world. What we see, in effect, as previously alluded to, is the transformation of Hegel's conception of the dialectic of mastery and slavery as outlined in the *Phenomenology of Spirit* to a conception of the relation in the work of Friedrich Nietzsche, in particular the *Genealogy of Morals*, in which slave morality constitutes the inscription of a psychology of weakness, victimhood and a corresponding spirit of revenge.

Such knowledge was grounded in the immediacy of the experience of oppression in much the same way that workers' direct experience of the oppressive nature of wage slavery would generate specific knowledge about the nature of exploitation and the domination of the value form within capitalist society. Although we need to be clear that this was not exactly faithful to Lukacs' more dialectical position. Nevertheless, Lukács accepted Lenin's suspicion in *What is to Be Done?* that left to its own devices, the working class could only achieve what Lenin derisively called "trade union consciousness."[18] In other words, collective experience without mediation evinced considerable limitations.

Fredric Jameson grounds the politics of a vast range of oppressed groups in Lukács' notion of standpoint epistemology or collective experience.[19] Yet he misses the way in which Lukács' standpoint of emancipation has turned into a standpoint of naturalized domination in the emergence, for example, of Afropessimism, especially in the work of Frank B. Wilderson III. According to Wilderson, the very condition of the personhood of what he calls "the Human" necessitates the "social death" of Black people, expressed in most obvious form in slavery. It is at this point, as well, that—in marked contrast to the Combahee River Collective—the idea of human emancipation is resolutely abandoned. Accordingly, Wilderson disavows Black solidarity with the anti-colonial and emancipatory aspirations of the Palestinian people—which cannot but strike us as particularly poignant today. The critique of reification in standpoint theory remains reified and results from an abandonment of universalism.

Standpoint theory understood in this sense arguably entails a very dubious relation of ownership to experience. And it is precisely this condition that gives the oppressed a stake not in the transformation but in the maintenance of such conditions, lest it lose its voice and fall silent once again. *The oppressed are driven, as it were, to identify with rather than to challenge the aggressor, which is to say: to identify with conditions of their own domination.* This might explain what can be regarded only as the attachment to the conditions of one's own victimization and the consequent hindrance that this places on social transformation and, ultimately, the *dialectic of liberation*.

Of course, this logic is self-reinforcing as the marginalized and excluded are encouraged to constantly emphasize and perform their victimization, often in competition with members of other marginalized groups, to be heard. The assumption here is that the veracity of truth claims articulated by historically oppressed groups is directly proportional to the magnitude of their historical suffering. This is well exemplified by Wilderson in seeking, as it were, to corner the market on "real" or "authentic" suffering:

> To suffer like a White woman or Native Americans or postcolonial subjects would be heaven for us, because the suffering of the Slave would have Human resonance. And that Human resonance would lend itself to very Human answers to the question, What is to be done? or What does freedom look like? We could launch coherent liberation campaigns. However, that would be disastrous for the Human race. This is why Afropessimism has no prescriptive gesture because the end of our suffering signals the end of the Human, the end of world.[20]

It is here in Wilderson's work that identity politics as what could be called a *melancholic attachment to one's own suffering* becomes most explicit. How can we account for the emergence of such an attachment? It is possible to do so through a Nietzschean genealogy of the "new moralism."

A Genealogy of the New Moralism

Nietzsche can help us identify, in a way more illuminating than McWhorter, why "woke anti-racism" can be construed, despite its good intentions, as *racist.* What would a genealogy of the new moralism look like? Nietzsche brings a philologist's perspective to bear on the origins of morality, prompting him to challenge the British empiricist's claim that the word "good" describes altruistic action or utility. In contrast, Nietzsche argues that Master morality is based upon self-regard and pathos of distance from the "low," the "bad," the "ill constituted." While noble morality affirms itself, Nietzsche suggests that slave morality "is constituted by what he calls the inversion of the value posting eye."[21] By this he means that, by virtue of a priestly caste's triumph over the warrior caste and consequent transvaluation of values, slave morality considers the nobles first as evil and then the slave as the embodiment of the good. This is what he calls the "venomous eye of réssentiment." It is the very powerlessness of the slave that is made into a virtue. What the slave cannot carry out in the world, he carries out in the imagination. And such imagination produces revenge fantasies to compensate for past privations and indignities, rather than the pursuit of justice or truth.

It is possible to understand what McWhorter calls "third wave anti-racism" as arising out of precisely such a profound sense of powerlessness. Yet, McWhorter's account misses a key aspect of this history and that the anti-racism represented by projects such as the Black Lesbian socialist Combahee River Collective, by figures like Angela Davis working within the Communist Party and the Black

Panthers whose leadership was systematically liquidated by the FBI through COINTELPRO. With genuine social movements for transformation in the 1960s having been forestalled or reversed - symbolized by the figure of carceral feminist and zealous public prosecutor Kamala Harris, the uncanny double of socialist-feminist prison abolitionist and revolutionary Angela Davis—a certain harshly moralizing discourse has returned embodying what Nietzsche himself identified as an unmistakable cruelty and lust for revenge. *Such an impulse is an effect not of strength but of weakness*.

Contemporary anti-racism could be said to embody the inversion of what Nietzsche calls the value-positing eye, precisely through its fetishization of "White Supremacy Culture," as we have seen. All the seemingly antithetical values to those of such a culture are affirmed as good while of course such a putative White Supremacy Culture is to be denigrated. In this we see the workings of a spirit of revenge that is less geared to assisting and improving the lives of Black and racialized peoples—as the Black Panthers clearly did with their school lunch programs and sickle cell anemia testing along with aggressive, armed community self-defence—than it is directly attacking White culture and individual White people. In fact, the young BPP organizer, Fred Hampton, shortly before his assassination by COINTELPRO, sought to bring together poor Blacks, Latinos, and Whites in what he called a "Rainbow Coalition."

There are two ways in which the spirit of revenge is expressed: by racialized people lashing out at White people and White people, consumed by guilt, attacking Whiteness, as it were, from the inside. As an example of the first, we may cite psychiatrist and psychoanalyst Aruna Khilanani's on-line lecture entitled the "Psychopathic Problem of the White Mind," at the Yale School of Medicine in the spring of 2021 in which she confessed that she "had fantasies of unloading a revolver into the head of any White person that got in my way, burying their body and wiping my bloody hands as I walked away relatively guiltless with a bounce in my step."[22] Donald Moss' 2021 paper entitled "On Having Whiteness," published in the *Journal of the American Psychoanalytical Society*, exemplifies the second instance. The abstract of the article claims that the condition he calls "parasitic Whiteness" is:

> a condition one first acquires and then has—a malignant, parasitic-like condition to which "white" people have a particular susceptibility. The condition is foundational, generating characteristic ways of being in one's body, in one's mind, and in one's world. Parasitic Whiteness renders its hosts' appetites voracious, insatiable, and perverse. These deformed appetites particularly target nonwhite peoples. Once established, these appetites are nearly impossible to eliminate. Effective treatment consists of a combination of psychic and social historical interventions. Such interventions can reasonably aim only to reshape Whiteness's infiltrated appetites—to reduce their intensities, redistribute their aims, and occasionally turn those aims toward the work of reparation.
>
> (p. 356)[23]

Daniel Burston observes that

> Dr. Moss is saying, in effect, that white-skinned people are extremely susceptible to acquiring a sadistic and exploitative mode of relatedness towards non-whites that leads them to control and enslave them. Once acquired, this rigid and internalized "taxonomy" is basically locked in and insusceptible to external influences that might take their development in a pro-social direction.

Burston concludes that in cases of both Khilanani and Moss,

> The stark, Manichean simplicity of binaries like these afford people a false sense of moral clarity, multiple opportunities for virtue signaling and a sense of pride for being on what they imagine is "the right side of history". But clinical experience demonstrates that simple binaries often belie much that lies beneath the surface, and psychoanalysis was designed to wrestle with ambiguity, contradictions and complexity in the individual psyche and society at large.[24]

So, not only does the new morality embedded in contemporary anti-racism entail a naturalized view of racialized people as inherently disempowered, generating a spirit of vengeance against both "White Supremacy Culture" or what Khilanani and Moss both refer to in an essentializing key as the "White mind." A further implication, insofar as anti-racism repudiates individualism or individuality, is that all persons, Blacks and Whites alike, must continue to be subordinated to reified group categories. Anti-racism as the manifestation of Nietzsche's "inversion of the value-positing eye," doesn't challenge the underlying subsumptive logic of racism. Rather, it simply aims to alter the poles of valuation. If historically the racial category "White" was held to be *normal*, as the basis of the European civilizing mission that lay at the heart of the colonial project, and non-White or Red, Black, and Brown, were held to be *pathological*, today the binary hierarchy is simply inverted, giving rise to new forms of oppression and mystification.

As a result, the notion that racism harms us by undermining of the possibility of the *free development of the individual*, which must today as it was in Marx and Engels' time be taken to be a key left demand, is ignored or dismissed. As I noted above, insofar as individuality is dismissed as a pillar of White Supremacy Culture, as it clearly is for Jones and Okun, the idea that the reduction of the individuality of the person to group categories is detrimental to human flourishing is ruled out in advance. Yet we know that such a reductionism, or what Theodor W. Adorno calls "identity-thinking," entails a sacrifice of the excessive heterogeneity or the "non-identical" dimension of the individual to identity. In "third wave anti-racism," as per Rose's "paradox of empowerment," cited above, the differences between groups' identities are emphasized in exact proportion to the elimination of differences *within* such groups. In other words, there simply is no remaining space available for dissent and consequently identity politics turns authoritarian. To merely express a heterodox perspective is to be complicit with White Supremacy Culture or to, always already, "identify with the aggressor."[25]

A key antidote to slave morality, for Nietzsche, was the idea of "active and interpretive" powers or the capacity to fashion new understandings of "being" out of the flux and flow of seemingly endless "becoming." He called this "Will to Power." Central to this was, of course, music and art. It is telling therefore that the artworld itself has become a site of identity anxieties and a disavowal of such fashioning. In the cases of artists whose work was deemed to be so egregious in its potentially *harmful effects* that anti-racist activists demanded that their work be placed beyond public purview, as in the cases of artists such as Guston, Arnautoff, Monkman, and Lum, or worse, that the work be destroyed—in the case of Schutz we see the rough equivalent of a book burning. One would have thought that rather than being pulled from public purview or destroyed, artworks that raise troubling questions would be placed within the space of aesthetic reason, that is, they would become objects of historically informed criticism or subjected to exuberantly conflicting interpretations.

In the foreshortening or indeed elimination of the space of aesthetic reason, and therefore a refusal of interpretation and counter-interpretation, we witness a stubborn refusal of the agon or hermeneutical contest. In a short early text entitled "Homer's Contest," originally intended for but not published in *Birth of Tragedy*, Nietzsche writes:

> And not just Aristotle, but the whole of Greek antiquity thinks about grudge and envy differently from us and agrees with Hesiod, who first portrays one Eris as wicked, in fact the one who leads men into hostile struggle-to-the-death, and then praises the other Eris as good who, as jealousy, grudge and envy, goads men to action, not, however, the action of a struggle-to-the-death but the action of the contest.

Nietzsche is suggesting, then, that Eris, the Goddess of strife, is inherently ambivalent: she signifies *antagonism* or war as the "struggle to the death," on the one hand, and *agonism* as competition or "contest," on the other. As Willow Verkerk writes in her book *Nietzsche and Friendship*

> The practice of agonistics in 'Homer's Contest' is explained by Nietzsche as providing a controlled release for impulses associated with cruelty and enmity that he later states are disciplined and spiritualized to allow for greater rigour in learning, psychological health, and creative development. In addition to the prevention of savagery and violence through sublimation, Nietzsche explains agon in antiquity as being performed by those who had a strong bond with their community and each other.[26]

In his first major work *Birth of Tragedy*, which he wrote, significantly, while working as a medical orderly during the Franco-Prussian War (1871), Nietzsche shows the origins of the dramatic form of tragedy in the festivals devoted to Dionysus—the Greek god of wine and song. Tragedy was born, argues Nietzsche, when what he calls perhaps in a somewhat "Orientalist" way the non-occidental, Dionysian idea of the unity of nature was met and tamed by the formative Apollonian principle of individuation.

During the festivals of Dionysus tragedians would engage in competitions or agonistics to determine who was the best poet. And, of course, as aesthetic phenomena, dramatic poetry was governed by the rules or laws of form. Aristotle made clear that tragic drama was defined by a plot that entailed *peripeteia* (reversal of fortune) and *anagnorisis* (recognition) and *hamartia* (fatal flaw) that leads the hero to his or her downfall and destruction.

If *agonism* is a form of contestation within or with reference to established rules (which are of course always open to modification and transformation), *antagonism* is a form of conflict that emerges when the rules or laws break down and represents a kind of regression to a condition that Thomas Hobbes called a "war of all against all," "Bellum omnium contra omnes." This is what Carl Schmitt, an important interpreter of Hobbes, called the "concept of the political."[27] For Nietzsche, as Verkerk explains, the agon is a competition between those who participate in amity or are friends, while for Schmitt antagonism is a struggle between those who harbor mutual enmity or are foes.

It is perhaps fitting, then, that tragic poets such as Sophocles and Aeschylus were, in fact, veterans of military campaigns and used their wartime experiences as raw material for their work. In these poets one can see a personification of the sublimation of violent destructiveness outside of or beyond law into form-giving activity within it.[28]

The anti-racist Left is beginning to mirror the Right in its refusal of agonism and an increasingly abstract criticism and rejection of liberal-democracy, not least its refusal of the idea that the political field is comprised of several vying, potentially hegemonic discourses that, as they contest with one another, make claims on the future. Instead, many segments of the Left simply assert and seek to crudely impose the validity of their own moralistic perspectives while at the same time closing off or cancelling contending perspectives without, that is, entering into discursive struggle with them. *The left does indirectly what the right does directly: this is to undermine the agonistic logic of liberal-democracy, itself.* In this, it contributes in its own way to a slide from *agon* to *antagonism*, amity to enmity and therefore a dangerous de-sublimation of political violence and the very real prospect of a descent into a kind of civil war from which it can never even hope to emerge victorious.

Notes

1 See John McWhorter in his 2021 book *Woke Racism: How a New Religion Has Betrayed Black America* (New York: Penguin Random House, 2021).

2 This chapter is based on a paper presented at a conference entitled "Nietzsche and the Genealogies of the New Moralism" co-hosted by the Nietzsche Archiv, the Akademie der bildenden Kuenste and the Institute for the Humanities at Simon Fraser University at the Klassik Stiftung, Weimar, October 28–9, 2022.

3 The triumphant neo-liberal iteration can be found in the right Hegelianism of Francis Fukuyama's *The End of History and the Last Man* (New York: The Free Press, 1992). See Amy Allen, *The End of Progress: Decolonizing the Normative Foundations of Critical Theory* (New York: Columbia University Press, 2017) for a critique of Habermas and Honneth's versions of Critical Theory.
4 G. W. F. Hegel, *The Difference Between Fichte's and Schelling's System of Philosophy*, edited and translated by W. Cerf and H. S. Harris (Buffalo, NY: SUNY Press, 1977).
5 G. W. F. Hegel, *Phenomenology of Spirit*, trans J. N. Findley (Oxford: Oxford University Press, 1977): 111–18.
6 Friedrich Nietzsche, *The Genealogy of Morals and Ecce Homo*, trans. Walter Kaufmann and R. J. Hollingdale (New York: Vintage, 1989): 24–56.
7 Gillian Rose, *Mourning Becomes the Law: Philosophy and Representation* (Cambridge: Cambridge University Press, 1996): 5.
8 This is no better exemplified than by contemporary Zionism's equation of anti-Zionism and anti-Semitism, which renders individual anti-Zionist Jews and progressive anti-Zionist Jewish organizations as "self-hating" or otherwise psycho-pathological.
9 See Joshua Bloom and Waldo E. Martin, Jr., *Black Against Power: The History and Politics of the Black Panther Party* (Berkeley: University of California Press, 2013).
10 "*Firing Line with William F. Buckley Jr*.: How Does It Go With the Black Movement," January 23, 1973. https://www.youtube.com/watch?v=XUicVnx1UKU Accessed December 15, 2023. This despite the fact that Newton clearly got the better of Buckley.
11 See Samir Gandesha, "Dictatorship Contra Critique." *The Conformist Rebellion: Marxist Critiques of the Contemporary Left* (New York: Rowman and Littlefield, 2022): 113–28.
12 Max Weber, "Science as a Vocation," *Essays in Sociology From Max Weber*, (Oxford: Oxford University Press, 1958): 23.
13 Nietzsche, *Genealogy*, 34.
14 A quick Google search reveals a wide adoption of this document from the Colorado Department of Education, National Child Welfare Workforce to Berkeley Public Schools to the Philanthropic Foundations of Canada and the Temerty Faculty of Medicine at the University of Toronto.
15 https://pfc.ca/wp-content/uploads/2022/01/dismantling-racism-workbook-en.pdf
16 *Woke Racism*, 15.
17 Fischer, *The Cut*, Aug 2, 2020.
18 V. I. Lenin, *What is to be Done: The Burning Questions of Our Movement* (Moscow: International Publishers, 1969): 17.
19 Fredric Jameson, "*History and Class Consciousness* as an 'Unfinished Project,'" in Sandra Harding (Ed.) *The Feminist Standpoint Theory Reader* (New York and London: Routledge, 2004): 143–52.
20 Frank B. Wilderson III, *Afropessimism* (New York: Liveright Books, 2020), 331.
21 Nietzsche, *Genealogy*, 36.
22 As reported in *The Washington Post*, June 9, 2021. https://www.washingtonpost.com/education/2021/06/09/yale-lecturer-talks-about-killing-white-people/ Accessed Dec 6, 2023.
23 Cited in Daniel Burston, "Mapping the White Unconscious: Critical Race Theory, Whiteness Studies, and Psychoanalysis," in *Critical Theory and Psychoanalysis: From the Frankfurt School to Contemporary Critique* Jon Mills and Daniel Burston (Eds.) (New York and London: Routledge, Taylor and Francis, 2023): 277.
24 Daniel Burston, "Mapping the White Unconscious: Critical Race Theory, Whiteness Studies, and Psychoanalysis," 283.
25 See also Ato Sekyi-Otu, *Left Universalism: Africacentric Essays* (New York and London: Routledge, Taylor and Francis, 2019): 165–6. It is also possible to argue that the IHRA definition of anti-Semitism, which equates anti-Semitism and criticism of Israel, enforces a kind of group think on the part of all Jewish people who either must

support the Israeli state or be branded as pathologically self-hating. The essence of identity politics is to maximize the difference between groups while minimizing, if not eliminating, differences within groups.

26 Willow Verkerk, *Nietzsche and Friendship* (London and New York: Bloomsbury, 2019): 48.

27 Carl Schmitt, *The Concept of the Political: Expanded Edition*, George Schwab (Trans) (Chicago: University of Chicago Press, 2007).

28 As Theodor W. Adorno puts it in *Aesthetic Theory*, "every work of art is an uncommitted crime."

Chapter 4

Questioning the University's "Anti-Blackness"

Charles Thorpe

Introduction

The University of California at San Diego (UCSD) is anti-Black. UCSD has anti-Blackness as a constitutive part of itself. Anti-Blackness is not contingent to UCSD but in some way essential. That is according to UCSD, anyway. A proposal drawn up in April 2021 for a new undergraduate college on the campus, focusing on addressing "structural racism and anti-Blackness," stated that

> In Spring 2020, the murder of George Floyd, Breonna Taylor, Daniel Prude, and countless other African American people, as well as Black Lives Matter activism, has caused the university to examine how structural racism and anti-Blackness is woven into the fabric of the institution.
>
> (UCSD, 2021: 27)

Since then, UCSD has been locked in an internal paradoxical struggle; if UCSD is really riddled with anti-Blackness, how can it be motivated to transform itself? If anti-Blackness is in the fabric of the institution, how can it be unstitched? This internal struggle might be understood as therapy (cf. Furedi, 2004). So that the institution may redeem itself, presumably, *all* its members must undergo their therapy.

This paper asks a question that must not be asked, namely, what is UCSD's anti-Blackness? The answer, I suggest, is ideology. Anti-anti-Blackness has become UCSD's institutional ideology. This functions to occlude the real contradictions that beset the institution internally (in terms of tension and conflict in the relations within the organization and on campus) and externally (in terms of the institution inhabiting a contradictory and conflictual social environment). UCSD utilizes moral panic (Cohen, 1973) surrounding racism, in a paradoxical way, as ideological legitimation. This is the use of racial politics in rationalization (in the Freudian/Marxist sense of defense mechanism or mystificatory self-justification). The politics of race ultimately resolve themselves in social and political pessimism, given expression in the "Afro-pessimism" advocated by Frank B. Wilderson III (Wilderson, 2020). This pessimism is a product and symptom of what Mark Fisher calls "capitalist realism," the underlying acceptance of capitalist society as the ultimate reality,

DOI: 10.4324/9781003389927-4

without horizon (Fisher, 2009). Racial politics on campus represent a form of false opposition from which there can be safely orchestrated what Erving Goffman called a "blow-up," a way of "cooling the mark out" through a controlled release of social tension (Goffman, 1952, 457; cf. Fisher ed., 2013). This pseudo-opposition masks the underlying contradictory position of the university in a context of capitalist crisis. It enables the continued legitimization of the university as the core institution of the "liberal class" but in a period in which social liberalism is routinely overridden by neo-liberalism, for which it acts as a mere cover (cf. Hedges, 2010; Kagarlitsky, 2021). This is reformism in an era in which reform is no longer possible (Thorpe, 2022).

The ideology of anti-anti-Blackness, or Afro-pessimism, cools out students, who are caught in a regime of neoliberal debt-schooling, by telling them, as did the new college proposal, that "While Black people and other people of color have always been aware of institutional barriers, many members of our campus community who benefit from unearned privilege have come to realize the importance addressing this challenge" (UCSD, 2021, 27). Beneficiaries of "unearned privilege," presumably, have nothing to complain about. Instead, "Self-awareness of one's position with respect to privilege, power, and identity forms the basis of the campus'[s] Diversity, Equity, and Inclusion graduation requirement… [and] can be further explored in the context of individual and community well-being" (UCSD, 2021, 25). The university takes the responsibility of exposing students to their privilege. So there can be no social movement of "the students" (connected with the working class, for universal goals) because the university has taught students to disaggregate themselves, into a list of potential clients for institutional patronage, or what Boris Kagarlitsky calls "targeted assistance" (Kagarlitsky, 2021, 17–18, 35–7). This disaggregation is therefore repressive diversity, a new form of repressive tolerance (Marcuse 1969 [1965]; Brookfield, 2007; Rahim, 2020). It ideologically supports the institution of the university as the arbiter of privilege and equity in a neoliberal system of controlled austerity. Professing the perspective of the "underdog" is a way of maintaining the top dog (Gouldner, 1973 [1968], 29; Thorpe, 2022, 223–8; cf. Žižek, 1997a, 1997b; Liu, 2021).

If a Protest Happens on Campus and No One is Around to Hear It, Does it Make a Sound?

On the morning of June 13, 2020, a Professor in the Communication Department and member of UCSD Science Studies Program distributed, via email, a flyer for a Vigil for Black Lives, which was subsequently forwarded to program faculty and graduate students by the program's director. The vigil was to be held that evening in one of the campus's free speech zones. This area is marked by the "Silent Tree," a sculpture made from a metal-plate clad dead tree, part of the university's Stuart Collection of whimsical postmodern landscape art. It forms a triangle with the Singing Tree and the Talking Tree which are set in the eucalyptus grove opposite the library. (The campus is set, and continually expands, within a progressively thinning eucalyptus grove.) The Silent Tree stands in front of the main campus library, named after Theodore Geisel, the creator of Dr. Seuss children's books. Above the Silent Tree, on a mezzanine atop the library's first floor is a bronze sculpture of Geisel sitting at his desk, with paper and pencils, with his most famous creation, the Cat in the Hat, standing beside him. At the time of the protest, Geisel and his cat were conducting a lonely watch on a campus closed for classes at the height of the COVID-19 pandemic. On the same day, the undergraduate graduating class of 2020 was celebrated with a virtual, online Commencement ceremony (UC San Diego Today, 2020).

The email containing the flyer urged its recipients to meet at the Silent Tree and march. The attached flyer showed three hands in clenched fist salutes, and stated "Vigil for Black Lives: Join us in a night of remembrance and protest against UCSD's anti-Blackness." This occurred during a wave of Black Lives Matter protests across the United States in response to the May 25 murder in Minneapolis of George Floyd by police officer Derek Chauvin. These protests marked the largest protest movement in American history.

The vigil at UCSD was in "remembrance" of Floyd and other victims of police violence that year. But the flyer also called for "protest against UCSD's anti-Blackness." I replied to all, "I don't understand. The flyer says protest against 'UCSD's anti-blackness'. What does this 'anti-blackness' consist of?"After all, UCSD's Chancellor, Pradeep Khosla and senior leadership had sent out an email message two weeks previously to all academics, students, and employees: "SUBJECT: Statement on George Floyd, Breonna Taylor and Ahmaud Arbery." Chancellor Khosla stated:

> Today our hearts are burdened, our minds are searching, and our spirits are processing a mix of disbelief, anger and sadness. The news of George Floyd's death in Minneapolis on Monday night and the disturbing video of his final moments has shocked the world. Taken in context with the recent killings of Breonna Taylor (by police in her own home) and Ahmaud Arbery (by neighbors while jogging), our black community members, in particular, are outraged, traumatized, fearful and in profound pain.
>
> (Khosla et al., 2020)

Would an institution characterized by anti-Blackness express "[g]rief and concern" for African American victims and repudiate all forms of racism and discrimination (Khosla et al., 2020)? Holding a vigil for the lives of Black Americans lost to police brutality, which was also advertised as a protest against UCSD's anti-Blackness, implied a connection of shared guilt between UCSD and the perpetrators of violence against Black people. So, was the Chancellor's statement mere lip service? Or worse, was it covering up an underlying hostility to Black people by UCSD?

Many UCSD departments circulated statements expressing support for the Black Lives Matter movement and condemning police violence toward Black people. For example, the Dean of the Social Sciences Division sent an email on June 8 saying that "The grip of racism is killing Black people and killing the American values of justice and equal treatment under the law. It is time to take action." The Division stated that it was making funds available for "action research" to

> undertake meaningful actions together with our community. We will work to center and amplify the voices and roles of Black, Indigenous, People of Color. We want this to be the start of a financial commitment that will continue into the future, to realize the dreams and ideals of a just and actively anti-racist society.
> (Padden, 2020)

The protest organizers and my colleagues publicizing the protest were positioned in a contradictory way in relation to these statements by academic-administrative representatives of UCSD as an institution. In summer 2020, statements of support for Black Lives Matter were so *de rigeur* for academic institutions that *Inside Higher Ed* offered advice on how best to phrase them (McKenzie, 2020). The protest organizers and my colleagues shared with the university administration a comprehension of police violence in terms primarily of racism. Statements by administrators on behalf of the university institutionally distanced the university from this violence. My colleagues were, it might seem, following the lead of the university administration, and of the wider academic milieu, in choosing to explicitly align themselves with this public cause at this time. But they did so by condemning the university as complicit. So precisely what is it that constitutes UCSD's anti-Blackness?

Budget Crisis and "Black Winter"

Placing the protest of June 13, 2020 in historical context requires keeping in mind the following. UCSD was established in 1960 as the quintessential Cold War campus, a creation of the Manhattan Project, the post-Sputnik expansion of science education and research, and the post-war naval, aerospace, and military-industrial economy in the San Diego region (Anderson, 1993; Davis, 2015). In the 1980s the commercial biotechnology, pharmaceutical, and electrical engineering sectors became the center of gravity of the university. There was a reorientation of institutional culture around the neoliberal model of the entrepreneurial university, bolstered by the end of the Cold War and by what Alan Greenspan called "irrational exuberance" and resulting financial bubbles (Walshok and Shragge, 2013; Miyoshi, 2000; Pollock, 2017). The dominant culture of the university is technocratic and connected with the corporate cultures of the military-industrial and biotech-pharma sectors. The War on Terror prompted a revival of the military-industrial links of the university with the development of drones and electronic surveillance (Davis, 2015; Reese, 2016).

The dominant corporate-technocratic culture was challenged from early on by left-wing faculty in the humanities and social sciences, and by student activists. Frankfurt School philosopher Herbert Marcuse was on the philosophy faculty between 1965 and 1970 (Moore 1986; Juutilainen 1996). Angela Davis was his graduate student and in 1969 was part of the Lumumba-Zapata Coalition. This student collective intervened in the university's plans for a new "Third" College, demanding it be named after the Congolese and Mexican liberationists. They demanded that the curriculum "be devoted to relevant education for minority youth and to the study of the contemporary social problems of all people" (quoted in Ferguson, 2017: 16). Third College's curriculum was oriented toward Third World liberation and Black and Chicano nationalism. What was sparked by charismatic activism became routinized into the university. Nancy Scott Anderson writes, "In the end, the UCSD revolution was co-opted by moving into the campus mainstream, and two of Third College's academic pillars became independent departments: communication and ethnic studies" (Anderson, 1993: 200).

From that point onwards, the culture of the campus was split between a corporate-technocratic dominant culture and a Third World liberationist left which formed an institutional counter-culture in these latter departments, the Literature Department, and among some other humanities and social science faculty. This counterculture survived in routinized form, but became demoralized and frustrated in the context of a primarily neoliberal business-oriented academic culture which devalued the humanities (cf. Miyoshi, 2000; Thorpe, 2008). The Third Worlders were also frustrated by "a large influx of Asian students who were interested in medicine and science, not in revolution" (Anderson, 1993: 199).

As time passed, Third World politics at UCSD retreated from Marxism into forms of cultural nationalism promoted under the rubric of post-colonial studies, which in turn fed into the emergence in the 1990s of postmodern identity politics. These developments coincided with the rightward shift into neoliberalism of the New Democrats under Bill Clinton. Identity politics emerged as the new posture of progressivism of the Democratic Party, with its base increasingly in the Professional-Managerial Class (PMC), as unions declined in the face of globalization and the Democratic Party abandoned the manufacturing working class in favor of the PMC along with various ethnic and sexual minorities, a process which intensified in subsequent decades (Selfa, 2012; Liu 2021; Walsh, 2016).

On a technocratic campus oriented to the commercialization of scientific research, the humanities and social sciences already struggled for legitimacy. But then the California budget crisis that arose from the 2008 bursting of the housing market bubble and the subsequent financial crisis led to cuts to the University of California (UC), prompting sharp rises in undergraduate fees, spurring considerable anxiety among these departments about their future support. On July 16, 2009 the UC Regents decided on a furlough plan in order to save costs during the budget crisis: "Under the plan, UC faculty and staff will be required to take from 11 to 26 furlough days — amounting to a salary reduction of 4 percent to 10 percent — with higher earners being forced to take more furlough days and steeper pay cuts" (Jones, 2009). Just before the Regents meeting making that decision, the Chair of the UCSD Sociology Department wrote a letter signed by 23 department chairs calling for UC to cease treating itself as a system of equals and instead to prioritize funding to the "world class" three of Berkeley, UCLA, and UCSD. The letter called for the Regents to consider closing "one or more" of three campuses ranked lower in research—Merced, Riverside, and Santa Cruz (Sweeney, 2009). A former UCSD employee wrote in the *San Diego Union-Tribune* that "the letter seeks to address the system's budget problems through a process that would make it even more exclusive and exclusionary than it already is" (Shea 2009; Ruggiero 2009). The chairs' letter showed the state of panic among UCSD faculty about the implications of the budget shortfall. This was a neoliberal response which narrowed the scope and reach of public goods, while maintaining the economic benefits to business interests of UCSD's science-driven industry cluster. Indeed, the chairs' proposal exemplified what Henry Giroux (2019) calls the political, social, and economic paradigm of neoliberal "disposability" applied to the University of California.

On November 19, 2009, the governing body for the University of California system, the UC Regents, voted to raise (what were then still called) fees by 32%. Whereas in 2000, the cost of UC annual tuition and fees per year was $2,716, this almost doubled in 2003 to $4,271. With the increase in 2009, which went into effect as of January 15, 2010, the annual cost of tuition and fees at UC rose to $9,300. The Regents sought to soften the blow and, one may surmise, to pre-empt and demobilize opposition by introducing the Blue and Gold Opportunity Plan providing scholarships covering tuition for students from families with household incomes under the California median (which in 2009 was $60,000) (Office of the President, 2009; Freedman 2013).

Amidst growing student protests, planning began for a nationwide day of protest for the defense of public higher education on March 4, 2010. As part of this, a student coalition prepared for a demonstration at UC San Diego for that date. The recession had left the State of California with a $20 billion budget deficit, K-12 school districts had been hit by mass layoffs, and furloughs were put in place at both the University of California system and the California State University system. In 2009, State Governor Arnold Schwarzenegger cut Community College funding by $812 million. During that Fall, planning began for the March 4 protest:

> On October 24, 2009, more than 800 students, workers and teachers came together at UC Berkeley to defend public education. The Mobilizing Conference brought together representatives from over 100 different schools, unions and organizations from all across California. After hours of open collective discussion, they voted to call for a Strike and Day of Action on March 4th 2010.
>
> (AK Press, 2010)

The Mobilizing Conference put out a National Call, emphasizing the defense of public education as a dimension of class struggle:

> The politicians and administrators say there is no money for education and social services. They say that 'there is no alternative' to the cuts. But if there's money for wars, bank bailouts, and prisons, why is there no money for public education?

> We can beat back the cuts if we unite students, workers, and teachers across all sectors of public education — Pre K-12, adult education, community colleges, and state-funded universities. We appeal to the leaders of the trade union movement to support and organize strikes and/or mass actions on March 4. The weight of workers and students united in strikes and mobilizations would shift the balance of forces entirely against the current agenda of cuts and make victory possible.
>
> Building a powerful movement to defend public education will, in turn, advance the struggle in defense of all public-sector workers and services and will be an inspiration to all those fighting against the wars, for immigrants' rights, in defense of jobs, for single-payer health care, and other progressive causes.
>
> (California Coordinating Committee 2009)

At UCSD, the March 4 demonstration organized by the student-led UCSD Coalition for Educational Justice demanded " . . . that our state government and our administrators take immediate action to eliminate all student fees and restore our universities to what the California Master Plan for Higher Education intended them to be: $0 tuition public institutions." This went along with demands that the State of California properly fund higher education and that university workers be treated with respect and dignity:

> Our workers play an integral role in making the university function. Without them our university would cease to function effectively and there would be no learning and research. Our university should immediately desist from laying off lecturers and workers that provide crucial student and patient care services as well as from furloughing faculty and staff.
>
> (UCSD Coalition for Educational Justice, 2010)

The student coalition also called for the UC Regents to "reverse the emergency powers they recently bestowed upon the UC Office of the President. We also request that our administrators provide the university community with absolute transparency in how university budgets are drafted and how our money is spent" (UCSD Coalition for Educational Justice, 2010).

The *New York Times* reported on March 4, 2010:

> Angered by increases in tuition and cuts in state financing, thousands of students, parents and faculty members protested across California on Thursday at colleges, universities and even elementary schools to plead for help with the state's education crisis. Called a 'strike and day of action to defend public education' by organizers, the demonstrations were boisterous and occasionally confrontational.
>
> (McKinley, 2010)

There were over a hundred protest actions planned for March 4 in 32 US states. According to a student organizing website:

> The Day of Action was originally conceived in California as a response to the current crisis in higher education in that state, but it has since grown to encompass students and others at educational institutions at all levels in all parts of the country — from Berkeley and San Diego to Portland, Maine and Montgomery, Alabama.
>
> (Student Activism, 2020)

Solidarity protests were held internationally, for example at the University of Marburg, Germany. The March 4 strikes and actions at universities were joined by solidarity actions on the day by teachers at some California schools. Student protests continued in the UC system in 2010 (Education 4 the People!, n.d.). On November 17, 2010, UC Regents met at UC San Francisco and voted on an 8% fee increase on top of the previous year's 32% increase, bringing tuition and fees to $11,124. During protests outside the meeting, a police officer unholstered his gun and pointed it at a group of students (Preuitt, 2010).

The March 4 protest movement that began in California was significant also for the fact that it was part of a wave of protest globally between 2010 and 2012. In November 2010, there were large student demonstrations in London. In a notorious incident, students broke into Conservative Party headquarters at Milbank Tower. In 2011, a wave of student protest emerged in Chile (Somma, 2012). In 2012, in Quebec, Canada, students went on strike and marched against a 75% tuition hike (Mason, 2012; Michael, 2013). The 2010s also saw student protests in South Korea, India, Mexico, South Africa, Nigeria, Italy, and Germany. These protests had in common demands for "an end to the introduction (or increase) of student fees and a return to free education in a publicly funded system" (Cini and Ríos-Jara, 2023: 421). Occupy Wall Street protests emerged in New York City and spread across the country toward the end of 2011, fading away by the middle of 2012. At UC Berkeley, on November 9, 2011 an attempt to set up an Occupy encampment in the university's main plaza was violently dispersed by police who jabbed students and staff with batons. A little later, on November 18, an Occupy encampment was broken up by police at UC Davis and student demonstrators who were blocking a pathway were pepper-sprayed in what was widely seen as gratuitous police violence toward peaceful protesters. In January, 2012, student protesters outside a Regents meeting at UC Riverside were met by Riverside County sheriffs who struck students with batons and fired paint-balls into the crowd at close range, causing students to be injured with bruising and welts. UC President Mark Yudof asserted that the police action was justified due to the "angry mob" who "provoked the response from the police" (quoted in Thorpe 2013: 219).

UCSD's budget crisis also produced a leftist response through an attempt to organize non-unionized tenured and tenure-track faculty in the American

Association of University Professors. Activist faculty took over an existing campus branch of the AAUP, taking it out of political hibernation, with a view to organizing for advocacy of public higher education and against cuts and tuition increases. This continued through the Occupy protests and in 2012 the AAUP branch organized a protest event with the theme Occupy Education, opposing privatization (AAUP, 2012). This organizing lost pace after 2012 and today there is almost no institutional memory of this leftward turn.

At UCSD, the year 2010 is remembered exclusively as a moment of racial crisis. Why? In 2010, the campus came under national scrutiny following an off-campus fraternity-linked party on February 15 that was billed as "The Compton Cookout," in mock "honor" of Black History Month (Marez, 2020: 161–3). The announcement of the event overflowed with crude racial stereotypes, some of which portrayed Black women as lewd "ghetto chicks" (Archibold, 2010; Gordon, 2010). The Black Student Union called on the administration to take various actions and students turned out to protest this racist language and imagery in numbers rarely seen on campus. A television program by the satirical rightwing student newspaper, the *Koala*, mocked students protesting the Compton Cookout and used the "n-word" and other racial epithets. A noose was found in the library, hanging from a bookshelf. A student subsequently came forward on March 1, claiming responsibility for the noose, saying that she and friends had been tying knots in a piece of rope they had found, a friend had tied a noose, and she had thoughtlessly hung it on the side of a table. She said, "it was not an act of racism," although "I know what I did was offensive — regardless of my intentions." She described herself as "a minority student who sympathizes with the students that have been affected by the recent issues on campus" (*San Diego Union-Tribune*, 2010; Johnston, 2010). On the same day that she came forward, the Doctor Seuss statue, presumably the Cat in the Hat, was discovered with a pillowcase placed over it, fashioned crudely like a Ku Klux Klan hood, with a rose inserted between the fingers of the statue (the Cat in the Hat is gripping his Hat) (Showley, 2010). The perpetrators of this gesture remain unknown.

These events came to be known on campus as "Black Winter" (Robbins, 2020). The February 15 party was followed by a student walk-out of a faculty and administration "teach-in." After the *Koala* television broadcast, students occupied the Chancellor's office and the Black Student Union put 32 demands to the administration. The Associated Student Council froze funding across the board for 33 student media organizations for three weeks, restored only after the measure was condemned by the ACLU's San Diego Chapter (Wayland, 2010; Bonilla, 2010). In response to the BSU demands, the university committed to measures such as hiring in areas related to race and increasing diversity in faculty, the creation of resource centers for Black and other minority students and creating a Diversity, Equity, and Inclusion requirement for undergraduates. According to the *San Diego Union-Tribune*:

> Chancellor Mary Anne Fox, who has condemned both the party and the TV show, stood at a lectern and repeatedly tried to appease the crowd. She read

> aloud each of the demands from the Black Student Union and stated 'done' loudly after several. Among the demands she agreed to were providing solid funding for the African-American studies minor and ethnic studies programs.
> (Su, 2010)

The administration's formal accession to the BSU demands was announced to a mass protest in front of the library on March 4 by student and faculty activists. A Sociology professor told the assembled crowd "This is a day of victory!" A History professor compared the BSU's activism with the guerilla struggles of the Farabundo Martí National Liberation Front in Nicaragua, the anti-apartheid and Black liberation struggles of the African National Congress and the Pan-Africanist Congress of Azania, "the sustained activity of the Cuban Revolution," and the First Intifada in Palestine. He said that "The young people of today have not known what we have today They have not known victory." An English professor sang that "The tables are starting to turn" and that it was a "revolution" (IllegalFruitTrade, 2010; JusticeUCSD, 2010a; JusticeUCSD, 2010b; JusticeUCSD, 2010c). The Compton Cookout became the touchstone for all subsequent discussion regarding race on campus, establishing a new institutional ideology.

Many faculty who were involved in organizing the protest against the Compton Cookout were also active in the AAUP's efforts to rally faculty and students against the neo-liberal regime and in the service of economic justice. But the latter has been forgotten while the former completely reshaped the campus. The events of "Black Winter" were symbols. As a Theater and Dance professor put it during the March 4 rally, they were "performances" following and enacting "scripts" (George Graves, 2010). Most of the UCSD leftist faculty had long ago shifted away from class struggle to discursive and symbolic preoccupations and from Third Worldism to narrower identity politics. They were primed by their culturalist, postmodern orientation for the symbolic contestation of "Black Winter."

The slogan of the protests arising from the Compton Cookout was "Real Pain, Real Action." On February 19, 2010 BSU members chanted the slogan for over five minutes before the Chancellor, Vice Chancellor of Student of Affairs and the Chief Diversity Officer (Alvarez et al., 2010: 176). The rhetoric of pain served to give a certain materiality to the symbolic and gave force to the claims made by the BSU and their faculty supporters (cf. Meštrović, 1997). It also served to overshadow and distract attention from the economic demands for which many protesters turned out on March 4.

The fact that the March 4 protest was called against tuition fees and the creeping privatization of higher education has been erased. The history of economic struggle has been smothered by the creation of a racialist cultural ideology portraying the BSU and its faculty supporters as fighting against a racist institutional culture. In response to the noose incident, the BSU drew up a list of demands for the university administration, including a diversity sensitivity requirement for undergraduates, safe spaces on campus for Black students, and increased funding for minority recruitment and retention (Su, 2010). The administration's response included the creation a Diversity, Equity, Inclusion plan, with a DEI requirement built into the undergraduate curriculum for all students. The university also moved to create "safe spaces" such as the Black Resource Center and the Raza Resource Center. In 2016, the university created the Black Excellence Initiative which focused on hiring Black faculty and fostering the academic success of Black students, seeking to address the low numbers of Black students at the campus and longstanding concerns over the "campus climate" felt to be unwelcoming and even hostile by Black students and faculty.

The BSU demands on the administration in the wake of the Compton Cookout were ones that the university administration could meet despite the new austerity measures. The Coalition for Educational Justice demands for the end to fees were calls that went beyond the campus-level administration to challenge the University of California Regents, University of California Office of the President, the State of California, and ultimately the entire political-economic framework of neoliberalism. In the 21st century, the ruling class cannot accept free higher education without calling into question the ideological and material foundations upon which they organize accumulation. In contrast, the BSU demands only marginally touched the budget. Therefore, for the BSU and its faculty allies "victory" was possible. But this particularistic and opportunistic "victory," in the form of a quick deal, was achieved at the expense of diluting and disorientating of the student movement against tuition fees and privatization.

At UCSD, the economic struggle against privatization was coopted and sidelined by a symbolic struggle in which an allegedly pervasive but poorly defined racism among the student body was to be expurgated through various measures which strengthened the place of identity-political organizations in student politics and created positions among the faculty in research on race and ethnicity, adding strength to social science and humanities departments, with a DEI requirement increasing the pool of students, on which departmental funding is based, for social science and humanities departments. In the process, the movement against rising tuition fees was steered toward the identity-political demands arising from the Compton Cookout (cf. Alvarez et al., 2010: 88, 135). The crowd who had assembled to fight against tuition fees, carrying signs (shown in photographs on front and back cover and pp. 9, 22, 37, 80, 81, 84, 100, 124, 138, 149, 169 of Alvarez et al., 2010) concerning the defense of public K-12 and higher education against budget cuts and privatization, were characterized as merely "allies" of the BSU (JusticeUCSDb). The result was confusion and disorientation among the protesters who had turned out to fight against tuition fees and privatization. This economic struggle never regained momentum.

The economic demands of students were subordinated to a "symbolic crusade" which mainly benefited the faculty (cf. Gusfield, 1976). This symbolic crusade institutionalized the politics of Third College in the new form of identity politics, yielding increased administrative support to the humanities and social sciences since these were viewed as safety valves for what was now regarded as a high state of racial tension on campus. Instead of a student movement against higher tuition fees, which in 2011 surpassed the portion of undergraduate education paid for by the state, and which provided collateral for the university system's borrowing, the moral panic in reaction to the Compton Cookout generated a faculty movement against racist students, the "frat boys" and the *Koala* as now the "folk devils" (cf. Cohen 1973). This created a coalition between the faculty and the administration, which also helped to solve some of the status problems of the humanities and social sciences within the technocratic neoliberal university. These would henceforth be valued for socializing the students through moral education (cf. Furedi, 2017). The students themselves were now the problem, requiring not just intellectual but moral and political tutelage by the faculty and administration.

The BSU had encouraged its representatives negotiating with the university officials, by chanting "Inside! Outside! All on the same side!" (Alvarez et al., 2010: 134). Who was demonstrating against whom became unclear. The university's response to the Compton Cookout was to bring the activists inside (cf. Elliott, 2019). This could be understood as the institutionalization of the campus's post-Third Worlder postmodern left. The UCSD Cross-Cultural Center established in 1996 presents itself as providing "programs and services for students to develop and strengthen activism efforts while learning to become local and global citizens" (Cross Cultural Center, n.d; Cross Cultural Center, 2021). The Black Resource Center and Raza Resource Centro, created in the wake of the Compton Cookout, form the Campus Community Centers, together with the Cross-Cultural Center, the Women's Center, and the LGBT Resource Center, and since 2016 the Inter-Tribal Resource Center and the Asian Pacific Islander Middle Eastern Desi American (APIMEDA) Programs and Services (Coalition for Critical Asian American Students at UCSD, 2014; Office for Equity, Diversity and Inclusion, n.d.). During a public talk in 2011, the director of the Women's Center described how the Community Centers form a liminal, intersectional "third space" (Licona, 2005; Bhabha, 2009) in which

> We occupy this very organic tension-filled space. And so, for example when something happens on campus that causes turmoil, our spaces become these really interesting places where we are both representing the institution, we are, as campus staff we are administrators on this campus, but we are also advocating for students. Stuff is happening outside of the Centers and students are organizing to combat that inside of our Centers, so we become this very kind of fluid new space where it is almost undefinable if we are part of the home space or part of the public space… It's very messy and sometimes it scares people what is going on over there and it's really because we are in that tension-space.
>
> (UCTV, 2011: [video] 25:40 to 28:00 minutes)

The director of the Cross-Cultural Center added,

> and I think that that being ok and being comfortable being in that tension space, where it's not so explicit to define, and you don't really necessarily know the

> systems of power that are happening because it's so networked and it's so fluid and so dynamic, makes the work that we do very very fantastic and fabulous.
>
> (UCTV, 2011: [video] 25:40 to 28:00 minutes)

In other words, the university reflexively creates its own official, sponsored activism and in so doing blurs the lines of political cleavage. It also produces its own therapeutic anti-politics (cf. Elliott, 2019; Furedi, 2004; Furedi 2006: 152–5; Furedi, 2009; Furedi, 2017; Fisher ed., 2013; Meštrović, 1997).

The Compton Cookout moral panic at UCSD, which sidelined and disorientated the struggle against tuition fees and privatization, prefigured the racial protests that erupted at US campuses including the University of Missouri, Yale University, Ithaca College and Amherst College between 2015 to 2016. David Walsh commented on these in the *World Socialist Web Site*:

> The student protests initiated over the past two weeks have a decidedly upper middle class character, aimed not at fighting for social equality but at carving out greater privileges for relatively privileged African American and other minority professionals. This is reflected in many of the demands which have been raised: more African American faculty, more funding for 'ethnic studies,' the hiring of a diversity officer (at Ithaca College, for example), a new director of the Office of Multicultural Affairs (University of Kansas) and so on. This will benefit a small number of people and change nothing about the desperate social conditions facing large sections of the working class, including a large majority of African American workers and youth.
>
> (Walsh, 2015; see also London, 2015)

At UCSD, the identity politics student organizations and faculty proved their value as professional "coolers out" (cf. Goffman, 1952). On the basis of their ability to disrupt and disorient redistributive struggles, the post-Third-Worldist racial-identitarian pseudo-left has been institutionalized as an officially sponsored pseudo-opposition by the neoliberal university managers. Universities willingly accede to the racialist pseudo-left demands for hiring more proponents of this ideology, skewing the humanities and social sciences toward a racial framework, and creating racialist political cadres adept at confounding leftist discourse and diverting anti-capitalist struggle into the self-serving opportunistic promotion of affirmative action (cf. Ratner, 2022: 233–7).

The Anti-Blackness of Science

A decade after the Compton Cookout and the March 4 Day of Action, Donald Trump was President and the country, like much of the world, was locked down. By the early summer, US COVID-19 deaths were in the tens of thousands and Black Lives Matter protests were occurring across the country. The student protests for public education in 2010 and the Occupy Movement of 2011 to 2012 had, to some extent, found expression in the Bernie Sanders campaign for Democratic nomination for the 2016 and 2020 Presidential election. The Sanders campaign faced opposition from the perspective of Black identity politics, and such identity politics therefore proved useful for the Clinton campaign and the Democratic Party apparatus (Finkelstein, 2023: 73, 84–5, 312–16; see also Beck, 2018; Kagarlitsky, 2021: 126–38; Léger, 2022). The COVID-19 virus was causing tremendous hardship to the entire American working-class, with jobs gone for good, or facing death working as "essential workers" in automobile plants, warehouses and hospitals. The collapse of the social-democratic moment represented by Sanders meant that this suffering and discontent had no progressive political expression. The huge multi-racial protests against police violence in America expressed the revulsion of a large section of American society, especially youth, against racism and to a significant degree against the repressive forces of the capitalist state. This movement had the potential to develop into a more broadly framed challenge to capitalism as a system. But it had no effective political leadership.

"Black Lives Matter" was a slogan that effectively expressed one aspect of the boiling discontent under the surface of capitalism, but it did not provide a way to put together the sources of this discontent in a way that expanded struggle. Instead, it fragmented and narrowed the political currents into a politics of racial representation that benefited a small layer of the Black population. Black Lives Matter insisted that brutal and unwarranted killings by police were chiefly a question of race. Its mono-focus on race blotted out the political economy of class and the capitalist state and separated the question of police killings from the social structural causes of crime (Mateus, 2018; Johnson, 2023; Stokes, 2023: 4–7; Fryer, 2019; Usmani and Zachariah, 2021; Lewis and Usmani, 2022). While there is a lack of research on class, it seems clear that most victims of death at the hands of police share a *class* position, within the working class.

In late May of 2020, the university publicly apologized for an incident in which unknown persons hacked into a zoom call during which Black students were discussing race relations and shouted racial epithets at the students. The Education Trust non-profit in July 2020 ranked UCSD the seventh least accessible selective public university in terms of its enrollment of Black students, and it was joined in the top ten for exclusion by seven other UCs (Education Trust 2020: 18). A 2010 article in *Voice of San Diego* said that UCSD has had difficulty recruiting Black students because, "black acceptees often have other, better options, including private schools that can offer scholarships based on race. And UCSD has been handicapped by the fact that the city of San Diego has a smaller black population than Los Angeles or Berkeley" (Salas, 2010). There were no current African American faculty or graduate students in the Science Studies Program, a small graduate-level academic unit opened in 1989 with participating faculty from Sociology, History, and Philosophy, later adding Communication and in 2019 adding an affiliation with Anthropology.

In this context, my question "What anti-Blackness?" provoked a reaction of shock and dismay among the Science Studies Program graduate students. My question seemed incomprehensible. They thought maybe it was a joke, but it couldn't be because it wasn't funny. It must be disingenuous, and it was alienating, cruel, and harmful, they said in a rash of emails. It seemed obvious to them that anti-Blackness was deeply embedded and institutionalized within the university. Graduate students began to make the demand that the Program put forward its own statement of solidarity with Black Lives Matter.

The Communication professor who had distributed the protest flyer forwarded the graduate students' opening salvo to the faculty list, with their own cover note condemning my ignorance of racial capitalism. A chain of email back-channel chatter about me went on among the program's core faculty. There then appeared, just under two weeks after the campus vigil and the beginning of the email controversy, a petition signed by a large number of current graduate students and some recent program alumni. It treated my email as evidence of pervasive anti-Blackness, which it demanded the Program to redress.

In line with these demands, a group of graduate students and faculty drew up a statement of support for Black Lives Matter. Four years after the event, the statement remains prominent on the Science Studies Program website, functioning as a manifesto for the political-intellectual agenda that now guides the Program. It began:

> The UC San Diego Science Studies Program (SSP) stands in solidarity with those demanding justice for the recent brutal murders of Ahmaud Arbery, Breonna Taylor, Steven Taylor, George Floyd, and so many other Black Americans murdered by police and white supremacist violence—violence that is part of centuries of racist oppression. We recognize that white supremacy exceeds these horrific acts and pervades cultural life in more banal but no less brutal forms, and we condemn the ongoing systemic, structural, physical, and epistemological forms of anti-Blackness in our institutions. We also note that statements are not enough, and that movements against white supremacy and anti-Blackness, such as the Movement for Black Lives, are calling for immediate action and for commitments to redress these forms of violence wherever they are found.
>
> (Science Studies Program, 2020)

The statement devotes just half of a sentence to the victims with whom it expresses "solidarity" and to the question of police violence. This violence is not treated as an expression of any particular crisis in the present, but instead as a constant "white supremacy" passed on from time immemorial: "part of centuries of racist oppression." This effectively puts the concrete matter of the police violence in parentheses, since "white supremacy exceeds these horrific acts and pervades cultural life in more banal but no less brutal forms." The focus here passes from the material, kinetic force of the police to the immaterial, from matter to spirit, with the introduction of the term "cultural." Culture is "no less brutal." Hence, alongside the "systemic, structural, physical," there are the "epistemological forms of anti-Blackness." And the target of condemnation is no longer merely the police but, more encompassingly, "our institutions."

The next paragraph states:

> As science studies scholars, we are well aware that science, technology and medicine flourished through, and depend on, the disenfranchisement of Black, Indigenous and colonized communities globally.
>
> (Science Studies Program, 2020)

Note that the tense shifts from the past ("flourished through") to the present ("depend on"). Do science technology and medicine depend on the disenfranchisement of Black, Indigenous, and colonized communities globally? What is meant by colonization and disenfranchisement here? Is this referring to the literal political rule of colonies and denial of the vote or a more amorphous form of subordination? The language is vague and allusive because it expresses a *mood*: a pessimistic, petit-bourgeois, romantic rage against modernity *in toto* (cf. Caudwell, 1938).

Furthermore, this statement adopts a tone of denunciation, a moral indictment of science, technology and medicine. In effect, it represents the Science Studies Program denouncing itself, because the faculty writing the statement have no one to blame but themselves for the Program's anti-Blackness, if it exists, because they collectively run it, including staffing admissions and faculty-recruitment committees. So, it is self-denunciation, or a confession.[1] According to the Science Studies statement, "Despite familiarity with these histories and critiques, the field of science studies/STS has failed to address its own role in upholding and enshrining racism" (Science Studies Program, 2020).

The postcolonial critique of science that is gestured at indicts science for suppressing non-western and Indigenous cultural forms of knowledge, which are to be recognized as equally valid. This claim has been put forward most prominently by the philosopher Sandra Harding, as an extension of her earlier feminist standpoint theories of science as male suppression of women's experience and knowledge (Harding, 1998). So, the statement, which began with Black Americans killed by police, rapidly turned to postcolonial anthropological epistemological relativism, asserting the knowledge-value of non-western cultures (cf. Widdowsen, 2019: 49–79; Stokes, 2023). In so doing, the Science Studies Program seems to suggest that Black Americans belong to a non-western culture and that they represent a way of thinking that lies outside, and which in some way runs counter to, modern science. This depiction of Black Americans as existing outside the norms of scientific rationality unwittingly recapitulates a patronizing, romantic primitivized image of Blacks (cf. Steeves, 1973; Glenn and Cunningham, 2009; Hughey, 2012; McWhorter, 2021).

But apart from the orientalism evident in the Program's "anti-racist" statement, what is the role of Science Studies and STS in "upholding," indeed "enshrining" racism? No examples or any kind of support are offered for the claim that Science

Studies is racist. But it seems that the assertion of this obscure racism is itself an abreaction that has the power to release its grip. Hence it is claimed that science studies not only upholds and enshrines racism but that "anti-Blackness and white supremacy… animate the field." Anti-Blackness, it is thereby asserted, is what inspires the history, philosophy, and sociology of science and gives these fields of study vigor. Racism is the spirit or motivating energy of this field of inquiry. Racism is this academic field's raison d'étre. So says the UCSD Science Studies Program, about itself.

The Science Studies statement of solidarity with the Black Lives Matter protests frames police violence against Black people as a problem of anti-Blackness and anti-Blackness is presented as a cultural phenomenon, arising from an epistemology, and science is presented as at the center of this epistemic anti-Blackness. The university as an institution is presented as carrying anti-Blackness, because it is an institution of science. Blackness is thereby presented as standing in opposition to the essentially western and white project of science. The racism or anti-Blackness of some students or non-students (the identity of the zoom hackers has not been established) is presented as the anti-Blackness of the university as a whole, as an institution, continuous with the anti-Blackness of science itself. The Compton Cookout or the zoom hacking are not attacks *on* the liberal culture of the university; rather, in the view of the Science Studies Program, they are *of* the university; they are an expression of what the university really is.

The myopically racialist logic of the Science Studies' statement meant attributing police violence to anti-Blackness and ignoring class and the function of the state in a society of immense class inequality (cf. Johnson, 2023: 46–7; Michaels and Reed, Jr., 2022; Usmani, 2021). This racialist logic combined with romantic anti-scientism and anti-rationalism in leading the Science Studies statement away from the question of police violence and toward a wholesale denunciation of science and the university as western institutions irredeemably mired in anti-Blackness and colonialism.

The SSP statement concluded:

> Over the coming years, we pledge as a program to center anti-racist scholarship and pedagogy in the governance and daily life of UCSD's Science Studies Program and to develop a robust critique of our own field's complicity in perpetuating anti-Blackness and white supremacy through our own institutional systems, programmatic structures, and disciplinary practices.
>
> (Science Studies Program, 2020)

This translated into the establishment of a political committee, of activist faculty and graduate students, with unspecified powers to oversee all aspects of the program, including curricula, with the prerogative to condemn one's teaching and any other aspect of "daily life" in the program as racist.

To mollify my objections, I was offered the insertion of the word "any" in the following sentence from the Program's published statement:

> We take a first step in redressing this failure by making an ongoing effort to recognize and rectify *any* forms of anti-Blackness and white supremacy that exist in the field of Science and Technology Studies broadly, and UCSD's Science Studies Program in particular (emphasis added).

The word "any" was offered as a softening of the claim that anti-Blackness and white supremacy did "exist" in Science Studies. "*Any*," I was enjoined to believe, meant merely that *if* such forms were found, "we" would redress and rectify them. Perhaps they would not be found and all would be well. But perhaps the modifier "any" rendered the targeted anti-Blackness more all-encompassing and pervasive. The resonances with Arthur Miller's *The Crucible* ([1953] 2022) were becoming rather too close.

In mid-January 2021, I sent the Program director a resignation letter in which I stated,

> I do not wish to have my name associated with this statement on the website and I do not wish to have my name associated with a program that would put out such a statement and which demands political-ideological conformity to highly spurious ideas.

In late November of that year, the review committee released its report. The report began by the committee stating its charge "to address issues of diversity, representation and anti-Blackness in the program's composition, curricula, colloquia, graduate and faculty relations, and any other relevant areas" (Science Studies Review Committee, 2021).

The substantive part of the report opened with the following paragraph:

> The Fall seminar has for decades generally been dedicated to understanding the historical origins and trajectory of Science Studies, typically including canonical texts by Fleck, Merton, Popper, Kuhn, Bloor, Shapin and Schaffer, and Latour, among others. Our Committee found the goal of the Fall seminar has traditionally led to syllabi that consist almost exclusively of works written by white, male scholars. To some extent, this reflects a lack of diversity in the Science Studies canon, especially among texts written before 1980.
>
> (Science Studies Review Committee, 2021)

The Program's list of racially problematic authors includes Ludwik Fleck, a Polish-Jewish microbiologist, who was the author of the astonishingly original *Genesis and Development of a Scientific Fact*, published in 1935, which coined the term "thought collective," and anticipated the whole field and approach of the sociology of scientific knowledge (Fleck, 1979 [1935]). On June 30, 1941, Lvov, where Fleck was born and where he lived, carrying on his medical research, was captured by the Germans and Fleck was transferred to the Lvov ghetto, where he continued his medical work, developing a typhus vaccine to fight the disease that was rampant in the horrific conditions of the ghetto (Allen 2014; Sady 2021). He was later transferred to Auschwitz, where he worked as a slave in the concentration camp's laboratory and then at Buchenwald in the SS Hygiene Institute's Department of Virus and Typhus Research. Forced to work on producing a typhus vaccine for the Waffen-SS, Fleck sabotaged the work, sending fake, diluted, vaccine to the SS.

Robert King Merton, who founded the sub-discipline of the sociology of science, was born Meyer Robert Schkolnick (Calhoun, 2003). As an adolescent, Schkolnick adopted the name Merton, which he had used as his stage name in his hobby as a magician, as his personal and professional name when he entered Temple University as an undergraduate. Merton later said that he had "rather liked the sound of it, no doubt because it had seemed 'more American' back then in the 1920s" and he eventually legally changed his name (Merton 1994: 9). As a sociologist of science, Merton formulated the "normative structure of science" as consisting of universalism, disinterestedness, organized skepticism, and communism. In his discussion of universalism, Merton contrasted this ethos with the particularism of Nazi ideology with its condemnation of "Jewish physics" and its demand for an "Aryan physics." Historian David Hollinger has shown how Merton's sociology of science expressed a notion of science as supported by, and supporting, democracy, and as incompatible with totalitarianism. Merton's sociology was an important expression of a broader intellectual advocacy in mid-century America of a cosmopolitan, secular intellectual culture against the model of a Christian culture, which had been characteristic of the American liberal arts college in the 19th century. The German model of the research university, transplanted to America in the late 19th century by liberal academic reformers, was immensely strengthened by the role of science in World War II. It was in this post-war period that American universities' taboo against hiring Jews, which had broken down in the natural sciences in the interwar years, began to be lifted in the humanities. Hollinger writes that "Not a single Jew held a tenured appointment in any department within Yale College until 1946. In Columbia's English department, the appointment of Lionel Trilling as assistant professor in 1939 was a breakthrough" (Hollinger 1996: 159; see also Karabel 2005). The exclusions of Jews especially from Departments of English reflected the notion of the study of literature as the carrying of a specifically national, and linked to this, Christian culture.

Hollinger notes how C. P. Snow's *The Two Cultures* in 1959 expressed the notion, similar to Merton's, of science as affined to democracy. Snow attacked literary modernism for, as Hollinger puts it, "perpetuating and celebrating a mythology of blood and history that had politically reactionary consequences. The modernists were basically crypto-fascists, Snow implied, while the scientific professions carried 'in their bones' a humane and democratic orientation toward the future" (Hollinger 1996: 165). Hollinger observes that the outlook of the literary academics who denounced Snow "was more frankly elitist than the program for scientific culture, and it was often merely ambivalent rather than hostile toward the claims of blood and history opposed by the celebrants of science" (Hollinger,

1996: 165). Against science, portrayed by liberal defenders like Merton as an inherently collective activity, literary modernism celebrated "the creative genius of the individual, alienated artist" (Hollinger 1996: 166). Snow's attack hit a nerve and, despite their denunciation of Snow, literary modernists were entertaining their own misgivings. Lionel Trilling, for example, questioned the " 'sympathy for the abyss' and 'hostility to society' that Trilling acknowledged to be disquieting features of the modernist program" (Hollinger 1996: 166). However, according to Hollinger:

> Some of this literary cohort withdrew, one might say, and regrouped, and came out some years later under the cover of Michel Foucault and postmodernism to attack science as itself crypto-fascist and to claim for literature the badge of democracy and equality and human decency.
>
> (Hollinger 1996: 166)

It was Clark Kerr's California Master Plan for Higher Education in 1960 and the subsequent expansion of public higher education in the research university, with guaranteed entry for the top one-eighth of high school graduates initially with free tuition, that solidified the model of the secular university in which religion and class would not be a barrier to entry. In the process of establishing UC San Diego, in the same year as the Master Plan was adopted, university leaders had to persuade residents and realtors in surrounding La Jolla to abandon their long-standing practices of housing discrimination against Jews (Stratthaus, 1996). The decline of the Master Plan was linked with the rise of neoliberalism and the demise of the Keynesian model of public education (Marginson 2016; Newfield, 2011). The racialist ideology adopted by the Science Studies Program is symptomatic of the fracturing of the public sphere that has accompanied the neoliberal attack on the notion of the university as a public good.

Conclusion

"Black Winter" has a sacred place in UCSD's institutional memory, but the protests and struggles against tuition hikes and *de facto* privatization have been forgotten. Material struggles for universal economic rights have been subordinated to an abstract anti-racism in which inequality is blamed on an ethereal, all-pervading, anti-Blackness which can never be pinned down and so never expurgated. Third Worldism has morphed into identity politics, and claimed ownership and control of the terminology once used by the left. UCSD exemplifies what Simon Winlow and Steve Hall in their book *The Death of the Left* point to as the role of identity politics in forging a pseudo-left that functions to support the political and economic structures of neoliberalism:

> Notionally left-wing cultural activists can now draw upon the support of the corporate sector and find their way into influential positions within its structure. In return, neoliberals have received a willing new partner that can be trusted to

> foster division, steer popular discussion away from economic matters, seek the cancellation of opponents and generally do all that can be done to prevent the return of serious class politics.
>
> (Winlow and Hall, 2023: 266)

The role of identity-politics oriented pseudo-left faculty and student organizations at UCSD is a vivid example of this process in the context of American public university.

In 2017 a group of leftwing students and faculty sought to revive the slogans from the 1960s Third College. They said:

> We are the Lumumba Zapata Collective, an intersectional (multiracial, multigendered, multiabled) coalition of faculty, staff, graduate and undergraduate students at the University of California San Diego who have coalesced around the struggle for a truly public university that centers social justice, both in pedagogy and practice. We trace our genealogy to the 1968 UCSD Third (Lumumba Zapata) College struggle, during which students fought for an alternative education model that focused on the liberation of domestic and global communities of color, one that centered a critical analysis of racialized global capitalism and its discontents.
>
> (Lumumba-Zapata Collective, 2017)

Despite their impeccably intersectional rhetoric, the new Lumumba-Zapata Collective was denounced by the Chair of the BSU, Refilwe Gqajela, because: "The 'Lumumba-Zapata'… name has been co-opted from the long history of not just Black student but Latinx/Chicanx student struggles and labor" (Gqajela, 2017). Patrice Lumumba and Emiliano Zapata had become symbolic resources, to be hoarded and banked by those granted by the university administration with ownership of racial identity categories.

The term "anti-Blackness" has gained widespread currency only in the last 20 years. It was a keyword in the lexicon of Black Lives Matter in 2020. "Anti-Blackness" is not merely a synonym for anti-Black racism but rather carries a conception of a substantive Blackness that is permanent and unassimilable to any universalistic rational project. It is a heavily theory-laden concept, embedded in the philosophical framework of Afropessimism. According to Diren Valayden and Megan McCabe, "By the 2000s, the use of anti-Blackness increases exponentially with the appearance of self-styled 'Afropessimist' literature in the academy." The term conveys deep pessimism about the possibility of overcoming racism and the possibility of mixing on an equal level between Blacks and whites. Valayden and McCabe write,

> Anti-blackness, then, significantly shifts the terms of racial discourse. In contrast to critical theories of race and racism that have emphasized contingency

> and historicity, anti-blackness asserts a permanence that is theoretically explicated in Afropessimist literature. Afropessimism locates the origins of anti-blackness in slavery and then asserts its "relentlessness" or durability over time.
> (Valayden and McCabe, 2021)

The key exponent of this doctrine, UC Irvine philosophy professor, Frank B. Wilderson III writes in his book, taking the concept for its title, that when a Black female undergraduate told him about the emotional toll his philosophy was taking on her, he said that "the thing that prevented most students from getting their heads around Afropessimism was the fact that it described a structural problem but offered no structural solution to that problem" (Wilderson, 2020: 331). Not only does it offer no structural solution, but the philosophy denies the Enlightenment humanistic values on the basis of which opposition to racial oppression had been, until recently, based. He says that for non-blacks "anti-Blackness reproduces them as Human beings… [so that] the Human is unethical, whether she is a communist and a feminist, whether he is a fascist and a misogynist" (Wilderson, 2020: 333). Wilderson writes, "There is no interracial redemption. There is no Afrocentric redemption. Redemption is the narrative inheritance of Humans. There is no denouement to social death" (Wilderson, 2020: 325).

Afropessimism, presenting racism as fixed and immovable from its origin in slavery, goes along with the generalized political pessimism of "capitalist realism," or the inability to imagine and believe in the possibility of a world beyond capitalism (Fisher, 2009). The shift of the academic liberal-left to Afropessimism accompanies and masks acceptance of the tuition-based model of privatized public education, in which costs will continually rise and education will be more and more of a luxury commodity for each successive generation. It dismisses the very notion of a universal struggle for common goals. It is hostile to socialism. Wilderson takes the obligatory swipe at Sanders: "A Black radical agenda is terrifying to most people on the Left—think Bernie Sanders—because it emanates from a condition of suffering for which there is no imaginable strategy for redress—No narrative of social, political, or national redemption" (Wilderson, 2020: 15).

As with UCSD's "Real Pain, Real Action," Black "suffering" is used as a slogan to subordinate and delegitimize universalistic struggles and to legitimize instead the narrow institutional interests of Black upper-middle-class academics and professionals as the institutionalized spokespeople for, and interpreters of, this permanent, and ultimately private and incommunicable, pain (cf. Neiman, 2023, 49–51). Afropessimism is a philosophy that underpins a politics of "targeted assistance" in which increasing austerity and social inequality are made palatable by affirmative action, targeted subsidies, and philanthropy (cf. Kagarlitsky, 2021: 17–18, 35–7). These are measures that tend to render class inequality invisible and to preserve the veneer of equal opportunity and social mobility by which class inequality is legitimized in the American ideology (Karabel, 2005: 536–50, 554–7). This creates a clientelist politics that obligates identity groups to jostle for acknowledgment and favor from the economic elite. It is a politics fundamentally at odds with the universalistic principles of social and economic rights on which the struggles of the left were forged (Finkelstein, 2023; Anderson-Connolly, 2019; Ratner, 2022: 233–7; Lange and Pickett-Depaolis eds, 2022; Winlow and Hall, 2023; Neiman, 2023).

This is the new politics of American liberalism, signaled by *The New York Times*' "1619 Project," which stated that "Anti-black racism runs in the very DNA of this country" (Jones, 2019; cf. North and Mackaman eds, 2021). UCSD academics' claim that racism and anti-Blackness are woven in the "fabric" of the university is an echo of this ideological signal from *The New York Times*. The episode is an example of how American academics receive their political direction from the institutions of the power elite, and how they desperately and frantically ideologically contort themselves in order to align with the broader legitimizing strategies of the professional-managerial class (Schmidt, 2000, 43–4; Ungar-Sargon, 2021; Liu, 2021).

The economic has been replaced by the cultural and symbolic and the struggle of the university against racism has become the struggle of the university against itself, against science and supposedly "western" reason. Today, among the multicultural, intersectional identity-politics "left," it is axiomatic that "colorblindness is racism" and that the very claim of science to universality renders it oppressive of women and Black people. This claim is further bolstered by postcolonial theory in which science is a western construct and non-western cultures are in opposition to the epistemic colonization of the world by western reason (Stokes, 2023). The valorization of (what are presented as) racially defined and demarcated cultures against an ostensibly oppressive universality revives the reactionary valorization of "blood and history" with Blackness as the romanticized, orientalized "other" to "western" reason. This Manichean philosophy of mysterious metaphysical forces—Blackness versus anti-Blackness—is a tragic worldview for a degenerated "liberal class" that fundamentally accepts capitalism (Hedges, 2010). It is a pseudo-progressivism that obstructs progress, the sickly involution of progressivism after the death of reform.

Note

1 In 2019, the Anthropology Department became a participating department in the Science Studies Program (Gere, 2016; Lerner, 2019), bringing into the Program anthropologist Saiba Varma, who has aligned herself and her work with critiques of "anti-Blackness" and with "feminist and decolonial critiques of anthropology" (UC San Diego, School of Arts and Humanities, 2020; Günel, Varma, and Watanabe, 2020). In 2022, Varma was disaffiliated from UCSD's program in Critical Gender Studies in a controversy regarding her alleged lack of transparency about her father's role operating in Kashmir in the 1990s as an officer of the Indian government's Research and Analysis Wing (RAW) intelligence agency. It was suggested that this might have an ethical bearing on her anthropological research with psychiatric patients traumatized by the violence in the province (Settler Scholarship, 2021; Ganai, 2022; Bhardwaj 2001; Akhauri, 2021; Mountain Ink, 2022).

Bibliography

AAUP 2012 University of California, San Diego (May–June). https://www.aaup.org/article/university-california-san-diego

Akhauri, T. 2021 "Who is Saiba Varma? Author's Book on Kashmir Stirs Controversy." *Shethepeople*, September 23, https://www.shethepeople.tv/news/who-is-saiba-varma-father-raw-occupied-clinic-militarism-yoda-press-controversy/

AK Press 2010 "March 4 Strike and Day of Action to Defend Public Education, Revolution by the Book." *AK Press Blog*, March 3, https://revolutionbythebook.akpress.org/2010/03/march-4-strike-and-day-of-action-to-defend-public-education/

Allen, A. 2014 *The Fantastic Laboratory of Dr. Weigel: How Two Brave Scientists Battled Typhus and Sabotaged the Nazis*. New York: W. W. Norton.

Alvarez, Luis et al. (Eds.) 2010 *Another University is Possible*. San Diego, CA: University Readers.

Anderson, N. S. 1993 *An Improbable Venture: A History of the University of California, San Diego*. La Jolla, CA: The UCSD Press.

Anderson-Connolly, R. 2019 *A Leftist Critique of the Principles of Identity, Diversity, and Multiculturalism*. Lanham, MD: Lexington Books.

Archibold, R. C. 2010 "California Campus Sees Uneasy Race Relations," *New York Times*, February 26, https://www.nytimes.com/2010/02/27/education/27sandiego.html

Bady, A. and Konczal, M. 2012 "From Master Plan to No Plan: The Slow Death of Public Higher Education." *Dissent* (Fall), https://www.dissentmagazine.org/article/from-master-plan-to-no-plan-the-slow-death-of-public-higher-education

Beck, J. H. 2018 *What Happened to Bernie Sanders*. New York: Hot Books.

Berger, M. T. 2013 "After the Third World? History, Destiny and the Fate of Third Worldism." In Berger, M. T. (Ed.) *After the Third World?* (pp. 1–31). London: Routledge, 2004.

Bhabha, H. 2009 "In the Cave of Making: Thoughts on Third Space." In Ikas, K. and Wagner G. (Eds.), *Communicating in Third Space*. (pp. ix–xiv). New York: Routledge, 2009.

Bhardwaj, A. 2001 "Book on Kashmir Puts Author's Father, an Ex-RAW Official, in Spotlight." *ThePrint*, September 18, https://theprint.in/india/book-on-kashmir-puts-authors-father-an-ex-raw-official-in-spotlight/735700/

Bonilla, D. 2010 "Behind the Scenes at UCSD: 'Guardian' Shows the Lengths Student Government Went to Gain Control of Media." *Foundation for Individual Rights and Expression*, March 12, https://www.thefire.org/news/behind-scenes-ucsd-guardian-shows-lengths-student-government-went-gain-control-media

Brookfield, S. 2007 "Diversifying Curriculum as the Practice of Repressive Tolerance." *Teaching in Higher Education*, vol. 12 no. 5–6. 557–68.

Calhoun, C. 2003 "Remembering Robert K. Merton," *Items and Issues*, Vol. 4 Nos. 2–3, 12–14.

California Coordinating Committee 009) "National Call for March 4 Strike and Day of Action to Defend Public Education, https://ucsdcoalitionforeducationaljustice.wordpress.com/march-4-organizing/

Caudwell, C. 1938 *Studies in a Dying Culture*. New York: Dodd, Mead & Co.

Chibber, V. 2013 *Postcolonial Theory and the Specter of Capital*. London: Verso.

Cini, L. and Ríos-Jara, H. 2023 "Contemporary Student Movements and Capitalism. A Marxist Debate." In Hall, R., Accioly, I., and Szadkowski, K. (Eds), *The Palgrave International Handbook of Marxism and Education* (pp. 413–28). Cham: Switzerland, 2023.

Coalition for Critical Asian American Students at UCSD (2014) Open Letter (February 26), https://apimeda.ucsd.edu/_files/ccaas-open-letter.pdf
Cohen, S. 1973 *Folk Devils and Moral Panics*. London: Paladin.
Cross-Cultural Center (2021) TWOW: Welcome to the Cross-Cultural Center and UCSD Activism, Cross-Cultural Center Channel, YouTube, September 30, 2021, https://www.youtube.com/watch?v=vGGEXIV7HY8
Davis, M. 2015 Why UCSD Loves Big Brother, May 27, Mike Davis @ UCSD' Mike Davis @ UCSD, YouTube channel xicano san diego, https://www.youtube.com/watch?v=-RwnG3RmPlw
Education 4 the People! (n.d.) https://defendcapubliceducation.wordpress.com/page/2/
Education Trust (2020) *Segregation Forever? The Continued Underrepresentation of Black and Latino Students at the Nation's 101 Most Selective Public Colleges and Universities*. Washington DC: The Education Trust.
Elliott, J. E. 2019 "Insourcing Dissent: Brand English in the Entrepreneurial University." *Telos*, vol, 187 (Summer) 129–55.
Ferguson, R. A. 2017 *We Demand: The University and Student Protests*. Oakland: University of California Press.
Finkelstein, N. 2023 *I'll Burn that Bridge when I get to it*. Sublation Media.
Fisher, M. 2009 *Capitalist Realism: Is there No Alternative?* London: Zero Books.
Fisher, R. (Ed.) 2013 *Managing Democracy, Managing Dissent: Capitalism, Democracy and the Organisation of Consent*. London: Corporate Watch.
Fleck, L. 1979 [1935] *Genesis and Development of a Scientific Fact*. Chicago: University of Chicago Press.
Freedman, Z. 2013 "Yudof Brought Students Financial Help, not Just Tuition Hikes." *Daily Bruin*, September 3, https://dailybruin.com/2013/09/03/zoey-freedman-yudof-brought-students-financial-help-not-just-tuition-hikes
Fryer, R. J. 2019 "An Empirical Study of Racial Differences in Police Use of Force." *Journal of Political Economy*, vol. 127 no. 3. 1210–61.
Furedi, F. 2004 *Therapy Culture: Cultivating Vulnerability in an Uncertain Age*. London: Routledge.
Furedi, F. 2006 *Where Have All the Intellectuals Gone?* Second edition. London: Continuum.
Furedi, F. 2009 *Wasted: Why Education isn't Educating*. London: Continuum.
Furedi, F. 2017 *What's Happened to the University? A Sociological Exploration of its Infantilisation*. London: Routledge.
Ganai, N. 2022 "University of California, San Diego Drops Author Saiba Verma [sic] from Curriculum." *Outlook*, January 6, https://www.outlookindia.com/website/story/university-of-california-san-diego-drops-author-saiba-verma-from-curriculum/408530
George-Graves, N. 2010 "UCSD Teach-in Address. Performance is Not Benign." In Alvarez et al., *Another University is Possible*, 9–15.
Gere, C. 016 Anthropology and Science Studies. Science Studies @ UCSD, October 15, https://knit.ucsd.edu/sciencestudies/2016/10/15/anthropology-and-science-studies/
Giroux, H. A. 2019 *Neoliberalism's War on Higher Education*. Chicago: Haymarket.
Glenn, C. L. and Cunningham, L. J. 2009 "The Power of Black Magic: The Magical Negro and White Salvation in Film." *Journal of Black Studies*, vol. 40 no. 2. 135–52.
Goffman, Erving 1952 "On Cooling the Mark Out: Some Aspects of Adaptation to Failure." *Psychiatry*, vol. 15 no. 4. 451–62.

Gordon, L. 2010 "After 'Compton Cookout' Scandal, UCSD Forges a More Positive Association with the City," *Los Angeles Times*, May 3, https://www.latimes.com/archives/la-xpm-2010-may-03-la-me-compton-20100503-story.html

Gqajela, R. 2017 "Refilwe Gqajela: The 'Lumumba-Zapata' Collective should Change their Name." *The Triton*, February 13, https://triton.news/2017/02/refilwe-gqajela-lumumba-zapata-collective-change-name/

Gouldner, A. 1973 [1968] "The Sociologist as Partisan: Sociology and the Welfare State, in idem, *For Sociology: Renewal and Critique in Sociology Today*. (pp. 27–68). New York: Basic Books.

Günel, G., Varma, S., and Watanabe, C. (2020) "A Manifesto for Patchwork Ethnography. Member Voices." *Fieldsights*, June 9, https://culanth.org/fieldsights/a-manifesto-Publication

Gusfield, J. 1976 *Symbolic Crusade: Status Politics and the American Temperance Movement*. Urbana: University of Illinois Press.

Harding, S. 1998 *Is Science Multicultural? Postcolonialisms, Feminisms, and Epistemologies*. Bloomington: Indiana University Press.

Hedges, C. 2010 *Death of the Liberal Class*. New York: Bold Type Books.

Hollinger, D. 1996 *Science, Jews, and Secular Culture: Studies in Mid-Twentieth-Century American Intellectual History*. Princeton: Princeton University Press.

Hughey, M. W. 2012 "Racializing Redemption, Reproducing Racism: The Odyssey of Magical Negroes and White Saviors." *Sociology Compass*, vol. 6 no. 9. 751–67.

IllegalFruitTrade 2010 UCSD Protest Rally – March 4th 2010 (Part I), YouTube, https://www.youtube.com/watch?v=JuCsAljfBZU

Johnson, C. G. 2023 *After Black Lives Matter: Policing and Anti-capitalist Struggle*. London: Verso.

Johnston, A. 2010 "UCSD Student Paper Runs 'Verified' Apology from Student who Hung Noose." *Student Activism*, March 1, https://studentactivism.net/2010/03/01/ucsd-student-paper-runs-apology/

Jones, D. 2009 "Furlough Plan Takes Effect." *UC Davis News*, September 4, https://www.ucdavis.edu/news/furlough-plan-takes-effect-systemwide

Jones, H. N. 2019 "Our Democracy's Founding Ideas were False when They Were Written. Black Americans have Fought to Make Them True." *New York Times*, August 14, https://www.nytimes.com/interactive/2019/08/14/magazine/black-history-american-democracy.html

JusticeUCSD 2010a K. Wayne Yang @ March 4 Rally, UCSD, March 4, https://www.youtube.com/watch?v=P0pRIFi6FxI

JusticeUCSD 2010b Ivan Evans, March 4 Rally @ UCSD, https://www.youtube.com/watch?v=Hves_6npSHk

JusticeUCSD 2010c BSU victory @ March 4 rally, UCSD, https://www.youtube.com/watch?v=20f3PSQmSGI

Juutilainen, P. A. 1996 *Herbert's Hippopotamus: Marcuse and the Revolution in Paradise*, video documentary, https://www.youtube.com/watch?v=vnZ8WaiXnBY

Karabel, J. 2005 *The Chosen: The Hidden History of Admission and Exclusion at Harvard, Yale, and Princeton*. New York: Houghton Mifflin.

Kagarlitsky, B. 2021 *Between Class and Discourse: Left Intellectuals in Defence of Capitalism*. London: Routledge.

Khosla, P. K. et al, 2020 Statement on George Floyd, Breonna Taylor and Ahmaud Arbery, May 29, https://chancellor.ucsd.edu/chancellor-khosla/letters/statement-on-george-floyd-breonna-taylor-and-ahmaud-arbery

Lange, E. L. and Pickett-Depaolis, J. (Eds.) 2022 *The Conformist Rebellion: Marxist Critiques of the Contemporary Left*. Lanham, MD: Rowman and Littlefield.

Lazarus, N. 2013 " 'Third Worldism' and the Political Imaginary of Postcolonial Studies." In Duggan, G. (Ed.) *The Oxford Handbook of Postcolonial Studies* (pp. 324–39). Oxford: Oxford University Press.

Léger, M. J. 2022 *Bernie Bros Gone Woke*: *Class, Identity, Neoliberalism*. Leiden: Brill.

Lerner, S. 2019 Letter to Professor Cathy Gere and Professor Steven Parish, Subject: Proposal to add Anthropology to the Science Studies Program, January 28, https://senate.ucsd.edu/media/348979/anth-proposal-to-add-anthropology-to-science-studies-program.pdf

Lewis, C. and Adaner Usmani, A. 2022 "The Injustice of Under-policing in America." *American Journal of Law and Equality*, vol. 2, 85–106.

Licona, A. C. 2005. "(B)orderlands' Rhetorics and Representations: The Transformative Potential of Feminist Third-space Scholarship and Zines." *NWSA Journal*, vol. 17 no. 2. 104–29.

Liu, C. 2021 *Virtue Hoarders: The Case Against the Professional-Managerial Class*. Minneapolis: University of Minnesota Press.

London, E. 2015 "Woodrow Wilson and Black Lives Matter: The Political Consequences of the Racial Evaluation of History." *World Socialist Web Site*, December 4, https://www.wsws.org/en/articles/2015/12/04/wils-d04.html

Lumumba-Zapata Collective 2017 Principles and Points of Unity. https://lumumbazapataucsd.com/2017/02/20/principles-and-points-of-unity/

Marez, C. 2020 *University Babylon: Film and Race Politics on Campus*. Berkeley: University of California Press.

Marcuse, H. 1969 [1965] "Repressive Tolerance." In Wolff, R. P. Barrington Moore, Jr., B., and Marcuse, H. (Eds.), *A Critique of Pure Tolerance*. (pp. 95–137). Boston: Beacon Press.

Marginson, S. 2016 *The Dream is Over: The Crisis of Clark Kerr's California Idea of Higher Education*. Berkeley: University of California Press.

Marx, K. 1843 *A Contribution to the Critique of Hegel's Philosophy of Right*, https://www.marxists.org/archive/marx/works/1843/critique-hpr/intro.htm

Mason, P. 2012 *Why it's Kicking Off Everywhere: The New Global Revolutions*. London: Verso.

Mateus, B. 2018 "Behind the Epidemic of Police Killings in America: Class, Poverty and Race." *World Socialist Web Site*, December 20, https://www.wsws.org/en/articles/2018/12/20/kil1-d20.html

McKenzie, L. 2020 "Words Matter for College Presidents, but so will Action." *Insider Higher Ed*, June 7, https://www.insidehighered.com/news/2020/06/08/searching-meaningful-response-college-leaders-killing-george-floyd

McKinley, J. 2010 "California Students Protest Education Cuts." *The New York Times* (March 5), https://www.nytimes.com/2010/03/05/education/05protests.html

McWhorter, J. 2021 *Woke Racism: How a New Religion has Betrayed Black America*. New York: Penguin.

Merton, R. K. 1994 *A Life of Learning*. New York: American Council of Learned Societies.

Meštrović, S. 1997 *Postemotional Society*. London: Sage.

Michael, L. 2013 "Quebec's Student Tuition Protest: Who Really Won the Dispute?" *CBC*, August 18, https://www.cbc.ca/news/canada/quebec-s-student-tuition-protest-who-really-won-the-dispute-1.1327562

Michaels, W. B. and Reed Jr. A. 2022 *No Politics but Class Politics*. Jäger, A. and Zamora, D. (Eds.), London: Eris.
Miller, A. [1953] 2022 *The Crucible*. London: Bloomsbury.
Miyoshi, M. 2000 "Ivory Tower in Escrow." *boundary 2* vol. 27no. 1 (Spring). 7–50.
Moore, J. 1986 "Marxist Professor Herbert Marcuse's Years at UCSD." *San Diego Reader*, September 11, https://www.sandiegoreader.com/news/1986/sep/11/angel-apocalypse/
Mountain Ink 2022 "California University's AP Resigns after Statement on Indian Scholar over 'Kashmir Controversy' Taken Down." *Mountain Ink*, February 8, https://mountain-ink.com/california-universitys-ap-resigns-after-statement-on-indian-scholar-over-kashmir-controversy-taken-down/
Neiman, Susan 2023 *Left is not Woke*. Cambridge: Polity Press.
Newfield, C. 2011 *Unmaking the Public University: The Forty-year Assault on the Middle-class*. Cambridge, MA: Harvard University Press.
North, D. and Mackaman, T. 2021 *The New York Times' 1619 Project and the Racialist Falsification of History: Essays and Interviews*. Detroit, MI: Mehring Press.
Office for Equity, Diversity, and Inclusion (n.d.) "A Community with a Heart," https://diversity.ucsd.edu/edi-centers/community-centers.html. Accessed November 8, 2023.
Office of the President 2009 Office of the President to Members of the Committee on Educational Policy, Action item, for meeting on February 4, https://regents.universityofcalifornia.edu/regmeet/feb09/e3.pdf
Padden, C. 2020 Dean of Social Sciences, to Division of Social Sciences Lists, Social Sciences' Commitment to Action on Racial Injustice and Social Inequality, June 8, https://diversity.ucsd.edu/_files/Campus%20Statements%20-%20Racism/Social%20Sciences%20commitment%20to%20action%20on%20racial%20injustice%20and%20social%20inequality%20-%20June%208%202020.pdf
Pollock, A. J. 2017 "Alan Greenspan's 'Irrational Exuberance,' then and now." *RStreet* (August 16), https://www.rstreet.org/commentary/alan-greenspans-irrational-exuberance-then-and-now/
Preuitt, L. 2010 Video: UC Protesters Clash with Police, *NBC Bay Area*, November 17, https://www.nbcbayarea.com/news/local/uc-regents-meeting-sparks-protests/2089186/
Rahim, A. 2020 "Diversity to Deradicalize." *California Law Review*, vol. 108 no. 5. 1423–86.
Ratner, C. 2022 *Cultural Psychology, Racism, and Social Justice*. Cham, Switzerland: Springer.
Reese, T. 2016 "Drone Valley: The University of California and the Business of High-tech Slaughter." *World Socialist Web Site*, September 12, https://www.wsws.org/en/articles/2016/09/12/ucsd-s12.html
Robbins, G. 2020 "UC San Diego Apologizes for Racist Comments on Zoom Call." *San Diego Union-Tribune*, June 1, https://www.sandiegouniontribune.com/news/education/story/2020-06-01/ucsd-apologizes-racist-comments
Robbins, G. 2020a "Black Students Pressure UC San Diego to Expand their Tiny Presence on Campus." *San Diego Union-Tribune*, August 8, 2020, https://www.sandiegouniontribune.com/news/education/story/2020-08-08/black-students-uc-san-diego
Ruggiero, A. 2009 "UCSD Professors Suggest Closing UCs." *The California Aggie*, August 13, https://theaggie.org/2009/08/13/ucsd-professors-suggest-closing-ucs/
Sady, W. 2021 "Ludwik Fleck." *The Stanford Encyclopedia of Philosophy*, https://plato.stanford.edu/entries/fleck/#LifeWork
Salas, D. 2010 "Why Black Students are so Scarce at UCSD." *Voice of San Diego*, https://voiceofsandiego.org/2010/03/10/why-black-students-are-so-scarce-at-ucsd/

San Diego Union-Tribune 2010 "Student: Noose in UCSD Library a 'Stupid Mistake.'" *San Diego Union-Tribune*, March 2, https://www.sandiegouniontribune.com/sdut-noose-in-library-a-stupid-mistake-ucsd-student-2010mar02-story.html

Schmidt, J. 2000 *Disciplined Minds: A Critical Look at Salaried Professionals and the Soul-battering System that Shapes their Lives*. Lanham, MD: Rowman and Littlefield.

Science Studies Program 2020 UC San Diego Science Studies in Solidarity with the Movement for Black Lives, August 18, https://sciencestudies.ucsd.edu/_files/Science-Studies-in-Solidarity-with-the-Movement-for-Black-Lives-8-18-20-Updated.pdf

Science Studies Review Committee 2021 Science Studies Review Committee Recommendations, November 21. California Public Records Request R003585-042022.

Selfa, L. 2012 *The Democrats: A Critical History*. Chicago: Haymarket.

Settler Scholarship 2021 https://twitter.com/Settler_Scholar/status/1437837980618706952?lang=en

Shapin, S. 2010 *The Scientific Life: A Moral History of a Late Modern Vocation*. Chicago: University of Chicago Press.

Shea, J. T. 2009 "No: Proposal is an Elitist Vision for the System." *San Diego Union-Tribune*, July 24, https://www.sandiegouniontribune.com/sdut-no-proposal-elitist-vision-system-2009jul24-story.html

Showley, R. 2010 "KKK-style Pillowcase Found at UCSD; Noose Case Sent to City Attorney." *San Diego Union-Tribune*, https://www.sandiegouniontribune.com/sdut-kkk-style-pillowcase-found-ucsd-2010mar02-htmlstory.html

Somma, N. 2012 "The Chilean Student Movement of 2011-2012: Challenging the Marketization of Education." *Interface: A Journal For and About Social Movements*, vol. 4 no. 2 (November). 296–309.

Steeves, E. L. 1973 "Négritude and the Noble Savage." *The Journal of Modern African Studies*, vol. 11 no. 1. 91–104.

Stokes, D. 2023 *Against Decolonisation: Campus Culture Wars and the Decline of the West*. Cambridge: Polity Press.

Stratthaus, M. E. 1996 "Flaw in the Jewel: Housing Discrimination against Jews in La Jolla, California." *American Jewish History*, vol. 84 no. 3 (September). 189–219.

Student Activism 2020 "March 4 Map Updated, with Much More to Come." *Student Activism*, March 2, https://studentactivism.net/2010/03/02/march-4-map-updated-with-much-more-to-come/

Sweeney, J. P. 2009 "Proposal to Shutter Some UCs Hits Nerve." *San Diego Union-Tribune*, July 19, https://www.sandiegouniontribune.com/sdut-1n19uccuts221810-ucsd-profs-say-some-campuses-can--2009jul19-htmlstory.html

Su, E. 2010 "New UCSD Racial Incident Sparks Rage, Confrontation." *San Diego Union-Tribune* February 20, https://www.sandiegouniontribune.com/sdut-new-ucsd-racial-incident-sparks-rage-confrontation-2010feb20-htmlstory.html

Thorpe, C. 2008 "Capitalism, Audit, and the Demise of the Humanistic Academy." *Workplace: A Journal for Academic Labor*, vol. 15 (September).

Thorpe, C. 2013 Repression in the neoliberal university. In Fisher (Ed.) (pp. 217–31). 2013.

Thorpe, C. 2022 *Sociology in Post-normal Times*. Lanham, MD: Lexington.

UC San Diego, School of Arts and Humanities 2020 *Let's Talk about Anti-Blackness*, November 18, https://www.youtube.com/watch?v=iMK6uFOnPTg&t=50s

UC San Diego Today 2020 "Virtual Commencement uses Creative Ways to Infuse University Tradition with Interactive Fun." *UC San Diego Today*, June 4, https://today.ucsd.edu/story/virtual-commencement-uses-creative-ways-to-infuse-university-tradition-with-interactive-fun

UCSD 2021 *Proposal for an Eighth Undergraduate College at UC San Diego*, https://evc.ucsd.edu/_files/Eighth-College-Proposal-Final.pdf

UCSD Coalition for Educational Justice (2010) *About our Coalition*, https://ucsdcoalitionforeducationaljustice.wordpress.com/about/

UCSD Cross Cultural Center (n.d.) *P.L.A.C.E.S. Philosophy*, https://ccc.ucsd.edu/about-us/PLACES%20Philosophy.html. Accessed October 29, 2023.

UCTV (2011) IDEaS: Beyond Identity Politics, University of California Television, June 10, https://www.youtube.com/watch?v=6yAi7sHPHEM&t=33s

Ungar-Sargon, B. 2021 *Bad News: How Woke Media is Undermining Democracy*. New York: Encounter Books.

Usmani, A. and Zachariah, D. 2021 "The Class Path to Racial Liberation." *Catalyst*, vol. 5 no. 3. 51–88.

Valayden, D. and McCabe, M. 2021 "Out of History: Against the Self-evidence of Anti-Blackness." *Boiling Point* (March), https://uchri.org/foundry/out-of-history-against-the-self-evidence-of-anti-blackness/

Walsh, D. 2015 "The Class Character of the Student Protests on US Campuses." *World Socialist Web Site*, November 17, https://www.wsws.org/en/articles/2015/11/17/prot-n17.pdf

Walsh, D. 2016 "The Socioeconomic Basis of Identity Politics: Inequality and the Rise of an African American Elite." *World Socialist Web Site*, August 30, https://www.wsws.org/en/articles/2016/08/30/pers-a30.html

Walshok, M. and Shragge, A. L. 2013 *Invention and Reinvention: The Evolution of San Diego's Innovation Economy*. Stanford: Stanford Business Books.

Warth, G. 2015 "UCSD Student Leaders Criticized for Cutting Media Funds." *San Diego Union-Tribune*, December 7, https://www.sandiegouniontribune.com/news/education/sdut-ucsd-students-koala-cuts-2015dec07-story.html

Wayland, M. 2010 "Funds Frozen for 33 UCSD Media Outlets." *NBC 7 San Diego*, February 23, https://www.nbcsandiego.com/news/local/funds-frozen-for-33-ucsd-media-outlets/1865849/

Widdowsen, F. 2019 *Separate but Unequal: How Parallelist Ideology Conceals Indigenous Dependency*. Ottowa, Ontario, Canada: University of Ottowa Press.

Wilderson, F. B. 2020 *Afropessimism*. United States: Liveright.

Winlow, S. and Hall, S. 2023 *The Death of the Left: Why we Must Begin from the Beginning Again*. Bristol: Policy Press.

Žižek, S. 1997a "Multiculturalism, or, the Cultural Logic of Multinational Capitalism." *New Left Review*, vol. 225 (September-October). 28–51.

Žižek, S. 1997b *The Ticklish Subject: The Absent Centre of Political Ontology*. London: Verso.

Chapter 5

Silencing Dissenters

Academic Authoritarianism in Response to Two Hoaxes

Neil McLaughlin and Neil Wegenschimmel

Concerns about societal extremism have mounted in recent years, but a topic of analysis that is seldom addressed is how we think about, theorize, and study authoritarianism among left-wing and liberal academics. As such, the following chapter will explore the institutional and scholarly reaction to two instructive and well publicized controversies that occurred in the modern peer review system: the Sokal affair of the 1990s and, more centrally, the "Grievance Studies" affair (also referred to as "Sokal Squared" (Hopper October 5, 2018)) that took place two decades later. First, we present brief chronologies of the two cases, beginning with the Sokal affair. This sets the stage for the Grievance Studies affair, which illustrates the polarization that has taken hold in the academy during the second decade of the 21st century, as the identity politics of both the left and right have collided.

The original controversy took place in 1996 when a New York University physics Professor named Alan Sokal published a spurious article on postmodern theories of science in the (non-peer reviewed) cultural studies journal *Social Text* before revealing his hoax to the media (Sokal, 1996). *Social Text* was a leader of radical identity politics at the time, and Sokal meant to expose what he viewed as a completely vacuous and untenable philosophy of science being promoted in the social sciences and humanities. Sokal, who is left wing, was also concerned that postmodern critiques of science were undermining scientific literacy and damaging the credibility of the political left (Hilgartner 1997).

More than two decades later, James Lindsay, Peter Boghossian, and Helen Pluckrose orchestrated a scaled-up version of Sokal's hoax. Until the *Wall Street Journal* uncovered their hoax they managed to publish four articles, and gain acceptance for seven more (Lindsay January 11, 2019, 38:56), in respectable but relatively low status academic journals, with over a dozen more languishing in "revise and resubmit" status (Peterson Interview January 2019). In this new, "Sokal Squared" hoax, only Lindsay had a science background (a PhD in mathematics), while Peter Boghossian and Helen Pluckrose were philosophically-oriented pedagogy and literary scholars respectively. This group was less identified with the left than Sokal was. Lindsay was a moderate Democrat who supported Obama, Boghossian a classical liberal from Portland, and Pluckrose a left-leaning scholar based in London, England. As a result, perhaps, the Grievance Studies Affair (as it

DOI: 10.4324/9781003389927-5

came to be known) quickly became a lightning rod for the polarized politics of the United States during the Trump era.

Despite these and other differences, many academic responses to the Sokal affair and its Grievance Studies ("Sokal Squared") cousin displayed a worrisome form of left-liberal academic authoritarianism that is mobilized when the conceits of post-modernism and identity politics are subjected to cogent criticism. Sadly, this contributes mightily to the creation of right-wing reaction, something we see vividly in the case of James Lindsay, who has become a notable figure in the conspiracy-driven Trumpist wing of the Republican Party. Boghossian, a centrist, was more concerned with intellectual dialogue, scientific skepticism, and pedagogy than political polemics, having developed an approach he calls "Street Epistemology," and written a book with Lindsay on participating in difficult political conversations (Boghossian and Lindsay 2019). He remains a moderate, albeit one with more right-wing connections and sympathies than he had formerly, because many liberals and leftists will not engage with him, and have even attempted to ruin his career (Boghossian January 11, 2019, 39:29). Pluckrose maintains her leftist values despite being unfairly attacked as a right-winger because of her involvement in the project.

Setting the Stage: Alan Sokal and the Science Wars

In the early 1990s, academic and public intellectual opinion spaces in North America (Jacobs and Townsley 2011) were polarized by a "science war." In the book *Higher Superstition: The Academic Left and its Quarrels* (1997), scientists Paul Gross and Norman Levitt offered a forceful critique of various postmodern, relativist, and social constructionist perspectives on science that were influential in this period. Gross and Levitt suggested that postmodernists did not understand the scientific method, were promoters of a toxic form of relativism, and were pushing a negativistic approach to radical politics in the form of even worse scholarship. The book inspired New York University physics professor Alan Sokal to take the culture wars of this period to a new level by publishing a hoax article called "Transgressing the boundaries: Toward a transformative hermeneutics of quantum gravity" in the cultural studies journal *Social Text* in 1996 (Sokal 1996).

Sokal's article was written in the postmodern style, stating that cultural studies'critiques of natural science were right: that it was largely socially constructed, citing cultural studies icons like *Social Text* editor Stanley Aronowitz. This felt like a coup to many in the *Social Text* network and readership, because they briefly imagined that a well-known physicist at a major research university (and an open leftist) had vindicated the view of science being promoted by radical cultural and science studies scholars.

Arguing for what he called a "liberatory" science, Sokal claimed that "post-modern science provides a powerful refutation of the authoritarianism and elitism inherent in traditional science, as well as an empirical basis for a democratic approach to scientific work" (Sokal 1996: 11). Espousing the critique of natural science that the *Social Text* network was arguing for (previously articulated in Stanley Aronowitz's book *Science as Power* (1988)), Sokal's article reviewed what he suggested were new developments in physics—particularly in his own specialization where versions of string theory and other cutting-edge approaches had led to a new framework called quantum gravity—stressing issues of uncertainty, complementarity, and discontinuity highlighted in cultural studies accounts of science. In fact, quoting Einstein, Niels Bohr, and Werner Heisenberg, as well as Stanley Aronowitz, Andrew Ross, and Jacques Lacan, Sokal claimed that the great scientists "foreshadowed postmodernist thinking." Going further, he suggested that quantum gravity would have profound implications in developing the content of a future postmodern and liberatory science.

Social Text editors were not unanimous in their admiration for this piece, but published it nonetheless because it reinforced their own position in the science wars with a perspective that appeared to emanate from inside theoretical physics itself. Aronowitz was particularly pleased, and perhaps flattered (as was Sokal's intention) to see his views quoted and linked to the work of great scientists and to cutting-edge theoretical physics.

The problem for *Social Text*, and the larger cultural studies-critical science perspective, was that the article made absolutely no sense to anyone with even a basic background in the science that Sokal was "reviewing." Rather, it was full of inside jokes and absurd statements that the *Social Text* editors could not possibly have understood, disguised in jargon Sokal believed the editors would appreciate (Ruark 2017). The real story behind the hoax was published in *Linga Franca,* the influential magazine on insider academic news and commentary (Hilgartner 1997), after which all hell broke loose between postmodern cultural studies theorists and mainstream social and natural scientists.

In normal circumstances, the exposure of this hoax would have, at a minimum, led to a major review of the editorial policies at *Social Text*, or at least a stepping back from some of the more outlandish claims made by cultural studies and critical science studies scholars. Instead, the literary scholar Stanley Fish accused Sokal of acting in bad faith and suggested that such a clandestine hoax constituted an ethical breach, amounting to a bad joke that establishes a legacy of fraud (Fish 1996: May 21, *The New York Times*). Sociologist Stanley Aronowitz accused Sokal of ignorance about philosophy, critical thinking, Marxism, and the politics of *Social Text*, completely sidestepping how such a nonsense piece could have been published to begin with (Aronowitz 1997). In both cases, the problem was deemed to be Sokal himself, and not the tendentious "scholarship" that he skewered so effectively.

Sokal went on to write more about the perspectives of cultural studies in a book, offering several commentaries on the incident and its significance, after which he largely went back to doing science (Sokal 2000; Sokal 2010; Sokal and Bricmont1997). He now teaches at the University College of London (UCL). His critique of the ignorance of science in the left-liberal academia has recently become inclusive of identity, seen in his option piece called "Sex and Gender: The medical establishment's reluctance to speak honestly about biological reality," written with Richard Dawkins in *The Boston Globe* (April 8, 2024).

Sokal Squared: Fanning the Flames of the Culture War

Sokal's hoax paper eventually inspired the "Grievance Studies" project undertaken by Peter Boghossian, James Lindsay, and Helen Pluckrose. This took place during a period of increase in many of the excesses Sokal had critiqued, and social media had come to play a major role in disseminating information about the hoax to a wider public. This "sequel" illustrates even more vividly the corrosive political effect of left-leaning authoritarianism in the academy today than Sokal's original hoax.

In 2017, Lindsay, Boghossian, and Pluckrose surreptitiously published four nonsense articles, and got three more accepted, in reasonably credible journals such as *Gender, Place and Culture*, *Hypatia*, *Fat Studies*, and *Sex Roles*.[1] At the time, Lindsay was a moderate Democrat with a PhD in math who ran in "new atheism" online circles. Boghossian was a talented philosophy teacher in pedagogy, critical thinking, and scientific skepticism at Portland State University and held classical liberal views. Pluckrose was a socialist-leaning British literary and religious history scholar, writer, and editor (Pluckrose 11 January 2019, 6:39). The project was exposed by the *Wall Street Journal* in 2018 before it concluded, making headlines in elite opinion journals and generating widespread social media coverage. It caused a major controversy within the academy, with a strong ripple effect in mainstream American politics (Hopper 2018).

The most notorious of these articles was "Human Reaction to Rape Culture and Queer Performativity at Urban Dog Parks in Portland, Oregon," published in the feminist geography journal *Gender, Place and Culture*. The article claimed the authors had closely examined 10,000 dog genitals and interrogated their owners as to their sexual orientation, ultimately concluding that dog parks were a major site for the expression of rape culture. Another article, "Who Are We to Judge? Overcoming Anthropometry and a Framework for Fat Bodybuilding" appeared in *Fat Studies*, and three equally absurd articles were accepted for publication in the feminist philosophy journal *Hypatia*, *Journal of Poetry Therapy*, and *Affilia*. However, these articles never made it to print because the hoax was exposed when the dog park article was questioned by skeptics, and journalists could not identify the authors because a fake name and university had been listed in the submission (Lindsay 11 January 2019, 38:59; Hopper October 5, 2018; Schuessler October 8, 2018).

Four other articles that the team generated for this purpose were given "revise and resubmit" decisions at *Porn Studies*, *Hypatia*, *Feminist Theory*, and *Women Studies International Forum*. Nine others were rejected from various social science and feminist journals, and one more was under review at a feminist work and organizations journal. This effort was strongly reminiscent of the Sokal affair, but scaled up several levels in an attempt to demonstrate how far identity politics and postmodernism had spread in the academy in the 25 years since the original hoax—intentions that go well beyond a childish desire to fool editors and trick reviewers at certain journals. Lindsay and Pluckrose then went on to develop a broader critique of the modern university in a book called *Cynical Theories* (2020). Endorsed by Andrew Doyle and Alan Sokal himself, the book gained massive attention and influence, becoming a best-seller on the *Wall Street Journal*, *USA Today*, *Publishers' Weekly* book lists and spending some time as a number one philosophy bestseller on Amazon.

The response to the Grievance Studies affair was quite different from the original hoax because of the changed media landscape after 1996. By now, social media had become the dominant form of communication and information sharing in North American society. The reception of their project was also deeply impacted by the political climate of the Trump era, and, crucially for our analysis, the status differences between the hoaxers impacted the reception of their project. After all, Sokal was a respected academic who held a tenured professorship at New York University in one of the most prestigious fields in the natural sciences. The Grievance Studies hoaxers, by contrast, were relative outsiders to the research university. Boghossian was a non-tenure track Assistant Professor working on a contract, with an EdD from Portland State where he taught.[2] Neither Lindsay or Pluckrose were working academics or positioned to attain tenure stream positions at major universities in math or the humanities respectively. Lindsay, despite his mathematics PhD, worked as a massage therapist upon completing graduate school, and Pluckrose had left the academy after finishing her MA (11 January 2019).

It is likely that these status differences had a profound impact on how these two hoaxes played out in intellectual circles and academic fields. The original Sokal debate unfolded in elite newspapers and magazines, in-house outlets for debates about the academy like *The Chronicle of Higher Education,* and in books published by high status commercial publishers such as Sokal and Jean Briemont's *Fashionable Nonsense: Postmodern Intellectuals' Abuse of Science* (1999). By contrast, Boghossian, Lindsay, and Pluckrose were not primarily talking to and engaging with the intellectual and academic elite, but were attempting to mobilize lay opinion against what they viewed as academic elitism (Bourdieu 1988; Bourdieu 1975) and the corruption of scholarship. Nevertheless, their hoax did get coverage in mainstream elite media outlets, many of which were apt to disparage them because of their marginal status vis à vis the university. As a result of these fierce dismissals, Lindsay underwent a right-wing political transformation. Boghossian remains hard to classify politically, and only Pluckrose continues to speak from the perspective of an intellectual trying to save the left from its own folly—similar to Sokal.

The fact that the Grievance Studies Affair happened during the Trump years, in an environment that did not exist when Sokal published in *Social Text* also impacted its reception. In the 1990s, Sokal controlled the narrative to a significant degree through his detailed account of his intentions and views on the issues—helped, to be sure, by thoughtful pieces by others that helped to frame the issues as not being against the left generally speaking, thus having a calming rather than hysterical effect. The polarization of the Trump years, however, along with the diverse politics of the hoaxers and the fast moving, uncontrollable, and monetizable nature of social media meant that the Grievance Studies affair quickly became a lightning rod for political partisanship in the United States.

The Cancellation of a Liberal Arts teacher

Peter Boghossian's experience provides the most clear and dramatic example of how academics responded to the Grievance Studies hoax with sustained efforts to destroy the careers of the hoax's authors. A EdD who did his dissertation on the use of the Socratic method to help prison inmates desist from criminal behavior, Boghossian was on a non-tenure track teaching contract at Portland State University when he participated in the Sokal Squared project. Boghossian was an innovative teacher, who wrote a book called *A Manual for Creating Atheists* (2013) where he developed the practice of "Street Epistemology," a non-confrontational technique for examining and challenging deeply held beliefs.

Boghossian was a talented, engaging, and committed teacher whose public philosophy, all things considered, could easily have found a valued place at Portland State or many other colleges in the past—politics aside. Times have changed, however, and Boghossian's teaching style ran against the grain of where things have gone, despite his innovative work teaching prisoners. And as noted previously, Boghossian was not tenured, nor had he achieved a particularly high status as a researcher. He was also an open critic of the various kinds of diversity training and hiring programs that were being introduced at Portland State and nationally during the 2010s. Finally, research universities value teaching and engaging with people in prisons and streets much less than publications on narrowly defined topics, technical articles, and books in peer reviewed outlets.

Furthermore, Boghossian invited controversial speakers to his classes, including Flat-Earthers, Christian fundamentalists, climate skeptics, and Occupy Wall Street activists, urging students to engage with their ideas with respect and care. Boghossian's dissatisfaction with Portland State, and the general intellectual climate of modern universities, stem from his allowing a wide range of views to be expressed in his class, something it was possible to do before new regulations around content and a new university culture that stressed the need for safe spaces took hold. This new culture is justified and enforced by theories of microaggressions, diversity offices, and growing numbers of administrators who constantly revaluate policy and implement yearly "action plans" to combat racism, transphobia, colonialism, misogyny, and so on. Like many professors of his generation, Boghossian was increasingly concerned that canonical texts were getting attacked as mere expressions of bigotry under these rubrics.

All hell broke loose in the wake of the publicity generated by the Sokal Squared project, and a set of conflicts and controversies emerged that ultimately led to Boghossian's resignation in 2022. After the minimal publicity from publishing

"The Conceptual Penis as a Social Construct" with James Lindsay in *Cogent Social Sciences* (2017) (Shermer 2017), the new batch of articles written by the trio landed like a bomb.

The beginnings of Boghossian's institutional problems at Portland State date from a Title IX investigation opened by a white male student.[3] The process led to unfounded rumors that Boghossian beat his wife and children, and although the initial allegations were deemed spurious, he received a recommendation for coaching (Boghossian, 8 September 2021). As a result of these trials and tribulations, Boghossian became more connected to like-minded scholars, especially on social media, concerned with academic freedom and viewpoint diversity on the nation's campuses. While on the Portland State campus itself, he was subjected to harassment with his office door marred by swastika graffiti and bags of feces left in front of it.

Boghossian was later brought up on research misconduct charges because it was claimed that the journal editors were unwilling human subjects and the Sokal Squared hoax articles had not been cleared by the university's research on human subjects' process (Boghassion 2021). He was also accused of data fabrication (Boghossian 11 January 2019, 39:25), to which he replied that he had no intention to take credit for false data, but was simply attempting to document a problem with peer reviewed journals in certain fields. He was also finally officially charged with plagiarism—specifically of Adolph Hitler's *Mein Kampf*, to which he pleaded guilty and for which he was declared innocent. Along with the others, he became nationally known as his critics on and off campus mobilized to silence him and drive him out of the university, while his supporters, including many famous intellectuals, rallied to his defense. Major scholars such as biologist Richard Dawkins, skeptic Michael Shermer, Harvard psychologist Steven Pinker, New York University social psychologist Jonathan Haidt, the newly famous Canadian psychologist and internet sensation, Jordan Peterson, and Alan Sokal himself and other highly prominent scholars and public intellectuals all came to the defense of Boghossian, arguing that the ethics review against him was politically motivated.[4]

In the end, Boghossian did not lose his job. Instead, he was instructed instead to undertake training on the issues before he engaged in another research project. The whole process was widely covered in the media; a first shot across the bow following several years of attempts to either marginalize or fire Boghossian based on partisan views—a form of institutional and academic harassment, one that carries many of the characteristics of what we could call liberal or left-wing authoritarianism (Fromm 1984; Bruner 1994; Kaufmann 28 February 2021; Costello et al. 2022). Boghossian experienced the constant investigations themselves as punishment, and they spelled the beginning of the end of his career at Portland State.

During this period of higher education in United States and Canada, a new wave of cancelations and harassment of campus speakers had becoming unfortunately common (Lukiannoff and Haidt 2018). As an innovative teacher, Boghossian had demonstrated a commitment to political diversity in education and an interest in social media controversies, and so it makes sense that he responded to his new-found micro-celebrity status by bringing controversial speakers to campus. As a result of this approach, anonymous articles criticizing him appeared in the student newspaper and the talks he organized on campus (such as with author Christina Hoff Sommers, the renegade "factual feminist," and Bret Weinstein and Heather Heying, at the time newly cancelled liberal professors form nearby Evergreen College[5]) were disrupted by tenured professors, while someone else triggered a fire alarm and the speaker cables were pulled in an effort to shut down the planned talks. Things went further downhill when flyers were circulated on campus that featured a Pinocchio nose imposed on Boghossian's picture and he was spat on, threatened, and harassed, all while being subjected to more investigations while the university ignored the campaign of harassment directed at Boghossian himself (September 8, 2021; Boghossian 11 January 2019). Boghossian finally quit, though one could also argue he was forced out, resigning in the spring of 2022 (Boghossian 2022).

The major claim against Boghossian from his on-campus critics and an increasing number of social media users calling for his head following the hoax was that he was right-wing or even far-right (Boghossian 11 January 2019), a serious charge in Trump's America, as fear of rising fascism grew. It is true that Boghossian associated with some very conservative social media innovators such as the Canadian professor Gad Saad and the British men's rights and Brexit activist Carl Benjamin. In an earlier book about atheism, Boghossian had also collaborated with Canadian Stefan Molyneux, who, it later become clear, was a white nationalist. At that time, however, Molyneux styled himself as a public philosopher on YouTube with right-leaning libertarian views. It was clear that Boghossian wished to use social media to do public philosophy himself, so the brief association with Molyneux in the nascent years of the culture wars makes sense.[6]

Clearly, Boghossian was increasingly pushed towards others who were also being harassed by the authoritarian left both in the academy and in the digital public sphere (4 January 2023). When Boghossian brought the conservative Carl Benjamin, the liberal Christina Hoff Sommers, and at the time left-liberals Bret Weinstein and Heather Heying to Portland State, they all shared a common experience of being attacked by social justice activists and had a mutual interest in using social media for political and intellectual discussions. To suggest that Boghossian was conservative because he did not dialogue with leftists ignores the reality that many liberals and leftists would have nothing to do with him following the Grievance Studies affair (Boghossian 11 January 2019, 45:42; Boghossian 27 February 2023, 28:34). Boghossian also got to know conservative political scientist Bruce Gilley (also from Portland State) after he was viciously attacked online for publishing a controversial case for colonialism in *Third World Quarterly* in 2017 (Howard-Hassmann and McLaughlin 2022). As Boghossian's fame grew on the internet, his associations with Jordan Peterson and other figures in what came to be known as the "Intellectual Dark Web" (IDW) solidified his reputation as a right-wing activist, in spite of being a self-described classical liberal who never voted republican and endorsed democratic candidates. During this time, the administration at Portland State did nothing to back Boghossian, who was depicted as far-right all over the internet as well as on his own campus. It must be noted that Boghossian's sharp criticisms of religion, his social liberalism, tendency to want to examine the evidence for all views, along with his willingness talk to representatives of all political camps, raise serious problems with the kind of guilt-by-association arguments that were being made against him.

By 2022, Boghossian had become far more linked to conservative political perspectives than he had been before Sokal Squared. The ideas he opposed included extremist transgender ideology, the authoritarian implications of Ibram X. Kendi's anti-racism, and the radical postmodern and social constructionist ideas that had consolidated their dominance in American universities by the time of the Grievance Studies hoax. Boghossian's YouTube critiques of *NPR* may have solidified his reputation as on the right side of the political divide in the eyes of many, though there remains much of value in his criticisms (28 August 2022), which were later echoed by Uri Berliner, a senior editor at NPR, as recently as April 2024 (Berliner 2024).

It may be too simple to say that Boghossian was driven to the right by the left-liberal authoritarianism, but it is certainly the case that he is now a less interesting and innovative intellectual and teacher and has increasingly dug into positions in the culture wars over identity. It is also the case that universities have become less interesting places without him. The great strength of Boghossian prior to his participation in the hoax was his willingness to go into prisons, walk the street, dialogue with student groups, and hold open sessions for students to listen and talk about ideas from all sides of controversial debates. Despite the new political space we might say he occupies, he continues to do such work with his "reverse Q and A," and "Street Epistemology" sessions filmed at universities and posted on YouTube. He remains open to a remarkably broad set of positions on a variety of issues—even if some of these are themselves deserving of criticism from the perspective of the authors of this chapter and the larger volume it is published in.

Boghossian, thus, is not right-wing in the ways his critics unfairly allege, and he is rightly critical of the very categories of left-versus-right that have shaped our discourse about politics in Europe and North America since the French Revolution (Boghossian December 14, 2022). He is, for example, very critical of Matt Walsh, the conservative Catholic activist who produced the controversial *What is a Woman?* documentary for the conservative outlet *The Daily Wire*. This is despite the fact that Boghossian agrees with elements of the critiques directed at radical trans ideologies that deny biological sex as an important and meaningful category. For Boghossian, Walsh's stated desire to use military force to shut down and arrest drag performers is profoundly authoritarian. The willingness to use violence to enforce a certain point of view is something he rejects, and this kind of behavior matters more to him than political categories of left and right. Boghossian has been fair-minded and consistent on such issues.

Still, Boghossian is now more of a crusader against "woke" ideology than an innovative teacher, and he operates on the margins of academic work. Whether through his associations with the so-called "Intellectual Dark Web," or his YouTube critiques that mock *NPR,* he is operating from the center-right of current global debates. Furthermore, Boghossian's involvement as a Founding Faculty Fellow of the nascent University of Austin in the United States, a privately funded academic refuge for cancelled professors with a conservative funder and a right-wing reputation in the mainstream press was another signal of his right-of-center move (Boghossian 27 February 2023, 32:01). Though arguably conservative in orientation, the institution encourages a diversity of political voices, perhaps more so than many established universities today. Kathleen Stock, a left-wing British philosopher who was driven out of her faculty position in England because of her views on gender and sex is another Funding Faculty Fellow at the University of Austin. Jonathan Haidt, the NYU social psychologist is also involved in the Austin experiment, something that faces many funding and accreditation challenges but which has thus far received much publicity and sharpened the critique of left-wing authoritarianism on campus.

Of the three hoaxers, Boghossian is the most difficult to categorize. He remains connected to James Lindsay, describing him as a friend and going to bat in defense of Lindsay for being criticized as a conspiracy theorist (Zepps 2023). While having connections to various right wing internet figures, Boghossian continues to foster "impossible conversations" that demonstrate an openness to left and liberal views. And Boghossian is just as critical of Elon Musk's banning of left-wing accounts he does not agree with on X (formerly Twitter) as he was of the former Twitter leadership's tendency to ban right-wing account, most famously including Donald Trump himself (December 8, 2022, see April 26, 2022). Boghossian is pro-gay rights, critical of the perspective on trans rights articulated by Judith Butler and radical trans activists, and not particularly popular among gender critical feminists, as they are sometimes called. Clearly neither on the left or right, it makes sense that Boghossian is critical of thinking about the world in these categories.

It is hard to deny, however, that attempts to silence legitimate debate about quality control in humanities and social science journals, and the ideological blinders that have creeped deep into university life, have coarsened the subtlety of Boghossian's thought to some degree. However, it was James Lindsay who was most clearly driven off the rails in the wake of the Grievance Studies affair.

The Making of a Conspiracy Theorist

Among the Grievance Studies hoax group, James Lindsay was the only one to come from a hard sciences background. He is also the only member of the group who went on to become a genuinely right-wing conspiracy theorist. In the years just before Sokal Squared hoax, James Lindsay was a liberal, Obama-supporting math PhD who was smart enough in the sciences to succeed in graduate school (Thomas and Rabinowitz 2020, 16:07), though he chose not to pursue the cutting-edge research frontier of contemporary math, citing family reasons (Jordan Peterson interview with the hoaxers, Jan 11, 2019). In response to what were limited options within his field, and driven by his own intellectual ambitions and curiosity, Lindsay became focused on, and we might even say, obsessed with, the ways that the contemporary social sciences and humanities were becoming excessively ideological and unscientific.

This appeared at first as a logical outgrowth of his religious skepticism and participation in the atheist community—not unlike Boghossian. Reading widely and willing to take more explicitly polarizing positions in ways that do not come naturally to either Boghossian or Pluckrose, Lindsay cast himself as the defender of the hard sciences in the group. In this way, he shared an epistemological approach with Sokal himself, though Lindsay lacked the former NYU professor's secure position in academics. It is arguable that the Grievance Studies affair would never have succeeded to the extent that it did without Lindsay's energy, intellect, and passion for the scientific method in addition to his burgeoning obsession with all-things critical theory (Lindsay 11 January 2019; 1:26).

Lindsay was also the least connected to the academic field at the time of the hoax. Until *Cynical Theories* was published and became a best-seller, Lindsay looked to social media for an avenue to participate in discourse—especially Twitter. This digitally-mediated path eventually led him down a rabbit hole of conspiracy until he became the most vocal and aggressive voice among the three hoaxers. In the aftermath of the Grievance Studies affair, he become involved in many highly contentious debates with academics, graduate students, and faculty on social media. Lindsay weighed in aggressively on the 2 + 2 is always 4 discussions,[7] on science, sex and gender, the James Damore scandal at Google (31 July 2018, Lindsay 14 October 2018), and various diversity, equity, and inclusion programs at universities, in government, and in the business world (Thomas and Rabinowitz 2020, 35:55). He engaged in sharply antagonistic public debates about Marxism and Postmodern philosophy, censorship on Twitter, racism, police violence, the Black Lives Matter (BLM) movement,[8] and eventually vaccines, lockdowns, Donald Trump, and even the war in Ukraine.[9] Lindsay was pursuing a career as a social media entrepreneur and content provider who was indignant and contemptuous towards a left that depicted him as a racist, sexist, and fascist. The more they insulted him, the deeper he dug in. As a non-academic, however, Lindsay's income and career was not threatened by the hostility directed his way, unlike with Boghossian whose job was on the line (11 January 2019, 5:49). As Lindsay's book sales and speaking engagements gained market share and visibility, a new career path opened—that of a conservative pundit, and oftentimes, crusader.[10]

Lindsay faced a choice. Facilitating difficult or even impossible conversations requires taking the best version of various opposing arguments and encouraging discussion and debate on that basis. However, the social media career strategy that Lindsay embarked upon after the Grievance Studies affair relied upon focusing on the worst, least generous, and most implausible reading of the arguments made by people he disagreed with or using examples from the fringes of internet leftism to make arguments about the mainstream left, universities, and other institutions. While Lindsay presented this style as necessary in order to "save the west from itself" and to stop it from being seized by a Maoist inspired ideological regime, his approach ginned up some of the worst elements on Twitter. His audience consisted of both enemies and devotees, and the tawdry attention he received from both seems to have motivated him to some degree.

As activists in and around Black Lives Matter, the radical trans activist networks, and left-wing and liberal university faculty, graduate and undergraduate students took the lead in attacking Lindsay, he faced mounting accusations of being a white supremacist, far-right ideologue, misogynist, and transphobe (Takami 7 October 2018). While many scholars and readers agree with the basic critique of some postmodern ideas articulated in *Cynical Theories,* authoritarian defenders of these ideas responded to challenges from Lindsay with personal attacks. As these grew in number and intensity, Lindsay adopted a more scorched Earth approach to engagement. In the process, Lindsay's profile on social media increased and became more incendiary.[11]

Lindsay's increasingly polarizing positions prompted many former allies consider him deranged, and a conspiracy theorist more than a debunker of bad scholarship.[12] There is a rich literature on conspiracy theories, of course, and it is a contested concept as both a conceptual category and a trope used to demonize one's political opponents, and so we should not use this label lightly, but Lindsay fully embraced pandemic vaccine conspiracies, Trump's election fraud, and World Economic Forum (WEF) "great reset" views that share a border with traditional antisemitic tropes (22 March 2022). Lindsay has read extensively, if thinly, the works of Hegel, Marx, Marcuse, Fanon, Paulo Freire, and critical race and queer theory scholars. Despite this, he maintains that all the problems society faces today reflect an institutional takeover by communists and Marxists, rooted in ideas that were intentionally deployed to undermine Western society. Indeed, the relentless criticism and attacks Lindsay faced when he was still reasonable appeared to galvanize this view, offering a post hoc justification for his descent into vehement absurdities.

Lindsay is now in business with a far-right Christian nationalist Michael O'Fallon—an odd ally for a former militant atheist—though Lindsay contests this way of framing his collaborator. He also runs the website *New Discourses* where he crowd-sources for money while frequenting various rabbit holes encouraged by the emotional intensity generated by social media outrage. Lindsay's *New Discourses* website is dedicated to unpacking the inner workings of the various strands of critical theories that he believes are so dangerous. Significantly, however, neither Boghossian or Pluckrose appear to be involved in his project. Perhaps due to the absence of their moderating influence, *New Discourses* has adopted a conspiratorial perspective that suggests the various theories discussed in *Cynical Theory* were all designed to transform Western Liberal Democracies into a liberal simulacrum that was actually Neo-Marxism in disguise and little different from the Maoism of the Chinese Communist Party (2020). On *New Discourses,* Lindsay blends every kind of critical theory together, from Marcuse to Hegelian dialectics, Foucault and Queer theory, providing the sense of a vast conspiracy intent on subverting freedom and liberalism through "critical social justice." By 2024, he was speaking at length and in absurd terms about George Soros, standard fare for far-right conspiracy theorists (Lindsay 2024).

Though speculative, it is easy to see how Lindsay may have come to view the treatment of the Grievance Studies hoaxers as evidence of a winding conspiracy among intellectual elites which he intended to unmask through his website and presence on other social media platforms. It is true that there are a lot of unreasonable ideas promoted on college campuses, and that it was even more extreme on Twitter where Lindsay was attacked relentlessly, leading him to respond aggressively. And the attacks on Lindsay became increasingly nasty, personal and not always fair. This led him to embrace Trump in 2020, much to the dismay of his some of his former followers and collaborators.

Getting attacked for supporting Trump further led him to embrace versions of QAnon-influenced ideas and COVID-19 pandemic conspiracy theories—as well as frequent use of the word "groomer," which reduces progressive views on sex and gender as being akin to pedophilia. All of which served to feed polarized battles around sex education, gay and trans rights in American schools. Lindsay also collaborated with Christopher Rufo, a conservative American activist who has embraced illiberal censorship to "cure" America of wokeness and ban "critical race theory" from schools, and who is now reforming the New College of Florida in the role of trustee. Rufo, however, is politically astute in ways that Lindsay is not. Lindsay's aforementioned relationship with Christian nationalist Michael O'Fallon (Smith and Rabinowitz August 12, 2020, 11:19–11:37) and his *Sovereign Nations* organization is also notable. O'Fallon has been active in trafficking George Soros conspiracy theories that dabble in anti-semitism (Ibid; 26:25), along with other unpalatable ideas that are common among far-right extremists (O'Fallon September 22, 2021).

In August of 2022, Lindsay was given a permanent ban on Twitter for making the groomer accusation against a political opponent, though it was later lifted by Elon Musk when he took over the social media platform in the fall of 2022. Lindsay remains active on Facebook, Twitter, Instagram, YouTube, and Soundcloud where he promotes his videos and book, endlessly claiming that America and the world is under attack by a postmodern communist movement that has taken over our universities and schools, and made serious inroads into government, media, and corporate life. He has published books on what he calls "Race Marxism" (Lindsay 2022) and what he and Logan Lancing call the "Queering of the American Child" (Lancing and Lindsay 2024) both of which combine valid critiques of radical ideas with half-truths, distortions, and bizarre fantasies about the contemporary left.

Lindsay initially worked well with both Boghossian and Pluckrose on the Sokal Squared project and two books, adding a focus on the scientific method on a team with two humanities scholars (Lindsay and Pluckrose 2020, Lindsay and Boghossian 2019). But a steady diet of vilification and persecution can do strange things to one's mind. Watching the experience of Boghossian, and the similar experience of Pluckrose (which we discuss below) apparently strengthened Lindsay's conviction that the universities were not just part of the problem, but the ultimate source of what Gad Saad calls "idea pathogens," (Saad 2020).

That being said, it is worth remembering how his earlier, more reasoned attempts to combat rabid echo chambers and polarizing progressivism were met with harsh dismissals. The early Twitter response to the Sokal Squared group lumped them all together unfairly with the far-right Breitbart empire and Richard Spencer's white nationalists. Lindsay was also acutely aware of the polarized culture wars that took place at Evergreen College, Yale, and Google. Some people will look at Lindsay's trajectory and claim that these worrisome trends were already present in his early work and that his collaborators simply chose to ignore it. We disagree, but there is little doubt that, for a variety of reasons, Lindsay went from being a somewhat harsh, often obnoxious, but nevertheless evidence-based liberal critic of contemporary trends to one of the worst examples of today's toxic "anti-woke" discourse. But if Lindsay became a right-wing extremist, the British literary scholar Helen Pluckrose certainly did not. Her story is one of reasonable ideas and good intentions caught with no place to go in the polarized landscape of the contemporary culture wars and identity politics.

Caught between Left and Right

English literary scholar, feminist, and philosopher Helen Pluckrose was a pivotal player in the Grievance Studies affair largely because she was the most left-wing of the trio, and the most deeply versed in the academic literature in the humanities (January 31, 2021). Pluckrose was group's social theorist and her insights about critical theory's history and contemporary relevance were at the center of their project. Her case is also the most unfortunate, and even tragic, part of the story. Educated in literature and then early modern studies in London, England, where she lives with her husband, a working-class forklift driver, and their daughter, she is a clear and concise socialist-influenced writer with an egalitarian left-wing sensibility. It was Pluckrose, one could argue, who kept the book she wrote with Lindsay, *Cynical Theory* (2020), away from some of the nasty polemics that has characterized the latter's work since.

Being reasonable, nuanced, and balanced did not, however, help Pluckrose's career nor her mental and physical health in the wake of the scandal caused by the hoax. Pluckrose suffered enormously from being attacked as a right-winger for her role in the hoax by academic and social media leftists on Twitter (Pluckrose 26 July 2020, 24:34). She was also subjected to vicious critiques from the right and far-right for refusing to denounce her own left-leaning priors, and thus being seen as part of the left-liberal elite camp the hoax was supposed to expose and denounce. Caught between the partisan left and right, Pluckrose remerged only recently after a couple of years of struggle and recovery from the emotional turmoil the incident created in her life. This is particularly unfortunate as she was and remains the most consistent and principled of the Sokal Squared team, and the hoaxer least compromised by the search for fame, social media likes, retweets, and money.

At the time of the Grievance Studies affair Pluckrose worked as an editor at the heterodox left-liberal online magazine *Areo*, which provided high level intellectual commentary on contemporary political and cultural issues with an eye on evidence-based epistemology. As with any such editorial job in our social media age, Pluckrose was a prominent person on Twitter, speaking on a variety of issues and promoting the magazine. As her personal profile rose in the wake of the Grievance Studies affair, she found herself bogged down in testy disagreements with radical postmodern, third wave feminist, trans, and critical race theory activists who viewed her as supporting right-wing attacks on the academic left. The radical right, by contrast, were appalled that she refused to embrace hard right-wing talking points on various social and cultural issues.

In staying true to both her left-wing social justice commitments and her critique of what she viewed as nonsense coming from various postmodern, feminist, and critical race theory influenced literatures, Pluckrose came under constant harassment from both sides of the culture war (Pluckrose 11 January 2019, 1:12: 07).[13] Many painted her as fascist adjacent and an apologist for white nationalism and right-wing populism, an unfair criticism to say the least given her views on Trump, Brexit, and various other right-wing concerns (Pluckrose 6 October 2019, 16:30; 31 January 2021, 5:07). Far-right Twitter, meanwhile, painted Pluckrose and *Areo* as so-called "cucked" intellectuals not up to the task of resisting left-wing authoritarianism and political correctness. Many of the attacks on her were personal and nasty, with sexist tropes abounding. From the perspective of the far-right, Pluckrose was basically a socialist or a communist, undermining Western civilization in the same way James Lindsay came to believe, but unwilling to admit it.

The reality, however, is that Pluckrose's search for fairness and consistency is evident across her writing. In fact, it was likely this even-handedness that put her firmly in the crosshairs of both left and right activists and ideologues as she refused to kowtow to either's positions and was strongly critical of both—especially their internal contradictions and inconsistencies. Pluckrose's involvement in the Grievance Studies affair only increased her profile which in turn led to left-wing attacks on her character, associations, academic record, and ideological positions which were often mischaracterized as right-wing extremism, a claim that is demonstrably untrue.

Guilt by association, then, was a problem for Pluckrose because while she did not have direct connections with as many right-wing internet figures as Boghossian and Lindsay did, she was closely linked to both, and stood fully behind the hoax. Her involvement thus made her a target for "cancelation" from the left, particularly the academic left, who attacked her with partisan fury—particularly online. Pluckrose has since distanced herself from James Lindsay due to his descent into Trumpism, but she has been unwilling to throw him under the bus publicly, an act of personal loyalty to a former collaborator but one that further damaged her reputation in the eyes of progressives. It is clear, however that Pluckrose and Lindsay represent opposite positions in the ongoing culture wars. Pluckrose refused to sign up with the new, more extreme "anti-woke" agenda promoted by Donald Trump (Pluckrose 31 January 2021, 5:47), Christopher Rufo, Jordan Peterson (who she was consistently critical of right from the time of his emergence), and especially James Lindsay. As a result, the right has come to view her as a traitor to the cause.

Pluckrose instead chose to move towards what she saw as a more constructive project beyond critiquing "cynical theory" and cancel culture by forming the organization *Counterweight*. *Counterweight* describes itself as a "liberal humanist organization which provides educational resources, customized action plans, mental health support and community for people in trouble." The organization's goal is to fight political polarization, promote liberal values and provide support for cancelled or mobbed workers based on principles of individualism, reason, due process, freedom from unjustified coercion, and the free exchange of ideas. Pluckrose is no longer in a leadership position with the organization (another effect of the personal crises she underwent), although she is listed as the founder and continues to promote its agenda. A positive organization that promotes ideas in the form of articles, illustrations, videos, podcasts, books, and courses that promote critical thinking, dialogue, and an online educational platform, *Counterweight* provides personal support and guidance to people who suffer abuse at work, with a focus on non-academics. Pluckrose remains involved in this important work as applied postmodernism moves out from the university and into the workplaces of broader society, endangering free-speech and worker's rights.

Pluckrose suffered by far the most from the authoritarian response to the hoax, in her case from attacks from *both* the authoritarian left and authoritarian right. We strongly suspect the fact of her being a woman played a role in this. She was frequently attacked online by "social justice" supporters—disgusting bullying tactics we would expect to see from the Trumpist right, but which were deployed against Pluckrose from the left in the wake of Sokal Squared to discredit her for reasons that had nothing to do with her work or views (Pluckrose October 6, 2019 16:34). Ultimately, the bullying faced by Pluckrose became unbearable, and led to severe reoccurrences of chronic health conditions and a battle with depression, which forced her to retire from Twitter, *Counterweight*, and *Areo,* as well as major involvement in the culture wars (January 12, 2022). Pluckrose now works in social care, though she has recently returned to Twitter (now called X), and her commentary remains balanced, calm, and reasonable. Her theoretical role as an online public intellectual continues to provide creative and provocative insights on the culture wars even as established specialists and graduate students in the fields she is critical off remain wary of her and of her ideas.

Conclusion: How Authoritarian Academic Left-Liberals Feed Trumpism and Undermine the University

We have argued here that both the original Sokal affair and the more extensive Grievance Studies hoax exposed real problems in the system of peer review in the social sciences and humanities. More importantly, the authoritarian tactics used to marginalize Alan Sokal and the Sokal Squared group were appalling; a deeply reprehensible episode on the part of the online and academic left. During the Trump years, many thousands of academics, students, and administrators have defended the tactic of using research ethics review processes to punish professors who exposed real problems in research and elsewhere, mobilizing Title IX laws as a tool to attack cogent challenges to ideological orthodoxies, mobbing ideological opponents with insults, personal attacks, and even death threats online, and using charges of racism, sexism, transphobia, and fascism to silence debate along with tactics of guilt-by-association (Kipnis 2018). None of these tactics are democratic. They demonstrate a thoroughgoing authoritarian attitude of perceived self-evident "rightness" that justifies whatever might be deemed necessary to shut down opponents. The ultimate consequence of this has been damage to the credibility of our universities, and the left itself, in the eyes of the lay population and political moderates—a point made by Sokal in his original hoax, and one which we feel deserves considerably more emphasis than it has had recently (Lukianoff and Haiti 2018).

Another serious consequence of all this lies in the example of James Lindsay. What happened to both Boghossian and Pluckrose was wrong, and this sort of thing has had a chilling effect on debate and ideas on campuses and in public discourse. Organizations like Jonathan Haidt's Heterodox Academy are trying to address this problem with a program for political diversity on university campuses. But these efforts have become much harder because of the political polarization that is exacerbated when someone like James Lindsay is driven to such ideological extremes—arguably as a response to unfair criticism and unjust treatment. Lindsay now uses the "groomer" smear on anyone who disagrees with him, calls anyone remotely liberal a communist, and has created a new version of David Horowitz's earlier books and program of far-right McCarthyist opposition to the academic left. We do not absolve Lindsay of personal responsibility for his actions and beliefs, of course, but simply note that the mutually re-enforcing reactionary hysteria that the academic left participates in is creating major divides and political ugliness that in turn drives right-wing radicalism and authoritarianism.

This is all to say attack from the left on the Sokal Squared hoaxers played a significant role in expanding the ground for the left's worst nightmares—with the dark visions of Orwell casting a long shadow over the whole of events. Thus, it is well past the time to take a critical look at the tactics, attitudes, and ideas embraced within our own left-liberal elite universities if we wish to have a deeper understanding of the world and change it for the better. We should draw on the rich and powerful positive traditions of the left while rejecting left-wing authoritarianism in both its older, murderous Stalinist form and the newer forms of bullying and harassment that have emerged on social media and in the academy. We must also address the dreadful problems in peer-review and partisan knowledge production before reactionary right-wing forces seize on them, as they are currently attempting to do in places like Florida's New College and across the broader United States, turning the left's authoritarianism back on itself in a battle no one can win.

Notes

1 The published articles are "Human Reactions to Rape Culture and Queer Performativity at Urban Dog Parks in Portland," 2018. *Gender, Place and Culture*; "Who are they to Judge? Overcoming Anthropomentry and a Framework for Fat Bodybuilding," *Fat Studies*; and "Ethnography and Breastaurant Masculinity: Themes of Objectification, Sexual Conquest and Masculine in a Sexually Objectifying Restaurant," *Sex Roles* and "Going in Through the Back Door: Challenging Straight Male Homohysteria and Transphobia through Receptive Penetrative Sex Toy Use," *Sexuality and Culture*, 2018.

2 Boghossian did not have a strong academic publishing CV in formal academic philosophy although he did have an exceptional teaching record and was a successful writer. It can be difficult for non-academics to fully grasp the complexity of this, as successful teachers and writers of well-received books written to non-scholarly audiences are not always given high status in universities where individuals are largely engaged in peer-review-sanctioned status competitions.

3 Title IX is an American national law that deals with sexual discrimination on campuses. It is viewed as essential for woman's rights by its supporters, and a threat to due process particularly around harassment allegations by its critics (Kipnis 2018).

4 There is an argument that this kind of "audit" should have been put through the formal ethics review process at the university, something journalist Jesse Singal has reasonably noted (2019). Clearly the hoax would not have been successful if it has passed through the ethics process that very likely would have resulted in the plan becoming public thus defeating the purpose of the enterprise altogether. Moreover, the authors and Boghossian himself were not using these publications on their CVs as research, which arguably puts them into a different category. There is, however, a certain contradiction between their position that "our project is *not* best understood as a set of hoaxes but rather as a kind of "reflexive" ethnography, which attempts to elucidate features of a (moral) culture by reproducing it faithfully" (Pluckrose, Lindsay, and Boghossian 2021: 1917), and the view that it is not research subject to ethics reviews. Whatever one thinks of the specifics on this issue, however, these considerations were not what was being debated as actors took sides in a polarized cultural battle that revolved around various versions of identity politics.

5 Weinstein and Heying, not unlike James Lindsay, have become unfortunate examples of how cancellation, and then perhaps popularity with new, online audience, can cause a slide into conspiracy theorizing. For Weinstein and Heying, this has largely revolved around vaccines and the COVID-19 pandemic.

6 Boghossian also wrote an introduction to a new atheism book by Dan Arel, a left-wing journalist and author, demonstrating that he was talking and working with a range of people at the time, an orientation flowing from his Socratic commitments rather than from than right-wing politics.

7 "The real motivation for the Woke pushing "2+2=5." Well, that and tearing down the "hegemonic" system (Western Civilization) so that they can get it out of the way and replace it with their own system (Critical Theory, liberationism) where they have all the power by these tricks" (Lindsay 3 August 2020).

8 "WEF explains how supporting BLM raised your company's ESG score. It's not just a scam. It's a superscam. Scam of the century" (Lindsay, 25 May 2022).

9 "The conflict in Ukraine is most likely a coordinated push by WEF partners to drive up the costs of energy in the West, both to break it and to usher in support for a now-cost-competitive green revolution" (Lindsay, 2 February 2022).

10 While it is true that in the immediate aftermath of the affair Lindsay published a book with Peter Boghossian *How to Have Impossible Conversations: A Very Practical Guide* (2019) that focused on persuasion and dialogue, the logic of Lindsay's social media profile was leading him to the very opposite.

11 It must be noted that in cases such as this there tends to be a circular-symbiotic relationship between the extremes of left and right: his left-wing enemies on social media offered up the material that Lindsay in turn used to drum up outrage, new audiences, and attention in the social media sphere, which in turn led to more outrage. Many of his critics were engaged in the same thing with differing levels of success.

12 The best example of this general point is Claire Lehmann, editor of *Quillette*, the online opinion magazine that is associated with conservative ideas and unorthodox views. Initially sympathetic to the critics of post-modern neo-Marxism articulated by Lindsay and Jordan Peterson, she came to reject in no uncertain terms Lindsay's "peddling" of White Genocide Theory (Claire Lehmann June 16, 2021), and has even become a critic of Peterson and Bret Weinstein. Lindsay labelled Lehmann as a someone who is "crypto woke" and thus responsible for helping to bring about the Neo-Marxist totalitarian world government that Lindsay views as imminent.

13 For example, Pluckrose was invited on a panel on intersectional feminism and all of a sudden all of the other feminist panelists dropped out, refusing to participate with her (January 31, 2021, 34:16); she was publicly disinvited from Decolonize STEM symposium even though she was clear that her argument will be that STEM is masculine, white, and Western—she was told that her attendance was a danger to other attendees (34:54).

References

Adorno, T. W., Frenkel-Brunswik, E., Levinson, D. J., and Sanford, R. N. 1950. *The Authoritarian Personality*. New York: Harper.

Altemeyer, R. A. and Altemeyer, B. 1981. *Right-wing Authoritarianism*. Winnipeg: University of Manitoba Press.

Aronowitz, S. 1997. "Alan Sokal's' Transgression." *Dissent*, vol 44 no 1. 107–110.

Aronowitz, S. 1988. *Science as Power: Discourse and Ideology in Modern Society*. University of Minnesota Press.

Berberoglu, N. G. "The Bewildering Case of the 'Grievance Studies' Affair: Distorted Positioning of Cultural Studies within the Academic Industry." In *III. International Conference on Cultural Studies* (p. 189).

Blyth, M. 2016. "Global Trumpism: Why Trump's Victory Was 30 Years in the Making and Why It Won't Stop Here." *Foreign Affairs*, November: 1–12.

Boghossian, P. 2014. *A Manual for Creating Atheists*. Pitchstone Publishing (US&CA).

Boghossian, P. 2019. "Interview with Grievance Studies Hoaxers." Interviewed by Jordan B. Peterson together with Lindsay James, and Helen Pluckrose. YouTube video, 1:18:14. Published on 11 January on Jordan B. Peterson Channel. https://www.youtube.com/watch?v=xWhuQOVTFGw

Boghossian, P. 2021. "My University Sacrificed Ideas for Ideology. So Today I Quit." *The Free Press*. https://www.thefp.com/p/my-university-sacrificed-ideas-for

Boghossian, P. 2022. "NPR on Professor Harassment: Right or Left?" Published on 14 December by Peter Boghossian Channel. https://www.youtube.com/watch?v=5EZlKCEfcZs

Boghossian, P. 2022. "NPR: DANGERS of Elon Musk and Free Speech." Published on 13 December by Peter Boghossian YouTube Channel. https://www.youtube.com/watch?v=xoa2za05Dmg

Boghossian, P. 2022. "I Stopped Listening to NPR when…." Conversation between Peter Boghossian and Bret Weinstein. Published on 28 August on DarkHorse Podcast. https://www.youtube.com/watch?v=ZbQpXJBQhA0

Boghossian, P. 2023. "On the Downfall of Academia, Social Justice, Jordan Peterson & More." Published on Freedom Pact. https://www.youtube.com/watch?v=87dUU2_fROc

Boghossian, P. 2023. "My Conversation with Carl Benjamin ['Sargon of Akkad']." Published on 23 January on Peter Boghossian YouTube Channel. https://www.youtube.com/watch?v=xoa2za05Dmg

Boghossian, P. and Lindsay, J. 2019. *How to Have Impossible Conversations: A Very Practical Guide*. Da Capo Lifelong Books.

Boghossian, P. and Lindsay, J. 2017. "The Conceptual Penis as a Social Construct: A Sokal-style Hoax on Gender Studies." *Skeptic*, vol 22 no 3. 49–53.

Boghossian, P. and Lindsay, J. 2018. "The Socratic Method, Defeasibility, and Doxastic Responsibility." *Educational Philosophy and Theory*, vol 50 no 3. 244–253.

Brunner, J. 1994. "Looking into the Hearts of the Workers, or: How Erich Fromm turned Critical Theory into Empirical Research." *Political Psychology*, vol 15 no 4. 631–654.

Burgis, B., Hamilton C., McManus M., and Trejo, M. 2020. *Myth and Mayhem: A Leftist Critique of Jordan Peterson.* New York: John Hunt Publishing.

Burgis B. and McManus M. 2020. "Why Jordan Peterson is Always Wrong." *Jacobin.* 4:24.

Burston, D. 1991. *The Legacy of Erich Fromm*, Cambridge, MA: Harvard University Press.

Burston, D. 2020. *Psychoanalysis, Politics and the Postmodern University.* London: Palgrave MacMillan.

Christie, R. and Jahoda, M. 1954. *Studies in the Scope and Method of the Authoritarian Personality*. Glencoe, Ill: Free Press.

Costello, T. H., Bowes, S. M., Stevens, S. T., Waldman, I. D., Tasimi, A., and Lilienfeld, S. O. (2022). "Clarifying the Structure and Nature of Left-wing Authoritarianism." *Journal of Personality and Social Psychology*, vol 122 no 1. 135–170. https://doi.org/10.1037/pspp0000341.

Fish, S. 1996. "Professor Sokal's Bad Joke, Op-Ed." *New York Times*, May 21.

Foucault, M. 1980. *Power/knowledge: Selected Interviews and other Writings, 1972-1977.* Vintage.

Frickel, S., and Gross, N. 2005. "A General Theory of Scientific/Intellectual Movements." *American Sociological Review*, vol 70 no 2. 204–232.

Fromm, E. 1984. *The Working Class in Weimar Germany: A Psychological and Sociological Study*. Berg Publishers.

Gross, P. R. and Levitt, N. 1997. *Higher Superstition: The Academic Left and its Quarrels with Science*. JHU Press.

Guerrero, J. 2020. *Hatemonger: Stephen Miller, Donald Trump, and White Nationalism.* New York: Harper Collins.

Haidt, J. 2012. *The Righteous Mind: Why Good People are Divided by Politics and Religion.* New York: Vintage.

Hilgartner, S. 1997. "The Sokal Affair in Context." *Science, Technology, & Human Values*, vol 22 no 4. 506–522.

Hopper, T. 2018. "Academic Hoaxes a Hit: Hilarity Ensues when Studies Papers Fall for Left-leaning Ridiculousness." *National Post*, October 5, 2018.

Jacobs, R. N. and Townsley, E. 2011. *The Space of Opinion: Media Intellectuals and the Public Sphere.* Oxford: Oxford University Press.

Kaufman, E. "Academic Freedom Is Withering." *The Wall Street Journal*. February 28, 2021. https://www.wsj.com/articles/academic-freedom-is-withering-11614531962

Kipnis, L. 2018. *Unwanted Advances: Sexual Paranoia comes to Campus.* London: Verso.

Lancing, L. and Lindsay, J. 2024. *The Queering of the American Child.* New Discourses.

Lindsay, J. A. 2019. "Interview with Grievance Studies Hoaxers." Interviewed by Jordan B. Peterson together with Peter Boghossian, and Helen Pluckrose. YouTube video, 1:18:14. Published on 11 January on Jordan B. Peterson Channel. https://www.youtube.com/watch?v=xWhuQOVTFGw

Lindsay, J. A. 2020. "2 + 2 Never Equals 5." *New Discourses.* https://newdiscourses.com/2020/08/2-plus-2-never-equals-5/

Linsday, J. A. 2022. *The Marxification of Education. Paulo Freire's Critical Marxism and the Theft of Education.* Orlando: New Discourses.

Linsday, J. A. 2022. "Dr James Lindsay and the Great Reset." YouTube video, 5:26. Published on 13 January on Rebel News. https://www.youtube.com/watch?v=jvlVvS8a9tk

Lindsay, J. A. 2022. *Race Marxism: The Truth About Critical Race Theory and Praxis.*

Lindsay, J. A. *New Discourses*. https://newdiscourses.com

Lindsay. J. A., 2024. "The Reflexive Alchemy of George Soros." New Discourses, Podcast Episode 138.

Lindsay, J. A. and Boghossian, P., 2019. *How to Have Impossible Conversations: A Very Practical Guide.* Hachette Books.

Lindsay, J. A. and Pluckrose, H. 2020. *Cynical Theories: How Activist Scholarship MadeEverything about Race, Gender, and Identity- And Why This Harms Everybody.* Pitchstone Publishing.

Lindsay, J.A., Boghossian, P., and Pluckrose, H. "Academic Grievance Studies and the Corruption of Scholarship." *Areo,* October 2, 2018.

Lukiannoff, G. and J. Haidt 2018. *The Coddling of the American Mind: How Good Intentions and Bad Ideas are Setting up a Generation for Failure.* New York: Penguin.

McLaughlin, N. 2019. "The Coming Triumph of the Psychosocial Perspective: Lessons from the Rise, Fall and the Revival of Erich Fromm." *Journal of Psychosocial Studies*, vol 12 no 1–2. 9–22.

McLaughlin, N. 2021. *Erich Fromm and Global Public Sociology.* Bristol: Bristol University Press.

Nayna, M. 2018. "James Damore, Helen Pluckrose & The Second Culture." YouTube video, 17:13. Published on 14 October on Michael Nayna Channel. https://www.youtube.com/watch?v=87e1aXxruTo

O'Fallon. Michael. 2021. "Soros vs. China. Public Occurrences, Ep. 29." YouTube video, 27:43. Published on 22 September on Sovereign Nations. https://www.youtube.com/watch?v=nQkmf3vpGX4&t=67s

Peterson, J. 2018. *Twelve Rules for Life*. Toronto: Random House.

Peterson, J. 2021. *Beyond Order: Twelve more Rules for Life*. Toronto: Random House.

Pluckrose, H. 2017. The Problem with Intersectional Feminism. *Aero Magazine*.

Pluckrose, H. 2019. "Interview with Grievance Studies Hoaxers." Interviewed by Jordan B. Peterson together with Lindsay James, and Peter Boghossian. YouTube video, 1:18:14. Published on 11 January on Jordan B. Peterson Channel. https://www.youtube.com/watch?v=xWhuQOVTFGw

Pluckrose, H. 2019 "Fighting Postmodernism from the Left, Helen Pluckrose & Peter Boghossian" YouTube video, 39:44 Published on October 6, 2019 by Rebel Wisdom. https://www.youtube.com/watch?v=x1VQJXZ9y14

Pluckrose, H. 2019. "Fighting Back Against Cancel Culture with Helen Pluckrose." YouTube video, 59:52. Published on January 31, 2021 by Triggernometry.https://www.youtube.com/watch?v=UwUGa5HVNyM&t=1820s

Pluckrose, H. and Lindsay, J. A. 2020. *Cynical Theories: How Activist Scholarship Made Everything about Race, Gender, and Identity—And why this Harms Everybody*. Pitchstone Publishing (US&CA).

Pluckrose, H., Lindsay, J., and Boghossian, P. 2021. "Understanding the 'Grievance Studies Affair' Papers and Why they Should be Reinstated: A Response to Geoff Cole. *Sociological Methods & Research*, vol 50 no 4. 1916–1936.

Ruark, J. 2017. "Anatomy of a Hoax: How a Physicist Hoodwinked a Group of Humanists, and Why it Still Matters 20 Years Later." *The Chronicle of Higher Education*, vol 63 no 18. B6–B6.

Schuessler, Jennifer 2018. "The Nonscience of Dog Sex and Hooters: Academic Hoaxes." *The Toronto Star*, October 8: A12.

Shermer, M. 2017. "Failure to Communicate: Why we Published 'The Conceptual Penis as a Social Construct' Hoax Expose. *Skeptic (Altadena, CA)*, vol 22 no 3. 48–49.

Shils, E. 1954. "Authoritarianism: 'Left' and 'Right.'" In Christie and Jahoda, *Studies in the Scope and Method of the Authoritarian Personality* (pp. 24–49). Glencoe, Ill: Free Press.

Siler, K. 2020. "Demarcating Spectrums of Predatory Publishing: Economic and Institutional Sources of Academic Legitimacy." *Journal of the Association for Information Science and Technology*, vol 71 no 11. 1386–1401.

Singal, J. 2019. "Is a Portland Professor Being Railroaded by his University for Criticizing Social-Justice Research?" *Intelligencer*. Jan 11.

Smith, Thomas and Aaron Rabinowitz 2020. "James Lindsay's 'New Discourses' Funded By Far Right Christian Nationalist." *Serious Inquires Only*. Episode 250. https://seriouspod.com/sio250-james-lindsays-new-discourses-funded-by-far-right-christian-nationalist/

Sokal, A. D. 1996. "Transgressing the Boundaries: Toward a Transformative Hermeneutics of Quantum Gravity." *Social Text*, no 46/47. 217–252.

Sokal, A. 1996. "A Physicist Experiments with Cultural Studies." *Lingua Franca*, vol 6 no 4. 62–64.

Sokal, A. D. (Ed.), 2000. *The Sokal Hoax: The Sham that Shook the Academy*. University of Nebraska Press.

Sokal, A. 2010. *Beyond the Hoax: Science, Philosophy and Culture*. Oxford: Oxford University Press.

Sokal, A. 2017. "What the 'Conceptual Penis' Hhoax Does and Does not Prove." *The Chronicle of Higher Education*. Retrieved from https://www.chronicle.com/article/What-the-Conceptual/240344.

Sokal, A. and Bricmont, J. 1999. *Fashionable Nonsense: Postmodern Intellectuals' Abuse of Science*. Macmillan.

Sokal, A. and Dawkins, R. 2024. "Sex and Gender: The Medical Establishment's Reluctance to Speak Honestly about Biological Reality." *Boston Globe*, April 8.

Chapter 6

Back to School

Academic Dogma Invades Public Life

Russell Jacoby

"We have to kill the narrative that the Vice President is making all the decisions." So opined Mark Meadows, Trump's chief of staff, amid the attack on the Capitol. We must "establish the narrative" that Trump is in charge. Was Trump in charge? That is not relevant.

Once upon a time a narrative meant an account of true happenings. *A Narrative of Events That Have Lately Taken Place In Ireland* runs the title of a typical early 19th-century book. The narrative could be challenged for its accuracy, but the idea of replacing it with another had not yet been hatched.

That idea emerged from the university. Narrative became a field of study, narratology, with journals, conferences, and experts. The dons taught that no singular events underpin a narrative. The narrative depends on who relays it and who reads it. A thousand segments constitute a narrative, which can be assembled in countlessly valid fashions. As one professor stated—actually my professor, Hayden White—in "Historical Text as Literary Artifact," narratives are "as much *invented* as *found.*" If they are invented, everyone can invent their own. Nowadays much talk flows about how the narrative of this or that event should be or has been presented.

Narrative is not the only item that has moved from the campus into the public square; it joins diversity, hybridity, binary, intersectional, marginalization, power differentials, microaggression, and group safety as well as approaches to free speech and gender that build on these terms. Something is happening in American culture. No one doubts the importance of American universities. But the direct impact of the humanities on American society as a whole—as compared to schools of medicine and science—has always seemed limited. For years I have asked my students to name a living American philosopher. Universal response? Zilch. Perhaps once students could name William James or John Dewey. Even among educated adults few today could name a living American philosopher. A list of the most influential contemporary philosophers begins with: Sally Haslanger (Ford Professor of Philosophy at MIT), Daniel Dennett (Austin B. Fletcher Professor of Philosophy at Tufts University), and Linda Martin Alcoff (Professor of Philosophy, Hunter College and City University of New York.) Who?

Yet my question misdirects attention. For the question is not who, but what, a trickier proposition. While the names of people in the humanities, including law

DOI: 10.4324/9781003389927-6

schools, may not be widely known, their ideas and lingo have filtered into the public arena—and not for the better. We are witnessing the invasion of the public square by the campus, an intrusion of academic terms and sensibilities. As Andrew Sullivan declared, "We all live on the campus now." While "narrative" has been adopted by all political sectors, this is largely the story of the left-liberal campus exporting its wares to government agencies, foundations, NGOs, and corporations, all of the liberal stripe.

The issue is both the notions and language that have been developed in humanities departments. The buzz words of the campus—diversity, inclusion, microaggression, power differential, white privilege, group safety—have become the buzz words in public life. Already confusing on campus, they become noxious off campus. "The slovenliness of our language," declared Orwell in his classic 1946 essay, "Politics and the English Language" makes it "easier for us to have foolish thoughts." Nowadays, we have lot of foolish thoughts. But slovenliness does not capture the problem.

Orwell targeted language that defended "the indefensible" such as the British rule of India, Soviet purges, and the bombing of Hiroshima. He offered examples of corrupt language. "The Soviet press is the freest in the world." The use of euphemisms or lies to defend the indefensible has hardly disappeared. Putin called the invasion of Ukraine "a special military operation"—and anyone calling it a "war" or "invasion" has been arrested. "The purpose of this operation is to protect people," declared Putin. We seek to "demilitarize and denazify Ukraine." Kindred examples drawn from China or North Korea or Iran are easy to multiply.

But today, unlike in 1946, political language of Western progressives does not so much as defend the indefensible as defend the defendable. This renders the issue trickier than when Orwell broached it. Apologies for criminal deeds of the state almost denounce themselves. Justifications for liberal desiderata, however, almost immunize themselves to objections. Who could oppose the goals of more diversity or group safety? If you question the diversity mania, you support Western imperialists. Wonder about the significance of microaggression? You are a microaggressor. Have doubts about an eternal all-inclusive white supremacy? You benefit from white privilege. Skeptical about new pronouns? You abet the suicide of fragile adolescents.

Moreover, the stakes may be higher today than they were when Orwell addressed political language. Dogmatic pronouncements of the left and right bothered him, but they mainly addressed issues outside of England—Soviet trials, Nazi aggression, British imperialism. His *Homage to Catalonia* corrected the record of the Spanish Civil War. But the foreign focus has abated, perhaps in tandem with an almost universal isolationism. The war in Ukraine sparks much attention but barely constitutes a divisive subject. A recent issue (October 2022) of the progressive *New Republic* features articles on Democratic messaging, economic democracy, reparations, and new pandemics. A new issue (Spring 2022) of the leftist *Jacobin* magazine runs pieces on American transit, nuclear power, crypto, and water. Political feuds now are less about foreign than domestic policy. This means they connect more closely to everyday life than when Orwell offered his thoughts. It is one thing to denounce the coverage of the Spanish Civil War; it is another to denounce the teaching of sexuality in American elementary schools. The latter owns an immediate impact.

"Diversity" is exhibit A in the campus invasion of the public square. Like "narrative" it is not a new term, but obsession with it stems from the campus. Its modern status dates from a Harvard admissions statement that figured in a 1978 Supreme Court decision which allowed affirmative action under the rubric of diversity. The court leaned on a Harvard College admissions document that stated, "The belief that diversity adds an essential ingredient to the educational process has long been a tenet of Harvard College admissions…In recent years, Harvard College has expanded the concept of diversity to include students from disadvantaged economic, racial and ethnic groups." The blockbuster of all campus exports, diversity has taken over not only universities with their diversity campaigns and officers, but government and corporations and everything in between.

Everyone loves diversity. Why not? As a human quality it is better than the reverse, homogeneity. Yet diversity exemplifies the murky lingo that defends the defensible. What does diversity entail? More representation of every group? Fair enough, but is this diversity if every individual must incarnate the group, a notion almost the antithesis of individual diversity? Moreover, diversity focuses on visible group markers—gender, race, ethnicity—which sidelines diversity of ideas, politics, and religion as well as economic class, which are less easy to track. If all agree, but partake of different groups, where is the diversity?

Does diversity mean that every sector of society demographically should mirror the composition of the country as a whole? Apparently so, but does this make for a more diverse world? A new study of diversity in Hollywood run by UCLA, and sponsored by blue-chip corporations, uses demographics of gender, race, and ethnicity as the self-evident standard to measure diversity. Of course, working class does not figure in diversity studies, if only because it cannot be easily charted. The Hollywood study reports that "People of color accounted for 38.9 percent of the leads in top films for 2021…At 42.7 percent of the U.S. population in 2021, people of color were again just short of proportionate representation among film leads." The gap of 3.8% troubles the diversity mavens. Work to be done, comrades! Redouble your efforts, however, for screen writers! "People of color would have to increase their 2021 share by about 10 percentage points to reach proportionate representation." Is this diversity or its opposite, paint-by-numbers? Moreover, where does diversity defined as the proportionate representation lead or stop? Indian Americans are overrepresented among motel owners. What to do? Vietnamese Americans largely staff nail salons. A problem! Too many Jewish lawyers—and too few Jewish NBA basketball players. None! Has the NBA addressed this crisis?

Compared to diversity, the other campus exports are small potatoes, but loom larger and larger. Take free speech. In recent years, the academics have given it a new cast that has migrated into the public arena. Like narrative or diversity, the new arguments that question free speech comes out of the academic left, an irony sometimes noticed. The Free Speech Movement at UC Berkeley virtually inaugurated the Sixties student protest. Historically on and off the campus leftists fought censorship and defended free speech. No longer.

The origins of this new argument against free speech derive mainly from leftist law professors, often calling themselves anti-pornography feminists and critical race theorists. In their tortuous writings, one finds all the terms that they picked up from the post-modern Marxists or the post-Marxists or post-something—hegemony, discourse, power, invention. To this they add misogyny, white supremacy, and a dash of paranoia. For all their sophistication these learned professors are continuously gobsmacked by the most elementary facts of society. Society is hierarchal. The rich have more clout than the poor. The powerful dominate the weak. They repeat these observations endlessly, as if they just discovered them. Apparently, they just did.

The first sentence of an article by Catharine A. MacKinnon, a chaired professor at the University of Michigan and Harvard Law Schools, who is the leading anti-pornography feminist, runs: "The First Amendment over the last hundred years has mainly become a weapon of the powerful." She specifies: "A First Amendment appeal is often used to support dominant status and power, backing white supremacy and masculinist misogynistic attacks." It is a means for "dominant groups to impose and exploit their hegemony." Note all the buzz words: dominant power, white supremacy, hegemony. The position marks a sharp shift from the traditional civil libertarians, who prized free speech as an arena for dissenters. These civil libertarians are now dismissed as misguided First Amendment absolutists.

A problem emerges from the half-baked Marxism of these law professors. Marx did declare that the ideas of the ruling class are the ruling ideas, but qualified that both cleavages exist in the ruling class and that a new revolutionary class challenges the dominant ideas. Perhaps he was wrong, but at least he posited movement and conflict. It could also be noted that the term "hegemony," a favorite of campus leftists, probably derives from the Italian Marxist Antonio Gramsci. For all his subtlety and inconsistencies, the imprisoned Gramsci saw social antagonisms as ever-present. As one commentator has put it, "Gramsci's concept of hegemony" provides the basis for an intellectual elite to engage in a "war of position" that will prepare the way "to overthrow the existing order."

War of position? Nothing could be further from the minds of these professors, who portray power as omnipresent and static. That the First Amendment is a tool of the powerful, Professor MacKinnon's pathbreaking insight, comes right out of hackneyed Marxism; it could be said with equal truth about any sector of society. "Housing is a weapon of the powerful." "The media is a weapon of the powerful." "Education is a weapon of the powerful." For that matter Professor MacKinnon, who teaches to the most privileged at the most elite schools, is a weapon of the powerful.

These propositions are not wrong but are not 100% true—and exactly where they are not true defines the space where many of us operate, including these law professors, as well as writers, activists, and critics of all stripes. But the critical anti-pornographers and race theorists, who otherwise damn binary thinking, view the world as a dualism, the dominators and the dominated. The latter become their concern, but only insofar as they are victims. They offer the victim's interpretation of history. This is how they see the history of free speech and racism, a history of victims. Moreover, they enlarge victimhood from an individual to a group matter; the group suffers threats to its safety or well-being. What are the boundaries to free speech? It becomes a psychological issue. Who has to listen and at what cost? The approach has spread far beyond the university.

The endless controversy about free speech circles around its limit: under what conditions should it be restricted? In the classic American case of 1919, Justice Oliver Wendell Holmes Jr. set out the criterion of "a clear and present danger" to the state as reason to curb free speech. Holmes wrote the opinion in which two socialists, who had distributed leaflets that encouraged peaceful resistance to the draft, were arrested. The leaflets proposed among other things that draftees "Assert Your Rights." In 1919 such talk constituted "a clear and present danger" to the government. They were convicted and jailed.

Holmes in subsequent cases, as well as commentators and judges over the years, have retreated from that standard as too lax or dangerous; that is, it gives the government too much latitude to censor. In general, civil libertarians have always argued that restrictions on free speech should be few and far between, confined to direct threats to institutions or people—in later lingo, "fighting words." We find this already in John Stuart Mill's *On Liberty*:

> An opinion that corn dealers are starvers of the poor, or that private property is robbery, ought to be unmolested when simply circulated through the press, but may justly incur punishment when delivered orally to an excited mob assembled before the house of a corn dealer.

The new free speech restrictors balloon the category of injury and replace individual harm with group harm. "We have not listened to the real victims," declares Charles R. Lawrence III, one of the principals in critical race theory. We have shown "little empathy or understanding for their injury." For Lawrence "insulting words" are "experienced by all members of a racial group who are forced to hear or see these words." For Mackinnon pornography injures all women. "The free so-called speech of men silences the free speech of women." She catalogs the ways pornography harms women, not only directly in its production, but by its readers and viewers. Pornography "objectifies" women and leads to devaluing them. She cites a zillion studies of this caliber as proof: some diligent scholars found "a statistically significant [positive] relationship between rape rates and adult magazine circulation rates by states." The same relationship can probably be found between rape and NASCAR viewers by state.

On and off the campus these arguments lead to new restrictions on free speech and charges against the offending parties. Laura Kipnis, a film professor at Northwestern University, has written about her ordeal when she upset campus tranquility. Her offense? She penned an article in *The Chronicle of Higher Education* that questioned what she called the sexual paranoia on campuses. Repeat: an article in a trade newspaper upset students, who felt threatened and unsafe by her piece. The students marched through the campus, lugging a mattress, a new sign of something. "We, the undersigned, are therefore calling for a swift, official condemnation of the sentiments expressed Professor Kipnis in her inflammatory article." One of the principals complained the article "harmed" students. The University readily opened an investigation that dragged on for months.

Jump off campus to the offices of *The New York Times.* The newspaper published an opinion piece by Senator Tom Cotton that called for the national guard to stem looting in the wake of the George Floyd riots. Employees of *The Times* protested and charged that the piece put Black staffers "in danger." Again: this was an article in the editorial section of the paper, page 14, not a speech before a corn dealer. In the American adaption of Stalinist show trials, the editor of the opinion section confessed. He regretted "the pain" he caused. He resigned.

In a mini version of *The Times* incident that highlights kindred realities, a stalwart progressive magazine, *The Nation,* apologized for a short poem it published. A white poet assumed the voice of a Black homeless woman. The magazine now appends to the poem an apology—longer than the poem—which regrets that the poem contains "disparaging and ableist language that has given offense and caused harm to members of several communities." The poetry editors are "sorry for the pain we have caused to the many communities affected by this poem." Note the idiom and ideas: "ableist" language and the bloated notion of pain and communities. Of course, the poet apologized "for the pain I have caused." In accord with the new Criminal Code, section 44.03 "Unintended Injuries to Communities by Means of Poetry," he has been sent to a re-education camp.

Or take another incident, not with the same outcome, but one that shows the same alignment of forces. In early 2015, two French Muslims forced themselves into the French satirical journal, *Charlie Hebdo,* which published caricatures of Muhammed. They shot twelve people point blank—writers, cartoonists, and others. In the Spring of that year the American branch of PEN, the international association of writers, wanted to bestow on the magazine its "freedom of expression award." It would seem cut and dry: writers and cartoonists killed in cold blood for their satirical work.

But no. Some of Americas most celebrated writers protested the award to *Charlie Hebdo.* They did not exactly support the murders. "An expression of views, however disagreeable, is certainly not to be answered by violence or murder," they opined. The "certainly" is a nice touch, as if doubt arises. It does, for it is followed by the inevitable "but" and the school-grade truism about power. But "power" exists and the "inequities" between those who write and those written about "cannot, and must not, be ignored." Guess what? The writers, who were killed, had power. The written about, and killers, not so much.

> To the section of the French population that is already marginalized, embattled, and victimized, a population shaped by the legacy of France's various colonial

> enterprises, and that contain a large percentage of devout Muslims, Charlie Hebdo's cartoons of the Prophet must be seen as being intended to cause further humiliation and suffering.

Note the buzz words: "marginalized" and "victimized."

To this letter several hundred very righteous writers, including Teju Cole, Deborah Eisenberg, Michael Ondaatje, Joyce Carol Oates, and Francine Prose fixed their signatures. Cole backed out of the awards ceremony and added his own thoughts. People "much more progressive" than *Charlie Hebdo* cartoonists should be honored; and he mentioned Edward Snowden and Chelsea Manning. Those suggestions might summarize the new model for free speech. Attack the US government—a powerful institution that operates more-or-less by laws and that cannot claim victimhood. You do get punished; but you can lead a life, win a book contract and some acclaim. This is much superior to attacking marginalized Muslims; this leads to no book contract and no acclaim, in part because you may get murdered.

The approach might be called the social-psychological interpretation of free speech. The power constellation and group sensibilities determine the boundaries of free speech. To the extent that writers possess power, compared to non-writers (or non-cartoonists)—as indicated in the PEN protest letter—the inequalities might block all writing, except about oneself, a temptation many writers already find irresistible. Apart from this quandary, marginalized groups, of course, should never be attacked or criticized. Only attack the government, white supremacy, Trump, colonialism, and the like.

In any event, how do you determine marginality? In the university everyone and every ethnicity claims to be marginalized. Outside the campus, increasingly every group sees itself as marginalized. With marginality as the limit for free speech, how might have the new arbiters viewed Voltaire and his brethren of 18th-century France. The *philosophes* were an elite who attacked the benighted Catholics, who probably felt injured and disrespected. The power of the Church was fast crumbling—it would soon be disestablished in the French Revolution—and the good Catholics were often rural and poor. Weren't they marginalized?

In 2004 Theodoor van Gogh, a Dutch actor and film producer, was murdered in the streets of Amsterdam—on his bicycle—by a Muslim extremist. He had made a ten-minute provocative film with Ayaan Hirsi Ali, the feminist born to a Muslim Somalian family, that denounced the treatment of women in Islamic societies. The assassin pinned a note to van Gogh's body with a knife that threatened Hirsi Ali. In his book *Murder in Amsterdam* Ian Buruma considers the events and its principals, but like today's free speech sceptics observes that Hirsi Ali attacked a marginalized community, "a minority within an embattled minority." In that sense, he comments, Hirsi Ali is no Voltaire.

Yet the same issue emerges. What makes a marginalized community, which constrains free speech? The 1989 fatwa against Salman Rushdie ordered Muslims anywhere to execute the author—with a fat reward bankrolled by Iran for this pious deed—and it encompassed not only Rushdie but also his publishers and translators. There are well over one billion Muslims. Rushdie himself noted that over the decades support for him has ebbed. People who once defended me, he observed, would now "accuse me of insulting an ethnic and cultural minority."

Of course, the literary professors never supported him, a move that seemed too crude and binary. "Instead of reproducing binary stereotypes," declares one brave critic, about his discussion of Rushdie and the fatwa, I will use "the concept of critical constellations: that is, a number of competing and even contradictory perspectives...creating diverse patterns or interpretative frameworks." Call this author if the Red Guard or Al-Qaeda comes a knocking. The essay on *The Satanic Verses* and the fatwa by Gaytri Spivak, a doyen of marginality studies, earns special mention in the category of opaque equivocation. Her discussion opens this way: "I come now to the cultural politics of the specific (mis)reading of the book as disposable container of blasphemy, signifier of cultural difference, rather than the field of the migrant's desiring/social-production." She comes to this ringing conclusion: "It is only if we recognize that we cannot not want freedom of expression as well as those other normative and privative rational abstractions that we on the other side can see how they work as alibis. It is only then that we can recode the conflict as Racism versus Fundamentalism." Thank you, Professor, but where does that leave Rushdie?

The situation of the estimable Voltaire could not be more different than the current critics of Islam; he lived at the border of France and Switzerland, so he could quickly flee if French authorities sought to arrest him. Along with other *philosophes* he never dreamed he could be killed either by the state or angry Catholics anywhere. Detained, censored, or exiled yes. Murdered, no. An angry mob once stoned Rousseau's house. According to a biographer he faced an "untenable" situation and fled. Voltaire had no security detail—unlike Rushdie and Hirsi Ali, who still has one. For critics of religious dogmatism in 18th-century France, the possibility of getting killed was zero. For critics of Islam in the 20th-century world, the possibility of injury or death is real—as the critics know. The comment by Buruma, which is seconded by others, could be more justly reversed: Voltaire was no Hirsi Ali.

I myself have missed this take-over of the public square by the campus, and I have written extensively on university events. In 1987, I published *The Last Intellectuals: American Culture in the Age of Academe* which elicited heated responses. Only now do I see I got something wrong—as did my critics. Some had objected to the term I introduced, "public intellectual," as redundant and misleading. Others rejected the main argument. I proposed a generational account of American intellectuals. For earlier American intellectuals the university remained peripheral because it was small, underfunded, and distant from cultural life. The Edmund Wilsons and Lewis Mumfords earlier in the 20th century to the Jane Jacobs and Betty Friedans later saw themselves as writers and journalists, not professors.

What I called a transitional generation, the largely Jewish New York intellectuals, ended up later in their careers as professors, but usually they lacked graduate training. When Daniel Bell was appointed to the faculty of Columbia University in 1960, officials discovered that he did not have a Ph.D.—and bestowed it on him for his collection of essays (*The End of Ideology*). This incident indicates something of the commitment of these men—and they were men; they wrote essays for a public, not monographs or research papers for colleagues. This orientation was as true for a confrere of Bell, like Irving Howe, who also ended up as a professor without graduate training. He observed that like himself Bell did not want to write long-winded treatises; nor did they want to specialize or get pigeonholed. Or as Bell phrased it for all of them, "I specialize in generalizations."

But the story changes for the next generation—my 60s generation. In prose we were much more radical than previous American intellectuals. We were the leftists, Maoists, Marxists, Third Worldists, anarchists, and protesters who regularly shut down the university in the name of the war in Vietnam or free speech or racial equality. Yet for all our university bashing, unlike earlier intellectuals, we never exited the campus. We settled in. We became graduate students, assistant professors and finally—a few—leading figures in academic disciplines.

To be sure, this was not simply a series of individual choices. The conditions that funneled the transitional generation onto campuses were hard to resist. The life of the free-lance intellectual, always precarious, had become virtually impossible. Living in cities turned increasingly expensive as the writing outlets diminished—and their pay hardly budged or even diminished. When Edmund Wilson wrote for *The New Republic* in the 1920s the proceeds of one article could foot the bill for room and board for several months. Sixty years later the payment had hardly increased—and could fund a few meals. At the same moment, in the 1950s and 60s, students poured into campuses and faculties enlarged. For young intellectuals, the signs all pointed in one direction: an academic career. Earlier American intellectuals imagined moving to New York or Chicago or San Francisco to join an urban bohemia; my generation imagined moving to college towns like Ann Arbor or Berkeley or Austin to join the conference-going set.

Within 30 years the timber and tone of faculties were refashioned. In 1950s the number of public leftists teaching in American universities could be counted on two hands. By the 1980s, they filled airplanes and hotel conference rooms. In the 1980s a three-volume survey of the new Marxist scholarship appeared (*The Left Academy: Marxist Scholarship on American Campuses, vol. 1-3*). Endless new journals with their own following popped up such as *Studies on the Left*, *Radical Teacher*, *Radical America*, *Insurgent Sociologist*, *Radical Economists*. In the coming years leaders of the main scholarly organizations like the Modern Language Association or American Sociological Association elected self-professed leftists.

Herein the story gets tangled. In a series of bestselling books—*Tenured Radicals*, *Illiberal Education*, *The Closing of the American Mind*—conservatives raised the alarm: radicals were taking over the university and destroying America, if not Western Civilization. In *The Last Intellectuals* I differed. The new radical scholars were proving to be obliging colleagues and professionals. The proof? They penned unreadable articles and books for colleagues. They were less subversive than submissive. Earlier American intellectuals wrote for a public; the new radical ones did not. They were not public intellectuals, but academic intellectuals.

The "famous" Marxist literary professor was famous only to graduate students in literature. From Homi K. Bhabha at Harvard to Gaytri Spivak at Columbia, Fredric Jameson at Duke and Judith Butler at Berkely the leftist politics of these scholars could not be doubted, but what was their impact inasmuch as they could not write? A half-serious bad-writing contest awarded a prize to Professor Butler for this sentence:

> The move from a structuralist account in which capital is understood to structure social relations in relatively homologous ways to a view of hegemony in which power relations are subject to repetition, convergence, and rearticulation brought the question of temporality into the thinking of structure, and marked a shift from a form of Althusserian theory that takes structural totalities as theoretical objects to one in which the insights into the contingent possibility of structure inaugurate a renewed conception of hegemony as bound up with the contingent sites and strategies of the rearticulation of power.

I argued that the conservatives should awake from their nightmare of radical scholars destroying America and relax; academic revolutionaries preoccupied themselves with their careers and perks. If they made waves, they were confined to the campus pool. In my more paranoid moments, I wondered if a larger plan had been enacted. Conservatives pretended to be outraged at radicals on campus, but faced with a generation of subversive students, they judged it would be better to keep them locked up in the university, which would limit the damage. The secret appendix to *The Conservative Strategy for the Twentieth First Century* declared, "Let us give the radicals English and Comparative Literature, gender studies, sociology, history, anthropology and whatever other departments and cockamamie centers they want on campuses, while we take over the rest of America." The plan largely worked. I wrote at the time, if given the chance it would be worth trading every damn left-wing English department for one Supreme Court. It would still be worth it.

My critics charged that I suffered from nostalgia for some old White dudes. Intellectual life had markedly improved and diversified. Moreover, I overgeneralized; they presented names of a half-dozen stalwart free-lancers or well-known professors. This argument continues.

But my critics and I both missed something that might not have been obvious 30 years ago. By the late 1990s the rapid expansion of the universities came to a halt, especially in the humanities. Faculty openings slowed or stopped in many fields. Graduate enrollment cratered. In my own department in ten years we went from accepting over a hundred students for graduate study to under 20 for a simple reason. We could not place our students. The hordes who took courses in critical pedagogy, insurgent sociology, gender studies, radical anthropology, Marxist cinema theory, and post-modernism could no longer hope for university careers.

What became of them? No single answer is possible. They joined the workforce. Some became baristas, tech supporters, Amazon staffers, and real estate agents. Others with intellectual ambitions found positions with the remaining newspapers and online periodicals, but most often they landed jobs as writers or researchers with liberal government agencies, foundations, or NGOs. In all these capacities they brought along the sensibilities and jargon they learned on campus.

That explains what is happening in the larger culture. The leftists who would have vanished as assistant professors in conferences on narratology and gender fluidity or disappeared as law professors with unreadable essays on misogynist hegemony and intersectionality have been pushed into the larger culture. They are everywhere. They staff the ballooning diversity and inclusion commissariats that assault us with vapid statements and inane programs.

When employees protest that they feel unsafe because their company is publishing an offensive article or book, we know what courses they have taken. When the ACLU drops any mention of the First Amendment from its annual reports; when one of its directors declares "First Amendment protections are disproportionately enjoyed by people of power and privilege;" and when it counsels its own lawyers to balance free speech and "offense to marginalized groups," we know they studied critical race theory. When women are dropped from Planned Parenthood literature with the explanation, "It's time to retire the terms 'women's health care' and 'a woman's right to choose'...these phrases erase the trans and non-binary people who have abortions." Or when the NARL (National Association for the Repeal of Abortion Laws) announces it is replacing the phrase pregnant women with "birthing people" and declares "We use gender neutral language when talking about pregnancy, because it is not just cis-gender women who get pregnant;" we know those who authored these changes majored in gender studies and critical blather.

We know this, but we have to suffer the consequences. The self-righteous professors have spawned self-righteous students who filter into the public square. The former prospered in their campus enclaves by plumping each other's brilliance, but they left the rest of us alone. The latter, their students, however, constitute an unmitigated disaster, intellectually and politically, as they enter the workforce. They might be the American version of the old Soviet apparatchiks, functionaries who carry out party policies. Intellectually, they fetishize buzz words (diversity, marginality, power differential, white privilege, group safety, hegemony, gender fluidity, and the rest) that they plaster over everything.

Politically, they mark a self-immolation of progressives; they flaunt their exquisite sensibilities and openness, and display incomparable narcissism and insularity. Once upon a time leftists sought to enlarge their constituency by reaching out to the uninitiated. This characterized a left during its most salient phase of popular front politics. No longer. With a credo of group safety, the newest generation of leftists does not reach out but reaches in. It operates more like a club for members only than a politics for everyone.

Chapter 7

The Transformation of *Woke*

Weighing the Mischievous Role of the Right

Lauren Langman

In his book, *The Selfish Gene*, evolutionary biologist Richard Dawkins (1967) coined the word *meme* as "a unit of cultural transmission," a henceforth common symbol, meaning, or trope within a culture. It amounted to a cultural version of a gene whose DNA and RNA stores a great deal of information. A meme acts a "as a shortcut that conveys wider social meanings." "Woke" is just such a meme that today, as used mostly (but not always, as this volume attests) by authoritarian actors on the right wing. Certain journalists, bloggers, influencers, celebrities, and conservative politicians deploy "woke" as an umbrella term, an all-inclusive designation, and indeed denigration, of the many and various people and/or institutions deemed undesirable. The meme has changed meaning over a remarkably short period of time, as McWhorter noted:

> It seems it was 10 minutes ago that it was the hot new badge of enlightenment, shared warmly as a kind of lexical bonding ritual, usually in the expression "stay woke." To be woke was to be in on a leftist take on how American society operates, especially in reference to the condition of Black America and the role of systemic racism within it…In 2012, people were using "stay woke" on Twitter with unalloyed pride. As late as 2016, you could find rosy-cheeked teens and 20-somethings all but chirping "woke," [as} the latest slang. No more. These days "woke" is said with a sneer. It's a prisoner in and typically uttered with a note of condescension. (McWhorter, 2021) somewhere between the way comedians used to talk about hippies …, here, I will sub in "jerks."

How did this happen? To understand how and why "woke" became a meme of denigration, we need to consider political-economic conditions, deeply impacted by neoliberalism and the legacies of progressive social movements. Economic systems and practices, however, don't always act in straightforward ways. Their impact is mediated by culture and character in which unmoored feelings, slanted understandings, and a mixture of motives affect impact. To understand authoritarianism, and especially right-wing reactionary movements which were its first (and continuing) subject, we need to consider authoritarianism as an aspect of character. Authoritarians need to exert power over others and given the onset of system

DOI: 10.4324/9781003389927-7

crises, discussed below, they especially crave scapegoats. Candidates for the latter designation are not only the weak and powerless, but elected corrupt, if not "evil," elites, most likely to be socialists or globalists (read Jews) who are indifferent to the "real people," and who cannot help but shove alien, progressive agendas down others' throats.

In recent years "woke" and wokeness, like other derogatory memes initially utilized by the right wing, such as sheeple, libtards, or snowflake, has been weaponized into a toxic designation of despicable enemies such as corrupt elites, "trouble-making" minorities, parasitic, criminal and usually darker skinned immigrants, nasty feminist women, perverted gays who "groom" children for pedophilia, the transgendered (especially transitioned male athletes who beat cis-gendered women in sports and then use unisex bathrooms), and finally, loony environmentalists who peddle the deception that climate change is a genuine danger tied to fossil fuel usage. Then of course there are "woke" organizations that includes socialists, communists, globalist elites, and the "deep state"—otherwise known as career government workers—who hate America, loath its freedom, reject its virtuous exceptionalism and its capitalism, and seek to implement totalitarian communism. Today, there are many "woke" cities that celebrate perversion and pedophilia by hosting "pride" parades of scantily clad marchers while "woke" corporations like Disney or Budweiser embraced these despicable Others and conspire to integrate workforces, attract multicultural multiracial customers and, not incidentally, thereby enhance corporate profits.[1]

One must keep in mind that the original meaning of woke meant "sensitized to stay or become awoken," literally getting "woken up," having a better understanding of racism, especially the injustices of systemic, structural, institutional racism. This original meaning was not censorious or self-righteous, and indeed seemed firmly aligned against any censorious forces. Emerging in the 1930s among African Americans when used most notably by music legend Leadbelly, in his 1938 song "Scottsboro Boys" chronicling the unjust plight of nine Black teenagers. It signaled to be awoke, to have an understanding that racism was not reducible to attitudes of bigoted individuals or cross-burning racist organizations. Rather, structural racism was rooted in unjust political and economic practices and laws. This view was central to a long line of African American intellectuals and writers: W.E.B. Du Bois, James Baldwin, Richard Wright, Langston Hughes, Toni Morrison, bell hooks, to start. Still, in the new millennium, Derrek Bell's (1989) text on race and the law, critical race theory, and Kimberly Crenshaw's (1989) paper on intersectionality were beheld by right-wing conservatives as a grave threat to the American way of life.[2] CRT must not be allow to poison young minds, so teaching anything resembling it is now prohibited in places like Florida, while some communities actually burn library books, such as Mark Twains' *Huckleberry Finn* where Tom Sawyer has a Black (and, for some over-the-top wokeists, definitely not N-worded) friend named Jim, or Judy Blume who dares suggest that teenagers have sexual feelings. *Die guten alten Zeiten sind wieder zurüc* (The good old days are back).[3]

Mimetic Inversion

Lest anyone imagine that "Woke" as a term is in itself anti-progressive or fanatical it is well to recall its origins. Excesses there certainly have been, and they are well documented in other essays, but in this piece, I look at far more benign beginnings and how right-wing authoritarians, the standard specimens of the authoritarianism literature, worked assiduously to render the term, and its agents, into figures of fear and ridicule. That some zealots operating under the banner of "woke" or "critical social justice theory" provided grounds for these attacks is a different matter altogether. Insofar as the term "woke" originally indicated a positive quality of enlightenment and understanding, how did it change? This transmutation is an example of "memetic inversion," that is to say, the meme, itself a social construction, becomes reinterpreted and reconstructed to acquire a very different, indeed often opposite, meaning. This has been called this "semantic pejoration" by Miles-Hercules as a process where a meme becomes transformed into a derogatory negative meaning (Tensley, 2022). Similarly, "semantic bleaching" is when a term loses its original meaning.

Consider how "queer" had been a derogatory term for gays, and LGBTQ in general, connoting inferiority, perversion, insanity, and/or deviance. It featured in male schoolyard bullying of seemingly effeminate boys who preferred art to sports. Over time progressive movements combined to challenge hidebound values and identities, often also winning legal battles, and so the term transformed from one saturated with denigration and subalternity to one of empowerment, pride, and dignity as homosexuality generally became acceptable.[4] Queer no longer has an exclusively derogatory meaning. Consider how many complicit large cities host annual Pride parades where governors and mayors lead the celebrants, and sponsors include major banks, airlines, or hotel chains[5]. Similarly, the term pussy, a vulgar term for female genitalia, has been altered into an expression of female empowerment especially by the notorious punk rock group, Pussy Riot, originally from Russia but given their progressive politics, as feminists, supporting gay rights, and critical of Putin, they had to exit and some of them were jailed. (Check their YouTube channel @wearepussyriot)

The same mimetic inversion has taken place among authoritarian right-wing groups for whom the meaning of "woke" morphed into an umbrella term of derision for all progressive groups, value agendas, and institutions that they deeply oppose and resent, beginning with effete metropolitan elites, then annoying minorities, feminine empowerment seekers, gay rights agitators, and so on. Woke has become a linguistic marker of a tribalist differentiation of "friend or foe" recalling Carl Schmitt's (1932[2007]) reactionary views. Given their right-wing character structure, their reactionary ideologies, and political mobilizations, we now see an all-out war on "wokeness" conducted in politics, education, and even in the military and corporate sectors. As Swearingen (2023) put it:

> The fight against "woke" (a term with a longer history than most of us may realize) is strikingly similar to the fight the right previously waged against

> "political correctness": *It's an existential battle against allowing people to be awakened — by reading novels and history, by attending plays, by watching and listening to actual news — through open discussion of privilege or systemic racism or, to use a different but related term, the underlying and nearly invisible structures of caste in America.* It is a fight to stop people from talking about those social structures, or about the combination of religious zealotry and political ideology at work to foreclose women's bodily autonomy. It's a fight to prevent young people from expressing their sexual and gender preferences, to make it more difficult for certain groups of citizens to vote, and to keep books that might make the most hypocritical and closed-minded evangelical Christian pastors uncomfortable off the shelves of public schools and libraries...
>
> (Swearingen, 2023, p. 1)

So, the recent mimetic inversion of woke/wokeness from an enlightened critical orientation regarding structural domination as fostering a variety of injustices (and embracing equality and inclusion) to a contemptuous meme for diverse "enemies" who dare challenge straight, white, male, privilege—portending the demise of "greatness" encapsulates the polarization of character, identity, and tribal political orientations today. Note especially the early link here between social structural change and recognition of group identity and rights, which need not be opposed to each other but can indeed become so. "Woke" is not exclusively to blame for a detaching of identity politics from class politics since the 1960s, but it is not innocent either.

Flipping the Meme: The "Double Whammy"

Since the 1980s neoliberal globalization has been a boon to many, especially old and new billionaires. At the same time many more people face or fear economic hardships. The progressive movements of the 1960s—civil rights, feminism, gay rights—gradually became more widely accepted. But, given generationally mediated cultural change and legislative changes, there have been systematic challenges and contestations to essentialist, hierarchical, privilege-granting identities. This combination, what I call a "double whammy" has led to antagonizing (not only) reactionaries in ways that get expressed as "morbid symptoms" when the old society is dying but the new has not yet been born. The second element of this double whammy preoccupies most essays here, but the first (economic status threat) component should not be underestimated.

The postwar years, roughly 1945 till 1975, the French call *Les Trente Glorieuses* (the Glorious 30 years) a period in which Keynesian economics was dominant, a period of unparalleled economic growth, relatively equally distributed: growing numbers of college graduates (G.I. Bill), relatively well-paid stable jobs, major expansion of corporations, an explosion of consumerism, shopping malls, and television advertising. But Vietnam War expenses and international trade pressures pushed Nixon to end the gold standard. By the late 1970's came a stagflation crisis and intense pressures from internationally oriented American capital. By the late

1970s Keynesian economics, it seemed, was sputtering out. To resolve this crisis, there was a renewal of classical Smith and Ricardo economics, largely via Hayek and Friedman. There was the embrace of neoliberalism, with market fundamentalism placing primary emphasis on corporate profitability, retrenchment of social investments, reduction if not elimination of government regulations, shrinking various government programs, cutting benefits and entitlements, and privatizing public resources—all in line with the entrenched decades-long Republican goal of reversing the New Deal.

Neoliberalism was embraced with dismaying alacrity by Democratic Presidents Clinton and Obama. At this time, the barrier between banking and investment, the Glass-Steagall Act, was shorn by the Gramm–Leach–Bliley Act. Financialization quickly swelled through mergers and acquisitions, or via investment holding companies such as Blackrock and Kohlberg Kravis, Roberts. Perhaps the most notable transformation of the economy, allegedly necessary for globalized commerce, was the explosion of the derivatives market, basically bets on future exchange rates, stock prices, etc. which burgeoned to 12 times the GNP of the world.

Neoliberal deregulation, globalization, privatization, financialization. offshoring of work to low-wage countries/regions and relocating factories, robotics (automation—CAD CAM), and digital communication led to rapid economic growth—albeit very unequally distributed. In ensuing years, capitalist profits surged along with incomes of CEOs and stockholders (who comprise at most the upper decile of the populace). But large numbers of workers and small business owners experienced economic anxiety and, in many cases, actual hardships, stagnant wages, declining benefits, and often unemployment. Many workers lost their jobs due to de-industrialization. At the same time, small businesses, especially in smaller, rural towns, could not compete with big box stores like Walmart. Factory workers, miners, truck drivers, and other blue-collar workers were discarded by the Democratic Party that hitherto had been very supportive of workers and unionization. Instead, its socially liberal but economically conservative agenda, appealed to hordes of university graduates, especially in/near large seaboard cities.

Neoliberalism as the current iteration of capitalism remained crisis prone, as became startlingly clear in 2007–08 when the sub-prime mortgage crisis hit, the housing market imploded, and the deregulated banks faced massive crises of liquidity, losing trillions of dollars.[6] Lehman Brothers did fail—the largest bankruptcy in American History. What next? Back to Keynes, now carefully recrafted to serve only high-income earners, and the US Treasury printed trillions to bail out banks, not excluding bonuses for bankers, for clearly criminal acts beginning with impossible teaser rates that brought masses into the housing market who could not afford mortgage renewals. Iceland knew how to deal with the fraudulent bankers—*jail!* And what happened to the millions of homeowners that lost their homes? Given the individualism of neoliberalism—tough luck! The other and larger effect of neoliberalism has been growing inequality and precarity, evoking fear, anxiety, and resentment which in turn foster the conditions for the rapid rise of social movements.

Identities and Values: From Deviant to Normative

Alternative progressive values and lifestyles were always limited to small minorities. The "Beat Generation" and even the counterculture of the '60s were not all that salient to the general population. The wider populace largely approved of the Chicago "police riot," as the Walker Report later depicted it, against demonstrators at the 1968 Democratic Convention. Still, there was an attendant upsurge in groups challenging traditional values in the name of civil rights, racial equality, feminism, gay rights, LGBTQ while a massive antiwar movement challenged John Wayne notions of patriotism. Marcuse (1969) characterized these movements as "great refusals," but at that time, they were largely limited to college students, some minorities, and progressives—a combination large enough to foster a backlash yet not large enough to implement desired changes immediately. As Mannheim (1972 [1928]) pointed out, social change is mediated through "cohort flow," that is to say, the events of the era in which people come of age, influences their attitudes, values, identities, and lifestyles, and tend to endure throughout the generational life span.

Soon it became evident that progressive values could arise as challenges, confrontations, and legal battles that would bring changes, but for many hostile traditionalist onlookers *these challenges were directed at undermining hierarchical, essentialist, privilege-granting identities—privileges underpinning status, power, and self-worth.* This was already evident in 1964–65 when the Civil Rights and Voting Rights bills passed and the southern racist Democrats (called Dixiecrats), suddenly became southern racist Republicans and, under demographic threat, set out to block voting rights through gerrymandering and restrictive tactics on voter registration. This backlash continues to this day, culminating in Trump and the quest to return to a mythical neo-medieval Golden Age (Norris and Inglehart, 2022).

By the end of the 1990s for many men, especially those without college degrees, the feminist movements, and the fact of more women in the workforce, challenged patriarchal male identities and power. Many men, if I may invoke psychoanalytic terms, felt castration anxiety. The result was a major backlash against women (Faludi, 1999). This backlash was observed most garishly in the growth of militias in which camouflage outfits and automatic weapons were sanctified expressions of real masculinity. Similarly, the gay rights movement, especially after Act-Up, rejected the essentialist basis of gender that normalized patriarchy, which also was widely embraced by many women at least until Betty Friedan's *The Feminine Mystique* (1963) rekindled the American feminist movement.

Capitalism and Crisis

Developing the insights of early Frankfurt School analyses, Fromm (1941) pointed out how the economic crisis of post–World War I Germany, with its combination of paying onerous reparations and a major depression, generated hyperinflation and high unemployment. A susceptible part of the frightened populace, alienated, powerless, and angry, sought palliatives, "mechanisms of escape." This considerable fraction, never an outright majority, were allured by an authoritarianism that ameliorated their fears through submission to a powerful leader, along with unleashing sadomasochistic aggression directed especially toward Jews, Slavs, and communists. Fromm saw it all as a grotesque form of idolatry.[7] Many Germans, especially in the lower middle classes and upper working classes, eventually voted for the Nazi movement.

Jürgen Habermas (1975), who lived through the rise of fascism, later developed his own updated theory of legitimation crises. Any social order needs to be considered fair and just to be accepted. Legitimation "deficits" signal a loss of public confidence when the economic system fails or falters, and the political system also fails to steer economic growth so as to protect or improve the average standard of living. The State therefore must regulate businesses but also ensure profitability. It must provide entitlements; guarantee rights and offer legal systems to secure justice. The cultural system (identities and values) must accordingly encourage motivation for work along with meaningful identities, lifestyles, and values. (Alienated labor, regardless of how economically rewarding, can never provide genuine fulfillment). *Dysfunctions and failures engender crises that migrated to life worlds impacting identities, motives, and emotions.* The specific reactions are shaped by one's underlying social character, which acts like "the switchman on the tracks of history." Lakoff (2016) contrasted traditional "strict father" morality with "empathic" parenting, seeing the family structure as preparing children for political orientations. The "strict father" demanding obedience fosters characters who embrace ideologies that prize power, hierarchy, order, and unquestioned loyalty to the ingroup. Empathic democratic parenting yields character types who gravitate to egalitarian ideologies that value individual freedom, curiosity, self-fulfillment, and sharing.

Crisis and Character

The last several decades can be seen in terms of multiple and overlapping crises beginning with the crisis of the Keynesian-Fordist era, which was followed by ongoing economic maldistribution via neoliberal policies. Between automation and other advanced elements of production and distribution, (e.g. import substitution and job export), workers and small business owners experienced acute economic anxiety, and in many cases actual hardships, stagnant wages, declining incomes and benefits, and often unemployment. Insofar as economic and technological changes impacted the jobs and incomes of workers and given the neoliberal valorization of individualism "justifying" the retrenchment of benefits and social programs, workers and small business faced hard times. And thus, we saw an incipient crisis of the legitimacy of the government, seen (accurately) as ever more subservient to the interests of big capital and ever more indifferent to the fate of a growing precariat, the jobless and homeless. Moreover, at the same time, the "double whammy" posed a problem of cultural legitimacy in its challenges to essentialist, hierarchical identities that had provided ever more insecure groups with some compensatory power, meaning, and self-esteem. But how were these challenges met?

The authoritarian character is initially shaped by strict and punitive socialization instilling obedience and supplication to authority, encouraging domination over subordinates and an aggression which is projected toward outgroups. Authoritarians, above all, value power, strength, and order. Only a strong leader can realize the will of the ordinary, "authentic people" and so it scarcely matters if that leader adroitly and even openly uses electoral politics to gain power in order to erode democratic freedoms and subvert the democratic process. Such leaders are prone to aggression and violence toward real or imagined enemies, and they tend to be directed via a highly selective form of nostalgia toward the past.

Central to every reactionary movement, Carl Schmitt (1) claimed, is a fundamental dichotomy of friend/enemy. The designated enemy is always a vulnerable group who supposedly victimized "the real people" and are thus legitimate targets for anger, hostility, opprobrium, and justifiable violence ranging from expulsion to extermination. Thus, authoritarians need a scapegoat or scapegoats as a legitimate target for pent-up aggression. The classical scapegoat has been the Jew and although contemporary right-wing authoritarians tend to be more subtle about it, many of our contemporary troubles are still blamed on the "woke" globalist and socialist Jew: witness George Soros who commands a fleet of Jewish flying saucers equipped with energy beams to start forest fires. As Sartre ([1944] 1995) put it, and it still rings true:

> all or part of his [the anti-Semite's] own misfortunes and those of his country to the presence of Jewish elements in the community, ... he proposes to remedy this state of affairs by depriving the Jews of certain of their rights, by keeping them out of certain economic and social activities, by expelling them from the country, by exterminating all of them .... (p. 7) Far from experience producing his idea of the Jew, it was the latter that explained his experience. If the Jew did not exist, the anti-Semite would invent him.
>
> (Sartre, ([1944] 1995 p. 12)

Authoritarians typically imagine that their impeccable moral community has been victimized, ignored, or subverted by self-serving, inept, and/or corrupt elites. Indeed, these enemy elites use their wealth and power to support unpopular agendas, including globalization and rigging of elections to secure suspicious cosmopolitan goals (such as "woke" political correctness in its extreme, which is the only way they can view it). These same alien elites for some undisclosed reason encourage the dragging of society down to promote a godless, multicultural, multiracial, multigendered, sexually immoral society of antifa communists, "deep state" traitors, and lazy parasites demanding expensive social benefits. As the Charlottesville Unite the Right marchers shouted, "the Jews will not replace us."[8] Multiculturalism, derided as "woke," rests upon a distorted perception that racialized minorities *have prospered, often via crime, or unearned economic support from the government, while hard working "real Americans,"—white men—have been left behind.*[9]

But given the adverse economic impacts of neoliberalism, the occluded nature of governance, and the drastic cultural changes that challenged essentialist identities, there are many vulnerable "enemies" to choose from, and thus the "woke" meme covers all the bases—a shorthand term that names enemies and justifies retribution. Perhaps the clearest example was the January 6th insurrection, where part of the aggression was aimed at "woke" supporters of Joe Biden such as Comrade Pelosi and RINO Pence, who both might have faced the gallows if caught that day.

"Woke" agendas need to be halted, indeed, undone, and reversed, in order to restore a now lost Golden age America. The "good people," mostly white, mostly rural, and often religious, fear "replacement," oblivion, and decline as "woke" spreads throughout the society.[10] And there is a moment of truth to these fears, in most large cities, especially when multi-cultural, tend to be progressive, most women support reproductive choice, young people appreciate diversity, few attend religious services of any kind. The Z generation, the most liberal generation, is beginning to assert its power and is poised eventually to displace the older conservative generations whose political identities are the legacies of a different and more prosperous era.[11]

For authoritarian actors, the intense existential/ontological anxiety of demise, especially of privileged identities, has fostered "morbid symptoms," from the MAGA support for Trump, bizarre conspiracy theories, aggression toward woke enemies, and all too often crazed mass shootings. We now see an all-out war on "wokeness" in politics, education, and even within the military and corporate sectors.

The Internet

One of the most important factors for the spread of reactionary ideologies had been the Internet where there lurks a plethora of information and misinformation. The early Internet was used by progressive activists supporting the EZLN (Zapatistas) and anti-WTO protests (Langman, 2005). There is now a wide variety of political websites ranging from the left, which may include socialist or communist perspectives, to the right, that may very well be extremist and border if not actually cross the line to fascism. Thus the "woke" meme quickly went viral, and moved from obscurity as enlightened to a widely used term of denigration and ridicule. Consider for example how Q-anon went insanely viral and soon had 20 million adherents, who actually believe that there is a conspiracy of cunning celebrities and left-wing politicians to kidnap, torture, rape, and then devour little children to gain their adenosine, which prolongs their lives. Hillary Clinton is actually a witch, 200 years old.

When there are thousands of websites from which to acquire "information," especially political data, people generally select websites consistent with their own viewpoints. Liberals may gravitate toward MSNBC or Rachel Maddow while conservatives, indeed reactionaries, become the faithful flock for the many conspiracy theories of Fox News or Alex Jones. (Leftists have nowhere to go in mainstream media.) Dare anyone question the "facts" and the reply is, "just do your research it's on the Internet." Thus the "woke" meme gained right-wing traction and displaced "political correctness" as the primary meme of denigration. As Ortiz et al. put it:

> With the advent of social networks, memes have become a practice to propagate and circulate communications, which has a significant dimension in cultural production ...The use of memes throughout social media is observed, [as a] tendency to satirize social events using laughter as a measure of collective coping with the news of public interest becomes evident . . . Collective coping consists of the learned and uniform responses that culture manifests with the purpose of eliminating a stressor to change the interpretation of a situation.
>
> (Ortiz, 2021)

The Four Horsemen of the "Woke"

To understand how "woke" became an all-purpose meme of denigration, we must not underplay political economy and cultural changes, as system crises that migrate to the life world. What has been essential is how these larger factors become mediated through the authoritarian character facing realistic economic threats and anxieties, coupled with progressive cultural changes, what was called the "double whammy," and enlisted intense feelings and emotions that undergird anger and aggression.

For Nietzsche ([1887] 2014) *ressentiment* had a specific meaning, an intense loathing and quest for harsh punishment as revenge toward the elites. When the once powerful warrior-conquerors of Israel were themselves conquered by the Romans who embodied power, wealth, and free sexuality, the subjugated Jewish priestly class embraced a "herd mentality," a transvaluation of values embracing subjugation, obedience, conformity, humility, poverty, kindness, mercy, and asceticism. The rich and powerful Romans, with their wealth, power, and sexual indulgence, might enjoy life, but they were "morally inferior"; hence, the Jewish priestly classes and their followers deemed themselves morally superior which provided compensatory status based on *ressentiment* toward the Roman elites, a *ressentiment* rooted in revenge and envy. The consequent erosion of their self-esteem and pride, fueled a simmering rage at their situation and hatred toward their conquerors (Morelli, 1998). The humbled slaves created "virtues" out of necessity; supplication, poverty, and sexual frustration—repression.

In much the same way, authoritarians are enraged at obscure elites, especially mainstream politicians in general, seemingly puppets of the "globalist socialists," (aka Jews) who contradictorily run the banks and media, and whose economic policies led to the declining standards of living that many people face, especially in rural communities and especially among those with no more than a high-school education.[12] *Ressentiment* is especially powerful in a society with formal rights of equality but with a great deal of inequality (Scheler 1994 [1912]). For current populist-reactionary movements, there is disdain toward distant elites and the "democracy" that grants the elites an inordinate degree of unresponsive power. They are not actually wrong, but their diagnostic capacities are scrambled by a blend of internal predispositions and a bombardment of external conservative messaging and so they are hard, if not impossible, for progressive forces to reach.

The vehemence and intensity of reactionary anger, rage, and *ressentiment*—classically located in the lower middle class—require us to consider how cultural changes challenging heretofore essentialist hierarchical identities, e.g. privileged selfhood based on race, gender, gender orientation, heteronormativity, and religious beliefs have been facing strong headwinds.[13] Progressive trends today, shorn of or slighting economic class remedies, move toward multiracial and multicultural inclusion, feminism, toleration for varied sexual identities, and growing secularism, especially among the college-educated. Particularly, the young generation, while seeming to sidestep class politics, can be seen backing the erosion and demise of identities which rested upon "eternal" notions of hierarchy which have depended on the recognition of their "superiority" by subordinates who internalized their subjugation as the "normal" order of things.

Given the headline-grabbing influx of immigrants and increasing proportion of domestic US minorities, there has been, especially among the MAGA crowd, a growing fear of replacement of the white majority. The fear of replacement evokes an "extinction anxiety" that is rooted in the fear of death (Becker, 1973; Freud, 1920). Terror management theory (Becker, 1973) argues that control of death anxiety is the supreme human concern, and therefore is a primary function of society. Fear of death fosters a resort to allegiance to seemingly eternal cultural beliefs; it spurs threatened people to double down on faith in the validity of inherited cultural worldviews, i.e. beliefs in essentialist, unchangeable identities that give their lives a degree of status, self-esteem, and meaning that buffers them against their own mortality. The terror is "managed" by socially constructed beliefs that minimize ontological dread by conferring meaning and values tied to institutions, such as religion or the "nation," that explain "the origin of the universe, norms for appropriate behavior, and promises of immortality for those who behave in accordance with cultural dictates…" non-conscious death thoughts come more readily to mind when cherished cultural beliefs or self-esteem are threatened (Becker 1973).

Social critics have long noted the salience of status anxiety when economic system stability becomes uncertain, when dependence on one's work, income, and the ability to accumulate property are indications of worth. Under macrosocial shifts, there is uncertainty of attaining and/or maintaining one's status. Economic conditions that erode security are often interpreted, especially in America, as a sign of personal shortcomings for having taken a job in a particular industry or in a region that faces economic peril. Scheff (1991) argues that the denial of unconscious shame and humiliation is the basis of violence and aggression. In Scheff's analysis of conflicts ranging from marriages to wars, the pain of shame/humiliation over lost honor is covered up and quelled by seeking violent revenge. For

Germany, the reparations paid to the French was a deep humiliation; the loss of honor from paying reparations was more painful than the loss of the war or the economic deprivations, which may be an explanatory stretch but ultimately is a factor portending German revenge and World War II.

The fear of "replacement," with many older and especially rural, unorganized, and less educated whites face stagnation and eventual social and economic demise, precipitates the fear of cultural death as "unworthy" immigrants and/or minorities ascending social ladders. While difficult for the rural lower middle classes, half of those arrested for the January 6 assault on the Capitol, the arrestees were from educated, professional, and managerial classes, likely to live in Blue States in relatively prosperous neighborhoods (Pape, 2021). But these neighborhoods were changing as affluent immigrants or minorities moved in—eroding the heretofore unquestioned status of whiteness. Feelings of shame and humiliation over losing status and honor disposed the participants to embrace violence to assuage those awful feelings.

Systems of domination, in general, and capitalism/wage labor, in particular in this case, stymie the human capacities for freedom and the realization of one's potential talents. Whether the alienated labor of industrial workers, the routinized office worker, or the canny selling of one's very soul typical of the "marketing personality," social life is fragmented, human fulfillment thwarted, and one reaction has been necrophilia: "the passionate attraction to all that is dead, decayed, putrid, sickly; it is the passion to transform that which is alive into something unalive; to destroy for the sake of destruction; the exclusive interest in all that is purely mechanical. It is the passion to tear apart living structures" (Fromm, 1973, p. 332). The attraction to death occurs when one fails or is thwarted in development of their potentiality, namely, to be related to life as something interesting, and to develop one's powers of love and reason. Then we see a rage that lashes out and seek to destroy anything or anyone in range. Vulnerable minorities are always in range; elites are not.

Braune (2010) notes that the necrophiliac loves "law and order" and bureaucracy, and "transform[s] all life into the administration of things." The necrophiliac is attracted to nationalism, since s/he loves what is "home-made" and that to which he is accustomed, while he is afraid of what is new or different. Fascism fosters a death-loving, necrophilic character orientation. Fromm states that necrophilia is closely related both to sadism and the death instinct, although neither concept fully explains necrophilia (Braune, 2010).

Conclusion

Neoliberal economic crises today foster economic anxiety, especially for those without university degrees who disproportionately (but, in a gig economy, not exclusively) face declining incomes and job precarity, and that these trends together with successful progressive changes regarding racial toleration, feminism, and LGBTQ, created a "double whammy." This engendered *ressentiment* toward elites for enabling policies which seem to help everyone but themselves, and toward the beneficiaries too. So racial minorities, women, gays, and environmentalists are collectively disparaged by designating such groups as insufferably "woke," which does not mean elements of "woke" cannot occasionally and justifiably be viewed as insufferable on the left side of the political spectrum too.[14] Given memetic inversion, "woke" moved from a notion of sober enlightened consciousness aligned with traditional left goals to a disparaging catch-all meme by right-wing authoritarians to express their superiority and disdain toward "woke." The left should be careful not to equate or lump together all "woke" phenomena in the same way as the right, however tempting it may be given the behavior of certain "woke" activists. One would be doing the work of the right for them, which is to sow divisiveness among progressive forces.

To fully understand right-wing authoritarians, we need to understand the real pains they suffer, and to do so, it is necessary to understand the consequences of neoliberal capital and apply a psychodynamic understanding of how these structural factors are mediated, experienced, and understood by people facing changes hitting their wallets and their hearts, and opt to embrace a politics of sustaining essentialist identities. But what my argument suggests is that to combat authoritarian movements, all attempts to open and change MAGA minds through facts, evidence, or logic are probably doomed to failure. There is perhaps a better strategy: organize the progressive, younger cohorts so as to challenge the reactionaries, and acquire the economic, political, and cultural power to make real the vision that "another world is possible."

Notes

1 Many gays, without the burdens of raising children, have greater disposable incomes, and are often targeted for luxury goods and travel.

2 Some of these ideas were anticipated by W.E.B. DuBois and the Cohambee Collective. Most of the critics of CRT have not read these works, but my having taught Crenshaw to graduate students, case law is not exactly material that gets your heart pounding and your blood pressure up, more likely it can put one to sleep.

3 The ironies arising around the issue of what to call Huck's companion signaled the problems that allegedly left-wing groups brought into play, the repercussions of which are the subject of this volume's essays. See, for example, David Mathews, "Dumbing and Numbing Down Jim," *New York Times* January 6, 2011.

4 The attempts to preserve identities, values, and lifestyle is a major factor mobilizing reactionary movements.

5 In many adverts today, major companies make explicit reference to having gay friendly policies—especially since gays often have more disposable cash for travel or luxury goods.

6 For discussions of the falling rates of profit, see Smith, 2018 and the nature of the derivatives market and 2008 collapse, see Sassen, 2018.

7 Freud (1921 [1990]) anticipated how the aim inhibited attachments to the leader cemented social bonds between the followers,

8 Replacement theory emerged in France where the followers of Le Pen, feared that White Europeans would be replaced by Muslims colluding with the left wing to take over Europe (Camus, 2024).

9 Samir Gandesha, "Understanding Right and Left Populism," in *Critical Theory and Authoritarian Populism,* ed. Jeremiah Morelock. (London: University of Westminster Press, 2018).

10 We should note that about half of those arrested on Jan 6 were from upper income levels such as CEOs, doctors, and lawyers, from urban areas of Blue States (Pape, 2022). They were not affiliated either to the Proud Boys, 3%, or Oath Keepers. What they had in common was living in upscale communities with changing demographics as affluent African Americans, Asians, and Latinos moved into their upscale neighborhoods, threatening a loss of status of their whiteness. One of the arrestees was a woman Professor Ob-Gyn at the Harvard Medical School.

11 In these times, smaller communities were more insular, and less exposed to and impacted by progressive trends and movements.

12 There is legitimate anger directed toward the transnational capitalist classes, especially its high-tech billionaires who promised that neoliberal globalization will free the shackles of government and bring everyone prosperity—but has instead created vast prosperity for the elites. The unintended consequence is precarity for all beneath the highest decile. The understanding of globalization, financialization, e.g. the derivatives markets, requires great effort to understand. It's easier to blame individual elites rather than the system, or believe that immigrants steal jobs while lazy minorities live well on welfare paid by the hard-working producers. The Biden administration has seen record employment, lower infections, and a record stock market, but the authoritarian right, who glean their information from reactionary websites and influencers, are generally not the kinds of people that pay attention to either the *Wall Street Journal* or *Financial Times*. Prices on store shelves, rents, and the "gig" nature of most new jobs tell them a different story and who to blame is not obvious or too obvious to them.

13 On lower middle class authoritarianism see Reinhold Niebuhr, "Pawns for Fascism," reprinted in Daniel Steinmetz-Jenkins (Ed.), *Did It Happen Here? Perspectives on Fascism in America* (New York: Norton, 2024).

14 Susan Nieman (2023) has argued that a problem of today's "left" has been the embrace of some of a tribalist, identitarian celebration of victimization that celebrate the oppression of particular groups, rather than confront the injustices causing oppression and victimization and rejecting the universalization of the Enlightenment as freedom, equality, recognition, and dignity for all, a major theme for Kant, Hegel, and Marx—dismissed as "grand narratives," further fragmenting an already fragmented left.

Bibliography

Adorno, Theodore; Frenkel-Brunswik, Else; Levinson, Daniel and Sanford, Nevitt 1950. *The Authoritarian Personality.* New York City: Harper & Row and W. W. Norton & Company.

Becker, Ernst 1973. *The Denial of Death.* New York: Simon & Schuster.

Bell, Derrick 1989. *And Are We Not Saved.* New York: Basic Books.

Braune, Joan 2010. "Erich Fromm and Thomas Merton on Biophilia and Messianism." Conference Presentation, International Erich Fromm Society. Ravenna, Italy.

Camus, Renaud 2024 *The Great Replacement: Introduction to Global Replacism.* Independently published.

Crenshaw, Kimberley 1989. "Demarginalizing the Intersection of Race and Sex: A Black Feminist Critique of Antidiscrimination Doctrine, Feminist Theory, and Antiracist Politics." *University of Chicago Legal Forum*, vol 1989 no 1 Article 8.

Dawkins, Richard 1967. *The Selfish Gene.* Oxford: Oxford University Press.

Faludi, Susan 1991. *Backlash: The Undeclared War Against American Women*. New York: Broadway Books.

Freud, Sigmund 1921 [1990]. *Group Psychology and the Analysis of the Ego*. New York: W. W. Norton & Company.

Freud, Sigmund 1920 [1975]. *Beyond the Pleasure Principle*. W. W. Norton & Company.

Friedan, Betty 1963. *The Feminine Mystique*. New York: W. W. Norton.

Fromm, Erich 1941. *Escape from Freedom*: New York: Farrar & Rinehart.

Fromm, Erich 1973. *The Anatomy of Human Destructiveness*. New York: Holt, Rinehart and Winston.

Gandesha, Samir 2018. "Understanding Right and Left Populism." In Jeremiah Morelock (Ed.), *Critical Theory and Authoritarian Populism* London: University of Westminster Press.

Habermas, Jürgen 1975. *Legitimation Crisis*. Boston: Beacon Press.

Habermas, Jürgen (1989) [1962]. *The Structural Transformation of the Public Sphere: An Inquiry into a Category of Bourgeois Society*. Cambridge, Massachusetts: The MIT Press.

Lakoff, George 2016. *Moral Politics How Liberals and Conservatives Think*. Chicago: University of Chicago Press.

Langman, Lauren 2005. "From Virtual Public Spheres to Global Justice: A Critical Theory of Internetworked Social Movements." *Sociological Theory*, vol 23, no 1. March, 42–74. https://journals.sagepub.com/doi/10.1177/0011392113479749https://journals.sagepub.com/doi/10.1177/0011392113479749

Mannheim, Karl 1972 [1928]. "The Problem of Generations." In *Essays in the Sociology of Knowledge* (pp. 276–322). New York: Routledge.

Marcuse, Herbert 1969. *An Essay on Liberation*. Boston: Beacon Press.

Mathews, David 2011. "Dumbing." *The New York Times*, 2011/01/05 https://www.nytimes.com › roomfordebate ›

McWhorter, John, 2021. "How 'Woke' Became an Insult." *New York Times*, Aug. 17, 2021 https://www.nytimes.com/2021/08/17/opinion/woke-politically-correct.html.

Morelli, Elizabeth Murray 1998. Ressentiment and Rationality. *The Paideia Archive: Twentieth World Congress of Philosophy*, vol 16. 80–86. https://philpapers.org/rec/MORRAR-14swea

Neiman, Susan 2023. *Left Is Not Woke*. Cambridge: Polity Press.

Niebuhr, Reinhold 2024. "Pawns for Fascism," reprinted in Daniel Steinmetz-Jenkins (Ed.), *Did It Happen Here? Perspectives on Fascism in America*. New York: Norton.

Nietzsche, Frederick. [1887] 2014. *On the Genealogy of Morals*, translated and edited by Douglas Smith, Oxford: Oxford World's Classics.

Norris, Pippa and Ronald Inglehart 2019. *Cultural Backlash*. Cambridge: Cambridge University Press.

Ortiz, Jose et al. 2021 Feb. "Analysis of the Use of Memes as an Exponent of Collective Coping during COVID-19 in Puerto Rico.", *Media International Australia*, vol 178 no 1. 168–181.

Pape, Robert 2022. American Face of Insurrection: Analysis of Individuals Charged for Storming the US Capitol on January 6, 2021. Chicago Project on Security and Threats. https://cpost.uchicago.edu/publications/american_face_of_insurrection/

Sartre, Jean Paul [1944] 1995. *Anti-Semite and Jew: An Exploration of the Etiology of Hat*. New York: Schocken Books.

Sassen, Saskia 2018. "Predatory Logics: Going Well beyond Inequality." In: Langman, Lauren and David A. Smith. (Eds.), *Twenty-First Century Inequality & Capitalism: Piketty, Marx and Beyond* (pp. 64–85). Leiden: Brill.

Scheff, Thomas and Retzinger, Suzanne 1991. *Emotions and Violence: Shame and Rage in Destructive Conflicts*. Latham: Lexington Books.

Scheler, Max 1994 [1912]. *Ressentiment*. Milwaukee: Marquette University Press.

Schmitt, Carl 1932 [2007]. *The Concept of the Political*. Chicago: The University of Chicago Press.

Smith. David N. 2018. "21st Century Capital: Falling Profit Rates and System Entropy." In: Langman, Lauren and David A. Smith (Eds.), *Twenty-First Century Inequality & Capitalism: Piketty, Marx and Beyond* (pp. 323–333). Leiden: Brill.

Swearingen, Kirk 2023. Why the Right is so Terrified of "Woke": There Are Truths it Just Can't Face. *Saon*, June, 2023.

Tensley, Brandon 2022. How 'Woke' Went from a Social Justice Term to a Pejorative Favored by Some Conservatives https://edition.cnn.com/2022/07/10/us/woke-race-deconstructed-newsletter-reaj/index.html

Chapter 8

Gender Trouble, Authoritarianism, and the Flight from Womanhood

Ilene Philipson

On a cool December afternoon in 1990, three colleagues and I walked into a small lecture hall on the UC Berkeley campus, having come from the university's feminist research institute where we were scholars in residence. We had arrived to hear a philosopher who had recently published a book on feminist theory that was receiving a great deal of attention. As we took our seats toward the back of a packed hall, Judith Butler strode to the podium. Wearing a sports jacket and Oxford shirt, she appeared sophisticated and utterly androgenous. The audience quieted. Butler opened with a single question:

Who here today thinks of themselves as a woman?[1]

I recall casting glances at my friends and exchanging quizzical expressions, looks of confusion, and perhaps suspicion or mistrust. We sat suspended, silent. And no one, in an audience of 150 composed largely of women, raised her hand. We seemed to intuit that this was a trick question, that something was being asked of us that we couldn't quite decipher. Retrospectively, I believe that none of us wanted to appear foolish or to be mocked, to be the lone hand that shot up only to be exposed as naïve, uninformed, stupid.

On reflection, the reluctance that I and the other audience members exhibited that day was born of the same emotions haunting those influenced by symbolic and identitarian politics today: a profound (if seldom fully conscious) desire to belong, to be a member in good standing of the morally righteous, the enlightened, and intellectually sophisticated elite. Symbolic feminism, with its obscurantist and ironic language, which provides adherents with a sense of being in the know and superior to others, and symbolic politics in general were introduced to me that day, December 6, 1990, in Wheeler Hall on the UC Berkeley campus.

The Question

In what follows, my intention is to show how that single question—and the audience's response—presages many features of what is widely considered as

DOI: 10.4324/9781003389927-8

progressive politics today. In asking her audience if any of us believed, or by implication, was uninformed enough to believe that she was a "woman," Butler implicitly introduced the main thesis of her 1990 book *Gender Trouble.* According to that argument, gender is a social artifice. Our ideas of what constitute men and women or male and female do not correspond to anything that exists in nature, but derive exclusively from the unwitting reproduction of power relations. When we speak or act in a gendered way, we "perform" gender, thereby reproducing gendered categories and reinforcing the mistaken belief that gendered natures actually exist. For Butler, however, the word "woman" does not denote an actual category of human beings but a "performance" that constructs gendered reality. It has no relationship to biology but is thoroughly socially constructed. It is what a person *does*; not what a person *is*. Thus, her project is the destabilization of accepted categories and the disruption of the norms associated with these categories. Liberation from categorization is her goal. For Butler, categorization itself is a form of "violence." Hence the central role of language and symbolization. As it is impossible to really remove oneself from social constructions created by language and discourse according to Butler, the best we can do is to disrupt and "trouble" them, opening up spaces for those who defy dichotomous categorization. Therefore, signing one's name on email according to gendered pronouns, e.g., "she, her, hers," is now required in many elite circles to convey to the recipients that because my name is "Ilene," for example, you cannot assume that I am a woman. Nor can you assume I am a woman in all categories of speech—nominative, accusative, possessive.

In Butler's question that December day, she deployed what Martha Nussbaum termed "the politics of parody," attempting to render gender categories "absurd."

In her well-known critique of Butler's work, *The Professor of Parody: The Hip Defeatism of Judith Butler*, published nine years later, Nussbaum excoriated "the new wave of symbolic feminism" that Butler ushered in. She characterizes this wave as representing

> . . .the virtually complete turning from the material side of life, toward a type of verbal and symbolic politics that makes only the flimsiest of connections with the real situation of real women. . . [S]ymbolic gestures, it is believed, are themselves a form of political resistance; and so one need not engage with messy things such as legislatures and movements to act daringly. . . Butler's focus on the symbolic, her proud neglect of the material side of life, becomes a fatal blindness. . . Women who are hungry, illiterate, disenfranchised, beaten, raped" are erased.
>
> (Nussbaum, 1999: 38–43)

As a result of Butler's influence today and that of many postmodern colleagues and students, policing speech, troubling gender categories, arguing for gender neutral bathrooms, advocating for the use of the term "pregnant people" in lieu of pregnant women, etc. becomes a form of political theater that allows its practitioners to feel virtuous and morally superior without mastering the intricacies of the legislative process, lobbying politicians, working in a soup kitchen, or volunteering on a crisis hotline for battered women. Indeed, a clear-eyed focus on the plight of battered women as *women* must rely on the very forms of categorization that Butler and other likeminded theorists wish to disrupt.

My colleagues and I found all this incomprehensible. We were socialist-feminists who believed that meaningful social change is rooted in political economy, promoting democratic institutions, and critiquing historically situated misogyny. The claim that resistance to the "sex-gender system" as anthropologist Gayle Rubin termed it, could be achieved through the relentless disruption of verbal categories, or the "troubling" of gendered experience, seemed naïve, and well, too simple. Creating "gender trouble" through enacting androgyny, glorifying camp, or more recently employing "they" as a third person singular pronoun (as does Butler) struck us as too easy and individualistic an approach compared with the formidable challenges of transforming a capitalist economy, redistributing wealth, and/or fighting for reproductive rights.

This difference in perspectives was highlighted in an article Butler published seven years after her talk at UC Berkeley. In "Merely Cultural" (*Social Text 52/53*, 1997), Butler claimed that "normative heterosexuality and its 'genders' are . . . essential to the sexual functioning of political economy," and sees the suppression of non-normativity as representing a challenge to the capitalist order (p. 42). Such assertions seemed improbable then and are even more improbable now, given the legalization of gay marriage in 2015, and the fact that gay relationships are now widely accepted and actively celebrated in American arts and popular culture. Economic inequality, unchecked by the state, is at the heart of the capitalist enterprise. Non-normativity is not. Today multinational corporations do not oppose the rights of queer and trans people. In fact, leading corporations in the technology, media, and consumer products sectors embrace them as potential consumers. It is cultural and religious conservatives who wish to turn back the clock and re-instate heteronormativity.

Finally, the larger context in which Judith Butler posed her question in 1990 is elucidated in the work of socialist-feminist philosopher Nancy Fraser. A long-time critic of Butler's work, Fraser notes that

> the feminist "movement shifted its attention to cultural politics, just as a rising neoliberalism declared war on social equality. . . that wanted nothing more than to repress all memory of social egalitarianism. . . Unable to transform the deep gender structures of the capitalist economy, they [the symbolic feminists] preferred to target harms rooted in androcentric patterns of cultural value or status hierarchies. The result was a major shift in the feminist imaginary: whereas the previous generation had sought to remake political economy, this one focused more on transforming culture."
>
> (2002: 1–6 *passim*)

Butler's symbolic feminism which focuses on representation, language, and performance arose in tandem with free-market fundamentalism and the most extreme forms of economic inequality. Like other critics of this perspective (cf. Lange and Pickett-Depaolis), I maintain that the current emphasis on language, representation, and culture over people's deteriorating economic circumstances and the steady erosion of democracy is a form of distraction, displacement, and obfuscation that now has entered mainstream political life. One could argue that symbolic politics have become the dominant ideology of late capitalism precisely *because* of these functions, that is, the displacement of materiality with identity, discourse, and cultural symbols as the focus of attention and resistance.

The Audience Reaction

In retrospect, the question Butler posed in 1990 elicited a variety of affects that now pervade feminist and progressive politics today. While we certainly experienced confusion or uncertainty about the purpose of the question, our shared reluctance to stand up or to assert our status as women was born of fear—the fear of getting it wrong, of being ridiculed, of being looked down upon, of appearing foolish, naïve, uninformed, un-hip.

By making parody a privileged mode of communication, Butler demonstrated contempt and separation from the past as well as a desire to subvert more common forms of understanding or representation. After all, Butler might have begun by simply stating "today I will argue that the category of *woman* has no relationship to anything occurring in nature and is constituted by performance." But instead, she chose to "trouble" conventional forms of presentation and attempted to lure unwitting audience members into becoming foils for mimicry and mockery. Intuitively, the entire audience knew not to take the bait. We sensed a hidden agenda and remained silent as a form of self-protection.

When my colleagues and I went to hear Butler, we carried with us the conviction that *sisterhood is powerful.* The eponymous book edited by Robin Morgan, published in 1970, was the handbook of what was then called the women's liberation movement (Morgan, 1970). In the following years we encountered some very cogent criticism of the idea that women should be seen as a discrete class or group, irrespective of their race or sexual orientation. But in 1990 this critique went further, questioning the very existence of the category *woman* outside of performative, social construction. The tacit implication of this critique was that "women's liberation" would eventually require our being "liberated" *from the very idea of womanhood itself.* As a result, today's obsession with symbols, language, and personal attitudes outweighs concerns about homelessness, the feminization of poverty, the increasing burdens of women parenting alone, and the damaging effects of pornography on women's sexual lives to name but a few. These pressing issues have much less cache than concerns about the existence of Civil War statues, the number of non-whites nominated for Academy Awards, serve on boards of directors, or pictured in advertising. The call for recognition of rapidly multiplying identities (e.g., we now have LGBTQIA2S+) has obfuscated and overshadowed what Nancy Fraser has termed "redistributive politics." She describes the difference between *redistribution* and *recognition* as the basis of political action as follows:

> "Members of the first camp hope to redistribute wealth from the rich to the poor, from the North to the South, and from the owners to the workers. Members of the second, in contrast, seek recognition of the distinctive perspectives of ethnic, racial, and sexual minorities. . ."
>
> (2001: 21)

At a time in which "an aggressively expanding capitalism is radically exacerbating economic inequality. . . questions of recognition are serving less to supplement, complicate, and enrich redistributive struggles than to marginalize, eclipse and displace them." Proponents of recognition or symbolic politics "suppose that maldistribution is merely a secondary effect of misrecognition. For them, economic inequalities are simple expressions of cultural hierarchies" so that "no explicit politics of redistribution is needed" (2000: 112). Thus, many people now imagine that if we only ended "systemic racism" and transphobia all would be well. Collective inattention to and apparent ignorance of the exploitation inherent in a capitalist economy is all too common.

An excellent example of the distinction between the politics of recognition and redistribution is described by Columbia professor and *New York Times* columnist, John McWhorter:

> In 2020, the long-serving curator of the San Francisco Museum of Modern Art, Gary Garrels, announced to his staff that he had successfully acquired new works by artists of color. He concluded his remarks by stating: "Don't worry. We will definitely still continue to collect white artists. Failing to do so would be reverse discrimination." This was met with outrage by his staff; he was branded a racist for even suggesting something such as reverse discrimination could exist, and forced to resign. As McWhorter concludes: "The Garrels episode bears some further examination. He was fired for using a term. Meanwhile, less than a mile's walk away, in the Tenderloin of San Francisco, there cluster legions of people who can't afford housing and live their lives in makeshift tents on the street. If censuring Garrels for his lexicon has any connection to the 'structures' keeping people on the streets, it's rather brutally indirect."
>
> (2021: 72–73)

If recent trends are any indication, this foregrounding of symbolic politics and what is considered allowable speech reaches it apotheosis in the struggles surrounding the issue of trans, even more so than with race. It is in the domain that Butler and many of her colleagues and disciples wished to trouble, that we see most clearly how the use of parody and derision has mutated into dogmatic belief, moral certitude, and in many cases, contempt, dismissal, and often pure hatred of anyone who holds onto "untroubled" categories.

The Trans Revolution

When Judith Butler addressed us in 1990, no one anticipated the upheaval in much of western societies' understanding of gender that would soon ensue. Her argument was posed in defiance of the universal and rigidly adhered to belief that gender was dichotomous and rooted in biology. This universality and rigidity were precisely what made her claims seem radical. She was taking on the given, the assumed, what seemed "natural." Today, as a result, the belief that human beings can be "born into the wrong body," and the right of people to declare themselves whatever gender they choose and have that declaration respected by law is defended by many with equal rigidity. In classrooms, passports, census records, criminal courts, public spaces, competitive sports, that is, virtually every aspect of our lives, trans identities are increasingly recognized. The United Nations and *The New York Times* have blithely replaced the term "pregnant women" with "pregnant people," and *The Cambridge Dictionary* has expanded its definition of the word "woman" to include "an adult who lives and identifies as female."

Transgender activism has become the main battleground upon which symbolic politics are enacted.[2] There is little question that transitioning benefits many people and improves their mental health. But it is important to distinguish what I am calling "trans activism" from "transgendered people or subjects." As Lisa Selin Davis and Christina Buttons have pointed out, these are separate categories. While there is some overlap, the majority of activists seem *not* to be individuals who are transitioning or have transitioned.

It is my assertion that those participating in trans activism increasingly have moved in an authoritarian direction. Its underlying premise is that liberation and freedom can be achieved through an ever-expanding celebration of diverse sexual and gender identities. Many of its supporters are engaged in a moral crusade to praise and glorify that expanding list, arguing for adherence to a set of principles that are considered incontrovertible, morally superior, and not open to argument or critique—a dogmatic stance often sustained through authoritarian behavior. Within the trans activist community, any feminist who disagrees with the current consensus among progressives is designated a TERF (Trans Exclusionary Radical Feminist) and is subjected to ridicule, public shaming, and sometimes literal death threats. Even more importantly, it is *not* typically people on the right who are subject to these forms of enforcement, but rather fellow feminists and progressives. We are the ones who are both open and vulnerable to the crusade in a way that people outside the left-liberal sphere are not. Why? Because for a person on the left, charges of being transphobic can entail irreparable harm to one's reputation and livelihood, rendering one a pariah, shunned by friends, left organizations, and/or employment.

This brand of left-wing authoritarianism conceals a fundamental contradiction undergirding the trans movement's symbolic politics, and prevents it from coming to light. As we have seen, Butler asserts that "a true gender identity" is "a regulatory fiction," and as such is maintained exclusively through performativity (1990, 192), because *woman* is not a biological entity, but rather a performance that constructs a gendered reality. It is what a person *does*; it is not who "she" *is*.

Nevertheless, large numbers of social media influencers, medical professionals, college students, and people who are wondering why they are depressed, isolated, and anxious are embracing the idea that being trapped in the "wrong body" is a common human problem. Presumably this misfortune is a sad trick of nature that can be remedied by a growing group of professionals and a pharmaceutical industry eager to release trans people into their "correct" bodies—albeit for a price. But this stance is based on the unproven assumption that one's "true" gender ***can*** be "known," and is ***not*** merely performed. Where this knowledge is derived remains moot, unspecified. Is the source of this "knowledge" psychological or neurological in origin? Apprehended with one's mind or heart or soul? There is little interest in such questions. Even expressing interest in pursuing such inquiry implies the existence of doubt, and by implication, a failure to wholeheartedly accept trans ideology, opening one to the charge of heresy, transphobia.

How can we reasonably maintain that gender is a "regulatory fiction," *and* that it is inherent, immutable, essential, and knowable at the same time? As sociologist Rogers Brubaker writes in his book *Trans:*

> "gender identity is at once subjective and objective. It is *defined* by one's subjective 'sense of self,' but the sense of self is understood as *grounded* in some objective---if at present still unknown---aspect of one's biological being. The sources of subjectivity are situated outside the realm of choice and reflexive self-transformation, outside the realm of culture, and even, paradoxically, outside the self. In this way the defense of gender voluntarism is pushed into essentialist terrain."
>
> (2016: 36)

The widespread failure to acknowledge this contradiction falls into the category of George Orwell's *doublethink*: "To know and not to know. . . to hold simultaneously two opinions which cancelled out, knowing them to be contradictory and believing in both of them. . ." (1949: 32). N.S. Lyons goes further, asserting that ". . . this is nihilism. It is like floating in a world without gravity; there is no way to know which way is up and which way is down and there is nothing that holds the world together. The result is the existential equivalent of vertigo and a society that is coming apart" (2022).

This vertiginous contradiction which is oblivious to itself is exacerbated and overlaid by an increasing acceptance of regressive gender stereotypes which are often misconstrued as heralding "a new stage in the mainstreaming of transgender identity" (Brubaker: 3). By way of example, consider Caitlyn Jenner's appearance on the cover of *Vanity Fair* magazine on June 25, 2015. Bruce Jenner, the Olympic gold medalist, willingly took cross-sex hormones, shaved his trachea, had all of his body and facial hair removed, his hairline changed, his forehead contoured, his jaw and chin surgically augmented, and his chest implanted with large, silicone breasts in order to resemble not what most natal women look like today, but rather a Hollywood movie star from the 1950s (think Jayne Mansfield). This resurgence of mid-20th-century gender stereotypes has strangely gained currency not only among adult transitioners, but within the medical profession itself. As Kathleen Stock has pointed out: "Many of the supposedly tell-tale signs of gender dysphoria among trans-identified children seem like stereotypes plucked out of ladies home-furnishing magazines from the early Cold War era" (2019).

This observation is born out in the work of Diane Ehrensaft, Director of Mental Health at the University of California, San Francisco Child and Adolescent Gender Center, an oft cited author and lecturer on trans children. In a lecture Ehrensaft gave, available on YouTube under the title, *Barrettes: Diane Ehrensaft*, a member of the audience asks if we can identify trans children who are preverbal, that is, between the ages of one and two. Ehrensaft replies that indeed we can. Such children, she says, are "very action oriented." She tells us of a colleague who was born female and that there is a video of her at two, tearing barrettes from her hair. "That's a gender message. . . And if it happens once or twice, that's a gender message. . . So, you look for those kinds of actions, like tearing a skirt off" or tearing barrettes from one's hair to discern gender dysphoria and the child's need to be recognized as transgendered. She then relates a story of a one-year-old boy who unsnaps his onesie to "make it into a dress" and let it flow. "That's a preverbal communication about gender" adding that "children will know by the beginning of the second year of life" that they are misgendered.

Ehrensaft is recognized by the US government as an authority in her field and has been chosen by the National Institutes of Health as a principal investigator in a five-year study of the medical and mental health outcomes of children receiving puberty blockers and/or cross-sex hormones. Yet, she asserts that preverbal children can express their inherent misgendering by an act as superficial as removing barrettes from their hair or unfastening constraining garments, producing virtually no compelling evidence in support of these extravagant claims. She ignores Occam's Razor, the methodological precept embraced by most scientists until now, namely, that the simplest explanation is usually the best. I am relieved that Ehrensaft wasn't around when I was a child, as my dislike of having my hair tied in a ponytail might have prompted my family to have me placed on puberty blockers.

Though it may not be immediately apparent, Ehrensaft seems to be taking the gender stereotypes of her own childhood in the 1940s and 50s as innate forms of gender expression. Traditionally, in most western countries, young children were dressed the same—white dresses for both boys and girls and each had long hair. According to Cydney Grannan, the "Baby Boomers in the 1940s were the first to be dressed in the sex-specific clothing that Americans are familiar with today.

Boys and girls were [now] dressed like miniature men and women instead of uniformly in children's dresses." Therefore, asserting that children's dislike of particular forms of dress that are characteristic of a particular society at a particular historical juncture has become a poor substitute for robust empirical verification of gender dysphoria. Moreover, Ehrensaft overturns the most basic premise of gender as social construction, claiming that children come into the world not only knowing the specifics of gendered clothing in their particular societies, but that they ended up in the "wrong" body.

The essentialist determinism reflected in Ehrensaft's pronouncements serves to ignore and obfuscate significant and disturbing trends in the numbers of young people seeking to transition. The number of youths who identify as transgender nearly doubled from 2017 to 2020 (Ghorayshi, 2022). But the more remarkable trend is the recent reversal of *who* is seeking to transition. Traditionally, it was males who wished to become females. This desire is not only reflected in the historical statistics regarding gender dysphoria but also in our cultural awareness of transvestites and drag queens. However, in 2012 that state of affairs began to change. Because Britain's National Health Service keeps detailed records of its medical services, NHS's Tavistock Gender Identity Development Service (GIDS) provides a wealth of information about patients seeking to transition.

> In 2009/10 there were 32 girls and 40 boys referred to Tavistock GIDS. In 2011/12 the sex ratio reversed and the gap between boys and girls has continued to widen year on year ever since. The total number of referrals for 2018/19 in England alone is 624 boys and 1,740 girls. In less than a decade there has been a 1,460% increase of boys and a staggering 5,337% increase in girls" (Transgender Trends, 2022).
>
> In 2016, natal females accounted for 46% of all sex reassignment surgeries in the United States. A year later, it was 70%.
>
> (Shrier: 33)

Today the adolescent girl is the more common but often less recognized trans identified subject. While political battles are raging over whether natal men who have transitioned to female should be allowed in female spaces, such as bathrooms, female prisons, and in women's sports competitions, the growing number of girls who wish to be boys remains relatively unnoticed. One might think that this phenomenon would be of profound interest to feminists. But it is not. To interrogate this desire, this flight from womanhood, remains uninteresting if womanhood is construed exclusively as performance, and if the process of altering that performance is privileged and venerated. Philosopher Kathleen Stock sees Butler and her followers as "sex eliminationists," who believe that "we should remove any social practice whatsoever that would serve to differentiate trans people from those who are born into their preferred sex category" (2019). To ask why a girl wishes to be a male, or more importantly, why increasing *numbers* of girls have this wish, might call attention to the reasons motivating such desire, which in turn detracts from the unquestioned and unqualified celebration of gender transitioning. It might, in fact, "serve to differentiate trans people from those who are born into their preferred sex category."

Trans As The New Penis Envy?

In 1925, Sigmund Freud asserted

> a momentous discovery which little girls are destined to make. . .
>
> They notice the penis of a brother or playmate, strikingly visible and of large proportions, at once recognize it as the superior counterpart of their own small and inconspicuous organ, and from that time forward fall a victim to envy for the penis.
>
> (1925/1974: 20)

Freud's disciple, Karl Abraham, embellished Freud's claim, noting that with "extraordinary frequency. . . a great number of women have repressed the wish to be male" and cope with this nagging though often unconscious desire by developing "the following idea: 'I had a penis once as boys have, but it has been taken away from me. . . She therefore endeavors to represent the painfully perceived defect as a secondary loss and one resulting from castration" (1920/1974: 109, 110).

Freud and Abraham's notion of an innate and universal penis envy was a reification and an evasion of historically constructed social relations that remained unseen by Freud. Given his tendency to construe traits and behaviors that he saw in himself and those around him in fin de siècle Vienna as universal and unchanging, Freud misread women's envy of what men possessed as some deep, essential, and biologically-based characteristic. Abraham deepened this misconception by suggesting that women who wish to be male are transforming "their primary defect," their lack of masculinity, into a belief that they had possessed a penis but it was taken away from them.

It wasn't until Karen Horney, Abraham's analysand, wrote "The Flight from Womanhood," in 1926 that a countervailing view was cautiously introduced into the psychoanalytic canon. While she too noted the widespread "desire to be a man, so familiar to us from the analyses of adult women," she asserted that this desire "had only very little to do with that early, infantile, primary penis envy. . ." Instead, she suggested another possibility:

> It seems to me impossible to judge to how great a degree the unconscious motives for the flight from womanhood are reinforced by the actual social subordination of women. One might conceive of the connection as an interaction of psychic and social factors. But I can only indicate these problems here, for they are so grave and so important that they require a separate investigation.
>
> (Horney, 1926/1994: 179/184)

Today we are also faced with the need to investigate into what Horney termed the flight from womanhood. Just as early 20th-century psychoanalysts were addressing their female patients' desire to be men, in the early 21st century we find a dramatic increase in girls and young women voicing the same desire. And as was the case with Freud, Abraham, and the majority of their colleagues, the response appears to be to posit an innate, essentialist explanation rather than a social one to account for the wish to be a man.

The "actual social subordination of women" that Horney identified in 1926 as a cause of women's envy of men looks quite different today. Economic, cultural, political, and ideological forms of sexism have changed radically over the last century. But the remarkable increase in the number of girls who claim they are trapped in bodies they despise and feel estranged from still serves as a displaced, concretized, and/or dissociated form of rebellion against societal norms focused on the female body.

With the pornification of our culture, male fantasies of what women should look like—enormous breasts, buttocks, and lips—have become increasingly prevalent. The average age at which girls first view online porn is 11 (Shrier: 23). Social media, with a global audience of three billion, telegraphs images of what female bodies should look like daily, minute by minute, second by second, to adolescent girls who are its most constant users. Hence, we see the advent of widely available forms of plastic surgery allowing females to resemble one of the Kardashians, as many girls and young women turn to breast augmentation, buttock lifts, lip fillers, and liposuction to comply with the interests and desires of the pornography-shaped male gaze.

An altogether different message comes from the fashion industry and celebrity culture that permeates the internet. Due to the rise of social media and its monopolization of many adolescent girls' lives, "pro-ana" sites, influencers, videos, and podcasts promote anorexia as an enviable means of coping with body dysmorphia or hatred of one's body. Celebrities such as Kate Middleton, Princess of Wales, singer Ariana Grande, and actress Angelina Jolie are widely followed, and their protruding bones and sleek figures reflect what is widely perceived as masterly control over their bodies. As author Lea Muldtofte describes in her essay, "The Grace of My Perfect Skeleton: An Autoethnographic Analysis of the Anorexic Body":

> I started talking through the visibility of bones, creating a space where no one could interrupt me. . . [T]he praxis of anorexia speaks just as much about the disorder of the culture surrounding body-ideals. . .as it does of the disorder with the anorexic mind, . . . a practice of protest with a high level of agency.
>
> (2018)

Expectations of surgically facilitated voluptuousness on the one hand, or "the visibility of bones" on the other, are not altogether new. However, their means of entrance into the minds of adolescent girls is. According to Lukianoff and Haidt, girls use social media more than boys and are more concerned about inclusion and conformity. As they point out,

> Another consequence of social media curation is that girls are bombarded with images of girls and women whose beauty is artificially enhanced, making girls ever more insecure about their own appearance. It's not just fashion models whose images are altered nowadays; platforms such as Snapchat and Instagram provide 'filters' that girls use to enhance the selfies they pose for and edit, so even their *friends* now seem to be more beautiful. These filters make noses smaller, lips bigger, and skin smoother. This has led to a new phenomenon: some young women now want plastic surgery to make themselves look like they do in their enhanced selfies.
>
> (2016: 155)

The adolescents who account for the remarkable increase in females seeking gender reassignment today discovered their trans identities in their teenage years, and in one study, only "after a prolonged period of social media immersion" (Shrier: 26). The CDC finds that 53% of girls reported extreme depressive symptoms in 2023 (Ghorayshi, 2024). I argue that, in part, the current flight from womanhood is an attempt to escape what Karen Horney referred to as the social subordination of women. Obviously, these are not the forms of subordination that existed in the 1920s, but rather are embedded in the visual, cultural norms that motivate women to look and be a certain way. In many cases, the adolescent onset of gender dysphoria can be viewed as a concretized and bodily-based form of rebellion against the confines of normative 21st-century femininity. Envy of what is perceived as men's freedom is at its root. Given the obvious monetary benefits to the pharmaceutical industry, to plastic surgeons, and therapists practicing affirmative therapy, transitioning has become a readily accessible choice, a choice that is increasingly celebrated and lionized.

The observation by psychoanalysts of a century ago that many of their female patients wished to be men, seems surprisingly salient in the 21st century. Why the flight from womanhood has reemerged now is as "grave and important" a question as it was in 1926 when Horney posed it. But it is ***not*** a question being asked by Butler and those influenced by postmodernism who maintain that the troubling of gender, symbolism, camp, irony, and parody are primary concerns, who are uninterested in such pressing questions.

A Case Study

"Olivia/Oliver" is a self-proclaimed gender fluid adolescent who came for therapy as a recent high school graduate. She was considering taking testosterone to transition to male from being a biological female. "O," as she and I agreed for me to call her, had never had close friends, suffered from tremendous social anxiety, but had excelled in school, particularly in math and science. As the only child of liberal professionals who spent inordinate amounts of time at work, O was accustomed to being alone and pursuing a variety of rather arcane interests on the internet (e.g., studying Finnish). O had been accepted into an elite liberal arts college on the East Coast and was extremely worried about leaving home and having to live in a women's dorm. She felt that girls demanded emotional involvement in their friendships, while boys seemed more interested in "stuff, things you can study and learn about." The thought of having to share a dorm room with a girl seemed terrifying. "A guy would just leave me alone," she confidently told me.

O had a long history of being bullied and made fun of. Socially and physically awkward, she would eat lunch in the library and dreaded field trips, team sports, and any extracurricular activities. She believed that transitioning would allow her to have a ready-made community as she observed that the trans-club at her school was remarkably welcoming of "people who don't fit in like me." She pointed out that in her large, public high school there were student organizations for Blacks, Latinos, Asians, queer, and trans students but nothing for her to join. "How does a white person fit in if you're not gender fluid or trans? There's no place, and it's not like I can join the women's basketball team!" O could not even catch a ball so certainly organized sports were not an option.

It did not take long for me to speculate that O was on the autistic spectrum, and I asked her if she had ever received any neuropsychological testing. O said she thought she had not, but would ask her mother. A day later I received an irate call from O's mother. She left a message for me saying decisively that there was nothing wrong with O that would require testing. Her daughter had gender dysphoria and needed to transition, period!

Over the next few months as O and I explored the deeper reasons for her desire to transition, we began to talk about the ways in which being trans felt like her only option, the only way out of a life of aloneness and misrecognition. By listening carefully to what she told me about conversations with her mother, I began to think that having a trans son was somehow more acceptable to this mother than acknowledging that her daughter was on the autistic spectrum. O not only wanted to escape the emotional demands of being in a dorm room with a girl, but wished to assume an identity that would give her social standing, a community, and maternal approval.

O's situation vividly illustrates how in certain circles transgenderism is not merely accepted but venerated. O's desire to transition was the means of escape from an unwelcoming world and simultaneously a profound collusion with her mother's intolerance of her autism and wish for her daughter to rank higher on the oppression hierarchy. I surmised that performing complete acceptance of a trans son also might place this mother on a hierarchy of her own, in the hip, politically progressive universe that celebrates gender non-conformity.

Why Trans is Good for Business

Today, left-wing politics are focused on diversity and inclusion of marginalized identities, but there seems to be little interest in *what* these identities are being included. As long as people of color and queer and trans individuals are represented in politics, film, boardrooms, classrooms, sports, etc., what these marginalized individuals believe in, or the nature of the enterprise into which they are included, is of little interest. Likewise, anyone or any organization that supports their inclusion is deemed worthy of support. It is out of this narrowness of vision that symbolic feminists and trans activists ignore the economic interests of Big Pharma, "trans-tech," and the medical profession enjoy from the growing acceptance of transgender ideology and the attendant increase in people transitioning. In stunning contrast to Butler's claim that heteronormativity and traditional genders are essential to the functioning of the capitalist economy, the process of transitioning has become a growth industry. And those benefiting from that growth are celebrating its ever-expanding market.

In the "U.S. Sex Reassignment Surgery Market Size, Share and Trends Analysis Report" for the American Society of Plastic Surgeons (Group View Research, 2022), the following is offered:

> The U.S. sex reassignment surgery market size was valued at USD 1.9 billion in 2021 and is expected to expand at a compound annual growth rate of 11/23% from 2022 to 2030. The rising incidences of gender dysphoria and the increasing number of people opting for gender confirmation surgeries are expected to boost the growth during the forecast period. . .
>
> Based on gender transition, the market is segmented into male-to-female and female-to-male. The FTM segment dominated the market in 2021 with the largest revenue share. This is attributed to continuous innovations in metoidioplasty, phalloplasty, scrotoplasty, and chest reconstructing. . .
>
> The companies contributing to the market growth are focusing on adopting several strategies to strengthen their market presence. They are offering advanced and innovative surgical solutions. . . Companies are investing in LGBTQ+ healthcare. . .

There is now a new "trans-tech" industry funded by venture capitalists who are seizing on those curious about transitioning. According to *Forbes Magazine*:

> Trans-tech is a budding industry. . . Our estimates place the average cost of transitioning at $150,000 per person. Multiply that by an estimated population of 1.4 million transgender people, we're talking a market in excess of $200 billion. That is significant. That's larger than the entire film industry.
>
> (Wright, 2020)

Eurphoria.LGBT, Inc is a for-profit company that offers "a complete suite of technologies, enabling a better transition." It advertises itself as "The All-In-One Prospecting Solution Built with You in Mind." It allows a member to "choose the right crunchbase solution for you," beginning at $29.00/month for a "Starter Membership," or a "Pro Membership (our most popular)" for $49.00. Euphoria. LGBT also offers a suite of for-profit apps, *Clarity*, *Solace*, and *Bliss*.

Plume and *Folx* are venture capital-funded, online subscription-based businesses that provide transitioners with online doctors' appointments, prescriptions, and drug delivery at the cost of $99 to $139 per month; although that does not include the cost of the drugs. Neither of these for-profit companies accepts medical insurance. *Plume* initially received $14 million in start-up funds, and in 2022, it took in another $24 million from venture capitalists who clearly are betting on trans as a growth industry.

Finally, there is little question that Big Pharma benefits from transitioners' life-long need for drugs to maintain their acquired identities. Makers of estrogen and testosterone clearly benefit from this market. But now Abbvie, the maker of Lupron, which was a drug developed to treat prostate cancer but is now used as a hormone blocker for gender dysphoric youth, reports that it made $726 million on this drug alone in 2018.

Many pharmaceutical companies fund transgender activism. An example is Gilead, ranked only #14 in global drug company profitability, due to the fact that it earned a meager $24.69 billion in 2020 as compared to the #1 ranked company, Johnson & Johnson, that took in $82.6 billion. Despite its relatively low ranking, Gilead doubled its grant award to the transgender community in 2019 to $4.5 million. Its stated reasoning was as follows: "Gilead's portfolio of HIV focused treatments, including medications such Biktarvy and Truvada, intersects with the needs of the transgender community, a community that's disproportionately impacted by HIV" (Bulik, 2019).

Through its compassionate language that recognizes the trans community's seemingly unfair treatment through it being "disproportionately impacted," Gilead positions itself as an enlightened and caring corporate entity. However, six days before this announcement, it was reported that Gilead was "converting Truvada PrEP users to Descovy faster than expected": "One big task for Gilead Sciences' HIV franchise in the coming year is to save some $2.5 billion in annual sales by switching as many PrEP patients as possible from Truvada to newly approved Descovy *before generics hit*" (emphasis added, Liu, 2019). In other words, Gilead is attempting to insure corporate profits over people's access to far more affordable generic drugs. Through promoting itself as a transgender supporter, it is attempting to secure its place in the trans marketplace that purportedly has a large segment of HIV patients. A $4.5 million grant to trans activists seems like a lot. But compared to the company's efforts to maintain $2.5 billion in annual sales, it is insignificant.

While all of these companies exploit trans people's interests, desires, and needs, they are offering services and drugs that actually can be used by that community.

However, we recently have witnessed the beginnings of corporations using trans to sell products that have nothing to do with serving transitioners. The most widely disseminated example of this, at the time of this writing, is a television commercial produced by J&B Whiskey. It is entitled "She" and has a running time of over three minutes with remarkable production values and a surprise ending. It opens with a grandfather in a rural Spanish village buying and applying make-up to his face so that he resembles an elderly woman. At a sepia toned, Christmas dinner, the grandfather coaxes his grandson into the bathroom and lovingly applies his newfound skills as a cosmetologist to his grandson's face. Viewers suddenly realize that the grandfather's efforts to learn about cosmetics was not for himself but his grandson. When the two enter the dining room together, family members look surprised and then tear up and embrace their new, trans granddaughter with a toast of. . . J&B Whiskey. The commercial has been watched by millions of people around the globe on YouTube and has been featured in news stories, such as "A Spanish Whiskey Commercial with a Trans Storyline is Making the Internet Cry," and "I Don't think I've Ever Watched a Commercial So Full of Love and Compassion" (Monteil, 2022).

This hardly is the first time social movements based in individual "freedom of choice" have been exploited by corporations to increase their profits. In the 1920s, the burgeoning tobacco industry encouraged women's smoking by exploiting the goals of the early feminist movement. In light of First Wave feminism's promotion of individual liberation after gaining the franchise in 1920, the advertising industry coined the term "Torches of Freedom," that is, cigarettes, as symbols of emancipation and equality with men. Individual choice, as opposed to the fight over political and economic concerns, can be easily incorporated into marketing portfolios and advertising campaigns. Thus, trans ideology may be less about social injustice, exploitation, or oppression as about individual journeys of being lost and then found, alienated from one's very self and then finding redemption. It is very much about individual choice, and as such, can be molded and preyed upon by corporate interests. Proponents of trans ideology think they are radical. But in many ways, they are unwitting accomplices and accommodators to corporate interests and those of elite professionals.

This strange symbiosis largely goes unnoticed due to the triumph of symbolic, representational, identity politics over those that recognize the larger role of political economy, social class, and the need for an explicit politics of redistribution. There are several feminist authors who have written books criticizing the widespread promotion and acceptance of trans ideology. Kathleen Stock and Helen Joyce from the UK, and Abigail Shrier and Janice Raymond from the US all have contributed important books on the subject. But none of them places trans in the overall context of the rise of identitarianism, and the ways in which the focus on marginalized identities, in general, allows us to ignore where real power resides. An early critic of this trend, sociologist Todd Gitlin, presciently wrote in 1996: "While the right has been busy taking the White House, the left has been marching on the English department." This pithy observation reflects the way the left has been enveloped in debates around politically correct language, symbols, and what gets expressed on college campuses and other elite institutions, while the right has been securing the Supreme Court, state legislatures, local governments, and now the House of Representatives. With their increasing political power, right-wing strategists and politicians consolidate the economic inequality and corporate domination that deformed American politics in the 21st century. As tears are shed around the globe for the acceptance of a trans granddaughter brought to us courtesy of a whiskey purveyor, we have stopped shedding tears for the tens of thousands of homeless people who fill our urban landscapes. We have become inured to the casualties of our neoliberal order.

Witch Hunt

> If *you wish to expel religion from our European civilization you can only do it through another system of doctrines, and from the outset this would take over all the psychological characteristics of religion, the same sanctity, rigidity, and intolerance, the same prohibition of thought in self-defense.*
>
> Sigmund Freud, *Future of an Illusion*

Greg Lukianoff and Jonathan Haidt point out that political witch hunts "arise quickly" and "appear in dramatic outbursts. . . Whether one thinks of the Reign of Terror during the French Revolution, the Stalinist Show Trials, or the McCarthy period in the United States, the phenomenon is the same: a community becomes intensely mobilized to rid itself of internal enemies." Another cardinal feature of witch hunts, they tell us, is the silence of others, that is, a fear of defending the accused. "When a public accusation is made, many friends and bystanders know the victim is innocent, but they are afraid to say anything. Anyone who comes to the defense of the accused is obstructing the enactment of a collective ritual" (2018: 101, 102).

Today, scholars who interrogate and criticize trans ideology are being harassed, erased, de-platformed, and threatened. To review but a sample: Kathleen Stock, a philosophy professor at the University of Sussex in England, was forced to resign her position due to her open and emphatic disagreement with Butler's basic thesis. In her book, *Material Girls: Why Reality Matters for Feminism*, she argues that biological sex is real and criticizes the idea that transwomen are "truly" women. In response, hundreds of British academics signed an open letter to the British government condemning it for its honoring Stock as an Officer of the Order of the British Empire. Large numbers of students called for her dismissal and took to the streets, clad in ski masks, brandishing flares and banners demanding "Stock Out!" Her office door was defaced and her lectures were disrupted. She resigned due to what she calls a "witch hunt." Kathleen Lowrey, an Associate Professor of Anthropology at the University of Alberta was dismissed eight months into what was supposed to be a three-year appointment as associate chair of undergraduate studies because she was creating an "unsafe" learning environment by expressing gender-critical feminist views. When Lisa Littman, a public health researcher, used parents' reports in an attempt to study why so many adolescent girls were claiming to be trans, Diane Ehrensaft told *The Economist* that such a study was akin to "recruiting from Klan or alt-Right sites to demonstrate that blacks really were an inferior race" (Shrier: 28–29). Professor Allan Josephson was fired by the University of Louisville School of Medicine for asserting: "the notion that gender identity should trump chromosomes, hormones, internal reproductive organs, external genitalia and secondary sex characteristics is counter to medical science" (Watkins, 2019). Graduate students at the University of Southern Maine staged a walkout of her class and demanded that Professor Christy Hammer be fired because she claimed that only two sexes exist (Levine, 2022).

I doubt that when Judith Butler asked who considered themself a woman she imagined the widespread dogma, hatred, and certitude her ideas, in many ways, would inspire. As part of the postmodern capture of the university that Butler heralded, we have witnessed what historian, Russell Jacoby has called "the invasion of the public square by the campus." He chronicles how, by the late 1990s, universities could no longer provide jobs for the growing ranks of doctoral students, particularly in the humanities. These PhDs ended up working in think tanks, NGOs, non-profits, and writing for all forms of media. Thus, the "buzz words of the campus–diversity, inclusion, microaggressions, power differential, white privilege, group safety—have become the buzz words in public life" (Jacoby, 2022). But of equal importance is the silence and implied tolerance of so many to the public bullying, censure, and denial of free speech that surrounds us. The lack of courage, the fear that I and every woman in the audience evinced in response to Butler's question still haunts me. My silence, my desire to fit-in and avoid potential ridicule now reverberates throughout vast segments of our society. Symbolic politics, the mob rule of the internet that enforces adherence to the ever-changing rules of correct speech, and threatens violators with expulsion—from social media, friendship groups, jobs, and careers—poses a formidable challenge to democracy and freedom of expression. Those of us who know this but do not speak out against this new religion, this new form of intolerance, do so at our own peril. After all, those who speak out today do not merely face mockery or ridicule as we may have in that lecture hall. Rather, they face both denigration and contempt on social media, death threats, and the very real possibility of losing their jobs, their funding, their reputations for the crime of using what is considered the wrong words or believing there is a necessary relationship between biological sex and gender. With the breakdown of civil society, of religion, and of agreed upon social norms, we are left with a new religion, a moral crusade that worships at the feet of marginalized identities and privileges language, more so than acts, as evidence of true belief. As Michael Lind observed, we are

> reviving the preliberal, premodern religious approach to society, conceived of as a congregation of the virtuous and like-minded. Either you are a true believer or you are a heretic. There can be no compromise with wicked people, and

> the chief measure of wickedness is not action—dumping toxins in a river or engaging in overt discrimination on the basis of race—but expressing disapproved attitudes and refusing to use ritualized politically correct language.
>
> (Lind, 2016)

If we returned today to Wheeler Hall on the UC Berkeley campus and Judith Butler asked "who here today thinks of themselves as a woman?" I imagine a similar silence would settle over the audience. But this time, a few hands would probably shoot up or a few audience members would stand, and they would stand tall, taller than most of those assembled. They would loudly and proudly proclaim "I am!!!" And those of us, born female, would likely cheer, in acknowledgment that those born male can now make this proclamation. And in our applause and acknowledgment, we would be cheering for the rights of all trans men and women to live free of fear and persecution, experiencing the same respect afforded everyone, and acknowledge that transitioning really does benefit many people's mental health. However, many—like myself—will also see that it is both a significant achievement these trans women can be so fearless and proud, and simultaneously a tremendous loss for those of us who still believe there is a substantive connection between sex and gender, biology and social construction. If there is any throughline from the audience reaction in 1990 to today, it is in the Orwellian idea of groupthink. Out of fear, cowardice, and/or the desire for acceptance, we go along, rationalize our silence, and permit the loudest, most fervent and determined to hold sway. Whether we like it or not, we are the ones who enable the witch hunt. It is in response to this reflection that I, at last, raise my hand and say yes, I am a woman. Hopefully, it is not too late.

Notes

1 Given that there exists no extant recording or transcript of this lecture to my knowledge, I have relied on my memory and that of my colleagues. Thus, the question may have been "who believes they are a woman," or "who considers herself to be a woman," or any variant thereof.

2 As author Lisa Selin Davis notes there is a Venn Diagram between Transgender Activists who may or may not be transgender themselves and transgender people. In the center of the interlocking circles are those who are transgender subjects and activists.

References

Abraham, Karl 1920/1974. "Manifestations of the Female Castration Complex." in Jean Strouse (Ed.) *Women and Analysis*. New York, NY: Grossman Publishers.

Brubaker, Rogers 2016. *Trans: Gender and Race in an Age of Unsettled Identities*. Princeton, NJ: Princeton University Press.

Bulik, Beth Synder 2019. "Gilead Doubles Transgender Community Awards to $4.5 Million." *Fierce Pharma* (online magazine).

Butler, Judith 1990. *Gender Trouble*. New York: Routledge.

Butler, Judith 1997. "Merely Cultural." *Social Text, 52/53.*

Fraser, Nancy 2000. "Rethinking Recognition." *New Left Review*, vol 3. 107–120.

Fraser, Nancy 2001. "Recognition without Ethics?" *Theory, Culture and Society*, vol 18. 21–42.

Freud, Sigmund 1925/1974. "Some Psychical Consequences of the Anatomical Distinction Between the Sexes." In Jean Strouse (Ed.) *Women and Analysis*. New York, NY: Grossman Publishers.

Ghorayshi, Azeen 2022. "Report Reveals Sharp Rise in Transgender Young People in US." *New York Times* June 10, 2022.

Ghorayshi, Azeen 2024. "Sadness Among Teen Girls." *New York Times*, August 6, 2024

Gitlin, Todd 1996. *The Twilight of Common Dreams: Why America is Wracked by Culture Wars*. New York, NY: Holt.

Grannan, Cydney. "Has Pink Always Been a 'Girly' Color?" www.britannica.com.

Group View Research 2020 "U.S. Sex reassignment Surgery Market Size, Share & Trends Analysis." https://www.grandviewresearch.com/industry-analysis/us-sex-reassignment

Horney, Karen 1926/1994. "The Flight from Womanhood: The Masculinity-Complex in Women as Viewed by Men and by Women." In Jean Strouse (Ed.) *Women and Analysis*. New York, NY: Grossman Publishers.

Jacoby, Russell 2022. "The Takeover" *Tablet Magazine* December 18, 2022.

Joyce, Helen 2022. *Trans*. London, England: OneWorld Publications.

Lange, Elena Louisa and Joshua Pickett-Depaolis (Eds) 2022. *The Conformist Rebellion: Marxist Critiques of the Contemporary Left.* Washington, DC: Rowman & Littlefield.

Levine, Jon 2022. "Maine University in Uproar After Professor Insists There are Only Two Sexes." *New York Post*, October 8, 2022.

Lind, Michael 2016. "What Politics Is(n't): In Defense of What Politics Is and Is Not." *The Smart Set*, September 30, 2016.

Liu, Angus 2019. "Gilead's Converting Truvada PreP Users to Descovy Faster than Expected." *Fierce Pharma* (online magazine).

Lukianoff, Greg and Haidt, Jonathan 2018. *The Coddling of the American Mind*. New York, NY: Penguin Press.

Lyons, N.S. 2022. "Reality Honks Back." *The Upheaval*, on Substack, February 16, 2022.

McWhorter, John 2021. *Woke Racism: How a New Religion Has Betrayed Black America*; New York: Penguin Press.

Monteil, Abby 2022. "A Spanish Whiskey Commercial With a Trans Storyline is Making the Internet Cry." *Them* (online magazine), December 19, 2022.

Morgan, Robin (Ed.) 1970. *Sisterhood is Powerful*. New York, NY: Vintage Books.

Muldtofte, Lea 2018. "The Grace of My Perfect Skeleton: An Autoethnographic Analysis of the Anorexic Body." *Capacious: Journal for Emerging Affect Inquiry*, June 30, 2018.

Nussbaum, Martha 1999. "The Professor of Parody: The Hip Defeatism of Judith Butler." *The New Republic*, 37–45.

Orwell, George 1949. *1984*. London: Secker & Warburg.

Raymond, Janice 2021. *Doublethink: A Feminist Challenge to Transgenderism*. North Geelong, Australia: Spinfex Press.

Selin David, Lisa 2023. "Stop Conflating Gender Ideology with Gender Dysphoria." *Broadside* on *Substack*, April 7, 2023.

Shrier, Abigail 2020. *Irreversible Damage: The Transgender Craze Seducing Our Daughters*. Washington, DC: Regnery Publishing.

Stock, Kathleen 2019. "Ignoring Differences between Men and Women is the Wrong Way to Address Gender Dysphoria." *Quillette*, November 4, 2019.

Stock, Kathleen 2021. *Material Girls: Why Reality Matters for Feminism*. London, England: Fleet.

Watkins, Morgan 2019. "Professor Sues U of L." *Courier Journal*, March 29, 2019.

Wright, Alyssa 2020. "Tech-Trans is A Budding Industry." *Forbes*, December 8, 2020.

Chapter 9

The Challenge of Jewish Difference

Antisemitism and the Progressive Left

Cheryl Goldstein

> The difference between sameness and difference is difference itself.
>
> —Joel Fineman

As the first quarter of the 21st century comes to a close, the world we inhabit grows increasingly complex, threatening and alien to us. Climate change transforms landscapes; advances in technology obscure distinctions between the human and the virtual; a global pandemic fostered rampant paranoia and distrust both within communities and internationally, leaving us physically and psychologically isolated. In the US political division and a growing gun culture prompt deepening anxiety regarding the future of democracy and the potential for civil unrest, while war and strife are rending nations apart or pitting them against one another all around the world. No one has been immune. In the face of so much that is frightening and unpredictable we are left feeling small and helpless, victims of systems over which we have less and less control. In the most elemental ways, we lack authority.

As a psychoanalyst, I'm not surprised that this sense of existential helplessness results in a manic defense where fear and dread are displaced and reappear as anger and hatred. When faced with our own insignificance and vulnerability some of us sink into despair, some of us mobilize, and some of us rage. But in the absence of more constructive and realistic outlets, anger provides people with a sense of agency in an overwhelming world. Rage feels empowering and expansive, and it engenders a sense of agency and purposefulness. Unfortunately, it also distorts our beliefs and narratives, generating fantasies of a world with clearly assigned categories of good and bad, oppressor and oppressed, etc., which seem to give our increasingly precarious and baffling world a measure of intelligibility, and by implication, a way to address and hopefully control inchoate threats. These narratives clearly identify who is "in" and who is "out," what is "good" and what is "bad," who is one of "us" and who is one of "them"; a starkly Manichean worldview where there is little ambiguity or room for nuance. According to this logic, if you aren't one of "us" you are considered "other" in a pejorative sense. We identify this "othering" as an indicator of a constraining and intolerant orthodoxy, the type of thinking we typically associate with the Far Right.

DOI: 10.4324/9781003389927-9

While the Right has always insisted on racial and/or religious purity, "othering" those who do not belong (according to their rigid and absurd criteria), it is surprising to see similar tactics now coming from the Progressive Left. Generally speaking, those on the Left see themselves (and wish to be seen) as being not merely tolerant, but positively inclusive of racial and religious "others." Rather than using identity as a way of shaming or marginalizing individuals and groups, the Left's concern for solidarity with the oppressed appears to engage with difference in multiple ways, often under the umbrella of "diversity."

Over the past few decades, however, the Progressive Left has also succumbed to more derisive forms of "othering," expressing its frustration with the liberal "status quo" through a growing tendency toward interpreting social reality in terms of binaries, exclusion, and intolerance. Feeling that they have little to no impact on governmental and political structures—an experience that was exacerbated by Trump's presidency and then brought home, quite literally, by the COVID pandemic—liberals and the Progressive Left found themselves struggling against forces that were impervious to their objections and concerns. It shouldn't be especially surprising, therefore, to find groups like Black Lives Matter (BLM) espousing positions that express this sense of futility. This would explain the diffusion of attitudes that originally emerged from the Afropessimism movement, such as the belief that anti-Black racism is *the* original and organizing racism defining Western culture. Viewed from this perspective, the world divides into a Black/White binary, making it incumbent upon those who are endowed with social awareness (i.e. who are "woke") to call out "privilege" and "Whiteness"—qualities which go inevitably together—as a means of acknowledging the foundational and entrenched nature of the American power dynamic.

Unfortunately, this type of binary thinking encourages the proliferation of further binaries, e.g. oppressor vs. oppressed, colonizer vs. colonized, bad vs. good, which soon take on an adversarial character. The social, cultural, political, and economic surround is then structured, at least in theory, by aligning binary terms, each one having its own proponents and theories, although there is inevitable overlap. For example, the binaries Black/White, oppressed/oppressor, colonized/colonizer are associated and organized in the work of Franz Fanon, while Edward Said in his groundbreaking book *Orientalism* advances a system of "Oriental"/Western, oppressed/oppressor, colonized/colonizer. Just taking these two cases as a sample demonstrates how shared elements within these binaries serve to reinforce one another.

In *The Identity Trap*, Yascha Mounk uses the term "identity synthesis" to refer to these constructions and their influence upon identity politics, an approach to politics that has become increasingly popular on the Progressive Left, that "draws on a broad variety of intellectual traditions and is centrally concerned with the role that identity categories like race, gender and sexual orientation play in the world" (Mounk, 2023, p. 9). The result, as the book's title intimates, proves problematic. "Despite the good intentions of its proponents," Mounk explains, "it [identity synthesis] undermines progress toward genuine equality between members of different groups. [...] it also subverts other goals we all have reason to care about [...]. Despite its allure, the identity synthesis turns out to be a trap"(Mounk, 2023, p. 12).

One way the identity synthesis "traps" people is by rendering them insensitive to complexity and ambiguity, thereby limiting their tolerance for individual differences under the auspices of advocacy. This is especially true when identities defy categorization into reductive binaries. Because the identity synthesis ultimately defaults to either/or, us/them dynamics, it generates communities premised upon sameness or homogeneity, erasing or minimizing individual and intra-group differences while dwelling on, exaggerating, and intensifying inter-group differences. The result is a resistance to "otherness" under the guise of empowering the "other."

The psychoanalytic project, both clinically and theoretically, involves confronting otherness on a variety of levels. Premised upon the existence of the unconscious—the "other" that lives within each of us—psychoanalytic work requires an openness both to the "other" that is the person in treatment and the "otherness" of the unconscious. Conceptualized as the "other" or "stranger" within us, the unconscious presents us with another other within, an otherness that is an essential component of who we are. This otherness is constitutional, woven (so to speak) into the human condition, and cannot be assimilated or superseded by a more totalizing sameness. Thinking psychoanalytically means accepting that we are destined, to a greater or lesser degree, to be at odds with others and at odds with ourselves.

Making otherness central helps when thinking in terms of our own inner dynamics and our relationships with other individuals, but is it applicable in a broader context? I maintain that a truly tolerant and liberal socio-cultural and political system *requires* a willingness to acknowledge, embrace, or if need be, simply endure otherness. Gerald Bruns makes this point when he uses the relationship between Judaism and Christianity to illustrate how otherness or difference operates in maintaining cultural identities. The relationship between these two traditions, Bruns explains, is not one of unity, but rather involves "entering into this relation as into a breach or wound that can never be healed." Relationship, Bruns explains, *requires* separateness and difference, and therefore Judaism and Christianity exist in a difficult and irreconcilable push and pull. Bruns observes that in a relationship of this type "...what is common, what is shared, is not an identity but a difference-and, moreover, not a dialectical or systematic difference within a totality but a *radical difference* that is not to be overcome or subsumed in a higher order..." (Bruns, 1991, p. 13).

Bruns suggests that radical difference, or "radical alterity," constitutes a fundamental structure of relating where the difficult and often painful tension of difference constructs the dynamic of interaction. Relating in this way opposes the assumption that we relate through a fundamental or negotiated sameness. (For Freud this concept also would hold true, since the presence of the unconscious indicates that we are not identical even *within ourselves*.) When relating upon the basis of sameness, one assumes that somehow understanding will transcend and ameliorate difference, as though difference is something to be overcome or assimilated rather than allowing it to remain as an inevitable quality of human interaction.

An example of a relational model that privileges sameness, presented as a "hermeneutics of trust" is exemplified in the work of Donna Orange, a psychoanalyst especially concerned with the study of philosophy and Phenomenological Contexualism. According to this model, Orange explains, "relating" occurs in an environment that privileges "what both partners hold in common to find understanding where difference exists" (Orange, 2011, p. 38). Relationships premised on this model erase "radical difference" by sublating difference and replacing it with "understanding." This logic appears to equate holding things "in common" with "understanding," thereby minimizing difference while implying that difference or "otherness" correlates with *mis*understanding.

Returning to Bruns' example of the relationship between Judaism and Christianity, we can see how seeking out "what's held in common" in order to arrive at "understanding," in the case of "reconciling" Judaism and Christianity—that is to say, in doing away with the "rift" that marks their difference—would not prevent, and could potentially promote, a historical repetition in which Christianity subsumes Judaism through its triumphalist tendencies. Stephen Frosh, a British psychoanalyst, remarks upon the banality of such supersessionist claims when he explains that

> the idea of 'Judeo-Christian civilization,' used loosely and as if it is unproblematic … is a misnomer. The 'Judeo-' in it is a construction of *Christianity*, a backward reading of Judaism and Jewish history in the light of the politics of the Christian mission […] What is the difference between 'Judeo-Christian' and 'Christian' in the resulting structure? The answer is — nothing at all.
>
> (Frosh, 2023, pp. 126–7)

In other words, what Orange presents as a catholic attitude toward interpersonal relating plays out problematically on the socio-political level. By privileging sameness, Orange's approach favors homogeneity, resulting in either discounting differences by treating them as incidental or irrelevant on the one hand or on the other hand repeating structural binaries, classifying and silo-ing relational interaction as "us=same" and "them=different." In either case, whether via discounting or distancing, difference and heterogeneity suffer when sameness and homogeneity are championed. Frosh also recognizes that the model of seeking out sameness under the auspices of "understanding" occurs at the expense of difference, remarking that "if we cannot imagine the experience of people *other than ourselves* and respond to the demands that are made on us by those experiences and by *their* articulation, then we are lost" (Frosh, 2023, p. 4) (italics added). Listening to the "other," specifically to the particularity of "*their* articulation"—what *they* are saying, what *they* are expressing as their own—allows for an interaction where difference can be discovered and engaged.

If recent experience is any indication, the Far Right and the Progressive Left now share a tendency for relating through sameness; a preference that results in an intolerance of otherness and an inability to sustain dialogue so that the "articulations" crucial to sustaining respect for radical difference are lost. This problem with "radical difference," or what I refer to as "cohering difference"—the difference that holds separateness together—serves as a point of convergence, an uncomfortable but significant place of contact, for Right- and Left-wing authoritarian movements, both of which are deeply enmeshed in binary thinking. This convergence manifests in each groups' attitudes toward Jews, highlighting the intolerance on both sides of the political and cultural divide. Whether expressed in overt or in more covert terms, the Progressive Left's antisemitism demonstrates an inability to contend with Jewish otherness, which defies categorization in terms of simple binaries and thus exposes the authoritarian and intolerant dimension of the contemporary Progressive movement.

There's nothing especially surprising about claiming that the Far Right has a problem with "otherness" or with Jews. We're accustomed to the racist, antisemitic, sexist, and homophobic positions espoused by the Far Right. As a movement that advocates for racial purity and "traditional Christian values," the Far Right's pursuit of "sameness," their definition of who is "in" and who is "out," one of "us" or one of "them," is distressingly familiar, and obviously premised on the pursuit of social and political uniformity. In contrast, the Left prides itself on not merely "tolerating" others but actively accepting them. In fact, however, the Progressive Left's tendency to valorize binary structures necessitates the development of an orthodoxy that categorizes people with the current iteration of this premised upon race and whether one is identified as BIPOC or White. Those who are identified as White benefit from having "Whiteness" and from the privilege "Whiteness" affords, distinguishing them from "others" (i.e. people of color) who are the excluded from "White" identity. In this version of identity politics, the Progressive Left creates a hierarchy of "others," establishing a system of categories and identities which one must accept to prove one's fidelity to the Progressive cause. This results in a form of intolerance that appears to champion "others," when, in fact, significant differences beyond skin color and gender identity, e.g. religion and class, are downplayed or thoroughly discounted. This reductive approach also fosters the harmful idea that understanding can only exist in a homogeneous environment where like-meets-like or where the White individual acknowledges his/her implicit and complete ignorance of the experience of the "other," a form of "identitarian deference" (Bernstein, 2022, p. 105). The insistence on declaring one's "antiracism" or on owning one's "White guilt" reflects the demand for an ideological homogeneity that assumes a uniformity of experience based largely, if not exclusively, on the color of one's skin.

The Progressive Left's disregard for the complexity inherent in otherness, their embrace of a culture of identity synthesis, and the requirement of identitarian deference results in a dynamic that is curiously reminiscent of the Far Right, namely, the embrace of sameness and homogeneity under the banner of ideological purity, rather than racial or religious purity. The Progressive Left's intolerance emerges when foundational binaries are challenged or complicated by groups or individuals that defy predetermined "either/or" identity dynamics, as Jews often do. Expressions of antisemitism, whether from the Far Right or the Progressive Left, demonstrate both groups' adherence to "either/or" thinking and their alignment with authoritarian discourse. Let me be clear, expressions of authoritarian intolerance are not exclusively directed at Jews, but they are more easily tolerated when expressed toward Jews. Why is this the case?

As noted previously, authoritarian ideologies (whether Right or Left) privilege binaries that allow for bifurcating human populations into "insiders" and "outsiders," "us" and "them." In discourses shaped by identity politics and binary categories like these, the Jew complicates and disrupts these categorizations. Echoing Theodor Adorno, Karin Stögner explains that "Jews do not so much represent a foreign hostile identity, but rather a non-identity, in other words the threat of the *dissolution* of identity itself, of unity itself" (Stögner, 2020). Stögner's reference to the "dissolution of identity" and "of unity itself" recognizes, albeit obliquely, the way that Jews as a heterogenous group, disrupt and disorganize the structural binaries.

By resisting assimilation into predetermined configurations, for example by remaining "foreign" without being "hostile," and therefore by refusing the terms of binary engagement, Stögner suggests that Jews call into question the value of binary logic altogether. The dawning awareness of this radical or cohering difference poses a threat to the whole system of categories, and relegates the Jew to the status of a maligned "non-entity." This defensive response provokes the emergence of antisemitic tropes that depict Jews as rootless, spiritless shape shifters who attempt to both hide *and* exploit their "non-being" (Di Cesare, 2018). Stögner reveals the Jewish other as the counterpoint to the Far Right *and* Progressive Left's conventional constructs of identity. As she explains, the Jewish "other" embodies *otherness* in a radical way, representing a difference that is experienced as nefarious because it dis-integrates the promise of an ideal unity. This is possible because the Jew undermines any potential for "unity" by compromising the very concept of a reconciliation by being more other than the "hostile" and "foreign" other. It is the absence of a classifiable identity that marks the Jews' radical difference and relegates the Jew to the status of a "non-entity."

Stögner's analysis explains one way that antisemitism takes root historically when Jews are not *visibly* different from their non-Jewish neighbors, that is to say when racial difference is *not* the issue. Since there are many different types of Jews—Black Jews, Mizrachi Jews, Sephardic Jews, Ashkenazi Jews—using conventional racial designations (skin color, for example) as a distinguishing feature of Jewish identity can only exacerbate the confusion and anxiety around Jewish "invisibility" and/or "Whiteness," because reducing Jewish "otherness" to skin color leaves large portions of the Jewish population unidentified, or at least unidentified as *Jews*. This tends to support a point made by Dara Horn, "One can believe that all humans are the same while being virulently anti-Semitic, because according to anti-Semites, Jews, with their millennia-old insistence on being different from their neighbors, are the obstacle to humans all being the same" (Horn, 2023). Horn's description, like Stögner's, explains that it is *the difference that we cannot see* that sets Jews apart. We see this happening when the Far Right identifies "elites," and "cosmopolitans," commonplace euphemisms for Jews, accusing them of appropriating power and attempting to infiltrate and pollute "Whiteness" and traditionally White spaces. When the Far Right voices concern about "cosmopolitans" it looks to expose Jews as a people lacking a sense of place or permanence and by identifying them, prevent them from being mistaken for those who are truly "White." Leaving Jews unrecognized increases the risk that Jews would gain additional power and control while further contaminating White identity and unity. The Progressive Left, by contrast, expresses its anxiety about Jewish invisibility by defending against the possibility that Jews will perform and appropriate non-White "difference." According to many on the Far Left, Jews falsely represent themselves as non-White and exploit their perceived historical victimhood by appropriating a position of marginality that more rightfully belongs to "truly marginalized" Blacks and people of color. Progressive claims of this type of Jewish usurpation both reinforce antisemitic tropes of exploitative domination and shapeshifting on the one hand while undermining the validity of Jewish identity by making it suspect, on the other.

What's especially disconcerting about this state of affairs is how unprepared we are to address the paranoid aspects these authoritarian discourses share. We're thoroughly familiar with the antisemitic tropes deployed by the Far Right ("Jews will not replace us," etc.) And because the Far Right engages in overt intolerance of others *and* otherness, it is easy to call out their antisemitism when we see it. However, Progressives often cloak their antisemitic intolerance in a discourse that champions the underdog and the oppressed, and we are often ill equipped to separate the social justice message from its authoritarian and antisemitic slant. Veiled expressions of antisemitism—designating Jews as "White" or "White adjacent" and expressions of antisemitic anti-Zionism which promotes violence against Jews—illustrate how Jews concretize the Progressive Left's discomfort with radical alterity and otherness in the pursuit of an idealized and ideological sameness.

Obviously, this leaves Jews in a difficult position. In the podcast "Adventures in Jewish Studies" Jeremy Shere points out that when Jews are asked if they identify as White "[T]he answer is obviously no, not all Jews in the United States or elsewhere are white, are seen as white, or see themselves that way"(Shere, 2019). Conflating Jewishness with "Whiteness" allows for the perpetuation of antisemitic attitudes since "the relevance of Jewish identity is neglected — which also means that Jews don't count in connection with suffering from racism" (Frosh, 2023, p. 123).

The tendency to label Jews as "White" exposes the Progressive Left's propensity toward a reductive sameness at the expense of Jewish difference. By dismissing Jews' right to define and determine their own identities, the Progressive Left willfully ignores the fact that, historically, groups organized around preserving the homogeneity of "Whiteness" have always left Jews vulnerable to discrimination and violence. While periods of relative peace and prosperity may lull Jews into a sense of complacency, the fact remains that Jews status as "White" is always tentative, precarious, and provisional. In truth, Jews are only "White" by sufferance, and when circumstances shift, they are promptly reclassified as *the enemies of Whiteness*.

Describing this homogenization of Jews into "Whites" as "erasive anti-Semitism," the Reut Group notes that such thinking "does not single out Jews. Rather, it indiscriminately lumps them within the dominant majority. This effectively erases the Jewish voice in defining Jewish identity" (Bernstein, 2022, p. 120). This is an example of what Stögner describes as "*over*-inclusion," an attitude that "leads to the problem of *under*-inclusion: [where] contemporary antisemitism is *not* viewed as racism at all," thus allowing the Progressive Left to deny Jewish otherness and precarity altogether (Stögner, 2020). Even worse, identifying Jews as "White" denies them the right of self-definition in a way that negates Jewish difference and thereby renders claims of antisemitism moot.

The erasure of Jewish difference via the over-inclusivity of "Whiteness" renders Jewish difference irrelevant, a form of passive antisemitism that erases Jewish difference and depicts Jews as complicit in maintaining White hegemony. In this situation "Jewishness is seen as adding nothing to a multicultural conversation; it is already implicitly included as part of the hegemonic 'White' conversation" (Schraub, 2019, p. 396). It also implicitly denies the multi-racial and multi-cultural aspects of the Jewish community. By making "nothing" of Jewish difference the Progressive Left remains locked in binary thinking, eliminating the possibility of a more complex third position, a position of cohering difference embodied by the Jew as in some cases "White," but, in any case, different for a number of compelling social and historical reasons. Admitting to the reality of such an identity, however, would problematize the Progressive Left's construction of a homogeneous Whiteness.

Neglecting Jewish difference by enforcing the "Whitening" of Jews not only negates authentic expressions of Jewish autonomy. As David Schraub points out, it actually intensifies antisemitism, since many of the negative qualities that attach themselves to concepts of "Whiteness" and the "upholding" of White hegemony are associated stereotypically with Jews. Writing about intersectionality and what the intersection of Jewishness and Whiteness does to Jews in the popular Progressive imagination, Schraub notes that "the prevailing view of Jews…is precisely that they are 'particularly powerful, or privileged, or influential.' And so, when the Whiteness frame…is overlaid upon the White Jew (as body or concept) it serves not as a counterweight but as an accelerant." This acceleration results in Jews being perceived as "hyper-White," or as a group that epitomizes Whiteness. As Schraub explains, "Pushed to its limit, 'Jewish simply displaces white.' Jews, as inherently avaricious, deceitful, domineering, and possessive, stand in for those Whites who are irredeemably supremacist in orientation; we end White supremacy at the point where Whites stop acting like Jews" Schraub, 2019, p. 393).

Schraub's observations confront us with the way Jewish difference is both denied and exploited by the Progressive Left. Since Whiteness functions by asserting power and control via its traditionally invisible and unquestioned hegemony, identifying and participating in the self-critique of Whiteness ostensibly exposes the invisibility that allows Whites to take their power for granted. Jews, however, who resist the designation of "White" and presumably seek to retain their hold on invisible power and control remain in or assume the position vacated by those now self-reflective Whites. That this results in greater hegemonic control by Jews, a common antisemitic trope, seems to elicit little concern in Progressive circles. As David Baddiel explains, "The problem is that Jews occupy a socio-cultural gray area. Jews, although marginal, are not thought of as *marginalized*" (Baddiel, 2021, p. 38).

Because the Far Right maintains that Jews deploy invisibility, i.e. "Whiteness," in order to exert control over and to corrupt "White power," additional differences like skin color become secondary to Jewish otherness because Jewish Whiteness was always and already a deception. Following in the footsteps of their European predecessors, the Far Right perpetuates the concept of the Jew as Black, a trope that historians like Sandor Gilman and Tudor Parfitt have explicated extensively, that was part of Christian European Anti-Judaism from the Middle Ages onward, and which the Nazis used to their advantage (Parfitt, 2021). For the Progressive Left's part, assertations of Jewish invisibility (i.e. Jews' *denial* of "Whiteness") functions as a strategic way of conflating Jewishness with Whiteness, allowing for the accusation that Jews deny their privileged positions in political, cultural, and economic hegemonies in order to replace those who are "truly" marginalized or discriminated against. For both ends of the political spectrum, then, the Jews' performance of "non-identity," embodied in their capacity to exploit all aspects of racial difference, reinforces anxieties about Jewish invisibility, an invisibility that undermines idealized constructs of unity and sameness held by both authoritarian movements.

Until recently, concerns about antisemitism on the Progressive Left have been met with denial a good deal of the time. Because the Progressive Left identifies Jews as "White" (or in a pinch, as "White adjacent") claims of antisemitism can be readily dismissed as expressions of "White fragility," requiring a recalibration on the part of *Jews* rather than an earnest reconsideration of Progressive platitudes. The irony is, of course, that this very demand would be experienced as a further symptom of racism by any other marginalized group but is deemed to be completely reasonable when it is expected of Jews. For the Progressive Left, Jews are the only minority whose lived experience is deemed to be intrinsically irrelevant, and called into question if not denied outright.

These denials are especially vexing when the Progressive Left insists that its peculiar brand of antisemitic anti-Zionism is not antisemitic, a response that has become the *de rigueur* disclaimer for academics and activists who hide their antisemitism—from themselves and others—under the guise of "principled" anti-Zionist rhetoric. Yet, as Schraub points out, "it seems clear that tropes of Jewish

Whiteness are quite implicated in how Israel is talked about *outside* Israel." More specifically Schraub asserts, "That Israel is viewed either as a subspecies of European colonialism or as a European cultural vanguard, rather than something at least sui generis, is reflective of the broader view of Jews as basically White" (Schraub, 2019, p. 399).

Since October 7, 2023 when Israel suffered a brutal terrorist attack by Hamas leaving over 1,200 Israelis dead, several thousands injured, and another 240 taken hostage, Schraub's analysis of antisemitic anti-Zionism has become increasingly salient. Almost immediately after the attack—the deadliest day for Jews since the Holocaust—there were numerous justifications and celebrations of Hamas' attack coming from groups affiliated with the Progressive Left. Organizations like Students for Justice in Palestine praised the attack. A group of 34 students at Harvard University wrote claiming they "hold the Israeli regime entirely responsible for all unfolding violence." The Democratic Socialists of America marched in support of Palestinians, and in the most direct link to the Progressive Left, the Black Lives Matter chapter in Chicago posted a graphic, which was subsequently removed, of a paraglider—a means of Hamas fighters' entry into Israel on October 7—with a Palestinian flag and the words "I Stand with Palestine."

These expressions of pro-Palestinian sentiment were not just poorly timed, nor were they merely anti-Zionist. Indeed, it is impossible to disentangle anti-Zionism from antisemitism in these cases. Statistics support this observation. Within two weeks of the October 7 Hamas attack the Anti-Defamation League reported a 400% increase in antisemitic incidents in the United States alone, while in France the number had nearly doubled, Germany saw a 240% year-on-year increase, and these are just a few examples (Reuters, 2023). It appears that amongst the Progressive Left, anti-Zionism dovetails with and quickly becomes conflated with antisemitism. Nowadays, and in the current climate, attempting to differentiate between the two often becomes an academic exercise.

The relationship between the Progressive Left's support of anti-Zionism with its mobilization of antisemitic tropes has a well-researched socio-political history [see for example (Tabarovsky, 2023)]. But the virulence of this conflation currently is just as much a direct result of the Progressive Left's intolerance of Jewish difference as it is of a historical comingling of Soviet era antisemitism, which also masqueraded as principled anti-Zionism, with today's Progressive politics. By that I mean that current Leftist anti-Zionism is driven by an insistence upon Jewish "Whiteness" and the erasure of Jews' radical difference.

Since October 7 we have seen how the Progressive Left's reliance upon the construction of identity as binary, a construction that insists on making Jews "White," reinforces both anti-Zionism and antisemitism. This happens because binaries allow for and even invite reinforcing associations. Put simply, the thinking goes something like this: Jews are White. Whites are European. Europeans are colonizers and oppressors. Israel is a Jewish State. Israel is therefore a White European, oppressive, colonizing state. This impenetrable circularity is the consequence of what I describe as an "associative binary cascade." This cascade occurs because a politics built upon "either/or," "Black/White" binaries actually diminishes the value and tolerance of difference.

Jews and Judaism have historically insisted upon their particularity in defiance of levelling or homogenizing trends. This privileging of difference, of respect for the stranger's strangeness is foundational. "You shall not oppress the stranger, for you know the feelings of the stranger, having yourselves been strangers in the land of Egypt" (Exodus 23:9). The experience of difference brings us together through a connection based upon an inclusion of difference rather than through a sublation or assimilation of it. This cohering difference maintains particularity in the face of the universal.

Writing about the dignity of difference, the eponymous title of his 2002 book, Lord Jonathan Sacks explained that just as the natural environment requires biodiversity in order to thrive, so the human environment requires cultural diversity. To maintain this diverse state requires more than mere tolerance, however. In looking at our current political culture, nationally and globally, we can ask ourselves whether it passes Sacks' fundamental test: does our culture make space for otherness? Does it acknowledge the dignity of difference?" (Sacks, 2002, p. 61)

The "space" Sacks references contains the field required for the relational "push and pull" inherent in Bruns' construction of "radical difference." It is a spaciousness of mind, a capacity, that exceeds "mere tolerance," and makes room for the connected distance that respectful differences require. In a world more populated than ever before, where we feel the crush as well as the crash of our differences and their impacts—economically, politically, environmentally—it can be difficult to imagine finding this "space." Recognizing the erosion of this necessary respectful distance in the discourse of the Progressive Left, as exemplified in its discourse about Jews, can help to shore up the foundations of liberalism rather than relegate it to crumbling into a pile of undifferentiated rubble beneath our feet.

Works Cited

Baddiel, D. (2021). *Jews Don't Count.* London: TLS Books.

Bernstein, D. (2022). *Woke Antisemitism: How A Progressive Ideology Harms Jews.* New York: Post Hill Press.

Bruns, G. (1991). "What is Tradition?" *New Literary History*, pp. 1–21.

Di Cesare, D. (2018). *Heidegger and the Jews: The Black Notebooks.* Cambridge, United Kingdom: Polity Press.

Frosh, S. (2023). *Antisemitism and Racisim: Ethical Challenges for Psychoanalysis.* London: Bloomsbury Academic.

Horn, D. (2023, May). Is Holocaust Education Making Anti-Semitism Worse. *The Atlantic*, pp. 24–39.

Mounk, Y. (2023). *The Identity Trap.* New York: Penguin.

Orange, D. (2011). *The Suffering Stranger: Hermeneutics for Everyday Clinical Practice.* New York: Routledge.

Parfitt, T. (2021, February 16). *Are Jews Black? Black History Month: A Brief History of an Often-pernicious and Persistent Question of Race.* Retrieved from Tablet Magazine:

https://www.tabletmag.com/sections/history/articles/jewish-whiteness-blackness-tudor-parfitt

Reuters (2023, October 31). *How the Surge in Antisemitism is Affecting Countries Around the World.* Retrieved from Reuters: https://www.reuters.com/world/how-surge-antisemitism-is-affecting-countries-around-world-2023-10-31/

Sacks, J. (2002). *The Dignity of Difference: How to Avoid the Clash of Civilizations.* London: Continuum Books.

Schraub, D. (2019, November). "White Jews: An Intersectional Approach." *AJS Review*, vol 43 no. 2. 379–407.

Shere, J. B. (2019). *Are Jews White.* Retrieved from Association for Jewish Studies: Adventures in Jewish Studies Podcast: https://www.associationforjewishstudies.org/publications-research/adventures-in-jewish-studies-podcast/are-jews-white-transcript

Stögner, K. (2020, May). *Intersectionality and Antisemitism: A New Approach.* Retrieved from Fathom: https://fathomjournal.org/intersectionality-and-antisemitism-a-new-approach/

Tabarovsky, I. (2023, November 12). *Soviet Antizionism and Contemporary Left Antisemitism [Webinar].* Retrieved from https://isca.indiana.edu/conferences/webinars/Fall23/izabella-tabarovsky.html

Chapter 10

Psychoanalysis, Authoritarianism, Antisemitism, and the Left

A Critical Theory Perspective

Daniel Burston

Authoritarianism Research: Weimar

Psychoanalysis was originally developed as a method for treating mental disorder, but was soon applied more widely to the study of social psychological phenomena and political movements, providing insights into trends in the collective psyche that might otherwise escape our attention. This is especially true with respect to the study of authoritarianism. The first psychoanalyst to undertake an empirical sociological study of authoritarianism was Erich Fromm (1900–1980), the Director for Social Psychological Research at the Frankfurt Institute for Social Research from 1928–1938. Fromm and his (mostly Jewish) colleagues were grappling with the horrifying spectacle of Hitler's steady rise to power. At the request of Max Horkheimer (1895–1973), the Institute's director, Fromm launched a study on the prevalence of authoritarian attitudes among (skilled and unskilled) blue collar workers, shopkeepers, and a sprinkling of white-collar workers and civil servants in the Weimar Republic that lasted from 1929–1931.

Fromm's concept of the authoritarian character was strongly influenced by the theories of Wilhelm Reich (1897–1957), a psychoanalyst whose book *The Mass Psychology of Fascism* had a profound influence on the entire Frankfurt School (Reich, 1933). Reich rejected the existence of the "death drive," and defied Freud's insistence on the centrality of the Oedipus complex to the history of civilization. He also revived Freud's (largely discarded) theory of the "actual neuroses," or of symptoms resulting from a patients' inability to find satisfactory outlets for their sexual needs and feelings. If prolonged, said Reich, the sexual anguish experienced by the average adult creates a "sexual stasis" that eventually causes their libido to regress to earlier—specifically oral, anal, and phallic—stages of development; a state of affairs which fosters the proliferation of sadomasochistic character traits. Reich's stance on these issues and his affiliation with the Communist Party made Freud profoundly uncomfortable, and as a result, Reich was summarily dismissed from the International Psychoanalytic Association (IPA) at the Lucerne Conference in 1934. But that, as they say, is another story. Meanwhile, before we go further, what is sadomasochism, and how does it express itself in social behavior?

DOI: 10.4324/9781003389927-10

Richard von Krafft-Ebing was a Viennese forensic psychiatrist who coined the term "sadomasochism" in *Psychopathia Sexualis* (Krafft-Ebing, 1886). By his account, "sadomasochism" denotes a kind of emotional numbness, or an inability to experience full sexual arousal and release without first inflicting pain on others, or having pain inflicted on oneself. Following Krafft-Ebing, Freud noted that sadism and masochism seldom appear in pure form, and that sadistic and masochistic tendencies are regularly found together in the same person. As a result, said Freud, a person who prefers the sadistic role harbors masochistic phantasies and inclinations in their unconscious and vice versa (Freud, 1905). But Freud and his followers expanded on this somewhat narrow definition of sadomasochism beyond the overtly sexual domain to include sadistic and masochistic character traits (e.g. Freud, 1905).

Taking his cue from Freud (Freud, 1924), Reich said that people with a sadomasochistic character structure need not engage in kinky sex. On the contrary, their sex lives may be quite dull and conventional. Nevertheless, people with a sadistic character take great pleasure in dominating, injuring, and humiliating others, robbing them of their dignity and their powers of autonomous action. They love power and control. Masochists, by contrast, take comfort in submission to the will of others, seeking solace and support from a "strongman" or charismatic leader. They feel anxious unless they are neurotically attached to a more powerful person who tells them what to do. They love power and control too, but typically seek it out in others, rather than trying to seize it for themselves.

Based on his clinical experience, Reich claimed that most of Hitler's followers fit this masochistic profile, offering their unquestioning obedience to *der Führer*, while channeling their latent sadism onto scapegoats and adversaries, real and imagined—Jews, Roma, Masons, gay people, etc. Furthermore, Reich said that the antisemitic and White Supremacist ideologies embraced by Hitler and his minions merely provided the pretext for acting on (and acting out) these deeply engrained characterological predispositions, and that most Stalinists were very similar, characterologically speaking, to their overtly Right-wing counterparts in this respect. Fromm concurred, though in *Escape From Freedom* (Fromm, 1941) and subsequent publications (e.g. Fromm, 1956), he suggested that the roots of sadomasochism are seldom the result of thwarted heterosexual desire, but stem primarily from a mode of relatedness toward paternal authority acquired in childhood as a result of harsh and defective parenting and socialization.

Meanwhile, because the Frankfurt School's flight from Germany in 1935 and their subsequent migration to the USA, it was not until 1937 that Fromm finally wrote a comprehensive overview of his study of authoritarianism in English. To Fromm's great disappointment, Max Horkheimer refused to publish it under the Institute's auspices, ostensibly on the grounds that it was "too Marxist." Horkheimer was never particularly fond of the USA, but he was mindful of the political climate in his adoptive home, where antisemitism and anticommunism were prevalent and intense, and often closely conjoined. As Left-leaning Jews, he and his Frankfurt School colleagues realized that to thrive here, to help America defeat Nazism, and (eventually) return to Europe rather than merely survive the war cowering in the shadows, they would have to downplay their Marxist sympathies. This was particularly true for Herbert Marcuse, Franz Neuman, and Otto Kirchheimer, who worked under "Wild" Bill Donovan for the Office of Strategic Services, the forerunner of the CIA from 1941 to the end of the World War II. Similarly, Leo Löwenthal worked for the Office of War Information, while Friedrich Pollack worked for the Department of Justice. By contrast with each of them, Fromm, the only clinician in their midst, had arrived in America earlier than the others, and had established a thriving private practice when his Frankfurt colleagues arrived in the USA. Unlike them, Fromm had no need of getting a security clearance to earn a living or to make himself useful in the fight against fascism, and never sought to minimize his Marxist leanings, then or later. But his good fortune on this score did nothing to blunt his disappointment at Horkheimer's refusal to publish his study.

However, the Marxist terminology that suffused Fromm's study of authoritarianism in Weimar was not the only "red flag" for Horkheimer et al. Fromm's increasingly outspoken objections to Freudian orthodoxy also provoked considerable ill-will between Fromm and his erstwhile colleagues (Jeffries, 2017). Indeed, the Institute's rejection of Fromm's request to publish his study, which was only published posthumously (Fromm, 1984), hinged as much on Fromm's evolving critique of Freud as it did on the actual merits of his study. Realizing this, Fromm left the Institute, which had relocated to Columbia University, in 1939, and was replaced by Theodor W. Adorno (1903–1969), who incorporated many features of Fromm's study in his own research design, rendering Fromm's early effort a kind of pilot study for *The Authoritarian Personality*, which appeared in 1950, becoming a classic text in mainstream social psychology (Jay, 1973; Burston, 1991; Brunner, 1994).

Adorno and *The Authoritarian Personality*

Sadly, the ill will resulting from Fromm's departure probably prompted Adorno et al. to give Fromm very little credit for his pioneering efforts. Indeed, in a paper entitled "Freudian theory and the Pattern of Fascist Propaganda." published one year after *The Authoritarian Personality*, Adorno didn't even mention Reich and Fromm, except in a dismissive footnote, where Adorno maintained that Reich and Fromm's ideas were all actually in keeping with Freud's original formulations about the central role of the Oedipus complex in human affairs. For example, in footnote number 12, Adorno wrote:

> The fact that the Fascist follower's masochism is inevitably accompanied by sadistic impulses is in harmony with Freud's general theory of ambivalence, originally developed in connection with the Oedipus complex. Since the Fascist integration of the individuals into masses satisfies them only vicariously, their resentment against the frustrations of civilization survives but is canalized to

> become compatible with the leader's aims; it is psychologically fused with authoritarian submissiveness. Though Freud does not pose the problem of what was later called "sadomasochism" he was nevertheless well aware of it . . .
>
> (Adorno, 1951, p. 89)

Was Freud "well aware" of the role of sadomasochistic dynamics in authoritarianism, as Adorno claimed? Perhaps, although Adorno provided no evidence whatsoever in support of this claim, and the term sadomasochism predates Reich and Fromm by several decades. More to the point, however, is the fact that in so saying, Adorno deliberately glossed over the fact that Reich and Fromm had developed their theories of authoritarianism and character structure quite deliberately as an *alternative* to Freud's Oedipal monism and his father-centered "group psychology," because they were convinced that Freud's insistence on the primacy of the Oedipus complex concealed patriarchal and ethnocentric biases. By minimizing Reich and Fromm's distinctiveness in this regard, Adorno effectively buried their contributions beneath a blanket of Freud piety, relying on the Oedipus complex and the relations between id, ego, and superego to explain authoritarianism instead.

That said, there is no denying that *The Authoritarian Personality* was a huge success, and that as a result, Fromm's initial study of authoritarianism in Weimar was largely ignored by scholars, social scientists, and critics. The tendency to ignore Fromm's work was reinforced (on the Left) by Herbert Marcuse's withering assessment of Fromm in *Eros and Civilization* (Marcuse, 1955) and by Russell Jacoby's book *Social Amnesia: A Critique of Contemporary Psychology from Adler to Laing* (Jacoby, 1975.) Taking their cue from Adorno—and to a lesser extent, from Otto Fenichel—Marcuse and Jacoby eviscerated Fromm for deviating from Freud's libido theories and his metapsychology (McLaughlin, 2021, chapter 4). Indeed, echoing Adorno and Marcuse, Jacoby complained that the patriarchal-authoritarian trends that Reich and Fromm discerned in Freud were merely myths designed to legitimate different varieties of psychoanalytic "revisionism," all of which were betrayals and/or an abandonment of Freud's materialist approach (Jacoby, 1975, p. 11). Jacoby's inability or refusal to acknowledge Freud's authoritarian and misogynistic tendencies—which Fromm first drew attention to (Fromm, 1951), and which many feminist psychoanalysts have since acknowledged and addressed in considerable depth (e.g. Chodorow, 1978; Benjamin, 1988; Chancer, 1992)—helped keep a lid on any discussion of the differences between Fromm and Adorno with respect to authoritarianism in general.

That said, *The Authoritarian Personality* was a marked improvement on Fromm's earlier study in one important respect. Those respondents who scored very high or very low on Adorno et al.'s celebrated "F" scale—which purported to measure the strength of their authoritarian and fascist sympathies—were invited for in-depth interviews afterwards, providing Adorno and his colleagues with a rich source of data that was unavailable to Fromm, who did not have the resources or the time to conduct in-person interviews. Even so, Adorno had his critics. In *The*

Authoritarian Personality: Continuities in Social Research, Robert Christie, Marie Jahoda, and Edward Shils took Adorno and associates to task for their refusal to acknowledge Left-wing authoritarianism (Christie & Jahoda, 1954). So did Milton Rokeach in *The Open and Closed Mind: Investigations into The Nature of Belief Systems and Personality Systems*, published in 1960 (Rokeach, 1960). Adorno did not take kindly to these critics, nor did he respond to them publicly, and as a result, these early critics of his are seldom heeded by the majority of researchers active in the field today. Indeed, Bob Altemeyer, a leading figure, once described Left-wing authoritarianism as "the Loch Ness monster of social psychology – lots of shadows, but no monster" (Altemeyer, 1996). The tacit implication of this remark is that while rumors of its existence abound, Left-wing authoritarianism (LWA) never actually shows up under intense scrutiny. Instead, says Altemeyer, Stalin's followers were just Right-wing authoritarians who adopted a Leftish ideology. Altemeyer's insistence on this score seemed to support the widespread belief that Left-wingers are inherently anti-authoritarian, and that Left-wing authoritarianism is therefore rare or non-existent (Altemeyer, 1996; Satel, 2021).

The Current Critique of Adorno et al.

That is basically where matters stood until 2018, when Lucian Conway and three colleagues published an article entitled *Finding the Loch Ness Monster: Left Wing Authoritarianism in the United States* (Conway, Houk, Gornick, & Repke, 2018). Conway et al. maintained that Altemeyer and associates did not find evidence of Left-wing authoritarianism because they had confounded political ideology with authoritarianism per se. That being so, Conway et al. proceeded to supplement and tinker with Altemeyer's celebrated Right Wing Authoritarianism (RWA) scale in various ways. Having administered it to 475 undergrads at the University of Montana, they concluded that Left-wing authoritarianism is as prevalent among "liberals" as RWA is among conservatives.

Then in August of 2021, Thomas Costello and five colleagues published a paper entitled "Clarifying the Nature and Structure of Left Wing Authoritarianism" (Costello et al., 2021). Echoing Conway, Costello et al. insisted that Altemeyer and associates could not find evidence of Left-wing authoritarianism because they were using inappropriate research tools. But rather than tinkering with Altemeyer's RWA scale, as Conway and associates did, they resolved to conceptualize Left-wing authoritarianism "from the ground up" in a process they called "boot strapping," and developed a list of ten "focal constructs" around which to question their respondents (Satel, 2021).

Having constructed new scales, and administered them to 7,258 adults, Costello and associates found that though Left-wing authoritarianism looks and sounds different, there are some significant areas of overlap or convergence between Left- and Right-wing authoritarians. When asked why Left-wing authoritarianism had been all but invisible till now, Costello traced the problem back to Theodor Adorno's landmark study, *The Authoritarian Personality* (Satel, 2021). In his own words:

> The possibility that authoritarianism research has a blind spot for LWA is perhaps unsurprising given that *The Authoritarian Personality* was an effort to describe the psychological appeal of fascism, a far-right ideology. But just as psychologists have recently acknowledged the prospect that a systemic overreliance on Western, Educated, Industrialized, Rich, and Democratic (WEIRD) samples has distorted our ability to make generalized claims about human behavior (Gurven, 2018; Henrich et al., 2010), the psychological processes underlying authoritarianism may be challenging to understand when only rightist authoritarians have been studied.
>
> (Costello, et al. 2021, p. 3)

Agreed. However, this state of affairs is both deeply unfortunate and extremely ironic because though he did not acknowledge the existence of Left-wing authoritarianism in his published work, Adorno was personally tormented by it toward the end of his life. Indeed, his lived experience of Left-wing authoritarianism is quite instructive, and prefigures trends in contemporary universities in several ways.

In "Critical Theory and the Newest Left: What the Frankfurt School has to say about Bureaucratic Progressivism," Alexander Stern describes Theodor Adorno's experience of "Left Fascism" among student radicals in West Germany in the late 1960s. Most of these students, notes Stern, came from privileged backgrounds and were alarmed and appalled by America's conduct of the Vietnam War, by German society's continuing silence and tacit disavowal of its Nazi past, and by the blandishments of consumerism in the West; issues that Adorno himself had drawn attention to. Knowing this, student radicals turned to him for support, putting Adorno in a very difficult position. Why so? Because as Stern points out, he was ". . . at the very least, uncomfortable with what he saw as creeping irrationalism in the New Left of his time, which in turn berated him for his lack of activist commitment." Moreover, says Stern, by 1968 the student movement had become increasingly violent, resorting to takeovers of administrative buildings, attacks on allies who refused their extremes, and classroom disruptions of various kinds. While acknowledging the merit of many of their aspirations and criticisms of society, Adorno refused to endorse these students' methods. As a result, he became a target for their anger, derision, and rowdy protests. Stern notes that:

> In one incident, Adorno called the police to clear student occupiers of the Institute. The hostility to Adorno came to a head the next year when students disrupted a lecture course to demand that Adorno engage in ritual self-criticism for his call to the police, and female students bared their breasts to him, ostensibly in an effort to expose his bourgeois prudery. The course had to be cancelled. Adorno died of a heart attack a few months later, at the age of 65.
>
> (Stern, 2021)

Adorno's tragic predicament had several dimensions that warrant attention today. First, despite his fierce critique of instrumental reason and advanced capitalist society, Adorno wanted to preserve and augment the best features of Western civilization, not to jettison them altogether. In this respect, he resembled Max Horkheimer who believed that ". . . a true conservativism which takes man's spiritual heritage seriously is . . . related to the revolutionary mentality, which does not simply reject that heritage but absorbs it into a new synthesis." The notion that Western civilization has a "spiritual heritage" worth preserving, and that we must avoid throwing the baby out with the bathwater was lost on many young radicals, which prompted Horkheimer to describe them as "pseudorevolutionaries" and their extremist Right-wing counterparts as "pseudoconservatives." Perhaps for that reason—among others, no doubt—Adorno opposed all attempts at using the university as a base from which to change society. On the contrary, as Stern points out, he said that "isolated attempts to introduce radical change in the university...will only fuel the dominant resentment toward intellectuals and thus pave the way for the reaction." (A prescient statement, if ever there was one!) Sadly, this sentiment led to a series of bitter disagreements and acrimonious exchanges between Adorno and Marcuse that shattered their friendship in the months immediately preceding Adorno's death (Jeffries, 2017, chapter 16).[1]

The last surviving member of Horkheimer's circle, Leo Löwenthal, passed away much later, in 1993, and the world has changed greatly in the interim. One notable feature of these changes is that Critical Theory, as Horkheimer, Adorno, and Marcuse conceived of it, has been overwritten or displaced by postmodernism, poststructuralism, Queer theory, Critical Race Theory, and so on. These later approaches to theory are often mislabeled as "Critical Theory," even by many self-styled Critical Theorists, although they rest on fundamentally different premises about the human condition. But now, the role of universities as sites or instigators of social change and/or as hotbeds of pseudo-revolutionary posturing is being widely debated once again. So, what does Left-wing authoritarianism on campus look like today? An inverted mirror image of Right-wing authoritarianism?

Yes and no. In some respects, these two forms of authoritarianism seem quite similar because they exhibit similar cognitive anomalies and distortions that Altemeyer documents thoroughly, including (but not limited to) double think, double standards, confirmation bias, and outright denial. But as a result of their sadomasochistic character, Right-wing authoritarians identify with the aggressor, value hierarchy, and are fixated in stage three or stage four of what Lawrence Kohlberg identified as "conventional normativity." By contrast, today's Left-wing authoritarians identify with the (real or imagined) victims of aggression and are wary of or hostile to hierarchy. Their ethical sensibility tends to be neither pre-conventional, conventional, or post-conventional (in Kohlberg's terms) but *anti-conventional* in character. As a result, rather than transcending the limitations of conventional moral reasoning, they move sideways, so to speak, opposing and inverting conventional normativity by enforcing new forms of obedience and conformity. An example of this among progressives today is the tendency to go beyond de-stigmatizing non-gender conforming identities and behavior and welcoming them into the mainstream to fiercely disparaging cisheternormative identities and behavior, treating them as intrinsically oppressive," putting the vast majority of the population on the defensive for merely being who they are.[2] While not stated explicitly, and not even necessarily conscious, the underlying intention here appears to be twofold: 1) a collective effort to de-pathologize many identities and behaviors that were formerly deemed to be evidence of mental disorder, while 2) simultaneously pathologizing or stigmatizing many forms of identity and behavior that were formerly deemed to be indicative of normality or mental health. The first objective is quite commendable, more often than not. The latter, by contrast, just sows more misery and confusion, and does nothing to advance the cause of general human emancipation.

Despite their preferences for different patterns of idealization and identification, Right- and Left-wing authoritarians both disdain liberal democratic norms and institutions, harbor intolerant or openly hostile attitudes toward those who don't share their world view, and share a pronounced willingness to resort to violence and intimidation to persuade others to dance to their tune. Finally, Right- and Left-wing authoritarians often embrace conspiracy theories, which give voice to their irrational fears and wishes, cover up contradictions, and fill in gaps in their explanatory models and narratives about the way the world works.

Nevertheless, the Leftish tendency to identify with the victim (rather than the aggressor) yields different ideological outcomes and cognitive distortions than one finds among extreme Right wingers. Right-wing authoritarians typically divide people into two categories, e.g. the strong versus the weak, the winners versus the losers, the superior versus the inferior, the pure versus the impure. By contrast, their Left-wing counterparts bifurcate humanity into the oppressed and their oppressors, imperialists and anti-imperialists, the good and the bad, BIPOC and White people. These different ways of carving up humanity prompt Right-wing authoritarians to insist on racial or religious purity as a condition of group membership. Left-wing authoritarians, by contrast, aspire to be more inclusive on race and religion, but nevertheless insist on *ideological* purity.

For example, consider this quote from John Molyneux of the *Socialist Worker's Party* (UK), who claimed that "an illiterate, conservative, superstitious Muslim Palestinian who supports Hamas is more progressive that an educated liberal atheist Israeli who supports Zionism (even critically)" (Quoted in Hirsh, 2018, p. 63). This scathing indictment illustrates the "progressive" authoritarian's tendency to idealize and identify with any member of a group he or she considers to be oppressed and conversely, to devalue, denigrate, or dismiss any member of a group he or she deems to be oppressors. The fact that the illiterate, conservative, and superstitious Hamas supporter is likely to be intensely patriarchal, misogynistic, anti-LGBTQ+, and that he embraces a political movement that is theocratic, authoritarian, and antisemitic to the core—while the Liberal Zionist has few, if any of these attributes—is irrelevant in this political calculus. The former is deemed more "progressive" by virtue of his membership in an oppressed minority, while the latter is cast out among the infidels because he failed the test for ideological purity, which consists—at a bare minimum—of a resolute rejection of Zionism, coupled with the tacit acceptance or active support of an Islamist organization; one that trains young children to hate and kill Jews, not just Israelis. In 2008, when Molyneux made this absurd claim, many people on the Left still regarded a statement like this as over the top, if not absolute rubbish. But not anymore. Now it is simply conventional wisdom in many, if not most activist circles, including many psychoanalytic ones.

Another closely related characteristic shared by Right- and Left-wing authoritarians is antisemitism, which is often disguised by (or channeled into) anti-Zionism and vocal support for Islamist organizations (Hirsh, 2018; Linfield, 2019; Randall, 2021). But what is antisemitism, exactly? For the sake of clarity and convenience, let's avoid the current controversies concerning the IHRA's "Working Definition" and *The Jerusalem Declaration*. Instead, let us define anti-Semitism simply as an irrational fear or belief that by virtue of their faith or heredity, Jews pose an actual or potential threat to the safety, well-being, or spiritual and ethical integrity of their non-Jewish neighbors. This inchoate fear (and the mistrust and hatred that flow from it) can vary in intensity considerably, depending on the person, their social environment, and their moment in history. Depending on circumstances, it can be mild, engendering casual disdain and microaggressions. At a more pronounced level, it produces outright discrimination and violence escalating all the way up to genocide (Burston, 2021).

Is antisemitism a form of racism? Probably so. However, Karin Stögner, quite rightly stresses the distinctive character of antisemitism when she points out that:

> Both colonial and apartheid racism is based on the hierarchical construction of supposedly superior and inferior races. The enemy, constructed as primitive and inferior, represents a lack of civilization and modernity, while racists consider themselves representatives of civilization. Absent are conspiracy myths presuming People of Color and colonized people secretly rule the world, control the media and finance, and accelerate the processes of modernization, globalization and cosmopolitanism. These are usually not part of racist ideology. Such conspiracy myths, however, are an essential feature of antisemitism, which suspects an intangible power resides among Jews, one that is ubiquitous and to which antisemites do not feel superior but rather inferior.
>
> (Stögner, 2020)

In other words, what differentiates antisemitism from other hateful prejudices are the characteristics attributed to the out-group in question and the tendency among antisemites to disseminate conspiracy theories. So, for example, White Supremacists often imagine that Jews possess a somewhat *superior* intelligence, but are also more devious, acquisitive, or power hungry than average, lacking loyalty to anyone but their own kind, or to any country but Israel. And needless to say, most Right-wing antisemites are *also* racists. But—and this is crucial—though they may vehemently deny it, so are many *anti-racist* and progressive activists, who hide their antisemitic prejudices (from themselves and from others) by saying that Jews, being White, enjoy unearned privilege, and therefore *must* have engaged in some sort of devious or deplorable behavior to achieve their place in the social order. Alternatively, they may rationalize their antisemitism by hiding it behind a barrage of fierce anti-Zionist rhetoric. And often enough, they employ both of these rationalizations concurrently.

It wasn't always thus. In the 19th century, Left-wing leaders like Wilhelm Marr, Eugene Dühring, and anarchists like Pierre-Joseph Proudhon and Mikhail Bakunin openly and repeatedly characterized Jews as an international cabal bent on infiltrating, subverting, and dominating the West through their market machinations and behind-the-scenes chicanery. They made no attempt to disguise or disavow their antisemitism, and openly shared antisemitic memes with their reactionary, Right-wing counterparts, like Richard Wagner and his son-in-law Houston Stewart Chamberlain (Wistrich, 2010). Among these were the bizarre fantasies of secret Jewish power disseminated in *The Protocols of the Elders of Zion*, a spurious document fabricated by the Czarist police to justify the lethal persecution of Jews in the Russian empire. One of Hitler's favorite books, *The Protocols* purported to be the proceedings of a meeting of Jewish leaders from all over Europe plotting to infiltrate and take over business, finance, the media, and all branches of government at the turn of the last century.

In our times, the conspiratorial thinking that gave rise to *The Protocols of the Elders of Zion* shows up vividly on August 18, 1988, in the Covenant of the Islamic Resistance Movement, otherwise known as Hamas. Article 22 of their charter reads (in part):

> For a long time, the enemies have been planning, skillfully and with precision, for the achievement of what they have attained. They took into consideration the causes affecting the current of events. They strived to amass great and substantive material wealth which they devoted to the realisation of their dream. With their money, they took control of the world media, news agencies, the press, publishing houses, broadcasting stations, and others. With their money they stirred revolutions in various parts of the world with the purpose of achieving their interests and reaping the fruit therein. They were behind the French Revolution, the Communist revolution and most of the revolutions we heard and hear about, here and there. With their money they formed secret societies, such as Freemasons, Rotary Clubs, the Lions and others in different parts of the world for the purpose of sabotaging societies and achieving Zionist interests. With their money they were able to control imperialistic countries and instigate them to colonize many countries in order to enable them to exploit their resources and spread corruption there.
>
> You may speak as much as you want about regional and world wars. They were behind World War I, when they were able to destroy the Islamic Caliphate, making financial gains and controlling resources. They obtained the Balfour

> Declaration, formed the League of Nations through which they could rule the world. They were behind World War II, through which they made huge financial gains by trading in armaments and paved the way for the establishment of their state. It was they who instigated the replacement of the League of Nations with the United Nations and the Security Council to enable them to rule the world through them. There is no war going on anywhere, without having their finger in it.

Apart from Hamas' lament for the demise of the Caliphate and their absurd claims about the United Nations, these remarks conjure with far-fetched and unsubstantiated rumors about secret Jewish power and behind-the-scenes influence lifted directly from the *Protocols of the Elders of Zion*; a scurrilous document which, ironically, was on display and widely distributed at the *World Conference Against Racism, Xenophobia and Other Forms of Intolerance* (WCAR) in Durban, South Africa in 2001 (Hirsh, 2018). This fact illustrates how deeply Nazi antisemitism influenced Islamist ideology, which in turn had penetrated Left-wing and "progressive" circles well before the turn of the century (Küntzel, 2024). It also helps explain why both Nazism and Islamism openly proclaim their goal of world domination, and are fiercely anti-democratic, misogynistic, and anti-LGBTQ as well as antisemitic.

But if Islamist fanatics and Right-wing extremists exhibit these stark similarities in the structure of their beliefs, why do many Left-wingers embrace conspiracy theories that are strikingly akin to—and often intricately interwoven with—theirs? And how can doing so possibly be construed as "progressive"? This is actually a *very* important question, but one seldom raised by people on the Left, who are reluctant to acknowledge the intriguing oddity of this situation for fear of being labelled Islamophobic. Nevertheless, if we're being honest, at the end of the day, Islamist movements and organizations like Hamas are really anything *but* progressive.

There are several reasons for this worrisome state of affairs. One is that Nazism and Islamism are both premised on a thorough-going rejection of the Enlightenment's legacy, as are postmodernism and poststructuralism, which are often confused with Critical Theory, as noted previously. Another reason is that, despite their differences, Nazism and Islamism both possess stark Manichean, world views constructed around rigid binaries—good and evil, pure and impure, oppressor and oppressed. Dogmatism and binary thinking are inimical to the development of *dialectical* reason favored by the Frankfurt School. Moreover, they stifle and/or displace what Erich Fromm called *rational doubt*. (Fromm, 1941; Fromm, 1947). Rational doubt is the foundation for critical thinking, or what Fromm's erstwhile colleagues in the Frankfurt School called substantive reason, which is not to be confused with *instrumental reason*—mere intelligence, cleverness, or cunning, which may be (and often is) harnessed in the service of authoritarian political agendas. In any case, extrapolating from Fromm's work, we can say that the absence or atrophy of rational doubt in any given population creates the ideal conditions for *irrational* doubt to flourish and grip large segments of a given population, spawning lurid conspiracy theories.

A prime example of this phenomenon is the belief shared by many Muslims and Left-wingers, namely, that the attack on the World Trade Center on September 11, 2001 was an "inside job" orchestrated by the Israeli government and/or by the Bush administration to justify launching a war on Islam. This narrative was repeatedly reinforced by the Iranian regime and its proxy, Hezbollah. Quite obviously, these claims are rooted in a profound mistrust of Israel and the USA. Less obviously, perhaps, this conspiracy theory was rooted in a fervent desire to cling to the victim role. In any case, doubts about bin Laden's culpability are irrational because they lack any evidentiary basis, conveniently shifting blame for his misdeeds onto Israel, rather than to Islamist terror, despite the fact that bin Laden had a long record of terrorist activity, and that 15 of the 19 terrorists aboard the planes were Saudi citizens, like bin Laden himself (Sardarizadeh, 2021).

Nevertheless, despite its manifestly irrational character, some version of this pernicious nonsense persists in Muslim countries and more importantly, in some Left-wing circles to this very day, attesting to a failure of collective reality testing fostered by dogmatism, binary thinking, and what psychoanalysts call rationalization and "splitting," e.g. the tacit assumption that devout Muslims are all innocent and good, and incapable of doing such evil deeds, while Israelis are all bad, and capable of doing anything to forward their agenda—even destroying the Twin Towers.

Another reason that Left-wing authoritarians embrace conspiracy theories is that despite (and because of) the fact that they are dogmatic, they are highly suggestible, and prone to uncritically accept the ideas of people they admire, especially if these influencers present themselves as champions of the underdog. When people like these tell them that Islamism is progressive, they tend to go along. No doubt this is what happened at Berkely in 2006 when Judith Butler said:

> I think: Yes, understanding Hamas, Hezbollah as social movements that are progressive, that are on the Left, that are part of a global Left, is extremely important. That does not stop us from being critical of certain dimensions of both movements. (…) So again, a critical, important engagement. I mean, I certainly think it should be entered into the conversation on the Left. I similarly think boycotts and divestment procedures are, again, an essential component of any resistance movement.
>
> (Quoted in Johnson, 2013)

Butler later insisted that her remarks were taken out of context. Perhaps so. But she cannot deny that her remarks, coming in the aftermath of the Durban conference in 2001, where Hamas were palpably present and heartily embraced by their conference hosts, had a tremendous impact on her audience, and on thousands upon thousands of her admirers around the world. A refreshing counterbalance to Butler's comments can be found in the work of Slovenian philosopher Slavoj Žižek, who decried the contemporary Left's

> uneasiness when it comes to unambiguously condemning anti-Semitism, as if by doing so one would be playing into Zionist hands. There should be no compromise here . . .
>
> (Žižek, 2011, p. 136)

Žižek then goes on to lament the

> . . . all too easy and uncritical acceptance of anti-American and anti-Western Muslim groups as representing "progressive" forms of struggle, as automatic allies; groups like Hamas and Hezbollah suddenly appear as revolutionary agents, even though their ideology is explicitly anti-modern, rejecting the entire egalitarian legacy of the French Revolution. (Things have gone so far here that some on the contemporary Left even consider an emphasis on atheism as a Western colonial plot.) Against this temptation, we should insist on the unconditional right to conduct a public critical analysis of all religions, Islam included – and the saddest thing is that one should even have to mention this.
>
> (Žižek, 2011, p. 137)

Coming in the wake of the Rushdie fatwa, the murder of Theo van Gogh, 9/11, and many other Islamist attacks in or on the West, Žižek certainly had a point. But let us not forget that Islamist groups do not merely export terror. They also terrorize their own people. As Susie Linfield quite rightly points out:

> There's little liberation, justice, or freedom to be found in Gaza, where there are no opposition political parties, no elections, and no freedom of religion, the press, or protest. Opponents are arrested, tortured, and sometimes executed. (Yahya Sinwar, a head of Hamas's armed wing, was known as "the butcher of Khan Younis" for his brutality toward other Palestinians.) Abortion and homosexuality are outlawed (what are those protestors with "Queers for Palestine" signs thinking?); mentioning trans rights would be unwise. It is legal for husbands to beat their wives, and so-called honor killings go unpunished. The ruling clique is notoriously corrupt, and though Gazans are very poor, Hamas is a very rich organization.
>
> (Linfield, 2023)

Furthermore, as recent events have reminded us, Hamas routinely and deliberately uses Palestinians as human shields and devotes the vast majority of its considerable resources to planning the destruction of Israel, rather than to ensuring the prosperity and safety of Gaza's inhabitants, a responsibility it outsources to UNWRA, and by implication, to a multitude of donors to the UN. Or consider the case of Hezbollah, the Iranian-backed Islamist militia to Israel's north. Hezbollah gave vigorous support to Bashar al-Assad's bloodthirsty regime in the Syrian civil war, in which more than 600,000 people perished and more than 11,000,000 were displaced. It also helped the Iranian regime suppress the massive demonstrations that erupted after the death of Mahsa Amini, a 22-year-old Kurdish woman, who was arrested in Tehran for wearing her hijab improperly and died in police custody on September 16, 2022. Hundreds of protesters, including many children, died in the demonstrations that ensued, that rocked the entire country for weeks. In addition to those who were killed, thousands more were blinded, and hundreds more were arrested, raped, tortured, or executed without a fair trial. Nevertheless, when explaining Hezbollah's involvement in suppressing the Iranian protests of 2022, Hassan Nassrallah, the former leader of Hezbollah, referred to Mahsa Amini's death only in passing, framing it dismissively as a "vague incident" orchestrated by hostile forces to undermine the Iranian regime. The silence that greeted Nassrallah's smug, callous, and blatantly dishonest remarks among many American "progressives" was deafening, foreshadowing their refusal to condemn and their frank celebration of the brutal horrifying and misogyny on display in the massacres of October 7, 2024, which sparked the latest Gaza war (Linfield, 2023).

In any case, the violence that Islamist groups practice is not merely visited on Israelis and Westerners, but on Muslims too; Muslims who, if they do not fall into line, are deemed to be traitors, or at best, completely expendable. Indeed, if one tallied up all the murders and human rights abuses perpetrated by Islamist movements and regimes against Muslim populations, that number would exceed Israel's many misdeeds against the Palestinians by a considerable margin. Yet many anti-Zionist and anti-racist activists—who routinely demonize Left-wing Zionists—maintain an alarming silence on this score. Why? Perhaps it is because they fear being labelled Islamophobic far more than they fear Islamism itself. Worse yet, they often celebrate these Islamist movements as "freedom fighters" and champions of human rights. Hence the blatant double standard that shapes so much Leftist discourse on the Middle East nowadays, criticizing Zionism with extreme ferocity, but praising Islamist groups, giving them a free pass, or at the very least, providing them with ample excuses to "explain," "contextualize," or avert attention from their dreadful human rights records. Yet these very same people never shrink from criticizing Christian nationalism or the perverse and bloody-minded messianism of Jewish extremists in the Occupied West Bank.

Sadly, this state of affairs is not confined to the fringes any more, and even shows up in psychoanalytic circles. Consider the case of Dr. Lara Sheehi, former President of the Society for Psychoanalysis and Psychoanalytic Psychology (SPPP), otherwise known as Division 39 of the American Psychological Association. Together with her husband, Stephen Sheehi, Sultan Quaboos Professor of Middle Eastern Studies at William and Mary, Lara Sheehi is the author of *Psychoanalysis Under Occupation: Practicing Resistance in Palestine*. In the week following the October Hamas murder spree, Sheehi posted frequently on Instagram, contesting reports of Hamas violence, making competing claims, such as: "The Zionist entity has a long history of sexual violence against Palestinian women." She decried "the claims of mass rape used to siphon off support from the Palestinian resistance." She urged widespread statements asserting that "the state of Israel is engaged in a war of extermination against the Palestinians," and that the October "armed resistance . . . is not only Hamas' but that of the entire Palestinian people," despite the well documented fact that many Palestinians emphatically do *not* support Hamas, or do so only episodically, and with considerable reservations. She also gave her vigorous support to George Washington University's chapter of Students for Justice in Palestine (SJP), who celebrated the events of October 7 and were subsequently banned from campus. Indeed, she echoed SJP when she castigated GWU's president as follows: "How dare you, Ellen Cranberg. How dare you call our mourning a 'celebration of terrorism.' How dare you slander the names of our martyrs as terrorists."

But Sheehi's recent advocacy on behalf of Hamas is nothing new. In an article entitled "The war tearing psychoanalysis apart" in *The Guardian* on June 16, 2023, J. Oliver Conroy cited a telling tweet on her now deleted Twitter account from May 22, 2021, where she declared: "If you see this and STILL entertain for even a split second that Hamas is the terrorist entity, there is literally zero hope for you, your soul, or your general existence as an ethical human being in this world."

While I commend Conroy for bringing this Twitter quote to light, I object to his way of framing her remarks here. Why? Because, according to him, Sheehi merely believes that "some human beings are beyond redemption." But that interpretation is so anodyne it completely misses the point. Sheehi referred specifically to people who entertain the idea that Hamas is a terrorist organization "even for a split second," calling them hopeless cases, lost souls who have forfeited any vestiges of ethical integrity they may once have had. It is not clear from context who authorized Sheehi to say which thoughts clinicians may or may not entertain without putting their souls in peril. But if we're being honest, we must point out that the notion that entertaining certain thoughts in consciousness *automatically* disqualifies one from being an ethical or worthy human being—and by implication, a competent clinician—runs completely contrary to the basic rule of psychoanalysis and the technique of free association. Besides, on reflection, the governments of the United States, the United Kingdom, Canada, Australia, New Zealand, the European Union, and several Scandinavian countries all deem Hamas to be a terrorist organization. The governments of Russia, China, North Korea, Cuba, Iran, Syria, and Turkey, in contrast, do not. So, most countries that deem Hamas to be a terrorist organization are democracies, albeit flawed democracies, whereas countries that do *not* are often governed by brutal, authoritarian regimes that crush dissent within their borders with a brazen disregard for human life and human rights. That being so, if the possibility that Hamas is a terrorist organization *never* crosses your mind, or if your assessment of Hamas aligns squarely with Sheehi's—and by implication, with some of the most belligerent and bloodthirsty regimes on the planet—perhaps you should wonder *why* this is the case.

In a videotaped interview for Jewish Voices for Peace earlier this year, Sheehi said:

> This is my own urgent call to the clinicians among us . . . from the river to the sea . . . we must center Palestine in every effort . . . This needs to be done not as an offshoot of our clinical work, but as a central working tenet of any clinical praxis that purports to be interested in alleviating the suffering of others.
> (https://www.youtube.com/watch?v=4JFqgJr9iJ4)

Demanding that clinicians "center Palestine in every effort" and treat the Palestinian people's struggle as "a central working tenet of any clinical praxis" is extremely problematic, because training in psychoanalysis (or indeed any mental health profession) should not demand adherence to any specific political ideology as a precondition for training. Nor should it require that practitioners become activists as well as clinicians. On the contrary, becoming an activist as well as a clinician should always remain a matter of individual choice and personal conscience.

To conclude, Adorno et al. discerned significant correlations between antisemitism and Right-wing authoritarianism (Adorno et al., 1950) but saw little (if any) correlation between antisemitism and those who embraced liberal or Left-leaning political views. In his day, perhaps, it seemed appropriate, indeed quite necessary, to distinguish between (Right-wing) authoritarians, on the one hand, and liberal or Left-leaning people with "progressive" political views on the other. And of course, only the former were deemed to be susceptible to conspiracy theories.

Many people still cling stubbornly to this outdated template for political psychology. But with all due respect to Adorno and his fans and followers, the entire political landscape in the West has shifted dramatically since 1950. The antisemitism roiling American campuses today, is often expressed or embodied in conspiracy theories of one sort or another and comes primarily from the identitarian Left, who call themselves "progressive," but often ally themselves with authoritarian and theocratic Islamist movements, and vilify and dismiss even the most progressive and humane Zionist voices and positions as reactionary or racist. Clearly, we need a new political vocabulary, and new analytical tools to ensure that the damage they do—and have already done—can be contained and, if possible, remedied with the passage of time. Finally, regardless of the outcome of the current Middle East war, we need to reconcile ourselves to the fact that antisemitism—which lay dormant, or dwelt on the margins of American civic culture for many decades—has returned with a vengeance and won't melt back into the ether any time soon.

Notes

1 Much as he disagreed with them about Freud, Fromm's ambivalent appraisal of student radicals in the late 60s was closer to Horkheimer and Adorno's than it was to Marcuse's, who tended to champion them without reservation. For more on this subject see (Jeffries, 2017).

2 For a fascinating case study of anti-conventional normativity among Left-wing authoritarians in the 20th century, see Alexander Stille's recent book *The Sullivanians: Sex, Psychotherapy and the Wild Life of An American Commune* (New York: Farrar, Straus and Giroux, 2023).

References

Adorno, T. et al. 1950. *The Authoritarian Personality.* New York: W.W. Norton.

Adorno, T. 1951. "Freudian Theory and the Pattern of Fascist Propaganda," reprinted in Sigmund Freud, Paul Roazen (Ed.) Englewood Cliffs, NJ: Prentice Hall, 1973.

Altemeyer, B. 1996. *The Authoritarian Specter*. Cambridge: Harvard University Press.

Benjamin, J. 1988. *The Bonds of Love: Psychoanalysis, Feminism and the Problem of Domination*New York: Pantheon.

Brunner, J. 1994. "Looking into the Hearts of Workers, or: How Erich Fromm Turned Critical Theory into Empirical Social Research." *Political Psychology*, vol. 15 no. 4. 631–654.

Burston, D. 1991. *The Legacy of Erich Fromm.* Cambridge: Harvard University Press.

Burston, D. 2021. *Anti-Semitism and Analytical Psychology: Jung, Politics and Culture.* London: Routledge.

Chancer, L. 1992. *Sadomasochism in Everyday Life: The Dynamics of Power and Powerlessness*. New Jersey: Rutgers University Press.

Christie, R. and Jahoda, M. (Eds.) 1954. *The Authoritarian Personality: Continuities in Social Research.* Glencoe, IL: The Free Press.

Chodorow, N. 1978. *The Reproduction of Mothering*. University of California Press.

Conway, L. G. et al. 2018. "Finding the Loch Ness Monster: Left Wing Authoritarianism in the United States." *Political Psychology*. Advance publication online. https://doi.org/10.1111/pops12470

Costello, T. et al. 2021. "Clarifying the Nature and Structure of Left Wing Authoritarianism." *The Journal of Personality and Social Psychology*. Online First Publication, August 12, 2021. http://dx.doi.org/10.1037/pspp0000341

Freud, S. 1905. *Three Essays on the Theory of Sexuality*. In *Standard Edition,* vol. 7. London: Hogarth Press.

Freud, S. 1924. "The Economic Problem of Masochism." *Standard Edition*, vol. 19. London: Hogarth Press.

Fromm, E. 1941. *Escape From Freedom.* Reprint, Avon Books, New York, 1965.

Fromm, E. 1947. *Man For Himself: An Inquiry into Psychology and Ethics.* Greenwich, CT: Fawcett Premier Books.

Fromm, E. 1956. *The Art of Loving.* New York: Harper & Row.

Fromm, E. 1984. *The Working Class in Weimar Germany: A Psychological and Sociological Study.* Cambridge: Harvard University Press.

Gurven, M. D. (2018). "Broadening Horizons: Sample Diversity and Socioecological Theory are Essential to the Future of Psychological Science." *Proceedings of the National Academy of Sciences of the United States of America*, vol. 115 no. 45. 11420–11427. https://doi.org/10.1073/pnas.1720433115

Henrich, J., Heine, S. J., and Norenzayan, A. 2010. "Most People are not WEIRD." *Nature*, vol. 466 no. 7302. 29–29. https://doi.org/10.1038/466029a

Hirsch, D. 2018. *Contemporary Left Anti-Semitism.* London: Routledge.

Jacoby, R. 1975. *Social Amnesia: A Critique of Conformist Psychology from to Adler to Laing*. Boston: Beacon Press.

Jay, M. 1973. *The Dialectical Imagination*. Boston: Little, Brown & Co.

Jeffries, S. 2017. *Grand Hotel Abyss: The Lives of the Frankfurt School*. London: Verso.

Johnson, A. 2013. "Book Review: Parting of Ways: Jewishness and the Critique of Zionism." *Fathom*. Spring issue.

Krafft-Ebing, R. 1886. *Sexual Psychopathy: A Clinical Forensic Study*, Rebman, F.J. (Trans.), New York: Rebman Company, 1903.

Küntzel, M. 2024. *Nazis, Islamic Antisemitism and the Middle East*. London: Routledge.

Linfield, S. 2019. *The Lion's Den: Zionism and the Left from Hannah Arendt to Noam Chomsky*. Yale University Press.

Linfield, S. 2023. "The Return of the Progressive Atrocity." *Quillette*, Nov. 18.

Marcuse, H. 1955. *Eros and Civilization*. Boston: Beacon Press.

McLaughlin, N. 2021. *Erich Fromm and Global Public Sociology*. Bristol, UK: University of Bristol Press.

Randall, D. 2021. *Confronting Anti-Semitism on the Left: Arguments for Socialists*. London: No Pasaran.

Reich, W. 1933. *The Mass Psychology of Fascism*. Reprinted by Pocket Books, New York, 1970.

Rokeach, M. 1960. *The Open and Closed Mind*. New York: Basic Books.

Sardarizadeh, S. 2021. "11 September 2001: The Conspiracy Theories Still Spreading 20 Years Later." London: *BBC News*, September 10, 2021.

Satel, S. 2021. "The Experts Somehow Overlooked the Authoritarianism of the Left." *The Atlantic*. September 25 issue.

Stern, A. 2021. "Critical Theory and the Newest Left: What the Frankfurt School has to say About Bureaucratic Progressivism." *The Hedgehog Review: Critical Reflections on Contemporary Culture*. Institute for Advanced Studies in Culture, June 25.

Stögner, K. 2020. "Intersectionality and anti-Semitism: A New Approach." *Fathom: For a Deeper Understanding of Israel and the Region*, May issue.

Wistrich, R. 2010. *A Lethal Obsession: Anti-Semitism from Antiquity to the Global Jihad*. New York: Random House.

Žižek, S. 2011. *Living in the End Times*. London: Verso.

Chapter 11

From Solidarity to Identity

Group Narcissism and the Demise of Left Politics

Michael J. Thompson

Introduction

American politics has witnessed a decisive shift in its civic culture. Where political liberalism was once the ideational ground for our political culture and institutions, anti-liberal values and ideologies are now gradually becoming more prevalent and robust, on both the political right and the political left. On the right, we can see the rise of authoritarian populism and neo-fascist impulses. A new authoritarian character has been shaped by a crumbling middle-class society, social anxiety amid social changes in our ethnic makeup, and more muscular right-wing media that has been able to create an alternate epistemic and moral ecosystem, exacerbating social ills and ramping up feelings of anxiety and insecurity. On the left, what now passes for "progressive" politics is largely defined not by movements for distributive justice and questions of concrete social, economic and political power, but by a new politics of identity and group-affiliation—a politics of culture has effectively displaced the traditional politics of power that once animated progressive movements.

Although it is tempting to see these changes on the political right and left as two sides of a singular characterological dimension, that of right-wing and left-wing authoritarianism respectively, I will argue that the transformation of the left is not adequately captured by the concept of authoritarianism but, rather, by a very different, more complex response. Right-wing authoritarians are sadomasochistically oriented toward a submission to perceived established authority (parents, police, figures that uphold traditional hierarchies, and so on), they believe that these authorities should be invested with the power to coerce and/or punish others to follow the norms they see as correct, and also are attracted to the security of hierarchy and order.

In contrast, the proliferation of non- and anti-liberal values and practices on the left does not predispose them to these orientations or beliefs but, rather, toward a structure of thinking, perceiving and feeling that is intolerant of views that encroach on their cathected beliefs about group identity. In contrast to those that see these trends on the left as an example of "left-wing authoritarianism," I think it is more useful and correct to understand this kind of political thinking (or non-thinking, as

DOI: 10.4324/9781003389927-11

it were) as the result of a specific kind of defect in the self-structure of modern subjects that predisposes them toward group-think and an intolerance of ambiguity and complexity. The need to belong to a group, to be recognized and find inclusion is a deep human need. But in contemporary left politics, this has become an inflamed and distended psychic even existential need—one that has been created by what I will call here a "psychic regression" where the ego's striving for autonomy or any other kind of self-reflective, critical agency becomes frustrated.

The kind of moral autonomy that is capable of tolerant, open-minded discourse requires a kind of psychic autonomy and ego-integrity that promotes synthetic capacities of thinking and consciousness that allows for more open, more critical forms of reasoning and reality processing. The focus on identity is a regressive desire rooted in the weakened ego's need for self-coherence; it allows for a kind of relatedness with others that communicates to the ego a sense of belonging and mitigates against existential and ontological forms of anxiety. Identity, in this sense, is a kind of fetish in that it takes a part, a feature of human existence that stands in for a richer form of object-relatedness. I will focus on both of these concepts—of group narcissism and the anaclitic self—in order to understand the psychic structure behind the kind of dogmatic and intolerant mind that characterizes much of contemporary left discourse and praxis.

This also finds resonance in the thesis introduced by Milton Rokeach, that of the "closed" or "dogmatic" mind. By applying the concept of the "dogmatic mind" I mean to convey a kind of lack of reflective thinking that is a response to ego-threat: that is, to the anxiety produced when one's values and convictions are called into question. For individuals suffering from anaclitic self-hood, the ideals they dogmatically defend are extensions of the fragile self. For those on the left, this means calling into question the forms of identity to which they cling in order to protect their sense of self. As the ego withers under conditions of post-industrial society, so too does the need grow for self-esteem and meaning. These are found through different forms of group narcissism and a need to seek out meaning, a coherent sense of personal identity, and what I call "surplus recognition" by members of a group with which one seeks some sense of identification.

The anaclitic self is impelled, due to its inherent weakness and lack of coherence, toward often masochistic relations to the group, but it can also turn into a sadistic relation to those objects that it cannot tolerate. But on the whole, I find it difficult to characterize the left as evincing a strong enough pattern of sado-masochism to qualify it as "authoritarian," since this would entail a devotion to hierarchical structures and deference to traditional forms of authority that do not appear in any meaningful way among left-wing groups or ideology. The extremes of the left are therefore not to be seen as "left-wing authoritarianism," but, rather, as the instantiation of the kind of closed or dogmatic mind that has become increasingly prevalent in an age of anxiety, oligarchic inequality, and mass/social media. This is the product of a withered ego that has been deprived of the kinds of basic security and meaning that has been stripped from modern cultures as a result of the alienation, reification and inequality that characterizes what we generally refer to as neoliberalism or what I will call the "cybernetic society."

The kind of self that results from this process of ego-regression is what call an "anaclitic self" where the psychic need for identity and for group belonging lead to a form of what Erich Fromm called "group narcissism." The dogmatic or closed mind is predisposed to anti-democratic forms of thinking: to intolerance, toward a simplification of moral categories, an incapacity to synthesize complex and contradictory ideas, and so on. This paper will explore the way that this dogmatic mind has come about and how it shapes "progressive" politics and its decidedly anti-liberal stance. This move to the anaclitic self, to group narcissism and identity as the basis of political consciousness effects a shift from the solidaristic politics of the pre-neoliberal age to an identitarian politics of the present.

Cybernetic Society and the Self

In order to get to the heart of my argument, that of the creation of the anaclitic self, a self that is impelled toward group narcissism and group identity, it is important to chart the social changes under capitalism that have made for the production of such a self. The transition from welfare-state capitalism to neoliberalism has meant a changed paradigm of political economy where social rights are privatized, income and wealth distribution de-democratized, and new forms of speculation emerge in order to generate surplus. Digging deeper into the social logic of this merging of technology, economic growth, and the need for control and securing streams of surplus extraction in mass societies is what I have called the *cybernetic* features of late modernity. This describes the ways that logics of control and planning, the maximization of economistic values such as efficiency and the cultivation of legitimacy of these system goals and processes. This was beginning to be seen in the 1950s and 1960s as an intrusion of private power into public ends and purposes. Henry Kariel, in his discussion of this shift in the late 1950s, describes the nucleus of this phenomenon of the imperatives of the managerial logics over the individual:

> [T]his should require little more than arranging his environment so as to make him truly comfortable, giving him the opportunity to become the communal, self-renouncing creature he naturally seems to be. Those who are assuming such managerial responsibilities may now purposefully intervene in the individual's life by administering what affects his drives. As they scrupulously observe whether his motions and emotions tend to conform to the ideal of social harmony, as they test whether the myths calculated to galvanize him will in practice induce him to behave appropriately, they make man's industry correspond with what has been identified as his true interest.[1]

As a result of these economic shifts there has been economic divestment in public goods and public ends. The secure social structures that were once rooted in the principles of the social welfare state have given way not only to new forms of economic precarity and inequality, they have diminished extra-material values that once gave liberal culture an impetus for cultural and political evolution and replaced them with values harnessed to system logics of organization, efficiency, productivity, control, and growth. At almost all levels, education has been rendered an extension of market forces and industrial needs. At the same time, as the middle segments of the income and wealth distribution fall behind the upper tail of the distribution, family and community life becomes subject increasingly to a temporal, spatial, and wage squeeze that creates pressures on the most intimate spheres of relatedness from the family to friendships to civic life. Social relations become increasingly brittle and shallow as communal forms of life are shattered. Add to this the expansion of technical modes of production and social control that seek to circuit affective drives and desire toward material consumption, commodification, and the legitimacy of system imperatives. The more insecure the individual is in modern society, the more anxiety begins to take over the mind and, with time, the relational matrix of which that individual is a part.

The self, then, as a result of these drastic social shifts, responds with anxiety. The kind of ego that develops is one that is focused on as a locus of manipulated desires and consciousness for the purposes of system legitimacy. At the same time, these same social logics actively shred and place pressure on increasingly brittle forms of relatedness, causing a pervasive ontological insecurity. The phenomenon of the weakened or withered ego has been at the center of critical theory's approach to understanding modern society from the beginning. The phenomenon appears in different theoretical languages, but in its most succinct form, it seeks to capture the ways that the critical capacities of the individual in modern society atrophy and its structures of autonomy and individual vitality wither. Marx's reflection on alienation were a first glimpse at this problem under the conditions of organized patterned forms of labor under capitalism. But other theorists from Simmel to Weber to Lukács also pointed to the process of atrophy of the self under the hypertrophy of modern social systems. In psychoanalytic terms, critical theorists saw this phenomenon in more nuanced light. For them, this problem existed as a result of structural changes in society and the ways that family life have been absorbed into the structural dynamics of mass society.

All of this has severe consequences on the structure and dynamics of the self. As Herbert Marcuse saw in during the welfare-state phase of capitalism:

> The immediate, automatic identification (which may have been characteristic of primitive forms of association) reappears in high industrial civilization; its new 'immediacy,' however, is the product of a sophisticated, scientific management and organization. In the process, the 'inner' dimension of the mind in which opposition to the status quo can take root is whittled down.[2]

Neoliberalism oversaw an expansion of both the exploitive as well as the managerial logics of capital. This has had a profound effect on the nature of identity and feelings of psychic security. The basic problem of identity under neoliberalism has been defined by (1) the erosion and negation of traditional structures of belief and disturbances in primary, familial relations; and (2) a result of the transformation of economic life from industrial to post-industrial and service-based economic activities, the undermining of secondary associational life which, under industrial society, once provided a stable, secure sense of self. Identity in the post-industrial context is a means to hold on to a stable sense of self, albeit not from a position of autonomy and creative self-assertion, but from a position of insecurity and need for narcissistic anchoring. The shattering of traditional forms of social traditions and practices results in a "homeless mind," or a form of life where "the pluralistic structures of modern society have made the life of more and more individuals migratory, ever-changing, mobile. In everyday life the modern individual continuously alternates between highly discrepant and often contradictory social contexts."[3] The ego therefore has no base, no ground for its autonomy.

This is an important point to stress. The development of a secure, self-confident ego requires a stable and secure foundation in the family's structure of authority. As Paul Verhaeghe has argued: "Identity develops optimally in a stable environment where clear authority figures ensure secure bonding. In other words, a child flourishes when people take decisions on its behalf in a consistent way."[4] The autonomy of the self comes about via a gradual integration of the capacity for decision-making and taking oneself more and more as an internal authority over those decisions. A coherent and integrated self begins to take shape as this process continues and interpersonal experiences validate one's understanding of oneself as possessing internal control mechanisms. But neoliberalism has gradually deprived the family of this function. Extra-familial authority has outstripped the privacy of the family. As Herbert Marcuse insightfully observed in the 1960s:

> The social development that has dethroned the individual as an economic subject as also reduced, to an extreme degree, the individualistic function of the family in favor of more effective powers. The younger generation is taught the reality principle less through the family than outside the family; it learns socially useful reactions and ways of behaving outside of the protected private sphere of the family.[5]

More recently, thinkers such as Anthony Giddens have charted the ways that this forms the basis for existential anxiety. Indeed, not unlike Fromm's ideas about the nature of social pathology or Harry Stack Sullivan's theories about the interpersonal nature of anxiety, Giddens shows that what he calls "high modernity" is characterized by "profound processes of the reorganization of time and space, coupled to the expansion of disembedding mechanisms – mechanisms which prise social relations free from the hold of specific locales, recombining them across wide time-space distances."[6] This has the effect of breaking down the traditional forms of protection to which the self had access in traditional societies. What comes to fill the void are abstract systems, mediated forms of self-understanding, commodified ego-ideals, and a shriveling of both the quality and quantity of organic social ties.

The commodification of every aspect of human existence—from the child in the womb to old age and death—has essentially made every element of living a space for market forces and, with it, risk, insecurity, and anxiety.

Add to this the intensified penetration of the commodity form into the lifeworld of individuals. With the decline of global profit rates in the 1970s emerged a continuous need for capital to transform all aspects of life into possible spaces for surplus extraction. With this has come the crowding out of extra-economic values from much of contemporary cultural life. Consumption and the need to turn oneself into that which can be consumed (by the market), into a commodity, has come with a psychic price: namely, the constriction of meaning provided to the self. As the organizational framework of values and meaning is gradually purged from the lifeworld, disorientation and anxiety begin to set in. As social relations become ever more brittle, contingent and shallow, to so too does the need for a sense of rootedness and belonging. The effect of this is that the ego begins to wither; it begins a process of disintegration as mutual forms of relational life devolve into competitive, instrumental, narcissistic, and objectifying forms of relating.

In the process of these changes, the colonization of the family entails a disturbance in the primary relational field of early ego development. Instead of a form of consistent authority for the child, modern forms of work and competitive education have spawned forms of child-rearing and family life that expose children to forms of anxiety and insecurity that disrupt basic internal structures of self-confidence and trust. Even middle and upper middle-class families have had their world infiltrated by uncertainty and risk. As parents work longer hours, have their children looked after by non-familial care-givers, race them back and forth between different extra-curricular activities, they undermine their very sense of security and basic trust in the world—a world that seems increasingly competitive, sadistic, and unrewarding. As Verhaeghe insightfully points out:

> The influence of parents and family has shrunk to a fraction of what it once was . . . . Because of the way in which work is organized, very few children enjoy a predictable and stable environment . . . this makes infants more insecure, with the result that many children fail to bond normally or to develop normal self-confidence and confidence in others.[7]

Of course, the over-riding influence of extra-familial authority and culture is that of the commodity form: of consumption, of the possibility that all forms of need can be satisfied via consumption.

Ego regression has taken on a much stronger role in post-neoliberal society, or what I will call here *cybernetic society*. This kind of social organization is typified by its near total commodification, not only of nature and human production, but of human experience and psychic dynamics. It is also characterized by deep forms of technical manipulation and organizational logics. Central to this social form is the undermining of social-relational webs that are constitutive of the human environment of the individual. To state my thesis with more succinctness: I believe left political movements (or what passes as "progressive" in today's political discourse) are attractive to those kinds of self that lack the requisite ego-functioning and ego-strength for autonomy. As a result, the self-structure of such individuals seeks to achieve self-coherence and stave off the anxieties that it entails via some form of group identity.

The regression of the ego, as I understand it, can now be seen to be a response to a world that is increasingly hostile to the self and its development—hostile in the sense that the world is rigid and distant, insecure and risk-filled, offering little soothing or a humane respite from the dangers it engenders. The phenomenon of the withering of the ego was pointed out in this context by Herbert Marcuse in the 1960s. For Marcuse, one core problem was the way that the ego was becoming separated from its ego-ideal, the latter being subsumed by the collective powers of organization.[8] The ego therefore relies less on its own internalized ideals, taken from his or her relatedness with others, and becomes alienated from real experience and posited by collective groups. Hence, on the reactionary end of the spectrum, we see increased aggressiveness being connected with identification with authoritarian leaders or aggressive social media stars. Identity plays an important role here in terms of white racial identification, or some other fetish of what constitutes one's sense of self. On the left end of the political spectrum, we see something similar, where the ego-ideal is attached to a similar fetich just without the aggressive authoritarian cathexis to a leader or to sadomasochism. But it can also be seen that as social inequalities have become increasingly acute under neoliberalism and the basic forms of security that characterized the welfare state phase of capitalist society, so too has a rise of anxiety as the self is increasingly atomized: "On a social level, neoliberalism increases inequality and divides people into winners and losers," writes Verhaeghe. This "imposes a constant threat on individuals, and those who aren't successful are told that they only have themselves to blame. The current tidal wave of anxiety disorders and depression is a result of this."[9]

Anxiety now becomes a core attribute of the pathology of the withered ego. Unable to live life autonomously, to create and sustain relationships from a position of self-confidence and self-worth, the withered ego becomes narcissistic, perpetually unsure of itself, questioning its own value. The key feature of this kind of anxiety, as Rollo May insightfully pointed out, was that it is: "objectless because it strikes at that basis of the psychological structure on which the perception of one's self as distinct from the world of objects occurs."[10] Now, seen from this vantage point, the self's insecurity about its own sense of existence, about its own positing in the world now becomes a crucial mechanism of anxiety. In a world of psychic fragmentation brought on by the vicissitudes of post-industrial life, the self is left to grab on to whatever shard of self-understanding it can in order to ground itself. This becomes the desire, the need for positing one's identity in the world: grasping on to a single or isolated feature of one's self (almost always socially constructed) and using that as a vehicle for group belonging, a regressive lapse into a sense of belonging to a collectivity that makes the ego feel secure and soothes the pangs of anxiety.

But this most fundamentally leads to a condition where the self essentially fails to develop autonomy—it fails to integrate a stable authority and, as a result, consistently looks to the external world to chart its own sense of agency. The self in such a context becomes *essentially heteronomous* by which I mean its sense of self is embedded in the external norms and values of the commodity world. The self strives to become a consumable object, to become an object that wants to be as desired as it desires other objects or commodities. One reflexively comes to understand oneself through the normative categories of value that the external world has stamped them with. The autonomous capacity to judge, to critique, to decide value for oneself is subsumed by the need for identity and the cathexis it invests in that identity. This is the condition of what I am calling the *anaclitic self*, and it is a crucial linking phenomenon in the psychic world that shapes the contours of group identification with implications for political consciousness and politics more generally.

The Anaclitic Self and Group Narcissism

The condition of the self I have just described leads to a more relevant development in social and political life. As I see it, the withering of the self that results from the shifts in post-neoliberal economic life results in a failure to achieve autonomy—both in psychological and moral-cognitive terms—and a need for incorporation by others in order to assuage anxiety and stabilize a weakly coherent sense of identity. Identification with a group secures for such a self a sense of integration that is not rooted within one's own self-structure, but transmitted via an identification with a group and the shared sense of identity that it constitute it. In the process, the ego's coherence and sense of integrity becomes increasingly dependent upon the identity that links it to the group. It is this dependence on group identity that comes to constrict thinking; to invest in the parametrical form of thinking that will secure group membership.

In order to understand this process, I will make use of Erich Fromm's thesis of "group narcissism," a concept that he began to elaborate in the early 1960s. For Fromm, group narcissism was a means for "the understanding of mass phenomena, such as the readiness of the suppressed classes to be loyal to their rulers."[11] It is a relational strategy employed by the withered ego that props up the self, granting it coherence via identification with a group organized around some identity formation. By belonging to the group, the ego is buoyed; it finds safety and a sense of protection and enhancement, even though it is through a heteronomous form of relational identification. The weakening of the ego and the dissolution of autonomy entail specific insecurities for the self. One's relations to others becomes shaped by the relative lack of autonomy. As R. D. Laing points out: "A firm sense of one's own autonomous identity is required in order that one may be related as one human being to another. Otherwise, any and every relationship threatens the individual with loss of identity."[12]

Freud's original understanding of group psychology held that identification was the primary mechanism that allowed for the formation of groups. Freud says that "identification is known to psychoanalysis as the earliest expression of an emotional tie with another person."[13] Identification is distinct from object-choice since the former entails a wish to take the place of the object rather than be related to the object as a distinct subject. Freud further says that "identification endeavors to mold a person's own ego after the fashion of the one that has been taken as a model."[14] But we can also see in Freud an early insight that distinguishes between different kinds of group psychology by outlining three different sources of group formation:

> First, identification is the original form of emotional tie with an object; secondly, in a regressive way, it becomes a substitute for a libidinal object-tie, as it were by means of introjection of the object into the ego; and thirdly, it may arise with any new perception of a common quality shared with some other person who is not an object of the sexual instinct. The more important this common quality is, the more successful may this partial identification become, and it may thus represent the beginning of a new tie.[15]

What we can discern here, I think, is a way of seeing two kinds of collective narcissism that plague the present. On the one hand, there is the malignant narcissism of the reactionary, of the weakened, damaged ego that looks for the leader as ego-ideal in order to attain some sense of potency in the world. To belong to this kind of narcissistic attachment to the group is to see oneself as reflected in its identity, in the shared sense of identity that is constitutive of the group. As Freud succinctly puts it: "Many equals, who can identify themselves with one another, and a single person superior to them all – that is the situation we find realized in groups which are capable of subsisting."[16] The "introjection of the object into the ego," in this sense, entails the kind of dogged following of the leader and attachment to the strongman characteristic of fascist and neo-fascist politics.

But there is also, in this passage by Freud, another mode of group attachment and affiliation, one he refers to as that "common quality shared with some other person who is not an object of the sexual instinct" and which implies the emergence of a group tie based on some trait that one possesses in common with others. Indeed, this can also be seen as a feature of right-wing authoritarian consciousness—as in racialized group identities, reactionary nationalism, and so on. But it is also the basis of what has infected and infiltrated left-wing politics: that of identity as a means to form group-affiliations which serve to protect the weakened ego from its own lack of potency and agency.

Here we can see what Fromm termed "group narcissism" come into view. For Fromm, group narcissism can be rooted in either of these two forms of group affiliation pointed out by Freud. I think that in order to understand the rise of group identity politics on the left and its effects on progressive politics, we need to consider how the pathologies of modern society and culture form the need for such group narcissism. Typically, it has been right-wing movements that have been described by these dynamics: the weakened ego compensating through an identification with the leader or the authority figure. Left political culture does not evince this in the same way—in other words, it is not simply a parallel form of "left-wing authoritarianism." Something different is at work: namely, the need for group belonging to quell the intolerable experience of a lack of authentic self-coherence and autonomous ego strength. The withering of the ego fostered by trends in the cybernetic society forge the basis for the psychic need for group-affiliation. What left-wing identity politics lacks is the sadomasochism of right-wing identity politics as well as the need for an authoritarian leader toward which one cathects. Instead, left-wing identity politics cathects to the fetish identity itself in order to access the experience of group membership that it facilitates.

The importance of narcissism here needs to be underscored. Fromm's view is that it emerges as a response to a lack of interest and connection to the outside world. The cybernetic society, as I outlined it above, is saturated with forms of risk and uncertainty that make anxiety a pervasive quality of the social contexts of modern life. The steep and rapidly increasing effects of social and economic inequality, technical mediation of experience, the fraying of social bonds and their capture by massive systems of technical control (social and other forms of mass media), the reification of previously spontaneous forms of human life from sex to work to play to aesthetic experience, as well as the bloating of administrative forms of control and surveillance, are not secure structures for the fostering of secure ties during ego-development. As Charles Thorpe insightfully points out: "Capital inserts commodities between us, and advertisers tout these gadgets or applications as bringing us together. Society becomes 'the network,' but the image of social networking hides increasing detachment and withdrawal."[17] Indeed, as anxiety penetrates family life, the rise of ontological insecurity also spawns a self that relies ever more on identification as a means to relate to self and world.

Narcissism now describes the kind of selfhood that looks for its own reflection in the world; a self that has been weakened by persistent anxiety throughout its developmental history and has consequently failed to achieve genuine psychic or moral autonomy. For such a self, the loss of identity is an existential loss of organized meaning—one cannot posit oneself in the world without some organized sense of what one is doing and how one matters to others. The fetishization of identity therefore plays a key role here in facilitating access to a pre-defined, pre-organized frame or meaning for self and world. Lack of this entails a kind of ontological insecurity that leads to despair and a sense of worthlessness that is deeply profound. A key component of the withered ego is therefore its need to *depend on the group* and the reified identity that makes it cohere—an *anaclitic self* therefore is a product of the damaged developmental contexts of neoliberal and cybernetic society. For Fromm, "the narcissistic person is unrelated to the world and as a consequence is alone, and hence frightened."[18] This unrelatedness to the world is not a personal pathology—it is not a personality disorder. Quite to the contrary, it is the product of the sick society, of a social world that fails to produce healthy, life-affirming, autonomous individuals capable of relatedness and rational self-legislation and self-directedness.

The obverse of this is what I am calling the *anaclitic self*: a self that relies on group identity in order for it to buoy itself, to achieve some kind of coherence and stave off the anxiety of loneliness and alienation. Since the "narcissistic person gains his sense of identity by inflation,"[19] we can say that this inflation is achieved by merging oneself with the group. This process of merger occurs by cultivating within one's own reflexive self-awareness the trait shared by the group. Now, as a result, Fromm notes: "I am 'great' because of some quality I *have*, and not because of something I *achieve*, I do not need to be related to anybody or anything; I need not make any effort."[20] The result is a kind of "group solipsism" where one's identification with the group can become the very source of its relatedness to existence or at least to the self's need for self-maintenance of identity. When one can do this on one's own, have a sense of oneself that is coherent and self-reparable when conflicts arise, then we can say one possesses a psychic form of autonomy.[21] But lacking this, we collapse into narcissism and the kind of defensive narcissism that requires us to stave off contrary ideas and experiences that may prove fatal to the self's security system. Autonomy and reason, critical reflection and genuine forms of solidarism are thereby rendered inert in the individual as he becomes increasingly in need of *surplus recognition*—or the excess of recognitive inclusion needed by a self that lacks the requisite resources for self-maintenance and self-coherence.

The Left and the Dogmatic Mind

It needs to be stressed that one of the most harmful effects of group narcissism is its impact on rational thinking. Because the anaclitic self is drawn, via the mechanism of identity, toward a group and its features (racial, gendered, political identity, and so on), this cathected position leads to a regression of critical reflective mentation insofar as the need for inclusion and surplus recognition supplied by being a member of the group (even if this membership is symbolic and not membership in an actual ensemble of others) mitigates critical awareness of aspects of the group that may be irrational or otherwise contradictory. The suppression of critical awareness is required for group membership to be sustained. When this process of politicized, it becomes toxic to liberal forms of political engagement and toleration.

The importance of the role of identity in the constriction of consciousness and the attacks on thinking and reflection that this entails needs to be explored. As I noted above, we should see identity as a kind of *fetishism*: a way of relating to self and other through a particularity of one or a cluster of our features or attributes, constructed or otherwise. This has the effect, as Virginia Goldner has argued, "that the construct of 'identity,' in any form, is problematic because it denotes and privileges a unity of experience."[22] Identity, seen in this way, entails a kind of conflation or collapsing of what Paul Ricoeur refers to as the *idem* and the *ipse*, aspects of our sense of identity that refer to traits or features we possess and that mark us off as distinct (*idem*) and those that we use to actively and reflexively inform our sense of selfhood, who we are, and construct our reflexive sense of self (*ipse*).[23] Viewed in this way, the pressure within the self builds to the extent that it cannot keep these two dimensions of self-understanding separate. As the collapse into one another, the very fragmented way we view ourselves constitutes the desire to extrude our sense of self through the shard of some identity as well as a means to interface with others and grant some form of relational security via group membership.

As I have been arguing, this identity cathexis is a means toward belonging in some basic sense to a group—whether actually in physical terms or in one's mind. By fusing with the group identity, one becomes a member of a larger whole; he or she feels a sense of security and assuages the anxiety suffered by the withered ego's incapacity for psychic or moral autonomy. The group membership itself has further regressive consequences, as pointed out by Wilfred Bion: "Substance is given to the phantasy that the group exists by the fact that the regression involves the individual in a loss of his individual distinctiveness, indistinguishable from depersonalization and therefore obscures observation that the aggregation is of individuals."[24] But this has regressive consequences on the capacity for thinking, on the cognitive, evaluative and affective dimensions of personality in that it constricts the horizon of reflective functioning. The individual's need to hold on to the identity cathexis means its protection at all costs: aggression against perceived threats becomes a basic feature of this kind of thought processing. One is placed within a hermeneutic position that is constrained by identity cathexis: the self interprets the world and experience from a defensive narcissistic position. Our mentation therefore is shaped in a way that highlights those aspects of experience that fortify that need; it filters out and/or highlights those aspects of experience that are resonant with the identity position that is adopted. The privileging of a unity of experience that Goldner above points to entails an incapacity for or intolerance of differentiation, complexity, and of reality.

Understood from this vantage point, dogmatism, or the closed mind characteristic of identity politics, is a mode of mentation that is marked by the need to satisfy knowing, but from a distorted and constricted position. What Milton Rokeach called the "closed" as opposed to the "open" mind is one that distorts knowledge about reality in order to stave off anxiety—to defend against the possibility of not-knowing:

> For the closed mind is *subjectively* experienced by the person who has it no differently from the way it is experienced by a person with an open mind. In this way the person's belief system may be thought of as a mechanism for having one's cake and eating it too. One can distort the world and narrow it down to whatever extent necessary, but at the same time preserve the illusion of understanding it. And if the closed or dogmatic mind is extremely resistant to change, it may be so not only because it allays anxiety but also because it satisfies the need to know.[25]

I think it is important to point out that this dogmatic structure of cognition is constituted by the deep insecurity that the anaclitic self seeks to assuage via its cathexis to the given identity and group membership. The identity position that one adopts, when it is cathected by the ego, is the container of experience and forms the perimeter of existential being. Any perceived attack (and this can come in the form of criticism, opposing views, and so on) is therefore felt as a deep narcissistic injury—a threat to undue the brittle relational security that has been achieved by the identity cathexis. This ego threat is met with a defensive aggression: with a need to destroy, eliminate or somehow neutralize the threat. Hence, we see that the dogmatic mind, in this instance, serves a fundamentally psychic function in that it is actually preserving the solipsistic space where the self is cocooned. It is a defensive operation to maximize security, to fend off the anxiety that will result and which threatens to destroy the self. I think this helps us understand the dogmatic, intolerant and anti-liberal nature of much of contemporary left politics. Its implications for the future of progressive political engagement therefore need to be assessed.

From Solidarity to Group Identity

What is the effect of this tendency in modern self and group dynamics? As I see it, it can be most succinctly described as a shift from a form of politics based on *solidarism* to one of *group identity*. Solidarism is a unique form of social cohesion where the bond between members of the group is not rooted in the anaclitic self's need for surplus recognition but through identification with an ideal, principle or interest. In solidarism, the members are therefore primarily motivated not by the impoverished inner world's incapacity for stemming off the anxiety suffered from the determinants discussed above, but from the capacity to enter into a truly reciprocal form of interdependence. Instead of being based on *identification*, as in Freud's theory of groups, it is rooted in a more mature capacity for relatedness and interest in another object. In solidarity, one's relation to the group is about shared concern or interest, the relatedness is itself secured by shared identification of a principle rather than that of a fetish-identity or a leader. The bond between members is therefore entered into out of *cooperation between autonomous individuals*—that is, individuals who enter the relation to the group rooted not in a need for self-coherence or identification, but through a desire to realize a principle or interest.

Instead of a need to adopt a cathected position toward an identity, a group, or a leader, solidarity requires psychic as well as moral autonomy. This opens an important distinction between dependent and interdependent forms of relationality. Relations of psychic *dependence* refer to the kinds where the self seeks them out and needs them to stabilize or in some way sure up one's sense of self. The withered ego depends on the group and identity is the connective tissue between them because he or she has not properly achieved psychic autonomy. By contrast, *interdependence* refers to a form of relationality where each relates to the other not out of a psychic deficit, but from a position of psychic autonomy. To be able to see oneself and others as members of a demos and adopt a demotic form of consciousness, it is requisite for there to be a breakdown of the more primitive forms of group-identification and the development of psychic capacities for mature relatedness. Central to solidarism as opposed to communitarianism or modern forms of group identity, is a capacity of autonomous selves to act in civic relations with others. Psychic autonomy therefore needs to precede a genuine form of moral autonomy insofar as psychic heteronomy, or the *anaclitic self*, deprives the ego of the requisite strength to be a democratic member of a group or community.

A central feature of democratic membership is reciprocal relational patterns and dynamics where group cohesion is rooted in the mutual needs and interests and validity of the members involved. It underscores what Aristotle referred to as the excellence (ἀρετή) of citizenship in a *polis*: that of the capacity to "rule and be ruled" (ἄρχειν καὶ ἀρχέσθαι), or the ability to identify with collective interests rather than one's immediate needs;[26] it entails a capacity to lead or follow according to the principle of common ends and goods rather than the self's particularist need for surplus recognition. Such an excellence gestures toward a psychic capacity to be secure in one's interdependent relations on others. One does not need to dominate in order to feel empowered or masochistically follow the herd or the leader in order to gain integrity, as the anaclitic self does. On the psychic level, this requires, as Erik Erikson pointed out, echoing Aristotle's political thesis, a sufficient degree of ego integrity which "implies an emotional integration which permits participation by followership as well as acceptance of the responsibility of leadership."[27]

This kind of ego structure is capable of solidarism, a kind of group affiliation that fuses autonomy with cooperation, mediates self with his relations to the group in such a way that he is both an individual who grasps a common identity with others, but in an interdependent rather than dependent manner. Solidarism therefore seems close to group identity, but it lacks a crucial orientation among its members. Whereas the members of the former interact interdependently, and therefore out of rational interest, members within a group-identity configuration are narcissistically dependent on each other and the group identity that confers on them a sense of meaning and self-coherence. It has been, from the beginning of the emergence of modern forms of democratic civic life, a core pre-requisite for a vibrant political culture. This was the form much of left political culture took throughout the modern world, from labor struggles in industrial society to civil rights and anti-colonial movements in the middle of the twentieth century. Only with the advent of post-industrial society do we begin to see the slide into identity politics and the politics of group identity.

Alain Touraine was able to see this emerging during the late 1960s with the advent of post-industrial society. As he was able to observe, the radical student movements were beginning to slide away from a politics of solidarity toward a politics of the group:

> The movement is defined less by its objectives than by the type of community that it creates. Just as, frequently, the principle function of a strike is to create solidarity among the workers rather than to win a salary increase, so also the student commune is its own reason for being. An antisociety is set up in opposition to the dominant social order.[28]

What Touraine was witnessing was, in many ways, the developmental path being born for much of contemporary left politics: a move away from solidarism based in class and social-structural commonality and interests to one rooted in the need for psychic forms of meaning and what Durkheim termed "collective effervescence." This smacks of Fromm's ideas about group narcissism insofar as the individuals involved seek out group affiliation on the basis of the narcissistic deficits that come from the withering of the ego.

The existence of the anaclitic self points to what Fromm calls "incestuous" relational forms versus that of "brotherliness." As Fromm explains this: "The incestuous desire has its strength not from the sexual attraction to mother, but from the deep-seated craving to remain in, or to return to the all-enveloping womb, or to the all-nourishing breasts."[29] The pull of the incestuous desire is a return "to the pre-individual existence of oneness with nature."[30] For Fromm, this longing for return to the pre-individual state manifests itself in a bonding with the family or the clan, with a kind of group-belonging that we can characterize as subsuming the self. The group or the family become crucial for the ego's coherence: "The individual leans on them, feels rooted in them, has his sense of identity as a part of them, and not as an individual apart from them."[31]

What we can see from this discussion is that the lack of ego integrity, the emergence of an anaclitic self from the ravages of anxiety and defective forms of primary and secondary social bonds resulting from the pressures of cybernetic society entails a heightening of the incestuous impulse, that is, of the desire for group identification in an attempt to grant the ego some degree of weightedness and meaning. But the individual motivated by these needs attains only a partial, disfigured form of self-understanding. The fetish of identity renders one's world more constricted and it is brittle, sensitive to attack, rejection or any form of criticism. The reason is, not unlike individual narcissism which has often been described as "hard-headed and soft-skinned." Since the ego invests so much into the fetish identity in order to cohere with the group, it is or paramount interest that this be kept safe. External criticism can lead to the possibility that the individual may come into contact with the unconscious fear that the identification with the group lacks rational validity and is a mere vehicle for more basic forms of security. Hypervigilance therefore becomes a central component of this kind of group-thinking and belonging, giving rise to the kind of anti-liberal politics around identity, race, gender, and so on.

Is There Left-Wing Authoritarianism?

I have sought to argue that current trends in late modernity, or what I have termed have termed *cybernetic society*, have effects on the social-relational world that undermines the capacity for the ego to form robust psychic autonomy. Primarily resulting from the strong forces of anxiety unleashed by neo-liberal changes in economy and society, the result has been a withered ego that seeks out group membership defined by some sort of identity in order to grant it coherence and a sense of ontological security. This anaclitic self develops a kind of narcissism that makes the toleration of ambiguity and difference difficult. Identification of oneself with a group occurs on the basis of a partial fetishistic aspect of oneself, rather than on the practices and projects that define one's sense of life. As a result, thinking become constricted: the psychic need to hold on to the identification that binds one to group membership evacuates any capacity to question it or to have tolerate the possibility of it being assessed, judged, or critiqued.

I think that this process holds as a general one for many people living in damaged social relations. But I also think that there is a crucial difference between how this manifests *politically*. Indeed, whereas right-wing forms of populism can be distinguished by an adherence to issues of identity and cultural forms of ego-threat, the left's populism has been generally associated with questions of structural, economic and corporate power. This distinction has been made by Samir Gandesha who argues:

> Right populism conflates "the people" with an embattled nation confronting its external enemies: Islamic terrorism, refugees, the European Commission, the International Jewish conspiracy, and so on. The Left, in marked contrast, defines "the people" in relation to the social structures and institutions – for example, state and capital – that thwart is aspirations for self-determination; a construction which does not, however, preclude hospitality toward the Other.[32]

Gandesha makes a clear distinction between right and left populisms, but this ignores a second dimension of left political culture: that of identity politics. As far as I can see, both the left and the right have been drawn into identity politics—the identities may be very different, but the pull toward identity and group identification is nevertheless real. This I attribute to the discussion I have been laying out above: to an increased anxiety made rampant by neoliberalism and cybernetic society.

The difference, it seems to me, is that *the left is not authoritarian*: for to be authoritarian it would require the addition of sadomasochism and a cathected position toward the leader that the right evinces robustly and the left decidedly lacks not to mention a desire to relate masochistically to traditional forms of hierarchy that is simply not a feature of radical leftist groups or their ideologies. Instead of characterizing these developments in left political culture as "liberal fascism," "left-wing authoritarianism," or some other moniker, I would suggest that we see it as the cumulative result of decades of identity politics and cultural politics that have been the hallmark of left movements since the 1960s. But the increasingly weak and incoherent nature of the anaclitic self motivates such an ego toward a kind of splitting that promotes the active destruction of the object that it sees as threatening. Such is the danger of any political radicalism rooted in archaic psychic needs and deficits. Nevertheless, it seems to me that authoritarianism is not the best way to describe this type of character structure nor the political moments and ideologies they espouse.

This still calls into question the very basis of modern left politics. By jettisoning class as a central variable in comprehending social power, these movements have shifted the focus toward those concerns with identity that privilege the particular, what is contingent, affective and irrational over that which is objective, material, universal and rational.[33] The New Left's move toward identity and culture and the postmodern and poststructuralist turn in academic theory impoverished the political imaginary that came down from the Enlightenment: one of inclusion, tolerance, equality, human development, and free thought. The character structure of recent generational cohorts since the 1960s has been a gradual shift toward the withered ego, the anaclitic self, and defensive forms of narcissism that reacted to with a cathexis of identity. As Daniel Rodgers observes: "Notions of power moved out of structures and into culture. Identities became intersectional and elective. Concepts of society fragmented. Time became penetrable. Even slogans of the culture war's conservatives were caught up in the swirl of choice."[34]

What this points to is the thesis that left identity politics and its dogmatic, intolerant dynamics are the result not of authoritarian strivings but a character structure rooted in the kinds of basic, ontological anxieties that such a sociocultural field produced. Indeed, in his description of the concept of left-wing authoritarianism, Bob Altemeyer saw that it was essentially constituted by three co-varying attitudes: "Left-wing authoritarians are revolutionaries who (1) submit to movement leaders who must be obeyed, (2) have enemies who must be ruined, and (3) have rules and 'party discipline' that must be followed."[35] This kind of political culture among the contemporary left is not very easy to find. The mere presence of intolerance of threatening ideas and the dogmatic adherence to group identity and membership does not really fit with the authoritarianism that Altemeyer describes. Perhaps further, Altemeyer himself admits to the difficulty in empirically verifying its existence: "when you find hostile and dogmatic 'political correctors' at a university advocating censorship, you might be dealing not to much with leftists as with Wild-Card Authoritarians."[36] Wild-Card Authoritarians are Altemeyer's words to describe those with attitudes that are authoritarian but are also anti-establishment, not exactly left or progressive. What this means is that authoritarian character structure can predominate *in either left- or right-wing contexts*, but that the crucial difference is in the actual values they espouse and which motivate them.[37]

Nevertheless, I think that it is worth considering the hypothesis that contemporary left politics is characterized more by the kind of defensive aggression brought on by a need to protect one's personalized cathexis to a given identity and the group or collective forms of identity to which that gives rise. It is the anaclitic self's need for relational security to soothe a fundamental sense of anxiety that bonds it to the group and to the identity discourse that sustains it. Attacks on it, threats to it, are met with aggression and intolerance; although indeed anti-liberal in leaning, this is not exactly authoritarian in nature. Although contemporary trends in left political culture and movements, no less than academic theory and ideas, has continued its drift against Enlightenment rationalism and liberal forms of tolerance and civic engagement. I believe that this trend will only continue: that political consciousness will remain largely a personal affair, a matter of identity, and that broader, more rational-democratic forms of solidarity will remain frustrated until a more psychically autonomous pattern of the individual is able to displace the anaclitic character structure that currently dominates.

Notes

1 Henry S. Kariel, *The Decline of American Pluralism* (Stanford, CA: Stanford University Press, 1961), 69–70. Also see my discussion in *Twilight of the Self: The Decline of the Individual in Late Capitalism* (Stanford, CA: Stanford University Press, 2022), 31–73.
2 Herbert Marcuse, *One-Dimensional Man: Studies in the Ideology of Advanced Industrial Civilization* (Boston: Beacon Press, 1964), 10.
3 Peter Berger, Brigitte Berger, and Hansfried Kellner, *The Homeless Mind: Modernization and Consciousness* (New York: Vintage, 1973), 184.
4 Paul Verhaeghe, *What about Me? The Struggle for Identity in a Market-Based Society* (London: Scribe, 2014), 146.
5 Herbert Marcuse, "Freedom and Freud's Theory of Instincts." In his *Five Lectures* (Boston: Beacon Press, 1970), 14.
6 Anthony Giddens, *Modernity and Self-Identity: Self and Society in the Late Modern Age* (Stanford, CA: Stanford University Press, 1991), 2.
7 Verhaeghe, *What about Me?*, 153–4.
8 See Herbert Marcuse, "The Obsolescence of the Freudian Conception of Man." In his *Five Lectures*, 44–61.
9 Paul Verhaeghe, *Says Who? The Struggle for Authority in a Market-Based Society* (London: Scribe, 2017), 11.
10 Rollo May, *The Meaning of Anxiety* (New York: W. W. Norton, 1950), 191.
11 Erich Fromm, *The Heart of Man: Its Genius for Good and Evil* (New York: Harper and Row, 1964), 62.
12 R. D. Laing, *The Divided Self: An Existential Study in Sanity and Madness* (London: Penguin Books, 1960), 44.
13 Sigmund Freud, *Group Psychology and the Analysis of the Ego*. In *Standard Edition*, vol. 18 (London: Hogarth Press, 1973), 105.
14 Freud, *Group Psychology and the Analysis of the Ego*, 106.
15 Freud, *Group Psychology and the Analysis of the Ego*, 107—8.
16 Freud, *Group Psychology and the Analysis of the Ego*, 121.
17 Charles Thorpe, *Necroculture* (New York: Palgrave Macmillan, 2016), 24.
18 Fromm, *The Heart of Man*, 75.
19 Fromm, *The Heart of Man*, 75.
20 Fromm, *The Heart of Man*, 77.
21 See the discussion by W. F. Pritz and B. Mitterauer, "The Concept of Narcissism and Organismic Self-Reference." *International Review of Psycho-Analysis*, vol. 4 (1977), 181–96.
22 Virginia Goldner, "Toward a Critical Relational Theory of Gender." *Psychoanalytic Dialogues*, vol. 1, no. 3 (1991). 249–72, 258.
23 See Paul Ricoeur, *Oneself as Another*. Trans. Kathleen Blamey (Chicago: University of Chicago Press, 1992), 113ff.
24 W. R. Bion, *Experiences in Groups* (London: Routledge, 1961), 142. Also see the discussion by Conrad Stephen Chrzanowski, "The Group's Vulnerability to Disaster: Basic Assumption and Work Group Mentalities Underlying Trump's 2016 Election." *International Journal of Psychoanalysis*, vol. 100, no. 4 (2019). 711–31.

25 Milton Rokeach, *The Open and Closed Mind* (New York: Basic Books, 1960), 68.
26 See Aristotle, *Politics*: 1276 b 16–1277 b 32.
27 Erik H. Erikson, *Childhood and Society* (New York: W. W. Norton, 1950), 269.
28 Alain Touraine, *The Post-Industrial Society* (New York: Random House, 1971), 89.
29 Erich Fromm, *The Sane Society* (New York: Rinehart and Co., 1955), 40–41.
30 Fromm, *The Sane Society*, 41.
31 Fromm, *The Sane Society*, 41.
32 Samir Gandesha, "Understanding Right and Left Populism." In Jeremiah Morelock (Ed.) *Critical Theory and Authoritarian Populism* (London: University of Westminster Press, 2018), 49–70, 63. Also see the discussion by Gregory Smulewicz-Zucker, "Democratic Socialism Contra Populism." In Gregory Smulewicz-Zucker and Michael J. Thompson (Eds.) *An Inheritance for Our Times: Principles and Politics of Democratic Socialism* (New York: OR Books, 2020), 365–78.
33 For an important critique, see Peter J. Steinberger, *Rationalism in Politics* (Cambridge: Cambridge University Press, 2022), 122ff.
34 Daniel T. Rodgers, *Age of Fracture* (Cambridge, MA: Harvard University Press, 2011), 16. Also see the rich discussion by John Sanbonmatsu, "Postmodernism and the Corruption of the Critical Intelligentsia." In Gregory Smulewicz-Zucker and Michael J. Thompson (Eds.) *Radical Intellectuals and the Subversion of Progressive Politics* (New York: Palgrave Macmillan, 2015), 33–68.
35 Bob Altemeyer, *The Authoritarian Specter* (Cambridge, MA: Harvard University Press, 1996), 219–20.
36 Altemeyer, *The Authoritarian Specter*, 233.
37 Altemeyer notes that: "In many instances the established authorities tend to be people who hold right-wing economic and political views – but not always. In Communist countries, the established authorities in society held a decidedly left-wing economic philosophy, but after so many years in power, the party leaders had become the Establishment. So I predicted persons who scored highly on the RWA (Right-Wing Authoritarianism) Scale in the USSR would support the Communist leadership and oppose democratic reforms, and by thunder they did." *The Authoritarian Specter*, 218.

Chapter 12

Center Askew

The Muddle over the Authoritarian Middle

Kurt Jacobsen

In London's Soho district in Autumn 1995, I attended a special preview of Ken Loach's *Land and Freedom*, a Spanish Civil War feature film focusing on the tragic consequences of deadly conflicts rending the anti-Franco Republican camp.[1] The film sided with the Left-populist perspective that George Orwell championed in *Homage to Catalonia*, his memoir of combat service in the semi-Trotskyite POUM component of the Republicans during their doomed struggle against fascist forces.[2] A key passage in Orwell's account is his evocation of the giddy early days in 1936 when jubilant working class denizens took charge of Barcelona and gained civic command over their own lives for the first time.[3] The film's protagonist is a kindred spirit to Orwell, an idealistic British trade unionist (and, unlike Orwell, a CP member) motivated to throw his lot in with the Republic, to risk life and limb "prematurely," as authorities later accused, to fight fascist predators prowling the continent.

In attendance that afternoon was a group of grizzled British veterans, including their surviving commander Bill Alexander, all former members of the British Communist Party, which had organized much of the International Brigade recruitment in the UK.[4] Director Ken Loach and screenwriter Jim Allen, as promised, appeared for a volcanic post-screening discussion. During the screening of this riveting film, I recall a few groans, sighs, and snorts emitted inside the cramped room (which sat about 40). Memorable film sequences depicted the Stalinists' crushing of POUM (and other rivals) in the Spring of 1937, and the cynical betrayal of peasants by the Republican courts so as to mollify landowners. The Communist Party saw no reason to suffer views that threatened their *realpolitik* path from the messy contentious reality of point A to the neat consensual paradise of point B. The Left-wing authoritarian way to achieve unanimity was a resort to the Machiavellian shortcuts of slandering, shouldering aside, and then, if necessary, snuffing other voices, especially those who reminded these uneasy authorities of their own betrayals of revolutionary aims, supposedly for the sake of attaining a democratic utopia.[5]

Loach's saga ends as the battered hero heads back to his native Liverpool, a sadder but still committed democratic Leftist (who rips up his Party card), as the displayed memorabilia of his later life attest. When the house lights came on, though, the real strife erupted. The British veterans were incandescently angry. They complained

DOI: 10.4324/9781003389927-12

that the POUM had been romanticized, and that good sound Communists like themselves had little choice but to subdue all the reckless anarchist and Trotskyite nuisances for the sake of the noble cause. The filmmakers gamely and grimly stood their ground.

Eons after the 1956 Hungarian invasion, Khrushchev's renunciation of Stalin and the confirmed gulag revelations was there a Leftist anywhere in the West who defended the Soviet record so unabashedly?[6] Yet here were a band of grey-beard diehards, in a tiny screening room, immaculately assured that their crucial failure in Spain was the incomplete carrying out of orders to liquidate anarchist and Trotskyite allies. (An academic friend in New York—hearsay alert—later told me that he overheard an American Lincoln Brigade veteran there opine that the only mistake the CP made in Spain was not killing enough anarchists.)[7] So there should be no need to remind anyone today that there is such a thing as left wing authoritarianism, even if the designation does not fit—and Altemeyer is correct in this stance—the original criteria that Adorno and his associates applied in their 1950 volume.[8] (Any social scientist conversant with Lipset's slant on working class authoritarianism—and, often glided over, middle class authoritarianism too—knows that the phenomenon drew plenty of attention with regard to political implications.)[9] Say what you like about the Brigade veterans, several of whom were Jewish, they doubtless would have easily surmounted lie detector tests or sodium pentothal injections in affirming that they were ardently anti-racist, pro-democratic and likely pretty bohemian too.

One can plead that such Left-wing authoritarianism is a perversion of true Left-wing values (as also can libertarian Right-wingers regarding their professed ideal)[10]—and that is the point.[11] Authoritarianism in its initial investigative incarnation was applied only to Right-wing attitudes and beliefs, which were xenophobic (especially at the time, antisemitic), racist, antidemocratic, "conventional," and rigid. Yet authoritarianism also has a behavioral style all its own—apart from this or that set of deformative personality traits—which attaches to any ideology and is exemplified in any martinet, whatever their political leaning, especially at the leadership level.[12] Strictly speaking, according to the Adorno volume and the estimable follow-up by Altemeyer, authoritarianism stemmed from reactionary spirits who combine a defensive devotion to a self-serving vision of the status quo with rampant ethnocentrism. Thus conceptualized, it made no sense to incorporate Leftist versions since they, albeit with some exceptions, plainly do not share these defining features.[13]

Yet it is hardly as if Soviet totalitarian behavior was ignored either, though its hideous manifestations were seen by Left critics as an avoidable effect of the degeneration of vibrant enlightenment values into Party handbook cant. Karl Korsch, Wilhelm Reich, and Paul Mattick number among many prominent Leftists who denounced "red fascism" in Stalin's Soviet Union. If you are, in Eric Hoffer's classic term, a "true believer" you allow no doubt to creep into your dogma, and react vehemently and even violently to heretical behavior.[14] There is no question, after settling on rigidity, conformity, and conventional thinking (adjusted to one's salient community) as criteria that any person of any ideological stripe—including especially those who profess to disdain ideology—can behave in an authoritarian manner to achieve cherished goals, including protecting themselves from contamination by leprous outsiders.[15] Thus, this attitudinal approach is juicily ripe for projection, whereby one attributes, consciously or otherwise, one's own unsavory motives onto disfavored and vulnerable others.

The rhetorical question arises, can one achieve liberty, fraternity and equality—let alone a democratic socialist regime—by imposition? A key lesson in a checkered Left-wing history is that oppression indeed can be fought by means that defeat their own end. Hence, the Frankfurt School critical theorists prized bourgeois rights and freedoms insofar as they could be extended to the rest of the population and thus form institutionalized steppingstones toward full emancipation. Free speech restrictions, in many instances, may be tempting to inflict on obnoxious opponents but the Left, customarily disadvantaged in terms of resources, has vastly more to gain by defending free speech. For at the first glimmer of an opportunity, right wing forces deploy restrictions against every miscreant meandering one millimeter to their Left port side. Yet plainly the Left, as a glance at the Soviet Union alone shows, has resorted to coercive and censorious methods anyway—and accordingly was rejected as a monstrous malformation by much of the world-wide Left.[16]

Since the 1920s an anti-Stalinist Left included Trotskyites plus a plethora of socialist and anarcho-syndicalist groupings within a fractious movement quibbling over matters of doctrine, but even then often at some to a free-thinking latitude. The attractiveness of Students for a Democratic Society (SDS) in the 1960s, and its founding Port Huron statement, was its sincere commitment to spur social change through participatory democracy.[17] No one needed to pledge groveling obedience to a central committee's "line" as to the correct agenda, and so there was scant need to fret about the "iron law of oligarchy" working itself out inside the organization (which shattered for quite other reasons).[18] A respect for the grass roots was wedded to a vision of achievable reforms when "reform" still meant measurable improvements in people's daily lives, and not just any whimsical alteration in rulers' preferences. Incidentally, and importantly, no member of the "New Left" SDS would ever label themselves as a liberal, no matter how much other parties' strain to lump them together. The term "Left" is so capacious a category today, and in some places in this volume, that Right wingers and allegedly neutral observers conveniently can shove into it anyone they designated as a nuisance.[19]

What historically united the Left, "New" or otherwise, was the goal of transforming the capitalist system and its political and cultural institutions so that, as the song, goes, the "Internationale will be the human race"—and not this or that identity segment, sect, or minor combination of them. Small gains, of course, were not to be disdained so long as they were conceived as tactical steps toward the socialist objective, as Andre Gorz argued.[20] Today the sectarianism that always afflicted Left groups is embraced in some circles to the point of conscientious self-disorganizing, which is a boon to status quo stalwarts. Earlier, Blacks, gays, women, and every other imaginable marginal group joined behind the universal cause, rather than pitted themselves against one another for a piece of a shrinking economic pie, shrinking because from the 1970s onward the postwar shift in wealth that enabled the "golden age" was assiduously siphoned again back to the top.[21] Postwar social contracts, wherever they existed in print or in practice, crumbled, and as they did a scramble for petty group advantages within this kingdom of crumbs ensued.[22]

Rueful analyses recount the dramatic counterrevolutionary shift enacted on a multitude of fronts—because the 1960s opened so many in areas such as ecology, women's liberation, gay rights—by what was quaintly reviled as "the establishment."[23] Falling profit levels in the 1970s had to be countered and so they were. Keynesian demand management strategies were seemingly unable to cope with the startling puzzle of stagflation (ignited by oil price hikes) and so social democratic reformism was slowly if quietly abandoned for the next likely savior, which turned out to be a well-managed resurrection of "free market" practices that begot the traumatizing Great Depression in the first place.[24] Stale Smithian 18th-century economic nostrums successfully were rebranded as fresh panaceas. Nearly all Left to Liberal-oriented Party leaderships accordingly cleaved to a "center" that moved, or arguably was moved, to the Right to the point that they all soon occupied ground formerly regarded as crackpot fringe terrain by Eisenhower just a few decades earlier.[25] The ensuing predicament is that, as Michaels astutely put it, "treating classes as if they were cultures or races is a strategy for managing inequality rather than diminishing or eliminating it."[26]

All this retrogressive activity harks to prescient critiques of the lack of interest by "house ideologue" Western intellectuals since the 1950s to attempt anything other than tinkering with—managing—state and economic arrangements, rather than ruthlessly scrutinize and/or challenge them.

The Tidy Center

Noam Chomsky in the midst of an escalating Vietnam War wearily noted:[27]

> the statement by fourteen leading political scientists and historians on US Asian policy, distributed last December (1967) by the Freedom House Public Affairs Institute. These scholars refer to themselves as "the moderate segment of the academic community." The designation is accurate; they stand midway between the two varieties of extremism, one which demands that we destroy everyone who stands in our path, the other that we adopt the principles of international behavior that we require of every other world power.

These options are what prudent centrists lodged themselves between, and it is usually where one finds even much-lettered sages, with their instinctive tilt toward the forces and figures of legitimate power. Chomsky was right. the tarnished centrists of the McCarthyism era—Democratic Party liberals—put up either a sporadic or else no fight at all against red hunts, and more often joined in the jamboree.[28] Recall that Adorno, Frankel-Brunswick, Levinson, and Sanford's book was published in the midst of the hectic HUAC sprees and, like many a hapless Hollywood target, they also did not miss the antisemitic as well as anti-labor undercurrents of the witch hunt.

A telling clue regarding centrist authoritarianism has been in plain sight since the 1960s: the fabled Milgram obedience studies. At Yale Stanley Milgram conducted what became monikered as the "Eichmann experiments" in his quest to uncover the roots of obedience and its link to fascism. Milgram planned to transport his controversial experiment—which no University today can be imagined to allow—to Germany but first tried it on students and ordinary Americans in New Haven. The experiment posed a collaborating actor as a "learner" who was to be tested and then punished for every obstinately wrong answer by electric jolts administered by the real subjects. So far as the subjects knew, the scale ratcheted in increments up to 450 volts (labeled "danger-severe shock") by which level the "learner" was screaming or ominously silent. As Pontius Pilates in reverse, white lab-coated confederates accepted all responsibility while urging often-tormented subjects to press on. Milgram swiftly discovered that one need not trawl Germany to find all the storm trooper and camp guard recruits of which any future *Fuhrer* could dream.

People from every walk of life were alarmingly inclined to succumb to authority, no matter what the orders were. Over 60% of Milgram's subjects, on average, obeyed urgings by authorities to complete the test and finish off hapless "learners."[29] (In Munich, Germans hit the 85% mark, nicely upholding wartime reputations.) Applications of the Milgram experiment to other groups varying by nationality and by demographic characteristics, yielded minor variations but the majority in all trials were willing to kill or knock unconscious an innocent person solely on the say-so of seemingly legitimate authorities. Even sophisticated people, Milgram concluded, can easily became "dominated by an administrative, rather than a moral, outlook," embodying Max Weber's feared hordes of "specialists without spirit, sensualists without heart."[30]

Kelman and Hamilton also found that a majority of Americans surveyed regarding the 1969 My Lai Massacre, and the trial of Lieutenant William Calley afterward, believed 67% of fellow Americans—and 51% of themselves—would and should murder unarmed men, women and children if so ordered.[31] Only 33% said no, which aligned all too neatly with Milgram's dismaying results. Predictably, those who would eagerly comply reckoned everyone else would too. The strongest indicator of "refusing to shoot" was high educational attainment, but even this august status was not a serious retardant on obedience.[32] In reflections about noncombat situations, Kelman and Hamilton surmised that the cumulative processes of "people keeping quiet, going along, not rocking the boat, and following orders when they knew better" underpins or instigates "crimes of obedience."[33]

Kelman and Hamilton offer the mildly mitigating point that the huge public disgruntlement with the Calley trial conviction verdict arose primarily from their suspicion of scapegoating at work, not from exculpating Calley, and that most Americans presume an unwritten "contract" with the state whereby citizens, especially conscripts, do as they are told despite misgivings so long as authorities assume blame. All this accords with Milgram, the subject of quite a few purse-lipped attacks.[34] It's as if the data derived from hellish experiments at Nazi concentration camps had been lifted by Milgram for modern scientific high jinks. The fuss over Milgram's methodology cannot help but come at the price of downplaying how necessarily distressing were his results. He shook up not just social scientists but entire post-industrial cultures that presumed that they were immune to the allure of fascist leadership, a shock every bit as disturbing, as Freud reckoned, as dislodging the Earth from center of the universe, demoting humans from fallen angels to risen apes, and the disclosing of humans as bumbling, bedevilled masters in their own mental houses. Nuremburg lawyer Telford Taylor recalled how vexing, indeed, impossible, it was for colleagues to comprehend that the Nazi leadership was clinically sane, and that extraordinary and "ordinary men" alike can indulge in mass murder, rape, and torture.[35]

Yet one cannot glance at the 60% plus compliance rates Milgram calculated and not realize that sensible folks nestled in the middle ground were implicated too. Any centrist scanning compliance figures might protest that a prudent 40% in the rock solid middle were exempt, and they would be flat wrong. For this sidestepped implication many such readers never forgave Milgram. It meant that *bien pensants* sporting Ivy League and Oxbridge degrees, and otherwise supping at the high table of Western culture, were really easy meat for "legitimate" authority. Few lessons are more important than that anyone, including middle-of-the-road savants, can be badgered, seduced, or propagandized into unfathomable cruelty, into becoming mirror images of nightmare figures. In this glum respect R.D. Laing justly observed that mass crimes are performed not by mad men but by ordinary individuals in thrall to trusted institutions.[36] None of these acrid insights would surprise anyone who contributed to Adorno's volume, worrying as they were at the time that red, white, and blue Americans were ripe material for fascism given conducive conditions. McCarthyism enveloped them. Decades later, Altemeyer was compelled by his data to wonder, "Are there so many people so generally submissive to established authority that they constitute a real threat to freedom in countries such as the Canada and the US."[37] The answer, he concluded, was "yes."

Hence, the purpose of this chapter is tease out the customarily ignored applicability of authoritarian personality work to the moveable and biddable middle. The center is where it is easiest hide one's suspected deviancies, repressed anger, and forbidden thoughts, where the pleasures derived from conformity and from punishing nonconformity are just as enticing as for the ultra-right, except that one can in good conscience despise those occupying either end of the spectrum as out of touch, inadequate, subhuman—as, indeed, "deplorables."[38] No less than anyone on the far Left or Right, however defined, do centrists suspect that beliefs they take for granted could be erroneous, doctrinaire, counterproductive, or match up eerily well with extremists. Stalking the "Loch Ness Monster" of Left-wing authoritarianism, Conway and coauthors conflate liberals with Leftists (which both groups would find insulting), regard strong conviction of any sort as suspect, and posit that looking askance at Christian fundamentalists—that is, the bulk leaning toward

Christian nationalism, mostly authoritarians[39]—is itself an authoritarian act and equates to hostility to Jews, Muslims or environmentalists.[40] Yet behavior they describe as "left-wing"—yearning for a "mighty and liberal leader" to "rule society with an iron hand and viciously punish societal offenders"—is at least as prevalent, and indeed far more so, among centrists.[41]

Niebuhr, echoing Marx' *Eighteenth Brumaire*, long ago detected that the petty bourgeoisie—what one might dub the volatile middle—is chronically insecure, intellectually incurious, untethered to a coherent political vision and therefore prone to embrace the strong man savior.[42] Recall too it was professionals—physicians, engineers, technicians of all kinds—in Germany who signed up in droves for advantageous Nazi Party membership.[43] Both middle and lower middle classes united during periods of crisis in their fear of and contempt for the working class who must be kept in their subordinate place. Lewis Lipsitz noted that middle class authoritarianism, if education were controlled for (through High School), surpassed that of working-class Americans especially regarding political preferences.[44] He cites neglected studies that indicate that "anti-elitist, out-spoken underdog and informality orientations among workers contribute to pro-democratic, equalitarian tendencies" while the middle class can experience painful economic and status insecurities, spurring authoritarian tendencies.

In the early postwar era Arthur Schlesinger hailed the American "vital center" which, if read with a wry eye, better fits Bernie Sanders' supporters than the managerialist mainstreamers of Hilary Clinton, Joe Biden, and Kamala Harris.[45] But if one postures as the repository of truth, as the Democratic National Committee or the British Labour Party Executive do, then no holds are barred in keeping mistrusted masses in line. Here is exemplified a robust post-war tradition of thinly concealed antagonism toward citizens making their needs known apart from however elites care to interpret them.[46] Most centrists also seem unaware or unconcerned that they inhabit a center that gets repositioned ever rightward according to pressures from the Tories in the UK and Republicans in the US.

Altemeyer aptly observed that a centrist or conservative within the social democratic consensus of Sweden of the late 20th century was quite a different creature than a counterpart in the neoliberal US or UK.[47] What constitutes a centrist depends not on personal views and commitments but on the intersection of personal qualities with social forces in the milieu. Nothing has served maintenance of the status quo more than the predilection of centrists to conform to what they reckon to be the sagacious middle. Hence, one witnesses their ready relinquishing of New Deal/Great Society achievements plus a resigned view that reinvigoration of those programs is unrealistic because corporate and financial titans plus suburban soccer moms won't cotton to them, all done with perfect assurance they represent the majority. Yet Page and Jacobs, among others, attest in their survey studies that Americans are well to the left of elites on nearly all policy matters.[48]

How do these foregoing observations about centrist behavior square with the authoritarian character? Centrists unabashedly exhibit authoritarianism, especially in the permission they grant themselves to behave as rigidly, high-handedly and acquisitively as—projection abounding—opponents. This classic defense mechanism, boundary-maintenance, and "making a display of their respectability" are Anglo-American social habits stretching back to the Puritans.[49] In what follows I examine purges of the Left undertaken by Labour Party centrists in the guise of extirpating antisemitism. The pattern apes actions embarked on by the Democratic Party in the USA to stifle Leftist-progressive influences.[50] Revelatory leaks of DNC emails in 2016 displayed the antics by contemptuous staffers to rig the primary system against Bernie Sanders and then, to diversionary perfection, blame Russia for unproven hacking.[51] The righteousness with which both these centrist Party elites conducted an unleashing of pent-up hostility upon approved targets is exemplary in every way of the authoritarian character in action yet, Houdini-like, escapes notice.

Labour Pains and Panics

In September 2007 then Tory Party leader David Cameron delivered a Fukuyama-esque speech "The End of Economic History," proclaiming:

> The debate is now settled. I'm proud that this is one of the few countries in the world where all serious candidates for high office support the principles of free trade and monetary discipline…Indeed the whole new Labour project was built on recognising, and accepting, the free market consensus.

Asked what her greatest legacy was, Margaret Thatcher infamously answered, "New Labour."[52] Left-wing hopes within the Party sank when in 1994, with Labour already well in the lead over the foundering Tories, party leader John Smith, no firebrand but no Blairite either, died.[53] The "control freak" nature of successor Tony Blair became apparent as his acolytes assumed command of key organizational nodes.[54] The Party's Clause IV commitment to nationalize major enterprises was dumped in favor genuflections to capitalism. The greater the Blairites' administrative power waxed, the fiercer were their attacks on "old Labour" redoubts. In 1997 Blair began government with a pledge not to raise taxes. Instead, he cut corporate taxes and simultaneously posed as a debt hawk. New Labour under Blair and then Gordon Brown were small "L" liberals (at best) in politics, centrists in economics, and perhaps socialists in culture with the consequences of generating a futile Iraq war, intensifying maldistribution of income and wealth, and proliferating dubious Private Finance Initiatives.[55] The internal Party modus operandi was to excoriate advocates of Leftist policies such as higher taxes on the rich, strict regulation of business, control of capital movement, and a "diplomacy first" position in foreign policy. The crusading moderates renounced links to Leftist redistributional goals, whether of money or power, and instead championed identity politics in all its divisive forms.

Labour between 1997 and 2010 consequently lost 5 million voters. Four out of 5 deserters did not turn Tory; one third voted Liberal Democrat and the rest just dropped out. By 2001 most nonvoters were deliberate abstainers, and a University of York study of local nonvoters found that "80% cited a lack of difference between the 2 parties."

In 2015, to the horror of Blairite grandees, Jeremy Corbyn, a standard bearer of the Bennite Left, was elected party leader, and overwhelmingly so.[56] The Blairites, who controlled the Party Executive and Headquarters and comprised most MPs, resorted to every stratagem to quash a revival of mortifying socialist aspirations. Few failed to notice the ferocity of the blunderbuss assaults.[57] The next four years witnessed internal strife designed to sabotage the party candidate in the next two general elections. Despite what should have been chastening defeats to the Tories in the preceding decade, the Blairites, united in accommodative attitude toward business and finance and a lack of for working class members, doubled down.

Among the myriad ruses was the charge that Corbyn, given his support for Palestinian rights, was an antisemite, as was anyone else who voiced similar views, not excluding Jewish Voices for Labour. The spectacle of the "swiftboating" of John Kerry earlier by the Republican Party likely emboldened Corbyn's enemies to believe such a preposterous charge would stick, and eventually it did. The bonus was that the people they fingered favored renationalization, redistribution of wealth, regulation of finance, jobs programs, regional aid, and a vibrant National Health Service—nearly all of which goals were anathema to Blairites, as leaked emails and the Forde Report attest. Corbyn had an impeccable record regarding defense of minorities, including Jews. What was not impeccable to some foes was the squaring of his anti-antisemitic stances with championing the Palestinian cause. Corbyn was caught off-guard by accusations regarding what should have been his strongest suit. The ensuing flap derailed not only Corbyn but a resurgent Left in Britain. If you want to watch Altemeyer's key three attitudinal clusters—authoritarian submission, authoritarian aggression, and conventionalism—blend in one heady but vanilla-flavored devils' brew, here it poured, decanted by people least disposed to admit it.[58]

As a reluctantly released 2020 Labour Report confirms

> much of the Labour Party machinery from 2015–18 was opposed to Jeremy Corbyn, and toiled secretly to undermine the elected leadership of the party. The priority of staff in this period appears to have been furthering the aims of a narrow faction aligned to Labour's right rather than fulfilling the organisation's objectives, from winning elections to building a functioning complaints and disciplinary process . . . Labour officials, including senior staff, expressed hostility towards Jeremy Corbyn and his staff, towards Labour MPs including Andy Burnham, Ed Miliband, Sadiq Khan, Emily Thornberry, Diane Abbott and Dawn Butler. Staff described 'most of the PLP' as 'Trots' or called them 'totally useless' in 2015 for not having yet launched a coup 30 against Corbyn. As one staff member commented, 'everyone here considers anyone left of [Gordon] Brown to be a trot.'[59]

So during the 2015 leadership election the GLU and Headquarters Labour staff described their work as "hunting out 1000s of trots" and a "Trot hunt," which included excluding apostates for having "liked" the Greens on Facebook. One high ranking GLU staffer, Head of Disputes Katherine Buckingham, admitted that "real work is piling up" while she and other staff were engaged in inappropriate factional work."[60] Even Ed Miliband's 2015 Manifesto was deemed "too far to the left in nationalizing railroad, landlord-bashing, and Trident"; corporation tax rises were deemed folly and the policy for free school meals was ridiculed by this neo-Dickensian wing. "I wouldn't want to win on an old-fashioned Labour platform," an out of office Tony Blair stated. "Even if I thought it was the route to victory, I wouldn't take it."[61] Jones tracks within the Labour party from the 1970s onward the influx of middle-class MPs and staff and their sheer scorn of the working class, with the consequent result that 60% of working-class voters in 2008 told BBC pollsters that no one represents their interests.[62]

"Many staff at Labour HQ," the Report explains, had a background in *Labour Students* [which] was an organisation historically, and then, run by people from the "right" of the party, as opposed to the "left" and "soft left." They appear to have had an internal culture of calling people to their left "Trots."[63] Chat logs reveal that HQ members "who denounced 'trots' were in turn themselves privately regarded as 'trots' by other staffers for being seen as insufficiently critical."[64] The comparability and function of this hostility is illuminated when one substitutes the word "trot" for "Jew" in a passage from *The Authoritarian Personality*:

> This anxiety is related to the imagery of Jews ["trots"] as prying and power seeking. If Jews ["trots"] are given the opportunity of free participation in community affairs, then granted they have these tendencies, they will form a small sectarian clique interested only in their own power and material interests. To gain these aims, they will shrewdly use even the most ruthless and dishonest methods.[65]

What is glaring here is, as in the classic F Scale, "stereotypy, rigid adherence to middle class values, the tendency to regard one's own group as morally pure in contrast to the immoral outgroup; opposition to and exaggeration of prying and sensuality; extreme concern with dominance and power (fear of Jewish ["trot"] power and desire for [their own] power), fear of moral contamination, fear of being overwhelmed and victimized, the desire to erect social barriers to separate one from another and to maintain the morality and dominance of one's own group."[66] All these characteristics were much in vogue among Labour Party centrist leaders and staff who, when scanning the excruciating record of emails and tweets, cannot help but remind one of the depiction of the anti-hero's hooting and braying accomplices in Martin Scorsese's *The Wolf of Wall Street.*

The staffers sedulously interfered with Corbyn's 2017 election run, diverted funds to factional favorites in safe seats, refused to streamline antisemitism complaint investigations (and blamed Corbyn for it), scrutinized the internet for potential infractions by "trots," assailed people of color within the Party who were regarded as "trots," and covertly cheered the Tories in hope of jettisoning Corbyn and his pariah supporters. Only 13% of UK press reports, even prior to the antisemitism row, were favorable to Corbyn.[67] Despite all this, Corbyn surged to within several thousand votes of winning the 2017 election, gaining the biggest Labour vote increase since 1945, outperforming Blair in 2001 and 2005. But a hung parliament enabled the Tories to scrape back into power alongside a well-remunerated coalition partner.[68] "Winning 40% of the popular vote, we were less than 2,500 votes away from forming a government," Momentum National coordinating group member John Taylor lamented. "Had we pulled together, we could have won. A Labour government could have revived crucial public services, built a more resilient economy, and saved lives by giving our NHS the resources it needs,"[69] Instead, the antisemitism bandwagon got under way, a spell when Labour Party members were five times more likely to be investigated for antisemitism if they themselves were Jewish.[70]

Was Labour really teeming with antisemites?[71] When pollsters in 2019 asked, at the climax of blanket negative media coverage, what proportion of Labour membership were antisemitic, respondents estimated an average of a third, which was about 660 times the validated figure, which was 0.05%.[72] The Home Affairs Select Committee uncovered "no reliable empirical evidence to support the notion that there is higher prevalence of antisemitism within the Labour Party than any other political party."[73] The number of antisemites in Britain, other investigators admit, is strikingly low—at 5 to 6%—and "strikingly lower than the corresponding views toward Muslims."[74] The Campaign Against Antisemitism in 2017 agreed that Labour member are less likely than the general public and no more likely than any other party to endorse antisemitic statements, although this finding sent them scrambling to chide Labour for not doing enough to root out lurking offenders. Citing surveys by the Institute for Jewish Policy Research in 2017 and a Pew Global Attitudes Survey in 2019 into the bargain academic investigators were puzzled by a YouGov poll in 2017 showing Conservatives are more likely to agree with antisemitic opinions, 16% versus 11% for Labour in one of five categories. Indeed, and curiously underplayed, in two of five categories the conservatives' antisemitism doubled Labour numbers. Although the investigators concede that the daft notion that "Jews control the media" might, in part at least, reflect the kid gloves media treatment that Israel gets versus Palestinians, their ultimate solution was to indelibly link any critiques of capitalism to invariable invocation of antisemitic imagery, going the Blairites one better. The only sure way out of antisemitic accusations is to cease criticizing not only Israel, but capitalism too, according to these value-free academics.

What of the Tories, on whom barely a media glove was laid? Wheatcroft provides a glimpse of their resplendent record on all things racial:[75]

> Churchill once told a colleague "The Hindus are a foul race" who deserve to be extirpated, and in 1955, at the last cabinet meeting over which he presided

> as Prime minister, he said that the Tories should fight the next election on the slogan "Keep England White." At the Conservative Party Conference the following year one of the speakers was Captain Charles Waterhouse, a veteran of the Great War, an MP since the 1920s, and great conference favorite. In his speech he used the phrase "nigger in the woodpile"; added in a stage aside, "Too many of them about anyway": and brought the house down with raucous laughter—a memory that must make today's Tories shudder, and not only them.

Memories indeed. In 1964 a Tory candidate in Smethwick told supporters: "If you want a n***** for a neighbour, vote Labour."[76] In April 1968 Enoch Powell's delivered his "rivers of blood" speech. David Hart, a storied Tory fixer, especially during the 1984 Miners' strike, rose to that esteemed status after undergoing and overlooking antisemitic bullying during his youth at Eton.[77] The *Jewish Chronicle* noted in 2019 that a Tory candidate who claimed events in the Holocaust have been "fabricated" and "exaggerated" was briefly suspended, but would be restored to the ballot.[78]

> Another Conservative candidate who described British Jews as "brainwashed extremists" was suspended too. In 2014 the Conservative party's inquiry into an MP who threw a Nazi-themed party and wore a Nazi uniform concluded that his behaviour was not antisemitic. The same year another Conservative MP was forced to quit over referring to someone as a "bloody Jew." A few years earlier a Conservative student society reportedly sang pro-Holocaust songs on multiple occasions.

All these incidents seem especially odd and ungrateful since British Jews overwhelmingly (ranging between 60 and 70%) and for many years supported the Tories, as befits so prosperous and secure a group, and so were highly receptive to discouraging words about Labour.

Has genteel antisemitism, and racism *in toto*, seeped away inside the upper crust Clubs? Some polls hint otherwise. "We were shocked by the extent to which those prejudiced views seeing minorities as a threat really carries across the full spectrum of society," said Kate Ferguson, director of research and policy, who oversaw a 2019 poll.[79] "You expect to see people with lower incomes have more prejudiced views, but a third of the respondents who we would consider well-off held those views." Meanwhile, hate crimes against Jews—ranging from shouting abuse to thankfully less common physical attacks—in Britain rocketed, especially after 7 October, by 147% in 2023 as hate crimes against Muslims rose 335%.[80] The Muslim population in the UK at 6% is ten times larger than the Jewish population.

Corbyn, caught in a fatal Brexit squeeze, even more damaging than the antisemitism flap, lost the 2019 election.[81] The pro-Brexit Conservatives won 44% of the vote and 365 seats despite a 72% disapproval rating in office.[82] In 2017 Labour "won 41% of the vote with 55% of remainers and 24% of leave voters," Ell Smith points out. In 2019 Labour's lead among remainers replicated 2017. But among leavers the Conservatives jumped from 41 up to 60 points, taking 74% of the leave vote (versus 14% for Labour). Of 54 Labour seats lost to Conservatives, 52 were in leave areas where Labour actually gained votes while Conservatives gained even more since 2017.[83] Brexit, not antisemitism alone, or Labour's manifesto, did it. In fact, 81% of voters backed spending on the NHS, 66% were for tax rises for those earning more than £80,000 a year, 66% were for building 150,000 council homes and 59% supported a green industrial revolution. Even 62.1% of Conservative voters (compared to 76.9% of Labour voters) supported energy becoming publicly owned, while 76.9% backed the NHS staying in public hands.[84] Despite this, Keir Starmer reneged on pledges to push for common ownership of "mail, energy and water" (though leaving the woeful rail system as a target) during his bid to succeed Corbyn.[85] But that is both another—and yet the whole point of the—story.

Conclusion

Authoritarianism evinces a behavioral style all its own—apart from any underlying ignoble personality traits—which attaches to any ideology. Altemeyer in 1981 accordingly worried that the notion that people cherish their freedoms may be "an untenable assumption."[86] The proposition that "a shared psychological core underlies different manifestations of authoritarianism" remains debatable, if not insupportable, but it is of scant concern here where personality traits, however interesting and important, need not be hauled in to explain ideology or political behavior.[87]

Antisemitism inside the Labour Party was never the menace it was assiduously made out to be. Corbyn's opponents cast around for ways to sabotage his movement and stumbled onto a winner, as Brits say. The supreme concern for elites across the United Kingdom was which faction in Labour would assume power in a future government, with attendant implications for taxation, wealth distribution, welfare state design, and foreign policy. "Liberalism [centrism] has ended up playing a useful and no doubt unintended role" Michaels presciently noted, as if he foresaw Keir Starmer, "the role of supplying the right with just the kind of left it wants."[88] Martin Forde, author of the Labour Party-commissioned Report, noted the indifference with which the Starmer-led Party treated his study, which inconveniently uncovered a "hierarchy of racism" inside the Party where concerns about forms of racism other than antisemitism were relegated to the margins.[89]

Anyone, including especially Corbyn, could have returned Labour to power in July 2024 just as any sentient MP could have done in 1997. The right "anyone" could have installed a vigorous social democratic program, instead of pallid austerity-lite policies. Starmer's Labour won fewer votes in 2024 than Corbyn did in 2017 and 2019, but emerged with a landslide in seats due to a Tory collapse and the vagaries of the first-past-the-post system. The centrists exercising iron control inside Labour's Vatican continued purges through the July election. Corbyn, who nonetheless retained his seat as an independent, was expelled from the Party under tenuous charges.[90] Diane Abbott, black and a Corbyn ally, experienced mistreatment in her quest to retain her Party's imprimatur and her seat.[91] A highly electable Muslim woman scholar of Leftward bent, Faiza Shaheen, was ejected as a Labour candidate too.

Politics remains a game brimming with deceit, ulterior motives, and misrepresentation. Power and privileges, after all, are at stake. What's new? Strenuously forgotten now in the US media is that the original leaked DNC emails at the heart of Russiagate revealed that hostile key DNC staffers all along sought to sabotage Bernie Sanders campaign in favor of Hilary Clinton (whose own considerable "Russia baggage" was duly eclipsed), for which an ineffectual and inconspicuous apology was offered.[92] The conscientious centrists so firmly in control of the Labour Party and the DNC today too (in the wake of Trump's reelection), demonstrate that just as one doesn't have to be a German to be a Nazi, one doesn't have to be Soviet fellow traveler to be in style, behavior and attitude a Stalinist. Any smug centrist will do.

Acknowledgment

For helpful comments and suggestions on this chapter I thank Steve Bronner, Russell Jacoby, and Robert Melville.

Notes

1 Noam Chomsky's essay "Objectivity and Liberal Scholarship" offers a concise discussion of the cynical antics at play in and around Spain over 1936–39. *Chomsky, American Power and the New Mandarins* (New York: Pantheon, 1969).
2 *Partido Obrero de Unificación Marxista.* The immense cost in blood and suffering, especially after the formal conclusion of hostilities, is recorded in Peter Preston's *The Spanish Holocaust* (New York: Norton, 2012). As many analysts point out, POUM policies were criticized by Trotsky too.
3 George Orwell, *Homage to Catalonia* (London: Penguin 1938), pp. 4–6. "There was much in it that I did not understand, and in some ways I did not even like it, but I recognized it immediately as a state of affairs worth fighting for." Also see Christopher Hall, *"In Spain with Orwell": George Orwell and the Independent Labour Party Volunteers in the Spanish Civil War* (Perth: Warren & Pell, 2009).
4 Overall, the bulk of recruitment to the International Brigades was conducted outside the Communist Parties. Tremlett estimates about half the total of International Brigades recruits were CP members. Giles Tremlett, *The International Brigades: Fascism, Freedom and the Spanish Civil War* (London: Bloomsbury, 2021), p. 3.
5 "Thus, though an irony of history, the revolutionary elements in the Republican zone – the anarchists and the quasi-Trotskyists of the POUM – would face the most determined opposition not from the Fascist forces of Franco, but from the Moscow-dominated Communists" Peter Preston, *The Spanish Civil War: Reaction, Revolution and Revenge* (New York: W. W. Norton, rev. ed. 2005) p. 151. On the purportedly temporary nature

of Stalinist-style authoritarian rule see Kendall Bailes, *Technology and Society Under Lenin and Stalin* (Princeton: Princeton University Press, 1978).

6 Several hundred Spanish Civil War refugees to the Soviet Union even wound up in gulags, with many perishing there. Adam Hochschild, *Spain in Our Hearts: Americans in the Spanish Civil War 1936-1939* (New York: Houghton Mifflin, 2016), p. 77.

7 This chilling sentiment also was expressed by a different New York-based Abraham Lincoln Brigade veteran Saul Newton, according to Alexander Stille, *The Sullivanians* (New York: Farrar, Strauss, 2023).

8 Bob Altemeyer, "Reply to Critics." *Canadian Psychology*, vol. 31, no. 4 (1990), p. 393. "The real issue is does the same kind of personality become a communist or a fascist?" Bob Altemeyer, *Enemies of Freedom: Understanding Right Wing Authoritarianism* (San Francisco: Josey-Bass Publishers, 1988), p. 259.

9 Seymour Martin Lipset, *Political Man: The Social Bases of Politics* (Garden City, NY: Doubleday, 1960), pp. 97–130. For a critique of Lipset on the incidence and causes of working-class authoritarianism, including the excluded role of precarity, see Jaime L. Napier and John T. Jost, "A Cross-National Investigation of Working-Class Authoritarianism." *Journal of Social Issues*, vol. 64, no. 3 (2008).

10 Ludwig Von Mises, *Planning for Freedom and Twelve other Essays* (South Holland: Libertarian Press, 1950), p. 27.

11 "In the Soviet Union a communist is a conformist rather than an attacker of the status quo, which in its authoritarian practices and denial of political and intellectual freedom bears little resemblance to historical aspirations of the Left." David Spitz, "Why Communists are Not of The Left." *Antioch Review*, vol. 9, no. 4 (Winter 1949), p. 496.

12 This seems to be the upshot of Edward Shils' tendentious cold warrior riposte, "Authoritarianism 'Left' and 'Right.'" in Richard Christie and Marie Jahoda (Eds.), *The Scope and Method of the Authoritarian Personality* (Chicago, Glencoe: Free Press, 1954), pp. 24–9.

13 That "cases of left-wing authoritarianism do exist cannot be denied but the idea that authoritarian personalities are equally drawn to communist and fascist movements now seem clearly false." William F. Stone, "The Myth of Left-Wing Authoritarianism." *Political Psychology*, vol. 2, no. 3 (Autumn-Winter 1980).

14 Eric Hoffer, *The True Believer: Thoughts on the Nature of Mass Movements* (New York: Harper & Row, 1951).

15 "In short, they seem to be all around us. There are authoritarians among the well-educated and the poorly educated, on the political left and the political right, among the rich and the poor, among the atheists and among the ardently faithful, among the young and the old, among males and among female, and – if anyone doubted it – among Americans as well Canadians." Bob Altemeyer, *Right-Wing Authoritarianism* (Manitoba, 1981), p. 250

16 See Herbert Marcuse, *Soviet Marxism: A Critical Analysis* (New York: Vintage, 1961).

17 Saul Landau and Paul Jacobs (Eds.) *The New Radicals* (New York: Pantheon, 1968).

18 See Kirkpatrick Sale, *SDS* (New York: Random House 1973) and Howard Brick and Gregory Parker (Eds.) *A New Insurgency: The Port Huron Statement and Its Times* (Ann Arbor: University of Michigan Library, 2015). Accessible at: https://quod.lib.umich.edu/m/maize/13545967.0001.001

19 Of great help on this crucial definitional issue is the discussion in Susan Neiman's, *The Left is Not Woke* (New York: Polity Press, 2023). Indeed, harking back to the Adorno volume helps too, where "Left of center" is defined as "opposition to the status quo, a tendency to think in sociological rather than moral-hereditarian terms; a tendency to identify with labor and the "common man" and to oppose the power of business, support for the extension of the political and economic functions of government." Adorno, *The Authoritarian Personality*, 157.

20 Andre Gorz, *Strategy for Labor* (Boston: Beacon Press, 1964).
21 See Thomas Piketty, *A Brief History of Equality* (Cambridge: Harvard University Press, 2022) and Michael Graetz, *The Power to Destroy: How the Antitax Movement Hijacked America* (Princeton: Princeton University Press, 2024).
22 See Russell Jacoby, *On Diversity: The Eclipse of the Individual in a Global Era* (New York: Seven Stories Press, 2020), and his essay in this volume.
23 See the Lewis Powell memo to Chamber of Commerce, "Attack in the American Free Enterprise System" (1971) https://scholarlycommons.law.wlu.edu/powellmemo
24 See Angus Burgin, *The Great Persuasion: Reinventing Free Markets Since the Great Depression* (Cambridge: Harvard University Press, 2015) and Kurt Andersen, *Evil Geniuses: The Unmaking of America* (New York: Random House 2020).
25 "Should any political party abolish social security and eliminate labor laws and farm programs you would not hear from that party again in our political history," Eisenhower famously reckoned during his presidency. "There is a tiny splinter group, of course, that believes you can do these things [but] their number is negligible and they are stupid." Geoffrey Kabaservice, *Rule and Ruin: The Downfall of Moderation and the Destruction of the Republican Party* (New York: Oxford 2013), p. 14.
26 Walter Benn Michaels, *The Trouble with Diversity: How we Learned to Love Identity and Ignore Inequality* (New York: Holt, 2006), p. 10
27 Noam Chomsky, *American Power and the New Mandarins* (New York: Pantheon, 1969), p. 14.
28 See Andrew Feffer, *Bad Faith, Teachers, Liberalism and the Origins of McCarthyism* (New York: Fordham University Press, 2019); Athan Theoharis, *Seeds Of Repression* (Chicago: Quadrangle Boks, 1971), Ellen Schrecker, *Many are the Crimes: McCarthyism in America* (Princeton: Princeton University Press 1999), and Paul Buhle and Dave Wagner, *Radical Hollywood* (New York: New Press, 2003).
29 Stanley Milgram, *Obedience to Authority* (New York: Harper & Row, 1974), p. 170.
30 Milgram, p. 186. Also, confining the shock limit to 150 volts, see Jerry Burger, "Replicating Milgram: Would People Still Obey Today?" *American Psychologist*, vol. 1 (January) 2009.
31 Kelman and Hamilton, *Crimes of Obedience* (New Haven: Yale, 1989), pp. 173, 174.
32 Kelman and Hamilton, p. 191.
33 Kelman and Hamilton, p. 308. Also see Christopher R. Browning, *Ordinary Men* (New York; HarperCollins, 1992).
34 See, for example, Gina Perry, *Behind the Shock Machine* (New York: New Press, 2013) and Cari Romm, "Rethinking One of Psychology's Most Infamous Experiments." *The Atlantic*, 28 January 2015.
35 See Telford Taylor's remarks in Studs Terkel's *"The Good War": An Oral History of World War II* (New York: New Press, 1997), p. 459. Arguments on the "banality of evil" come into play here too. See Hannah Arendt, *Eichmann in Jerusalem* (New York: Viking, 1963).
36 R. D. Laing, *The Politics of Experience* (London: Penguin, 1967), p. 28.
37 Altemeyer, *Right Wing Authoritarianism*, p. 7. To the dismay of some critics Altemeyer argued that ethnocentrism is no longer a key indicator of authoritarianism (pp. 29–32).
38 Josh Vorhees, "New Poll Finds that Hilary Supporters are Pretty Racist Too." *The Guardian*, 29 June 2016. A Reuter/Ipsos poll found that one-third of Hilary voters (versus one-half of Trumpers) regarded Blacks as "more criminal" and "more violent" than whites. One third of Trumpers, and almost a quarter of Clinton fans, thought Blacks were "less intelligent" than whites.
39 Ashley Lopez, "More than Half of Republicans Support Christian Nationalism, New Survey Reports." *NPR*, 13 February 2023: "45% of Americans say US should be a

Christian Nation." Pew Research Center, 27 October 2022. https://www.pewresearch.org/religion/2022/10/27/views-of-the-u-s-as-a-christian-nation-and-opinions-about-christian-nationalism/

40 The liberal political correctness ideology had "taken on the mantle of 'conventional morality' in that its endorsers score high on measures of authoritarian punitiveness towards transgressors.' Suedfeld, G., D. Steele, & P. W. Schmidt, "Political Ideology and Attitudes Toward Censorship." *Journal of Applied Social Psychology*, vol. 24 (1994), p. 777, cited in Lucien Gideon Conway, Channon C. Houck, Laura Janelle Gornick, and Meredith A. Repke, "Finding the Loch Ness Monster: Left-Wing Authoritarianism in the United States." *Political Psychology*, vol. 39, no. 5 (2018), pp. 1051, 1062.

41 Conway, Houck, Gornick, and Repke, p. 1063. As Sinclair Lewis' 1922 novel *Babbitt* attests, such inclinations go way back. "To the [Good Citizens] League belonged most of the prosperous citizens of Zenith. They were not all of the kind who called themselves 'Regular Guys.' Besides these hearty fellows, these salesmen of prosperity, there were the aristocrats, that is, the men who were richer or had been rich for more generations: the presidents of banks and of factories, the land-owners, the corporation lawyers, the fashionable doctors, and the few young-old men who worked not at all but, reluctantly remaining in Zenith, collected luster-ware and first editions as though they were back in Paris. All of them agreed that the working-classes must be kept in their place; and all of them perceived that American Democracy did not imply any equality of wealth, but did demand a wholesome sameness of thought, dress, painting, morals, and vocabulary."

42 Reinhold Niebuhr, "Pawns for Fascism" reprinted In Daniel Steinmetz-Jenkins (Ed.) *Did It Happen Here? Perspectives of Fascism in America* (New York: Norton, 2024). Also, Martin Trow, "Small Businessmen, Political Tolerance and Support for McCarthy." *American Journal of Sociology*, vol. 64 (November 1958).

43 See Philip Ball, *Serving the Reich: The Struggle for the Soul of Physics Under Hitler* (Chicago: University of Chicago, 2014), Robert Proctor, *Racial Hygiene* (Cambridge: Harvard University Press, 1988), Gotz Aly, *Cleansing the Fatherland* (Baltimore: Johns Hopkins University Press, 1994) and, of course, Robert J. Lifton, *The Nazi Doctors* (Basic Books, 1988).

44 Lewis Lipsitz, "Working Class Authoritarianism: A Re-Evaluation." *American Sociological Review*, vol. 34, no. 1 (February 1965), p. 105.

45 Arthur Schlesinger, *The Vital Center* (New York: Houghton Mifflin 1949).

46 See Sanford Levinson and Philip Green (Eds.) *Power and Community; Dissenting Essays in Political Science* (New York: Pantheon, 1969).

47 Altemeyer, *Enemies of Freedom*, p. 260.

48 On Americans as "conservative egalitarians" see Benjamin Page and Larry Jacobs, *Class War? What Americans Really Think about Economic Inequality* (Chicago: University of Chicago Press, 2010).

49 Kai T. Erikson, *Wayward Puritans: A Study in the Sociology of Deviance* (New York: John Wiley, 1966), pp. 4–13. Note especially the citation of Aldous Huxley on the antinomies of "tidiness" (p. 13).

50 Keith Spencer, "There is Hard Data that Shows that Bernie Bros are a Myth." *Salon*, 9 March 2020. https://www.salon.com/2020/03/09/there-is-hard-data-that-shows-bernie-bros-are-a-myth/ and David Marcus, "Burying the Bernie Bro Narrative." *The Gate*, 19 November 2019. chicagogate.com/articles/2019/11/24/burying-bernie-bro-narrative/ . On "Russiagate" see Matt Taibbi, *Hate Inc* (New York: OR Books, 2019).

51 See Sam Varghese, "CrowdStrike Chief Admits no Proof that Russia Exfiltrated DNC Emails." https://itwire.com/business-it-news/security/crowdstrike-chief-admits-no-proof-that-russia-exfiltrated-dnc-emails.html and Ray McGovern, "CrowdStrike Further Tainted by Worldwide Crash," 20 July 2024. https://consortiumnews.com/2024/07/20/crowdstrike-further-tainted-by-worldwide-crash/

52 Andy McSmith, Ben Shu, and Richard Garner "'Margaret Thatcher's Legacy' Spilt Milk, New Labour and the Big Bang." *The Independent*, 13 April 2013.
53 Anthony Barnet, "John Smith and the Path Britain Did Not Take." OpenDemocracy 12 May 2019. Accessed at: https://www.opendemocracy.net/en/opendemocracyuk/john-smith-and-path-britain-did-not-take/ Labour's rightward shift, though, arguably began forcefully under Neil Kinnock, Party leader from 1983 to 1992.
54 "Once I was working at Number 10 there was only one view that mattered: 'the line.' In effect this amounted to whatever Tony Blair thought about any particular issue" Lance Price, *The Spin Doctor's Diary: Inside Number 10 with New Labour* (London: Hodder & Stoughton, 2005), p. xii.
55 See George Monbiot, *Captive State* (London: Pan Books, 2001).
56 "In 2013 the Electoral College was abolished and the choice of leader – subject to minimum support in the form of nominations within the PLP – became solely the decision of individual members (and registered individual supporters). The ostensible aim was to reduce trade union influence," The Forde Report summarizes, "but it also eliminated PLP influence in the final vote and passed it to an – normally overwhelmingly Left – individual membership. Jeremy Corbyn was the first leader elected under this system." *The Forde Report* (London: Labour Party National Executive Committee, 2022), p. 29. https://labour.org.uk/wp-content/uploads/2023/01/The-Forde-Report.pdf. The implication is well worth noting that a "normally overwhelmingly Left" Party constituency is regarded as something to be contained, rather than represented.
57 For an account of orchestrated press ferocity against Corbyn in just his first year see Bart Cammaerts, Brooks DeCilla, Joao Magalhaes, and Cesar Jimenez-Martinez, "Journalistic Representation of Jeremy Corbyn in the British Press: From Watch Dog to Attack Dog" (London: Media@LSE Report, 2015). https://www.lse.ac.uk/media-and-communications/research/research-projects/representations-of-jeremy-corbyn.
58 "Authoritarian submission entails very strong submission to established authorities. Authoritarian aggression is directed at persons who are seen as deviating from social norms and/or thereby threatening the established authorities. Conventionalism is strong adherence to social norms (which are seen as moral) as well as the rejection of the idea that people themselves may decide what is good and what is bad." Altemeyer, *Right Wing Authoritarianism*, 1981, pp. 154–5.
59 The Work of the Labour Party's Governance and Legal Unit in Relation to Antisemitism, 2014–2019 (Labour Party March 2020), pp. 29–30. https://acrobat.adobe.com/link/review?uri=urn%3Aaaid%3Ascds%3AUS%3A445d2798-f676-473b-a1ab-daaf55ea804c#pageNum=1
60 The Work of the Labour Party's Governance and Legal Unit in Relation to Antisemitism, p. 31.
61 Richard Seymour, *Corbyn: The Strange Rebirth of Radical Politics* (London: Verso, 2016), p. 46.
62 Owen Jones, *Chavs: The Demonization if the Working Class* (London, Verso, 2011), pp. 9–10, 248.
63 The Work of the Labour Party's Governance and Legal Unit in Relation to Antisemitism, p. 74.
64 Jon Stone, "Anti-Corbyn Labour Officials worked to Lose to lose the Election to Oust Leader, Leaked Dossier Finds." *The Independent*, 13 April 2020.
65 Adorno et. al, *The Authoritarian Personality*, p. 98
66 Adorno et. al, *The Authoritarian Personality*, p. 100. In an Adornoesque passage the Forde Report notes, "One of the tragedies of this period for the Party is that so many have lost sight of the humanity of those who they see as being in an opposing faction." *The Forde Report*, p. 36.

67 Seymour, *Corbyn*, p. 28. The author notes that opening of leadership selection to a vote by all party members in 2015 was due to a misjudged "Blairite maneuver to weaken the union link and place the professional party caste in charge of atomized individual members." Democracy broke out instead.
68 Harriet Agerholm, "Jeremy Corbyn was just 2,227 votes away from chance to become prime minister." *Independent*, 9 June 2017. Seven extremely close seats, which would otherwise have enabled Corbyn to become prime minister, were lost by that total margin.
69 Stone, "Anti-Corbyn."
70 David Hearst and Peter Oborne, "UK's Labour Accused of Purging Jews from Party over Antisemitism Claims." *Middle East Eye*, 12 August 2021.
71 After confirming every charge in the leaked 2020 report, and allowing that internal antics contributed to Labour's 2017 election loss, The Forde Report portrays any hint that antisemitism was weaponized against Corbyn as "denialism." p. 13.
72 Oliver Eagleton, *The Starmer Project: A Journey to the Right* (Verso, 2022), pp. 143, 152.
73 Eagleton, *The Starmer Project*.
74 Ben Gidley, Brendan McGeever, and David Feldman, "Labour and Antisemitism: A Crisis Misunderstood." *Political Quarterly*, vol. 91, no. 2 (April-June 2020), p. 414.
75 Geoffrey Wheatcroft, "Bloody Panico." *New York Review of Books*, 23 March 1923, p. 46.
76 Sathnam Sanghera, *Empireland: How Imperialism has Shaped Modern Britain* (New York: Pantheon 2021), p. 108.
77 Seumas Milne, *The Enemy Within* (London: Verso, 1994), p. 32.
78 Jon Lansman, "Focusing only on Labour Whitewashes the Antisemitism and Racism of Other Parties." *Jewish Chronicle*, 20 November 2019.
79 Robert Booth, "Middle Income Earners Behind Rising Racial Tensions, Poll Finds." *Guardian*, 5 March 2019.
80 Michael Holden, "UK Redefines Extremism after Rise in Hate Crimes against Jews, Muslims." Reuters, 14 March 2024
81 On Keir Starmer's mischievous role in aggravating the Brexit plight in 2019, see Eagleton, *The Starmer Project*, p. 200.
82 Ell Smith, "It was Brexit, not Leftwing Policies, that Lost Labour this Election." *Guardian*, 21 December 2019.
83 Jo Mitchell and Rob Calvert Jump, "Labour, the 'Red Wall', and the Vicissitudes of Britain's Voting System." OpenDemocracy, 20 August 2020.
84 Xander Elliards, "Even Tories Support Publicly Owned Utilities." *The National*, 15 August 2022.
85 "Starmer Blames Retreat from Nationalisation on Post-pandemic Debt." *The National*, 26 July 2022.
86 Altemeyer, *Right Wing Authoritarianism*, p. 5.
87 Thomas H. Costello, Shauna Bowles, Irwin D Waldman, Arber Tasimi, Sean T. Stevens, and Scott O. Lillenfeld, "Clarifying the Structure and Nature of Left-Wing Authoritarianism." *Journal of Personality and Social Psychology*, vol. 1 (January 2022) pp. 40, 41.
88 Michaels, *The Trouble with Diversity*, p. 109.
89 Nadine White, "Labour Tried to Gag Black Lawyer who Wrote Party's own Racism Report." *The Independent*, 19 June 2024. https://www.independent.co.uk/news/uk/politics/labour-party-racism-report-martin-forde-starmer-b2564059.html.
90 Peter Isackson, "The Real Scandal of Jeremy Corbyn's Exclusion." *Fair Observer*, 5 November 2020. https://www.fairobserver.com/region/europe/peter-isackson-jeremy-corbyn-suspension-labour-party-uk-keir-starmer-united-kingdom-european-politics-79681/#

91 Maurice Mcleod, "Labour's Shocking Treatment of Diane Abbot Could Alienate Black Voters for Years to Come," Guardian 29 May 2024. Also see Albert Toth, "Labour MP Selections: Who's in and out amid Abbot and Shaheen Row." *The Independent*, 31 May 2024.

92 Eric Beech, "Democratic National Committee Apologizes to Sanders over Emails." Reuters, 25 July 2016. On Clinton's own Russia connections and for a summative debunking of Russiagate, see Jeff Gerth, "The Press versus the President, Part One." *Columbia Journalism Review*, 30 January 2023. https://www.cjr.org/special_report/trumped-up-press-versus-president-part-1.php

Index

Note: Endnotes are indicated by the page number followed by "n" and the note number e.g., 111n5 refers to note 5 on page 111.

For Product Safety Concerns and Information please contact our
EU representative GPSR@taylorandfrancis.com Taylor & Francis
Verlag GmbH, Kaufingerstraße 24, 80331 München, Germany